# Governance in China

# Governance in China

Edited by
Jude Howell

corporatism 169

ROWMAN & LITTLEFIELD PUBLISHERS, INC.
*Lanham • Boulder • New York • Toronto • Oxford*

ROWMAN & LITTLEFIELD PUBLISHERS, INC.

Published in the United States of America
by Rowman & Littlefield Publishers, Inc.
A wholly owned subsidary of The Rowman & Littlefield Publishing Group, Inc.
4501 Forbes Boulevard, Suite 200, Lanham, Maryland 20706
www.rowmanlittlefield.com

P.O. Box 317, Oxford OX2 9RU, United Kingdom

British Library Cataloguing in Publication Information Available

**Library of Congress Cataloging-in-Publication Data**

Governance in China / [edited by] Jude Howell.
    p. cm.
Includes bibliographical references and index.   ISBN 0-7425-1987-2 (alk. paper) —
ISBN 0-7425-1988-0 (pbk. : alk. paper)
  1. Public administration—China. 2.  China—Politics and
government—1976-  I. Howell, Jude.
  JQ1510.G68 2004
  320.951—dc21

                                          2003008631

Printed in the United States of America

∞™ The paper used in this publication meets the minimum requirements of
American National Standard for Information Sciences—Permanence of Paper
for Printed Library Materials, ANSI/NISO Z39.48-1992.

To my mother
and friends

# Contents

# Figures and Tables

# Abbreviations

| | |
|---|---|
| ACFTU | All-China Federation of Trade Unions |
| ACWF | All-China Women's Federation |
| APEC | Asia-Pacific Economic Cooperation |
| ADB | Asian Development Bank |
| BBC | British Broadcasting Corporation |
| CASS | Center for Applied Social Surveys |
| CCP | Chinese Communist Party |
| CCTV | China Central Television |
| CICPA | Chinese Institute of Certified Public Accountants |
| CPA | Certified Public Accountants |
| CPPCC | Chinese People's Political Consultative Conference |
| CYL | China Youth League |
| GATS | General Agreement on Trade in Services |
| GDP | Gross Domestic Product |
| ICT | Information Communication Technologies |
| IMF | International Monetary Fund |
| MII | Ministry of Information Industry |
| MoCA | The Ministry of Civil Affairs |
| NATO | North Atlantic Treaty Organization |
| NGO | Nongovernmental Organization |
| NPC | National People's Congress |
| NWCWC | National Women and Children Working Committee |
| OECD | Organization for Economic Cooperation and Development |
| PRC | People's Republic of China |
| RMB | *Ren Min Bi* (People's Money) |
| SARFT | State Administration of Radio, Film, and Television |

| | |
|---|---|
| SOE | State-Owned Enterprise |
| TRIPS | Trade-Related Intellectual Property Rights |
| TVE | Township and Village Enterprise |
| UNDP | United Nations Development Program |
| UNESCO | United Nations Educational, Scientific and Cultural Organization |
| VCD | Video Compact Disk |
| WTO | World Trade Organization |

# Preface

China seems to be a paradox. With a Communist Party at its helm, Deng Xiaoping and other reformers have embraced the market economy in pursuit of rapid economic development. They have decollectivized agriculture, expanded the private sector, welcomed foreign investment, opened up the Communist Party to private entrepreneurs, and joined the World Trade Organization, a global bastion of free trade. An authoritarian regime, with vestiges of socialist ideology, driving its populace to "get rich quick" by embracing the market, seems at first sight quizzical.

Though China's economic growth rates have been impressive, the stresses and strains of rapid socioeconomic change and of the paradoxical combination of socialist rhetoric and a market economy have already begun to manifest themselves: Rising unemployment as state enterprises can no longer compete against their private and global rivals; large-scale rural-urban migration as unemployed farmers pour into the cities in search of jobs; environmental degradation as local government officials and entrepreneurs pursue profit and development at any cost; a health care system in disarray; and widening inequalities between the rich and poor, and the urban and rural. Though some have become rich in the scramble for wealth and status, many are struggling at the margins. Social discontent and alienation have fuelled the rising number of demonstrations and protests. In urban areas, laid-off workers and unpaid pensioners have taken to the streets seeking their just dues. In rural areas, angry farmers have occupied government buildings, led petition drives and filed court cases to protest the overzealous and unjust exaction of fees by cash-strapped local governments.

For any government, such stresses and strains pose enormous challenges. How can growth be achieved without increasing inequality, and how much inequality is politically acceptable? What kind of institutions are needed to facilitate the deepening of the market, and how can existing institutions be reformed? How should the government manage social discontent? As interests become increasingly diversified and pluralized, how can the Party maintain legitimacy and power? Is political reform inevitable in the wake of increasing economic liberalization and globalization? If so, what form should this take and who will be its champions? These, and many more questions, are matters of governance. This volume takes up these matters of governance. In doing so, it goes beyond a narrow focus on the legal and managerial dimensions of governance to address broader issues around regime maintenance, political reform, institution-building, state-society relations, participation, and representation. The chapters in this volume emerged out of debate and discussion at an international forum on governance held at the Institute of Development Studies, University of Sussex, UK, on September 11-13, 2001.

Without the support and encouragement of many individuals, this forum and book would not have been possible. I am deeply indebted to Katie Lee and Natalie Cade for their enthusiasm and support throughout this process and for providing us with start-up funds to get the whole project going. I owe particular thanks to Ken Grimshaw for providing a generous grant for the forum. I am grateful to Sarah Cook for covering the costs of seven Chinese scholars to travel to the UK, and to Michael Edwards, for sponsoring two American scholars to present papers at the Forum. David Ellis helped enormously in identifying stimulating participants and in thinking through the shape of the forum. Jillian Popkins was constant in her enthusiasm and support of the idea. Rod Wye, Fiona McConnon, and Keith Bezanson all gave their unreserved backing for the forum. Bob Benewick was unstinting in his steady and calm support during the preparations and the unfolding of this event. Organizing an international forum involves considerable coordination and transnational communication. Here, thanks are due to Julie McWilliam and Julia Brown for keeping cool behind the scenes and for making it all happen and to Emily Delap for her contributions as research assistant and rapporteur.

Producing a volume with authors scattered across four continents is no easy task. Here I can only praise the efforts of Julie McWilliam, who kept the ball rolling with a great sense of humor and enormous patience. For final editing of the completed draft, I should thank Zaza Curran, whose careful eye ensured that punctuation was as it should be and references were present and correct. I am grateful to Julie McWilliam for assiduously and speedily inserting final changes into the pre-print copy. Not least I should thank the anonymous reviewer for a close reading of the manuscript, insightful and constructive comments, and enthusiastic endorsement of the project. For the prompt responses and constant encouragement, I owe much thanks to Susan McEachern, Dianne Ewing, and others at Rowman and Littlefield Publishers. Finally, thanks is due to all the contributors of this volume, who responded in timely fashion and with great patience to requests for changes.

# 1

# Governance Matters: Key Challenges and Emerging Tendencies

*Jude Howell*

With the end of the Cold War and the seeming vindication of liberal democracy and free markets, Western governments and international development agencies embarked upon a new agenda of "good governance." Taking the spotlight away from ideology and global political divisions, the good governance agenda focused its attentions on the internal failure of states in the South. The term "governance," like all political science concepts, is contested, and the juxtaposition of "good" augments the essentially evaluative nature of the concept. For international financial institutions such as the World Bank and the International Monetary Fund, the term "good governance" refers primarily to institutionalizing processes for achieving effective, efficient, transparent, and accountable government. It includes therefore establishing processes and mechanisms for holding public servants responsible for their actions, constructing a legal framework for development, decentralization, microlevel accountability to consumers, and making information available for policy analysis and debate (Turner and Hulme, 1997: 229–231).[1] While the World Bank, International Monetary Fund, and United Nations (UN) agencies have focused their assistance on the more technical dimensions such as accountability and transparency, not least because their associational principles bar them from engaging overtly in politics, bilateral development agencies and Western governments interpret the term more broadly to embrace also the processes of democratization, respect for human rights, and socioeconomic equity (Leftwich 1993[2]; Moore 1993).[3]

These debates have not only fuelled a host of practical programs and projects concerned with improving governance processes in the South, but have also spirited political scientists to move beyond the conceptual confines of formal political institutions and systems to consider more broadly the processes by which power, authority, and resources are negotiated both within the state and between the state and society. For the purposes of this book, we define governance as the totality of processes and arrangements, both formal and informal, by which power and public authority are distributed and regulated. The study of governance therefore encompasses the analysis of formal political institutions such as the government, the military, and the judiciary at national and local levels, as well as informal processes of rule such as patron-clientelism and networks. It embraces not only the study of states but also the arrangements and processes within political and civil society, the relations between these, and in turn their linkages with the state.

Understanding governance processes in China inevitably takes us beyond a narrow focus on political elites, the party system, or the military to a broader discussion of how state-society relations are shaped, how power and authority are distributed and maintained, and how claim-making processes are initiated, intermediated, and upheld. For over two decades, China has experienced phenomenal economic growth that has torn asunder the old building blocks of the economy and society, unravelled the knotted, cellular communities of the work unit and the commune, and unleashed a seemingly relentless tide of individual, creative energy. Yet not all have gained to the same degree in the race for wealth and status. There have been outright winners and losers, as well as those who have in part gained and in part lost.

The Chinese Communist Party's almost obsessive concern with economic growth has perhaps unsurprisingly stimulated a vast array of studies on the challenges of developing a socialist market economy. As the socioeconomic fault lines of reform became ever more visible during the 1990s, the problems of inequality, injustice, environmental degradation, and poverty began to draw the attention of Chinese and international scholars. Since the 1990s, social discontent has increasingly found expression in spontaneous political protest. Unpaid pensioners and laid-off workers take to the streets in cities across China on an almost daily basis to claim their dues, whilst aggrieved farmers resist the extractive demands of cash-strapped, and sometimes corrupt, local government officials. Reports of slowdowns, street demonstrations, occupations of government buildings, and physical attacks upon local cadres and factory managers filter through the increasingly permeable walls of government censorship and control. Governance is a burning issue. Yet the Chinese Communist Party drags its feet on political reform. The problems of inequality, poverty, environmental damage, and injustice are reduced to matters of geographical location, lack of human capital, or the inevitable consequence of rapid economic growth that will eventually be resolved through the equally inevitable economic processes of trickle-down. It is a key premise of this book that governance matters, and that it matters for the future of China.

It would be wrong, however, to suggest that nothing has changed in China's processes of governance over the past two decades. Indeed much has been written about the gradual spread of competitive village elections, the reform of the civil service, the changes in recruitment processes to the Party, the rise of civil society, the decentralization of power to local governments, the gradual spread of the rule of law, and the invigoration of national and local parliaments.[4] Despite the ongoing repression of political dissidents, spiritual sects, and ethnic minorities, the political space for open discussion and measured critique is still much greater than on the eve of reform. In the last five years, Chinese scholars have tentatively tried to reopen the debate about the need for political reform, warning that a failure to reform politically could in turn endanger the economic successes achieved to date. Top leaders have heeded these words of caution but held back from initiating any systematic and comprehensive program of reform or from encouraging a more open debate on the subject.

In this book we seek to contribute to the development of a debate on governance in China. We not only review past changes in governance processes but also look ahead to the future, taking into account the likely effects of the 2002 16th Party Congress and of World Trade Organization (WTO) entry. We focus on some of the particular governance challenges that demand rigorous analysis and creative thinking for their resolution. As it is not possible to cover all the dimensions of governance, the book takes up a selection of themes for exploration and reflection, namely, the need for political reform; processes of institution-building such as strengthening state capacity and improving the legal framework; enhancing regime legitimacy through the sharing of power at lower levels and promoting participation and voice through the development of civil society; and managing social discontent.

During the 1990s, Chinese scholars ventured with increasing boldness to open up a debate around the issue of political reform and its relationship to the dual processes of economic liberalization and globalization. Joseph Fewsmith skillfully explores the contours of this debate, reflecting upon both the responses of China's political elite to globalization and WTO entry and, conversely, the potential impact of globalization on political reform and governance. Whilst globalization was initially embraced with enthusiasm in the West and Japan, over the last decade it has become increasingly contested, as witnessed in the passionate street protests in Seattle and Rome. In contrast, the Chinese political mainstream elite, that is, those associated with the former General Secretary Jiang Zemin and former Premier Zhu Rongji, have remained much more sanguine about processes of globalization and the benefits to be gained by China. By defining globalization in narrow economic and technical terms and emphasising its inevitability, Chinese political leaders have skillfully sidestepped any intense debate around its political dimensions and consequences. In this way they have managed to deflect those criticisms that have warned of the dangers of rising transnational corporate power, U.S. interference, and the threat to Chinese sovereignty.

In reflecting upon the implications of WTO entry for political reform and governance in China, Fewsmith points to the socioeconomic factors that have already called forth incipient systemic changes, such as village elections and Party personnel selection procedures, and that are likely to continue to do so in the post-WTO context. He highlights on the one hand the rapid growth of the private economy and on the other hand the social consequences of state enterprise restructuring. Though the emergence of a middle class might promise to be a stabilizing factor, the stark increase in inequality—regional, urban/rural, and income—and the problems of labor market absorption bode less well for social stability. Once the heroes of Maoist communism, the Chinese working class has now become one of the prime losers. All these concerns underpin the New Left's critique of both capitalism and globalization, which, drawing upon nationalist discourse, seeks a "native" model of modernity. Fewsmith notes that other social trends, not directly related to globalization, such as tensions between the Party and elected leaders in villages, the rise of popular religions, and growing social protests, also increase the pressure for political reform in China.

Against this background of socioeconomic change, China's intellectuals are increasingly focusing on issues of political reform, underlining its inevitability and inseparability from processes of economic reform. The three driving factors here are the legitimacy of the ruling regime, the fear of social fragmentation, and globalization. In particular, Fewsmith argues that the logic of globalization, namely the need to compete in global markets, will require the government to change its relationship to the economy and to institute efficient and rule-based systems of governance. Economic competition will demand political reform; without political reform, China's economy will falter in the cutthroat sea of global competition. However, Fewsmith does not expect political reform to be quick or easy, or necessarily to lead to democratization. Indeed, he speculates that political reform will be a highly contested process, with winners and losers making conflicting demands, on the one hand demanding a more democratic and open system, and on the other hand pressing for the maintenance of an authoritarian status quo, not the least reason being to address issues of social unrest.

The processes of institution-building, such as enhancing the competence and capacity of different elements of state administration and establishing and consolidating rules and regulations that ensure transparency and predictability, are crucial for effective governance. They are also of particular relevance to China, where political loyalty rather than meritocracy and rule by man rather than rule by law have undermined the structures of governance for many decades. Moreover as the spectre of corruption continues to erode public confidence in the Party and state institutions, strengthening processes of accountability and transparency are vital for preserving the legitimacy of the regime. In their chapters on civil service reforms, the lawyers' system, and the regulation of cultural industries, John Burns, Zhu Sanzhu, and Michael Keane respectively explore these key issues of institution-building.

Taking the more technical dimensions of governance as his starting point, Burns considers the extent to which civil service reforms have steered China toward more accountable, transparent, and effective governance. Burns traces the evolution of these reforms from 1980 onwards, noting the gradual introduction of compulsory retirement, the recruitment of younger and more educated officials, and the overhaul of the salary system. He finds that significant steps have been made in enhancing the accountability of the state, though as in other countries, bureaucratic/political accountability remains stronger than legal and professional accountability. New civil service regulations, public sector reforms, the ministerial/cadre responsibility system, and performance contracts in local governments have all enhanced bureaucratic accountability. Though the Chinese Communist Party remains the main site of political power and authority, the more critical responses of some National People's Congress delegates to government work reports point to a growing political accountability. The legal accountability of the civil service has been enhanced through the rotation of jobs and law enforcement, though localism, poor training, and inadequate pay have all undermined the effectiveness of the police and judiciary in prosecuting civil servants. The rise of professional associations such as the Chinese Institute of Certified Public Accountants and the development of professional codes of conduct have likewise marked an important step in promoting professional accountability within the Chinese civil service.

The Chinese civil service has also become more inclusive and representative than in the past. It is no longer only Beijing residents who can compete for civil service positions in the central government. National minorities, women, and even private entrepreneurs are being urged to seek government posts. Though civil service reforms have fostered greater transparency in the recruitment and appointment processes, Burns notes that this continues to be undermined by the pervasive buying and selling of positions. While low pay continues to be an obstacle to attracting the best talent to the civil service and retaining those on staff, civil servants are now younger and more educated than in the pre-reform period.

Though WTO entry and China's expanding external economic relations will increasingly require a highly competent civil service, Burns argues that internal pressure will be much more significant in accelerating the pace of bureaucratic reform. However, as private entrepreneurs take up positions within the state and form closer alliances with state officials, the prospects for greater meritocracy within the state remain ambivalent. On the one hand, as the domestic business community comes to recognize the neutrality of the civil service and the law to be in its own interests, then the meritocratic direction of reforms can be strengthened. On the other hand, the potential capture of the state by private business could compromise these efforts.

Institution-building in the sphere of law is the key theme of Zhu Sanzhu's chapter. He traces the development of the lawyers' system in China from 1949 onward and looks critically at attempts to develop and modernize the legal profession in the reform period. Cooperative and partnership law firms began to emerge in 1988 and were granted statutory status upon the promulgation of the Lawyers' Law in 1996. By 2000, they accounted for 15 percent and 25 percent, respectively, of all law firms in China. The Lawyers' Law of 1996 brought about significant changes in the lawyers' system, pushing in the direction of greater autonomy for lawyers. The definition of lawyers changed from legal workers of the state to legal practitioners providing services to the public. With the establishment of the All-China Lawyers' Association in 1986, lawyers laid an organizational foundation for regulating their own affairs. Initially their regulatory functions were limited. However, as the reform of government administration accelerated in the 1990s, the national and local level lawyers' associations began to take on an increasing number of functions that were previously carried out by the Ministry of Justice. Zhu maintains, nevertheless, that the All-China Lawyers' Association cannot yet be described as an independent association, as key personnel in the Secretariat are closely linked to the Ministry of Justice. Zhu laments that the dual systems for regulating lawyers—on the one hand by lawyers themselves, and on the other hand by government—have only increased regulatory costs and distorted the legal services market. Partial and hybrid processes of institution-building do not necessarily lead to improved governance.

China's accession to the WTO has had both a direct and indirect bearing on the legal service market and lawyers' system. The legal service market has opened up as negotiations for WTO entry have continued. The number of foreign representative offices of foreign law firms has spiralled upward since 1992, and the new 2001 regulation relating to representative offices enlarged significantly the range of services they can provide. However, restrictions still remain on the business scope of these offices, the qualifications of foreign lawyers, and the employment of Chinese lawyers. Accession to the WTO has also raised a host of questions around the legal profession, including the quality of lawyers, their ability to compete with foreign firms, the standards of services, and the need to adapt to international practices. Faced with competitive challenges in business, expertise, management, and quality, Chinese law firms will have to surmount two major barriers according to Zhu, namely, their small scale and lack of specialization. Regulations issued by the Ministry of Justice since 1992 and a new code of conduct introduced by the Beijing Lawyers' Association in 2000 aim to raise professional and ethical standards in the profession, important not only for the public image of lawyers in China but also for their standing internationally. The new national examination system, which started in 2002, is yet another initiative in this direction. For Zhu, the development of a legal profession in line with that of developed countries hinges crucially on the government's success in readjusting the relationship amongst lawyers, judicial administrative organs, and lawyers' self-regulatory associations.

Developing new institutions and processes of regulation is a challenge confronting not only the civil service and the lawyers' system, but also the sphere of culture. The internationalization of cultural industries and the emergence of new electronic technologies have rendered invalid past conceptualizations of propaganda and culture as distinct fields that require regulating in different ways. Given the increasing demand for leisure time and consumption in China, Keane predicts that cultural industries are likely to be one of the most dynamic growth areas of the future economy. However, for China to compete in the global market in key creative industries such as music, publishing, and multimedia and technology-based cultural services, it has to address a number of issues. First, what is the actual and potential impact of WTO entry on China's cultural industries? Second, given the internationalization of the cultural industries, what kind of national regulatory regime should be set up to deal with the diffusion of global cultural goods and services via new media technologies? And how can such a regulatory regime be enforced, given the tendency for local governments and foreign business to collude in reinterpreting central policy to their mutual advantages? And third, what are the implications of a fragmentation of sovereignty and authority for the development of civil society, democracy, and pluralization?

Drawing upon the work of Tipson (1999), Keane puts forward three different scenarios depicting the Chinese government's response to the information revolution. The first is the Singaporean approach, which seeks to develop an integrated national information infrastructure; the second "Taiwan approach" involves a more relaxed control regime, allowing greater plurality of expression; and the third is the "North Korean approach," which attempts to keep the lid on the development of communications so as to avoid any challenge to its regime. Keane argues that the first scenario is the most likely. Over the last two decades, the focus has been on the development of information technology hardware through national economic planning processes. The convergence of once separated sectors such as broadcasting and telecommunications has in turn triggered institutional changes for the purposes of regulation. This is reflected in the formation of the Ministry of Information Industry in 1998, which has absorbed the functions of other related ministries. Culture has thus become a value-adding industry as well as a site of expression that requires control and monitoring.

Yet Keane fears that in following the Singaporean model, China may end up deterring potential foreign investors used to more autonomous business environments and inhibiting the development of China's own cultural industries. For China to become a significant global player in this sector, Keane suggests a more "light touch" regime that facilitates creative autonomy and industrial development. For Keane, whether China can reframe the relationship between culture, services, and the knowledge-based economy so as to compete globally depends crucially on getting the policy right.

At the heart of governance processes is the fundamental question of "who has the right to govern?" Who has power and who has authority, and how are the two related? How much can and do citizens participate in formal processes of governance and in the broad deliberation of public affairs? The distribution of power and authority both within the state and between the state and society underlies the characterization of a regime as variously democratic, authoritarian, or totalitarian. The chapters by Linda Jakobson and Zhang Jing explore in turn the contestation of power and authority at the level of the village and an urban residential community. Both pose fundamental questions around the changing nature of political participation in China and the implications for processes of democratization and citizenship.

Jakobson sets out by examining the gradual spread and institutionalization of competitive, direct elections for positions in village committees in Chinese villages. Enjoying the political backing of veteran communist Peng Zhen, then chair of the National People's Congress and known for his conservative stance in other political debates, reform-minded officials within the Ministry of Civil Affairs were able to push the idea of directly electing village heads. In the context of rising corruption, the declining legitimacy of the Chinese Communist Party, and a sense of growing unrest in rural areas, the direct election of village leaders promised not only greater accountability of leaders to citizens, but also greater rural stability. By making permanent the Organic Law on Villagers' Committees in November 1998, top Party leaders signalled their approval of a fundamental change in the way power and authority were distributed and shared in villages. The sharing of power never goes uncontested. Though the idea of direct village elections has gained in popularity and legitimacy amongst villagers, it has encountered resistance from township and county leaders, who are fearful that they will lose control and authority over village affairs. Hence the institutionalization of direct village elections across and within counties and the actual practices for nominating candidates remain considerably uneven across the country.

Nevertheless, as villagers have realized their newfound powers to oust unpopular, corrupt, or incompetent leaders, the demand for a greater say in governance processes has filtered upwards to towns and townships. In early 1999, the first relatively competitive, direct elections for the post of township head took place in Buyun township, Suining city, Sichuan province. Reported two weeks later in the Guangdong newspaper *Nanfang Zhoumou*, the event led to a surge in optimism amongst scholars, reform-minded officials, and Party leaders about the prospects for democracy in China. However, within only four days, the Ministry of Justice had declared the elections to be in violation of the Constitution and law. Yet, the fact that the elections were not annulled and no officials were punished suggested also that the top Party leaders were not unanimous on how to respond to these events. In the next six months, Zhuoli township, Shanxi province, and Dapeng township near Shenzhen also experimented with direct elections for the position of township head, though the degree of influence given to citizens did not match that provided in the Buyun elections. The holding of these other two elections in different parts of China pointed to a growing demand among town and township dwellers for the greater accountability of leaders.

In the long term, these changes in grassroots governance have far-reaching implications for the process of democratization in China and the continuing rule of the Chinese Communist Party. As Jakobson points out, the experience of direct elections raises the awareness of rural dwellers about issues of accountability and transparency and enhances their interest in governance processes. This in turn increases the pressure upon the Chinese Communist Party to implement political reform. From the point of view of the top Party leadership, competitive, direct village elections provide a way of dealing with problems of corruption and the crisis in legitimacy of the Party. As citizens become increasingly conscious of their legal rights, the need for outlets to air grievances, resolve conflicts, and demand accountability intensifies. For China's top political leaders, extending political choice might run the risk of losing their grip on local governance, but continuing with the status quo might well pose a more pessimistic scenario of rapidly declining legitimacy and spiralling social unrest.

In her paper on a dispute involving a property owners' committee, a private property management company, and grassroots institutions of governance, Zhang Jing explores the changing contours and complexities of local governance in the context of the liberalization of the housing market. Taking the case of Qing Shui Yuan residential estate in Pudong district, Shanghai, she describes the tensions and contradictions in the established modes of governance at neighborhood and street level and reveals the emergence of a new framework of social relations. The dispute revolves around a property owners' committee that sought to change the private property management company, which had contracted to provide services on the estate. As the company had failed to provide services to a satisfactory standard, the property owners' committee voted to invite another property company to take over this work. Fearing that it was now about to lose its contract, the original company approached the relevant administrative authorities and asked them to intervene. The local street committee not only instructed the company to withhold the transfer of the maintenance fees into the account of the property owners' committee, but also ordered the assembly of owner representatives not to proceed with competitive tendering.

Zhang argues that the intervention of the local administrative authorities in the affairs of the residents of Qing Shui Yuan estate inhibited the development of a new form of governance that was being developed through the property owners' committee. The property owners' committee is made up of accountable representatives of residents on the estate, selected through a competitive process. The prime purpose of the committee is to ensure that residents' interests are protected. By contracting a property management agency to provide services on the estate, the property owners' committee and the selected property management agency enter into an equal and contractual relationship. However, the outcome of the dispute on Qing Shui Yuan estate points to resistance by local administrative authorities to the devolution of power to self-regulating citizens' groups. At stake is the fundamental issue of how local communities should be governed: whether from above by government or from below by self-regulating communities. Zhang suggests that unless citizens are given greater powers to control their own affairs, we can expect ever increasing numbers of conflicts at the community level. The case study illustrates vividly the emerging conflicts of power and authority in the context of a deepening disjuncture between the needs of a rapidly liberalizing economy and an increasingly dysfunctional mode of local governance.

The sharing of power and authority opens up a range of issues around the institutions and mechanisms of participation, the spaces for association and self-organizing, and the avenues for citizens to engage in and deliberate upon public affairs. The nature of civil society and the presence or otherwise of critical, public spheres reveal much about the possibilities and limitations of citizen participation in governance processes. Both Jude Howell, in relation to marginalized interests, and Du Jie, with regard to women, reflect upon the development of spaces for citizen action in China. In particular they interrogate the role of more independent nonstate organizations and actors in articulating the interests of diverse groups and in creating critical public spheres that bring about policy change.

By focusing on processes of societal organizing around HIV/AIDs, labor rights, and gender in the workplace, Howell explores the changing nature of autonomous organization in reformist China and its implications for the consolidation of a corporatist framework governing the associational sphere. In doing so, she tackles the thorny issue of the usefulness and relevance of established social science concepts such as civil society, corporatism, and the public sphere. She argues that from the early to mid-1990s onward, two key changes in the development of autonomous organization occurred: first, the emergence of a new stratum of organizations concerned with those social groups that were marginalized in, or losing out, from the processes of reform; and second, the continuing, yet constantly contested, expansion of the space for societal organization, as new forms of association such as networks, projects, centers, and associations at several levels removed from a registered social organization began to proliferate.

The emergence of this new stratum of organizations took place in a context where the pace of retrenchment was accelerating and the need to provide an effective safety net to laid-off workers became ever more urgent. By devolving state responsibility for these functions to community and nongovernmental agencies, the Party/state created an opening for organizations to emerge that would address the interests of different marginalized groups. International events such as the Fourth World Conference on Women held in Beijing in 1995 exposed Party leaders and cadres in the All-China Women's Federation to the diverse roles played by nongovernmental agencies in many countries, creating a more open climate for the expansion of more autonomous organizations. The growing number of international development agencies operating in China in the 1990s catalyzed the development and consolidation of more independent organizations concerned with issues of poverty, marginalization, and injustice.

The increasing diversification of more independent organizations and the proliferation of new associational forms that maneuver around the registration processes point to the weakening rather than the consolidation of a corporatist framework governing intermediary associations. Aware of the advantages of allowing society to organize itself, and aware of their own incapacity, in any case, to regulate systematically the spread of associations, local government officials often cast a blind eye to emerging organizations that provide services to vulnerable groups, provided they do not espouse political agendas. As government officials are torn between trying to retain control against the odds and giving a clear sign to potentially beneficial forms of association, governance becomes increasingly fragmented and localized. At the same time, associational life is not only more complex and diverse, but also more differentiated and more contentious, as the winners and losers in the reform process become more visible and vocal. The emergence of protopublic spheres that venture upon critical debate of matters once the unquestioned prerogative of the Party/state provides a potential outlet for the conflict that is simmering within civil society. In the absence of sufficient institutionalized mechanisms for the open discussion of policy, voicing critical opinion remains a risky affair in China. Though the spaces for independent organizing may be expanding and diversifying, the lack of an institutional framework that can positively encompass the differentiated interests will only strain the legitimacy of the Party/state and risk knee-jerk responses of spasmodic repression.

Du discusses the changes in the All-China Women's Federation (ACWF) during the reform period and the proliferation of new women's organizations, particularly in the 1990s. Having become dormant during the Cultural

Revolution (1966–1976), the ACWF set about reestablishing its branches and networks from 1978 onward. In response to the changing and increasingly diverse needs of women, the ACWF began to extend its working areas and encourage the development of new professional women's associations. It gradually increased its autonomy from the Party/state and gained new sources of economic revenue. The hosting of the Fourth World Conference on Women in 1995 was a catalyst for change both in the ACWF and in the landscape of women's organizations in China. New, more independent women's organizations began to proliferate across major cities in China from the early 1990s onward. These included women's and gender studies centers, courses, and research projects, which began to engage with the international women's movement and gender theory.

Though the terrain of organizing around gender has pluralized and diversified in the reform period, the ACWF, as the largest organization representing women and the one most closely related to the Chinese Communist Party, has been the best positioned to bring about policy change in favor of women. Du discusses two significant moves by the ACWF to bring gender issues into mainstream policy making. The first concerned the ACWF's attempts to modify the new 1998 regulation on the contracting of rural land so as to safeguard women's interests. The second successful intervention related to the drafting of the 10th Five Year Plan and the ACWF's proposal to remove the notion of "phased employment," which would effectively hinder female participation in the labor force.

Whilst new women's organizations have less access to the policy-making process, they have made substantial contributions to other arenas. In particular, they have sought to address the practical needs of grassroots women, providing new kinds of services. They have carried out detailed empirical research, which has increasingly provided a base for the development of gender-sensitive policies. They have introduced the concept of gender planning into development programs in China. Particularly important has been their role in raising awareness of sensitive gender issues such as domestic violence. Du predicts that the gendered processes of socioeconomic change are likely to intensify with further reform and WTO entry, with both positive and negative outcomes for diverse groups of women. If the ACWF and the new women's organizations are to respond effectively to these challenges, then they will have to forge a common strategy based upon cooperation and mutual interests.

As rapid socioeconomic change undermines the certainties of the past and disrupts patterns of social relations and institutional configurations of participation, the risks of social discontent, alienation, and disaffection are high for any government. Under such circumstances, social malaise can translate with seeming ease, like a snake slithering through the long grass, into organized protest, spontaneous rebellion, and regime threat. The process of reform in

China has unsettled existing norms, values, and incentive structures, recasting the web of losers and winners. Social protest in the form of strikes, peasant uprisings, demonstrations, and physical assaults upon government officials and factory managers have become regular occurrences, though official reports veil their magnitude and frequency. How such events are managed has implications not only for the immediate aggrieved social groups, but also for the broader framework governing state-society relations and in particular the boundaries of association and critique. Marc Blecher and Clemens Østergaard explore this issue with reference respectively to urban workers and the followers of Falun Gong.

In his chapter, Blecher starts by asking how serious a threat the Chinese working class now poses to the state. He pursues this question by outlining the factors that could potentially galvinize labor discontent or promote quiescence. He considers the challenges the Chinese working class presents for the state and possible state responses. The decline in material conditions and the loss of social and political status experienced by retrenched workers creates a potential governance problem for the state. In the context of China, this relates not only to worker unrest around lay-offs and state incapacity to provide adequate safety nets, but also to the gradual dissolution of the old systems of institutional control and regulation such as the work unit and concentrated worker housing. New social welfare schemes for pensions, medical care, and unemployment may on the one hand be an attempt to establish a new system of governance, but on the other hand could provide a focal point for collective action when the state is not seen to deliver. Similarly, though the 1994 Labor Law seeks to develop a framework guaranteeing decent employment conditions, without proper enforcement, exploitative and unacceptable employment practices are likely to spark off spontaneous protests and unrest.

However, there are also a number of factors which make it easier for the state to govern the working class. Blecher suggests that social fragmentation amongst the working class has actually prevented the formation of a cohesive labor movement. The vast majority of protests, demonstrations, and strikes have been limited to single factories and to particular geographical locations. The coping strategies of retrenched workers, such as falling back upon the family and/or finding work in China's rapidly expanding informal economy, have taken the sting out of sudden unemployment. Furthermore, workers' resignation to, if not positive endorsement of, the overall reform process has subdued any major challenge to the political system. As Blecher notes, there is somehow an expectation that wealth will eventually trickle down. China's monopolistic trade union structure is also an asset to the state in containing potential unrest and ensuring social stability.

Taking into account the above factors, it would seem that the governance challenge posed by the working class is neither monumental nor miniscule.

Nevertheless, there are still significant political, social, and economic challenges that if not dealt with could unsettle the political status quo. These include the need to maintain political stability, prevent the rise of independent trade unions, and ensure social order and control. Dealing with corruption, enforcing labor policies, maintaining economic growth, and adequately resourcing a social welfare system are all issues that if not properly handled can provide the powderkeg for social protest. All these are contradictory processes requiring, as Blecher puts it, "much sophisticated statespersonship and a generous dose of good fortune."

How then can the state address the specific challenges posed by the working class in the context of rapid social and economic transformation? Blecher argues that continuing to strengthen the trade union and neighborhood committees as valuable institutions of social control no doubt makes sense, but the effectiveness of these measures will be limited by the decreasing influence of the state over enterprises and the ongoing reluctance by the Party to grant the unions any meaningful autonomy. Maintaining economic growth, too, will be crucial. Developing the social welfare system will be vital to removing the hard edge of the market economy, though the state will need to exercise caution in not raising expectations too high. Blecher concludes that the task of governing China's working class may not be so daunting, given that some of the most formidable undertakings have already been achieved. Yet the state's continuing efforts to stave off any independent organization by China's working class suggest an acute awareness within the Party leadership of the potentially destabilizing effects of worker unrest and the need for ongoing monitoring and alertness.

Collective action by discontented urban workers, rural-based social protest, the declining influence of Party ideology, public perception of serious corruption in the Party-state, and the widening income disparities along generational and regional lines have all contributed toward mounting social alienation and malaise. In the absence of a unifying ideology and with the gradual crumbling of the former institutional fabric of social solidarity, disillusioned sections of society, and, in particular, middle-aged, female, poorly educated city dwellers in the declining rustbelt of China, have sought spiritual sanctuary in both mainstream religions such as Buddhism and Christianity as well as in the profusion of what are often labelled as cults and sects.

In his chapter on the Falun Gong, Østergaard argues that this new religious movement represents a new kind of popular fundamentalism, distinct from other forms by its strong organization and its deft use of modern technology and modern marketing methods. Østergaard traces the gradual evolution of the Falun Gong from a religious movement offering spiritual salvation to an interest group making claims upon the state. Tolerated by the Party-state in its early years, the Falun Gong began to arouse suspicion and hostility as some qigong groups came under attack for propagating feudal, antiscientific, and superstitious beliefs. In 1996 the Falun Gong drew media criticism, leading to the eventual expulsion of Li Hongzhi, the charismatic leader of the Falun Gong, from the national Qigong Research Association and his subsequent exile to the U.S. By directing his followers to challenge the Party-state's depiction of the Falun Gong and to engage in demonstrative protests, Li Hongzhi turned the movement into a political force. This culminated in the collective surrounding of the Zhongnanhai by over 10,000 followers, an action that stunned Chinese political authorities and the public security and drew international attention.

Faced with this confrontational situation, the Party-state initially proceeded with caution, investigating the organization and holding back from immediate action. In the context of the May bombing of the Chinese embassy in Yugoslavia, the approaching tenth anniversary of Tiananmen, and strained relations with Taiwan, Chinese leaders called for a ban on the Falun Gong and mounted a strident campaign against its followers. By arresting followers and holding them in re-education camps and deprogramming centers, the Party-state sought to stamp out the organization through both repression and persuasion. Though the Party-state resorted to traditional campaign methods and repression, it nevertheless seemed to win the struggle against Li Hongzhi. However, this was also because Li Hongzhi had miscalculated the enormity of the state's response to the Zhongnanhai action. Furthermore, he had created a practical dilemma for his followers: though they sought an escape from the material world, its harshness and injustices, the politicization of the organization brought them directly back into the world of conflict.

Østergaard argues that though the response of the state has severely limited the growth of the Falun Gong, the resort to traditional methods of repression and persuasion have done little to enhance the legitimacy and standing of the Party. Moreover, this episode has led to tighter controls on society and inhibited the more open discussion of political reform in the late 1990s. The Falun Gong drama highlights the continuing inability of the Chinese Party-state to establish a modicum of balance with society that is premised on negotiation rather than force.

What then do these various explorations of governance reveal to us about the changing nature of governance in China? It remains, as ever, enormously difficult to capture in one neat phrase the "state" of governance in China. It would be wrong to suggest either that little has changed in governance processes in China and that China remains as authoritarian as ever, or that the changes that have taken place do add up to fundamental change in the direction of more accountable, transparent, effective, and even democratic governance. At the most, we can hope to tease out the emerging tendencies and patterns, to reflect upon the factors that may pull China in one direction or another, and to speculate with some modesty and caution on the prospects for the future.

The twelve chapters in this volume highlight a number of emerging tendencies and patterns. First, governance processes in China are increasingly fragmented and contradictory, as the central government struggles to enforce national and uniform policies and laws. Zhang's study of a residential estate in China and Howell's chapter on marginalized interests point to the localized nature of governance outcomes and processes, which are linked crucially to the fragmentation of governance processes across vertical and horizontal lines, illustrated in the chapter of Burns on civil service reform and Keane on the regulation of cultural industries.

Second, the process of reworking that totality of institutions and arrangements for distributing and regulating power and public authority has been partial and uneven. This has led in some instances to an institutional vacuum, where new institutions have not fully developed and old institutions have either collapsed or become increasingly irrelevant, as witnessed in the domain of social welfare or rural health care. In other cases it has given rise to hybrid, overlapping institutional forms and arrangements, as described in Zhu's chapter, which worsen rather than ameliorate governance outcomes. Patterns of governance are increasingly motleyed and varied, rendering the implementation of central policy more complex and haphazard.

Third, as economic liberalization deepens, there is a growing tendency for the legitimate scope and boundaries of public authority to be contested, as described in Zhang's chapter on the conflict in the residential estate and in Østergaard's chapter on the Falun Gong. Fourth, the Party/state has not yet established predictable and effective arrangements and processes, in the rapidly changing context of economic reform, for the articulation of societal interests. The corporatist framework is increasingly fragile as dynamic individuals and groups of individuals find alternative ways of organizing around their interests, as evidenced in the chapters of both Howell and Du. The weakness of this framework is underlined by the growing incidences of social protest in both urban and rural areas, by the ability of the Falun Gong to develop into a nationwide organization with the capacity to surround Zhongnanhai, and not least by the repressive responses of the Party/state to perceived threats to its power.

Finally, the chapters by Keane, Fewsmith, Zhu, Burns, and Howell all suggest that China is becoming increasingly subject to economic and social forces from the outside. Though the impact of external variables will by no means be comparable to national contexts such as Bangladesh, Mozambique, Argentina, and some Eastern European countries that are reliant on international aid and/or loans from international financial institutions, nevertheless, the influence of external economic, cultural, and social forces needs to be factored more consciously into analyses of politics and governance in China.

None of this points to an increasingly institutionalized and democratic set of governance arrangements and processes. The spread of village elections across the country and the gradual, yet tentative, percolation upwards of competitive elections suggest that democratic rules and practices may be starting from the bottom up. Similarly, the proliferation of nonregistered organizations that bypass the stringent regulations for registering social organizations points also to an increasingly tolerant Party/state, which is willing to extend the slack if the social benefits are perceived to outweigh the costs. Yet the agencies of repression are always at hand to respond to unwanted outbursts of dissent and to set with force the boundaries of legitimate association and critique. China remains authoritarian, but it is an authoritarianism that is increasingly, albeit haltingly, opening up, allowing the expansion of spaces for self-regulation and intellectual reflection, and even the competitive contestation of power at lower levels.

In the concluding chapter of this volume, we analyze the combination of political, institutional, and economic factors that combine in complex ways to shape the way power and authority are distributed and regulated and the nature of governance problems in China. We compare China's governance challenges with those of other countries in the South and transitional contexts and then consider the future prospects for governance in China. The deep-seated drive of the Chinese Communist Party to maintain power aggravates reform efforts to create autonomous spaces in the economy and society and to separate out the Party from government. Attempts to modernize the Party by recruiting popular, "clean," and technically competent members are weakened by the persistence of deeply embedded webs of personal obligation and loyalty and the economic gains that can still be reaped through a position in the Party. The pathologies of Leninist institutions such as the incentive structure governing bureaucrat's behavior; the tendency toward institutional protectionism; the resistance to sharing power, authority, and resources; elitism; and the politicization of the public administration hinder institutional adaptation and innovation. Contradictions amongst economic reforms such as decentralization and taxation, and the disjuncture between institutional and economic reforms, such as the development of a comprehensive social security system and state enterprise reform, contribute to the governance problems facing China at the turn of the millennium. Though China displays similar symptoms and causes of poor governance, such as corruption, lack of transparency, and the dominance of personalized rule rather than the rule of law, to many other countries in the South and the former Soviet Union, it is still better positioned than many countries to take up these challenges, not least because of its relatively strong economy, its long history of state administration, and a growth-oriented political elite. It is hard to speculate with any certainty upon the prospects for governance as China deepens its economic reforms and engagement in the global economy and polity. Political scientists and economists have often gotten their predictions for regime change and economic growth alarmingly wrong. However, if there is one certainty for China's future, it is that governance matters.

# NOTES

1. In the World Bank's report *Governance and Development* (1992: 1), "governance" is defined "as the manner in which power is exercised in the management of a country's economic and social resources for development." The World Bank has focused on those areas that relate directly to economic policy and management and has evaded broader concerns around regime type.

2. Leftwich (1993) distinguishes three levels of governance: first, the narrow, managerial definition adopted by the World Bank, which is concerned with public administration and the judicial system; second, a broader interpretation which focuses on legitimate, authoritative states, with a democratic mandate and clear separation of powers; and third, a systemic interpretation, which goes beyond government to include more broadly economic and political power, the structures and rules governing their production and distribution, or in brief, a system of political and socioeconomic relations.

3. Bad governance in turn is characterized by corruption, personalized forms of rule, unstable and unpredictable government behavior, a lack of accountability and transparency, incompetence and inefficiency, repression, and a lack of respect for human rights. For a further discussion of this see World Bank, 1992.

4. For a long list of the key initiatives taken to reform the state apparatus, see Oksenberg (2001: 24).

# 2

## Elite Responses to Social Change and Globalization

*Joseph Fewsmith*

Globalization in general and the World Trade Organization (WTO) in particular affect Chinese society in various ways, including influencing elite perceptions of the international economy, affecting social trends in China, and creating pressures for political reform. These impacts cannot be separated from domestic trends but are in fact part of the same broad issue that the Chinese political elite needs to think about as it considers adjusting its mode of governance. Because trends in Chinese society and the global economy are complex, different people draw different conclusions about how to respond, and unexpected international or domestic events could affect China's response in the future.

This chapter will consider these issues by looking first at elite responses to globalization, then looking at societal trends—particularly expressed dissatisfaction—and the challenge they pose for legitimacy, and finally at pressures for political reform. There are three basic arguments. First, elite political acceptance of globalization, even if limited by a relatively narrow, economic interpretation of that concept, was not inevitable and has prevailed against other more negative views. Second, the social dissatisfaction expressed in public opinion surveys and instances of collective protest pose a problem of governance for China. This problem centers on the issue of legitimacy. Finally, the Chinese Communist Party (CCP) faces pressures stemming both from globalization and social dissatisfaction to change its mode of governance. The CCP has begun to respond by adjusting its traditional understanding of Marxism-Leninism to permit and encourage the growth of a more institutionalized relationship between state and society. It has also undertaken reforms to change recruitment and promotion procedures within the CCP, and there seems to be widespread acceptance among the political elite for further political reform.

## GLOBALIZATION

The term "globalization" has evoked different responses from political elites and publics around the world. Many, like Malaysia's Muhammed Mahathir, have railed against the forces of globalization, at least during times of international economic crisis. Even Japanese attitudes have been ambivalent. In the 1980s, Japan used the term *kokusaika* (internationalization), which had a positive connotation, but in the 1990s, commentators have adopted the more ambivalent term *gurobaruka* (globalization) as concerns about the implications of "globalization" for Japanese society have mounted (Kim, 2000). Populist concerns about globalization have mounted since the 1997 meeting of the WTO in Seattle, and now a wide variety of groups protest international financial meetings on a regular basis.

In contrast to this international skepticism, mainstream political elite opinion in China remains remarkably in favor of globalization. By "mainstream political elite," I mean those associated with Jiang Zemin, former general secretary of the CCP until November 2002, and Zhu Rongji, former premier of the State Council until his retirement in March 2003, who have dominated the policy-making process in recent years. The emergence of such a positive evaluation of globalization seemed unlikely only a decade or so ago. In Jiang Zemin's National Day (October 1) address in 1989, the new general secretary declared, "A small number of people planned to create a so-called 'middle class' in China to act as their basis of support so as to overturn our socialist system. This proves from the obverse side that we must whole-heartedly rely on the working class" (Jiang, 1991). This negative evaluation of the development of a middle-class society, then as now seen as linked to the development of international economic relations and the creation of a private sector, was very much a part of the conservative political backlash following Tiananmen.

Skepticism of globalization began to fade following Deng Xiaoping's "journey to the south" in 1992, when Deng lambasted conservatives, suggesting that they should step down. As China's economic reforms were reinvigorated, foreign investment began to pour into China. In 1993 foreign direct investment in China shot up 1.5 times to $27.5 billion, and then increased to over $40 billion in the mid-1990s and since. Discussions on China's entry into the WTO resumed as Chinese skepticism faded and political relations between China and the United States began to improve.

By 1997, at the 15th Party Congress, Jiang Zemin could tell the assembled Party delegates (Moore, 2000):

Opening to the outside world is a long-term basic state policy. Confronted with the globalization trend in economic, scientific, and technological development, we should take an even more active stance in the world by improving the pattern of opening up in all directions, at all levels and in a wide range, developing an open economy, enhancing our international competitiveness, optimizing our economic structure and improving the quality of our national economy.

The following spring, Jiang declared, "Economic globalization is an objective trend of world economic development, from which none can escape and in which everyone has to participate" (*Renmin Ribao*, March 9, 1998).

At the 16th Party Congress in November 2002, Jiang presented a vision of an urbanized, professionalized, technocratically advanced, middle-class society (*xiaokang shehui*) being created by the year 2020—by which time he expects that China will have quadrupled its GNP over 2000. This type of society would not, indeed, could not, be created in isolation from the international economy but only through acceptance of the challenge of globalization. As Jiang put it (Jiang, 2002):

We [China] are willing to work with the international community to actively promote world multipolarization, to advance harmonious existence of diverse forces, to maintain stability in the international community, to actively promote the development of economic globalization in the direction conducive to common prosperity, and to seek advantages and avoid disadvantages so that all countries, particularly developing countries, can benefit from the process.

This was not an unreserved endorsement of global economic order—Jiang also declared that "the old international political and economic order, which is unfair and irrational, has yet to be changed fundamentally"—but it nevertheless clearly envisioned China as a beneficiary of the international economic order and the processes of globalization.

This positive evaluation of globalization has emerged despite opposition within the government and the emergence of a significant body of public opinion that was critical of capitalism in general and globalization in particular. In particular, Li Peng, the conservative premier between 1988 and 1998 and head of the National People's Congress (NPC) from 1998 to 2003, championed the preservation of the "socialist" economy in China and correspondingly saw close ties—either political or economic—with the West as a threat. Such views presented a considerable obstacle to Jiang Zemin, Zhu Rongji, and other reformers and slowed the acceptance of globalization in the 1990s.

Within society, criticisms of globalization have been even more visible and more pointed. One of the most interesting developments of the 1990s was the emergence of a school of thought (generally referred to as the "New Left") that has been highly critical of social trends within China and of globalization. More to the point, it has seen domestic trends within China as related to international pressures, either through the influence of economic forces or through the intellectual acceptance of "Western" ideas regarding "modernization." These new ideas regarding China's development fell on fertile soil as a new nationalism appeared, as income gaps within China—both intra- and interregional—grew rapidly, and as the collapse of socialism in Eastern Europe and the former Soviet Union was accompanied by serious economic dislocation as those nations adopted one form or another of "shock therapy" (the rapid and simultaneous implementation of price and ownership reform). The crux of the question, for these academics, was nothing more—and nothing less—than the definition of modernity (Wang, 1998: 7–26).

The New Left emerged against the background of the 1980s, when Chinese intellectuals sought to move the country away from the chaos of the Cultural Revolution by criticizing "feudal" traditions (which include the centralization of power and the absence of individual rights), "leftism" (meaning political, economic, and social trends that opposed any form of "bourgeois" lifestyle), and the planned economy (which focused on highly intensive and inefficient state-owned enterprises (SOEs)). Drawing on the May Fourth liberal tradition, such intellectuals inevitably saw the importation of economic, political, and social systems and lifestyles from the West as antidotes to the failures of Chinese Communist Party rule. These trends reached a popular climax with the broadcast of *River Elegy*, the six-hour miniseries that was shown on Chinese television in June and again in August 1988. The film argued that Chinese civilization, rooted in the now dry and withered upper reaches of the Yellow River Valley, was no longer capable of sustaining a developing and modern society. To "modernize" and move away from the "feudal" traditions of the past, it was necessary to open the country up to the "blue seas" of the Pacific and the economic and cultural influences of the West. Put another way, "capitalism" was the necessary antidote to "feudalism."

The collapse of the Soviet Union and the subsequent decline in the economies of the newly independent republics that emerged from it convinced many that privatization, especially rapid privatization ("shock therapy"), was not the answer. Worse, the importation of capitalism in the former Soviet Union entailed a decline in international status, the breakup of national territory, the emergence of large-scale criminal organizations, and the inclusion of Russia and other republics into the Western capitalist orbit. Combined with the emerging inequalities in Chinese society, many intellectuals rejected the 1980s agenda and argued that the introduction of capitalism had only made things worse. It was necessary to define a non-Western model of modernity.

This mode of thinking, known in China as the "New Left" (to distinguish it from the "Old Left," which is composed of orthodox Marxist-Leninist thinkers), was thus a critique of capitalism on the one hand and of globalization on the other. In this, it drew both on native traditions of "leftist" thought (of which there were many in modern China) and Western critical thought (including Michel Foucault, Fredric Jameson, Edward Said, Immanuel Wallerstein, and others). In its search for a "native" (*bentu* or *bentuhua*) model of modernity, these intellectual trends inevitably have a nationalistic component and overlap to some extent with more popular nationalism (as expressed in such books as *China Can Say No* and *China Under the Shadow of Globalization*). These trends are reflected in an article by Shao Ren (apparently a pseudonym) that appeared in the influential journal *Tianya*:

> The U.S. controls the regulations that have been formulated by the international economic organizations; all are designed to accord with the interests and needs of the institutional model of the strong capitalist states. As soon as China joins the WTO, the U.S. can at any time find an excuse to interfere in, sanction, and intimidate our country into accepting so-called "international norms" that do not accord with our national characteristics. And to help the multinational companies to control China's industrial and financial lifelines, it [the U.S.] will usurp our economic sovereignty and force us to carry out suicidal reforms just as it has in Latin America, Russia, Southeast Asia and elsewhere (Shao, 1999: 6).

Elite opposition to globalization converged with intellectual opinion and wider nationalist emotion in the spring of 1999 when President Clinton's rejection of Premier Zhu Rongji's bid for WTO membership was followed by the bombing of the Chinese embassy in Belgrade. The nationalist fury and political turmoil in China imperiled the premier's job and threatened Jiang's strategy of getting China into the WTO. It was not until the fall of 1999 that the immediate wave of passion passed and serious negotiations could resume (Fewsmith, 2001a).

This episode underscores the extent to which Jiang's adoption of the term globalization was a conscious choice that reflected basic decisions about China's development strategy and that it was made against others who disagreed strongly. Indeed, it appears that Jiang adopted the term "globalization" in the mid-1990s to shift the terms of the debate from emotional phrases such as "Westernization" and all-out "Westernization" (*quanpan xihua*), which had been employed extensively in the aftermath of Tiananmen, to more technical terms. Chinese commentators initially adopted terms like "joining the world" (*zouxiang shijie*) and "joining tracks" (*jiegui*) to depict bringing China into the international economic order. Eventually, the leadership accepted the term "globalization," which has the advantage of being seen as a global process; that is, a force to which all nations must adapt and hence not a matter of giving up "Chineseness" and yielding to "Westernization." Thus, the term "globalization" sidesteps, or tries to, that bugaboo of twentieth-century history, the Chinese-Western duality.

If China's leadership has been willing to accept, indeed to use, the vocabulary of globalization, they have also done so in a way that reflects their technocratic and hierarchical biases. The political leadership does not see globalization as *laissez-faire* and multidimensional. Indeed, globalization is linked to technological change, as expressed in such terms as the "information age" (*xinxi shidai*) and the "knowledge economy" (*zhishi jingji*). The pace of technological change is depicted as fast, as indeed it is; China must either get with the technological and economic changes of the age or miss yet another opportunity to catch up with the West. The rhetoric of missed opportunities curses through modern Chinese history and forms a powerful, nationalistic spur to carry out the necessary changes.

As Thomas Moore has argued, this program of change is cast in fairly narrow terms of economic and particularly national competition (Moore, 2000; Moore, 2002). Globalization is one part of a national strategy of developing "comprehensive national strength." This suggests that in China globalization will be led primarily by the production and organization of computer engineers and large-scale "national champions" that can compete with Western multinationals. Indeed, this was the vision set out in Jiang's report to the 16th Party Congress.

This vision may jibe with reality, at least in the short run. As Heike Holbig has argued, China's entry into the WTO will generate a need for greater expertise and enforcement of rules. This is likely, in the short run, to increase the weight of the central government *vis-à-vis* the localities and of technocrats vis-à-vis democrats (Holbig, 2001). Over the longer run, however, globalization is likely to stimulate important changes in China's governing structures, in part because of the massive social changes that economic development and restructuring have brought about in recent years. Indeed, there is already considerable discussion in China about the challenge globalization presents to government and Party institutions. Zheng Yongnian has argued that the Chinese government defused the tension following Tiananmen by "de-ideologizing" its governing philosophy (that is, by dropping the antagonism between "capitalism" and "socialism" following Deng Xiaoping's 1992 trip to the south) and by allowing the rapid emergence of a private economy. The result was the emergence of an interest-based politics, which, by the end of the 1990s, was already making new and perhaps more urgent demands for political reform (Zheng, 2001: 173–96).

This process of domestic social change will converge with the demands of globalization to open up new space in China's policy, bring about substantial change in state-society relations, and generate significant demand for political change. There are three broad trends that affect this dynamic. First, there is a concern with political legitimacy. As the appeal of Marxism-Leninism has waned, the CCP has placed greater stress on economic growth as a way to retain power. Jiang Zemin stated this with unusual clarity at the 16th Party Congress in November 2002: "If we deviate from development, it will be impossible for us to talk about upholding the Party's advanced nature and its steadfastness." Globalization has been seen as a way to promote economic development and national greatness. Second, over the past decade, there has been increasing concern with social fragmentation and instability as income differentials have widened dramatically and peasants and workers have taken up collective action in protest. Although critics would counsel keeping globalization at arm's length as discussed later in this chapter, mainstream political opinion has seen economic growth as the only way to deal with social issues. Nevertheless, this social fragmentation creates pressures for the CCP to reform as it attempts to cope with globalization. Finally, globalization generates international pressures to reform government; Chinese cities must compete with each other and with cities abroad to create a good investment environment. Thus, many reformers in China have welcomed globalization as a force that can help propel China's domestic reforms to a new level. These pressures will lead to new opportunities for different, and hopefully better, modes of governance. In the following subsections we look at each of the trends in turn and consider their implications for political reform and governance.

## LEGITIMACY AND SOCIAL INSTABILITY

The response of China's governing elite and intellectuals alike to globalization is very much influenced by perceptions of changes in domestic society. These changes have gutted traditional understandings of Marxism-Leninism (thus undermining the legitimacy of the government), have created new social forces outside the Party's direct control, have raised serious questions about who is benefiting from economic growth as sharp intra- and interregional income gaps appeared, and have fostered social frustration that constantly threatens to boil over into social instability and sometimes does. All these forces press against the Party, creating possibilities of political reform as the Party readjusts its relationship with society, the government, and the outside world.

The growth of the private economy in the 1990s was very rapid indeed. According to official figures, which no doubt understate the size of the private economy, the number of people working in the non-state sector grew from 21.51 million in 1989 to 87.01 million in 1998 (*Zhongguo siying qiye fazhan baogao, 1999* (2000): 33). According to a more recent source, by the end of 2001, there were some 21 million people working for 180,000 foreign-invested enterprises, suggesting that the private economy has grown very rapidly in recent years (Li Peilin, 2002: 61).

These trends reflect dramatic changes in China's social structure, though not all of these changes are good. On the beneficial side of the ledger, a middle class has begun to form, as indeed Jiang Zemin has hoped will happen. A recent Center for Applied Social Surveys (CASS) study estimated the size of this middle class at 15 percent of China's population. However, it seems to be the very wealthy who are benefiting more than the middle class. As a result, income inequality has grown rapidly and continues to grow. Twenty years ago, China was perhaps the most egalitarian society in the world; today it is one of the least. The difference between the top 20 percent and the bottom 20 percent at the beginning of the reform era was 4.5 to 1, but by the late 1990s, it had grown to 12.66 to 1. By the late 1990s, China's Gini index stood at 0.4577 (some privately estimate 0.5), whereas in the United States the Gini index was 0.38–0.39 (Lu, 2001: 93–94).

Although the number of peasants, in proportional terms, has shrunk from about 70 percent to about 50 percent, their absolute number has actually increased. In 1978, there were an estimated 298 million farm workers. The number increased to 350 million in 1991, before declining to 321 million in 1999 (Carter, 2001: 73). This means there has been an increasing number of farmers working a diminishing number of acres—and increasing pressure to break down the *hukou* (household registration) system that has kept the urban and rural areas largely separated from each other. Unless this system can be changed substantially, a very large number of peasants will remain at the base of the income pyramid, and the longed-for "olive-shaped" pattern of income distribution, indicating the formation of a middle class, will not take shape quickly or easily.

The biggest loser of the reform era, particularly in the 1990s, has been the traditional working class. According to official statistics, which apparently understate the reality, state-owned enterprises (SOEs) laid off 37 million people—33 percent of the total SOE workforce—between 1995 and 2001. At the same time, urban collectives laid off 58 percent of their workers, reducing their payrolls from 31 million to 13 million (*Zhongguo tongji nianjian* [China Statistical Yearbook], 1997 and 2002). These lay-offs have been particularly painful because of the difficulties of re-employing those laid off. In general, those laid off are older, female, lacking formal education, and the jobs they can get, if they can find them, tend to be lower-paying and with fewer benefits than their previous jobs. In 1998 50 percent of those laid off were able to find new jobs; in 1999 that figure fell to 42 percent, then to 35.4 percent in 2000, 30.6 percent in 2001, and an estimated 20 percent in 2002 (Mo, 2003: 36). Re-employment is particularly difficult in old industrial areas such as the northeast. Given that China's social security system is still embryonic, it is not surprising that these trends have spilled over into the streets as workers have protested their treatment (see Blecher, Chapter 10 in this volume).

Up until the mid-1990s, the township and village enterprise (TVE) sector was the engine that drove employment. Over the decade from the early 1980s to the early 1990s, TVEs were able to provide employment for some 100 million peasants, thus easing—but by no means solving—underemployment in the countryside. In the mid-1990s, however, TVEs stopped absorbing labor and indeed began dismissing workers. Employment in the TVE sector peaked in 1996 at 135 million, fell to 125 million in 1998, and has crept back up to 131 million by the end of 2001 (*Zhongguo tongji nianjian*, 2002: 121). These trends reflect one of the most anomalous characteristics of the contemporary Chinese economy—the tendency for industrial growth to be capital-intensive rather than labor-intensive. This trend perhaps reflects the barriers between regions. TVE growth has always been biased toward the eastern part of the country, where it is highly integrated with the global economy (two-thirds of the growth in Chinese exports in the 1978–1992 period came from the TVE sector). To date, interior provinces, where labor is highly underemployed and cheaper, have not been able to partake fully in the growth of TVEs. This may be due to local protectionism or high transportation costs, or both.

The slow growth of TVEs in the 1990s points to one of China's most serious social problems: jobless growth. Over approximately the last decade, China's economy has continued to grow impressively, but the number of jobs created has lagged behind. According to the research of Wang Shaoguang in the 1980s, every additional percentage point in GDP growth increased the number of jobs by 0.32 percent. In 1999, however, the GDP grew by 7.1 percent, but employment only increased 0.36 percent; thus every percentage point of GDP growth brought about only a 0.05 percent increase in the number of jobs (Wang, 2000: 383–84). Of course, the latter figure reflects in part the very large layoffs from SOEs that took place in the late 1990s, a situation that is limited in duration; nevertheless, the slow growth of employment relative to the need for jobs is very real.

These trends have clearly generated social frustration. A survey conducted by the State Reform Commission (apparently in 1998) revealed that 80.6 percent of the people are dissatisfied with the growing gap between rich and poor. It concluded bluntly that the idea of getting wealthy legally is widely ridiculed (*Dangjian yanjiu conghengtan*, 1998: 85–86). The sort of dissatisfaction such figures represent is widely spread across different strata of China, albeit for different reasons. For instance, 59 percent of workers and staff surveyed say that they believe that the status of workers has declined in China. When asked about the social situation (the term is not defined in the text but presumably measures specific concerns such as feelings about corruption and public order as well as more abstract expectations about whether life is improving), 45.7 percent of workers and staff said that they believe that there are quite a few problems (*wenti bu shao*), while another 42 percent believe the situation is serious (*Dangjian yanjiu conghengtan*, 1998: 73). That is a total of 87 percent who expressed considerable concern about the social situation. Corruption was cited as a prominent concern, but no figures were given. In conclusion, the book stated, "One cannot be optimistic about the attitudes of workers" (*Dangjian yanjiu conghengtan*, 1998: 75).

According to the same source, 40 percent of middle-aged intellectuals believe that China is working to build "Chinese-style capitalism" (rather than Chinese-style socialism). Among scientific and research units, SOEs, and institutes of higher education, 33.3 percent of intellectuals believe that China should "carry out general elections" and implement a "bicameral, multiparty, tripartite" political system. As to the nature of the Party, 24.3 percent of intellectuals responded that it was a "whole people's party" or "not clear" (rather than the vanguard of the proletariat) (*Dangjian yanjiu conghengtan*, 1998: 75–76).

The problem in contemporary China is not merely that income differentials are widening, but that it appears that large groups of people are simply being jettisoned. Workers who are unlikely to be rehired, peasants whose incomes have been declining and have difficulty migrating, and peasants who have moved into cities but cannot be integrated into urban societies because of rules governing residency are effectively excluded from mainstream society. The educational opportunities for their children are poor, the health care system is fragile, and the opportunities for upward social mobility are scarce. Thus, Qinghua University sociologist Sun Liping argues that China is developing a "fractured" society rather than a pluralistic society. Looking at social trends, Sun argues that a rather substantial part of the population is simply being cast off (*taotai*) and left outside of industrial and urban society. Sun worries that the WTO process will exacerbate these problems. More to the point, he is concerned that unless the state makes more efforts to integrate these social groups into society, the seeds of social turmoil will be planted (Sun, 2002: 9–15).

Similarly, there has been a growing amount of social protest, some peaceful and some violent, associated with peasant discontent, labor disgruntlement, and religious discrimination. Although these trends have been reported in many places, the *China Investigation Report*, edited by the CCP Central Organization Department in 2001, provided a systematic look at local governance problems across much of China. According to this book, most participants in rural social protest in the past had been farmers and retired workers, but now they include laid-off workers, individual entrepreneurs, demobilized soldiers, technicians, and even cadres. Whereas previously most such protests were spontaneous and uncoordinated, now they are gaining leadership and organization; some even hire lawyers and seek the support of the media (Zhonggong Zhongyang Zuzhibu Ketizu, ed., 2001: 285–86). Trust between rural cadres and the population is reported to be virtually nonexistent; cadres fear the farmers, viewing the populace as "wild animals or a flood" and fearing to go into villages alone (Zhonggong Zhongyang Zuzhibu Ketizu, ed., 2001: 221–22).

The chapter on Sichuan province states that collective actions of more than 50 people increased by 141.9 percent in 1999 over the year before and that the number of participants increased by 156.6 percent. In the first half of

2000, such instances increased 16.3 percent over the same period in 1999. It goes on to say that in the past, most participants had been farmers and retired workers, but now laid-off workers, individual entrepreneurs, demobilized soldiers, technicians, and even cadres were joining in (Zhonggong Zhongyang Zuzhibu Ketizu, ed., 2001: 285–86). Other reports in the same volume confirm the tense nature of Party-mass relations in other parts of China. For instance, the chapter on Hunan says that trust between rural cadres and the population is nonexistent; cadres fear the farmers, viewing the populace as "wild animals or a flood" and fearing to go into villages alone (Zhonggong Zhongyang Zuzhibu Ketizu, ed., 221–22). More recent accounts suggest that such social tensions continue. For instance, the 2003 edition of the annual *Blue Book of Chinese Society* reports that in the first half of 2002, Labor Dispute Resolution Committees at various levels accepted 70,000 cases affecting 200,000 workers, up from the year before (albeit by an unspecified amount). The rate of increase of collective disputes is higher than the increase in the overall rate of disputes, and the number of people affected is more than 50 percent of those involved in labor disputes. Such trends have led some people to speculate about the breakdown in political control at the local level (Tanner, 2001).

## PRESSURES FOR POLITICAL REFORM

The pressures of globalization, the emergence of a significant private sector, the laying off of millions of industrial workers, the increase of tensions in the countryside, and the gradual emergence of new forms of social and political organization (whether *qigong* associations or rural elections) have all generated pressures to reform the political system in significant ways. The CCP is intensely conscious of the failure of communist parties in the former Soviet Union and Eastern Europe, and it has studied those examples carefully with an eye to preserving its own power. One lesson learned, which accords well with China's own experience, is that economic reform and economic growth are essential to maintaining social stability, which, in turn, is the key to retaining political power. In the wake of Tiananmen, conservatives in the Party blamed the Dengist reforms for leading inevitably to the student demonstrations. In response, Deng staunchly defended the importance of reform and opening up, saying that, without it, China (he meant the CCP) would not have survived the political upheaval of 1989 (Deng, 1993: 370–83). Indeed, it can be argued that the relaxation of official attitudes toward private entrepreneurship and the growth of a consumer culture were critical to the relaxation of political tensions in the 1990s (Yan, 2000: 159–93). But as time goes on, the growth of economic forces outside the purview of state control have begun to generate new demands for change.

In February 2000, Jiang Zemin began to respond to these changes by introducing his concept of the "three represents" to express that the Party represents the most advanced productive forces, the fundamental interests of the broad mass of the people, and the most advanced culture. No doubt this ideological formulation was related to Jiang's desire to leave a mark in Chinese politics by inaugurating his own set of ideas, but it also paved the way for adopting policies that had heretofore limited the Party's adjustment to the changing forces in society. This became evident when, on July 1, 2001, Jiang gave an important speech on the 80th anniversary of the Party's founding. In this speech, Jiang called for admitting "private entrepreneurs"—capitalists—into the Party along with other social elements that had emerged in recent years. In practice, there were already quite a number of private entrepreneurs in the Party. Bruce Dickson estimates that some 20 percent of private entrepreneurs are members of the Party. Some of these entrepreneurs were Party members who then "jumped into the sea" of business and others were admitted to the Party after they had become wealthy. Even if Jiang's speech was simply reflecting this changed reality, it was nevertheless important not only because it largely jettisoned the class basis of the Party (hence the notion of class struggle), but also because it reversed the views expressed by Jiang Zemin on National Day 1989 that the Party opposed the formation of a middle class as well as the Party's declaration, adopted in the wake of Tiananmen, that forbid admitting private entrepreneurs into the Party. These changes were subsequently adopted at the 16th Party Congress and written into the CCP Charter.

Although the issue of admitting capitalists into the Party created headlines in the West and controversy in China (it was implemented extremely cautiously, if at all, in the first year after Jiang's speech), the most important point in the speech was its emphasis on regularizing the relationship between the Party and society. The speech made clear that the CCP should transform itself from a "revolutionary party" (*gemingdang*) into a "ruling party" (*zhizhengdang*). This terminology is a bit awkward since the CCP has been in power for over 50 years, but it is nevertheless highly important in suggesting that the CCP itself now sees the importance of changing from a Leninist structure designed for mobilization to a more bureaucratic structure suited to administration (Fewsmith, 2001b).

If taken seriously, such a transformation of the Party would change the governing structures of China—including the Party-state relationship, the state-society relationship, and the role of law—in fundamental ways (suggesting that such changes will take years to accomplish). Yet the fact that the CCP is using such language at the highest level and experimenting with a variety of reforms at lower levels suggests that this is a process that needs to be watched carefully and that the accumulated pressures from domestic social change and globalization are having an impact on governance in China.

Perhaps the most important change in intellectual concern over the past couple years has been the growing focus on issues of political reform after a decade of relative eclipse. The social cleavages outlined above (and developed in other chapters in this volume) have now moved to the center of intellectual attention. There is a growing belief in China today that social issues (as well as other such related issues as corruption) cannot be effectively addressed without political reform of one sort or another. Previously, the emphasis was on economic reform and growth; today there is a greater awareness of the need for political change.

This recognition is not limited to intellectuals and social activists. A recent survey of provincial departmental (*ting*) level cadres studying at the Central Party School asked about the primary factors influencing economic and social development in the first decade of the twenty-first century. The cadres overwhelmingly chose "political structural reform," followed by a "healthy legal system" (see table 2.1).

Some sense of what cadres mean when they speak of "political structural reform" can be obtained from the question about what needs to be done to attain success in political reform. As table 2.2 shows, in 2002, cadres saw inner-party democracy as the first priority, followed by changing the functions of government organs and straightening out relations between the Party and the state. Apparently, their understanding of political reform is limited to what we might call administrative reform. Only 1.5 percent make "strengthening supervision by public opinion" their first choice, and only 7.5 percent make strengthening the campaign against corruption their first

**Table 2.1.   Primary Factors Influencing and Constraining Economic and Social Development Prior to 2010**

| Factor | Percentage | Rank |
|---|---|---|
| 1. Political Structural Reform | 79.8 | 1 |
| 2. Healthy Legal System | 60.3 | 2 |
| 3. Development of Economic Structural Reform | 55.7 | 4 |
| 4. Level of S&T Innovation | 58.6 | 3 |
| 5. Labor Quality | 49.6 | 6 |
| 6. Excessive Population | 38.4 | 9 |
| 7. Job Creation and Unemployment | 39.1 | 8 |
| 8. Unequal Income Distribution | 49.6 | 6 |
| 9. Outward Flow of Talented People | 12.1 | 10 |
| 10. Corruption | 50.4 | 5 |
| 11. Other and left blank | 7.0 | — |

Source: Qing Lianbin, "Zhongguo dangzheng lingdao ganbu dui 2002-2003 nian shehui xingshi de jiben kanfa" (Opinions on social situation in 2002 by some officials), in Ru Xin, Lu Xueyi, and Li Peixin, eds., *2003 nian: Zhongguo shehui xingshi fenxi yu yuce* (China's social situation: analysis and forecast, 2003) (Beijing: Shehui kexue wenxian chubanshe, 2003), p. 136.

**Table 2.2.   Decisive Factors in Attaining Success in Political Structural Reform**

|  | First | | Second | | Third | |
|---|---|---|---|---|---|---|
| *Rank* | *2001* | *2002* | *2001* | *2002* | *2001* | *2002* |
| Decisive Factors | | | | | | |
| 1. Further Change Functions of Government Organs | 21.6 | 24.1 | 19.6 | 9.8 | 41.2 | 33.9 |
| 2. Manage Well Relations between Party and State | 30.4 | 13.5 | 12.7 | 6.8 | 43.1 | 20.3 |
| 3. Increase Inner-Party Democracy | 23.5 | 33.8 | 15.7 | 15.8 | 39.2 | 49.6 |
| 4. Increase Supervision by Public Opinion | 2.0 | 1.5 | 10.8 | 12.8 | 12.8 | 14.3 |
| 5. Strengthen Campaign Against Corruption | 3.9 | 7.5 | 2.9 | 13.5 | 6.8 | 21.0 |
| 6. Reduce Size of Party Organs | 3.9 | 2.3 | 3.9 | 4.5 | 7.8 | 6.8 |
| 7. Strictly Promote Term System for Cadres | 4.9 | 5.3 | 8.8 | 18.0 | 13.7 | 23.3 |
| 8. Increase Role of Democratic Parties | — | — | 1.0 | 1.5 | 1.0 | 1.5 |
| 9. Raise Function of People's Representative Congresses | 2.9 | 6.0 | 13.7 | 6.0 | 16.6 | 12.0 |
| 10. Improve Decision-Making System | 6.9 | 6.0 | 10.8 | 11.3 | 17.7 | 17.3 |

(Source: Qing Lianbin, "Zhongguo dangzheng lingdao ganbu dui 2002-2003 nian shehui xingshi de jiben kanfa" (Opinions on social situation in 2002 by some officials), in Ru Xin, Lu Xueyi, and Li Peixin, eds., *2003 nian: Zhongguo shehui xingshi fenxi yu yuce* (China's social situation: analysis and forecast, 2003) (Beijing: Shehui kexue wenxian chubanshe, 2003), p. 132.

choice. Only six percent make raising the function of people's representative congresses their first choice, and virtually no one saw increasing the role of democratic parties as important at all. Nevertheless, increasing inner-party democracy could enhance competitiveness within the Party, possibly breaking up personal networks and promoting coalition-building skills. Changing the function of government organs could give society a greater voice over time. But clearly these cadres view such reforms as limited.

## GLOBALIZATION

If social pressures and corruption have forced rethinking about the importance of political reform, even if political reform is understood in limited terms, then globalization is the other force propelling political reform. The real impact of globalization will be more on the government than on the economy, for the simple reason that the economy will not be able to compete unless the government changes its relationship to the economy rather significantly. Despite nearly a quarter century of reform, government officials remain far too likely to interfere with the economy—sometimes to uphold regional blockages, sometimes to tax businesses, and sometimes to enrich themselves. Globalization, particularly the rules of the WTO, will force enormous changes in Chinese governance because the WTO demands transparency and an end to government subsidies in most instances. Most of all, because globalization enlarges the scope of competition, various areas in China will be forced to compete with each other to create the best investment environment. Those areas in which there is less government interference in business, less corruption, and more service provided to business will do better. Globalization also means competition to recruit and retain the best people, precisely those who are most mobile. So those areas that make life more comfortable for skilled personnel will do better over the long run—and that generally means government becoming more responsive to the demands of the emerging middle class (Chen, 2002: 2–6). Such pressures will affect everything from the cadre recruitment system in the CCP to the way government operates.

Such changes are already apparent in various areas, primarily at the local level and out of the limelight. Nevertheless, this fermentation process can be expected to bring about significant change over time (either because it is successful in coping with difficulties or because it is not successful and therefore will bring about new demands for deeper reforms—or collapse). At the moment, a great deal of attention is being paid to reform of the Party personnel system. This focus no doubt reflects an unwillingness to adopt more open and democratic processes, but it nevertheless suggests a deep appreciation within the Party that the old way of doing things will no longer suffice.

Efforts to open up the personnel selection process might be traced to the mid-1980s, when such places as Ningbo, Shenzhen, and Guangxi began to implement a combination of recommendation by both the organization department and the masses, as well as testing and examination. In 1992 the Central Organization Department transmitted a report on Jilin province's effort to promote recommendation and testing in the selection of deputy office (*ting*) level cadres. In 1995 the Central Organization Department transmitted provisional new regulations governing the promotion and use of cadres. In addition to specifying procedures for evaluating cadres being considered for promotion, they endorsed the idea of a "public comment" period. In 1996 the Central Organization Department transmitted Jilin's provisional regulations governing the open recommendation and testing of "leading cadres." In 1998 Vice President Hu Jintao called for gradually increasing the open selection of cadres and increasing the participation of the masses. In 2000 Zeng Qinghong, head of the Organization Department, called for vigorously expanding the scope of open selection of leading cadres (Zhao Hongjun, 2001:

18–21), and in 2002 the Central Organization Department issued new, permanent regulations governing cadre promotions that largely endorsed the 1995 Provisional Regulations.

These efforts have by no means been an unqualified success, as the number of critical comments appearing in Party building journals makes clear. Leading cadres still manipulate selection results, cadres who want to be promoted still "campaign" for votes (lapiao), and corruption continues to be a problem. Nevertheless, the very continuation of such problems has prompted further reaching reforms in some areas. For instance, in Yuetang Administrative Village (xiang–an administrative village is at the same administrative level as a zhen, or township, and encompasses several villages) in Putian municipality in Fujian province, there was an experiment to select CCP cadres in a more open and democratic fashion. Under this "three recommendations, two tests, and one selection" system, those who wanted to compete for an administrative position had to submit their names; one position (not specified) attracted 66 applicants. Their credentials were checked not only by a special Party committee, but also by the discipline inspection, family planning, comprehensive, and other Party departments. Then the candidates took a test written by the provincial organization department. Then candidates were "recommended" by secret ballot by leading cadres, regular cadres, and representatives of the masses. The names of the top five candidates for each position, based on their written exams, were made public for a seven-day comment period. Then, based on comments and the results of the recommendation process, the organization department at the level above Yuetang Administrative Village selected two nominees per position. The final decision was made by vote of the Party committee at the level above Yuetang Administrative Village (Shi Wen, 2001: 8–9). While by no means a democratic process in the Western sense, this experiment suggests considerable pressure not only to open up elective processes for some government officials (such as village heads) but also inner Party promotions, even at levels above that of the village.

Another recent example comes from Guangdong Province in southeast China, where it was announced that all officials selected to be the "number one" official of municipalities and prefectures in the province would be determined by a secret ballot vote of the whole provincial Party committee. The system will subsequently be extended down to the county and administrative village (xiang) level. This method was adopted in reaction to the buying and selling of administrative offices in Zhanjiang municipality. Although this new process is intended to open up the appointment procedure, the report noted that there were many problems that still needed to be dealt with, including the nomination process (Tang, 2002: 17–19).

Most recently the Shenzhen Special Economic Zone unveiled plans to circumscribe the power of the CCP by separating the powers of the Party, the government, and the people's congress. This experiment, just in the formative stages, is directly linked to the pressure China is feeling from the WTO. As Yu Youjun, mayor of Shenzhen, stated, "Actually, our greatest challenge and our greatest mismatch in joining the WTO was our government. WTO required us to effect great changes to our governance systems, otherwise we would not be able to adapt to WTO admission requirements."

## CONCLUSION

China's effort to pursue globalization, whether one is referring to the earlier decision to open the country after the throes of the Cultural Revolution (indeed, of the whole Maoist period) or the more recent decision to pursue membership in the WTO, is a logical corrective to the largely autarkic and inefficient patterns of growth that China pursued for nearly three decades. Moreover, China has developed rapidly as a result of its decision. Export growth has been key in fueling China's economic development, and the attraction of foreign investment in recent years has deepened that process. In part because of this growth, China did not need to confront the inefficiencies of its state-owned enterprise and banking sectors for a long time. In the latter half of the 1990s, the burden became too great financially and left the country too vulnerable to international pressures as the nation prepared the way for WTO entry. By delaying lay-offs for so long, China made the pain of such lay-offs when they came all that much greater. Although Beijing can be rightly criticized for not working harder to build social security systems and job training programs to ease the pain caused by these lay-offs, criticism of the broader processes of globalization ignores both their inevitability and the degree to which China has benefited from them.

Globalization will inevitably increase pressures for political reform. It will do so because China will need more efficient and more rule-based governmental behavior in order to compete internationally. Moreover, the dual processes of economic growth and the international links forged by globalization will increase societal demand for political reform. Indeed, government officials who have been involved in the WTO process seem to regard globalization as much as a political process as an economic process. Government will need to compete for domestic and international investment alike. Domestic barriers will have to decline as interior provinces try to take advantage of globalization. The *danwei* (work unit) system will erode as labor mobility increases, and the pressures on the *hukou* (household registration system) are already evident.

To speak of pressures for political reform does not mean that it will happen quickly or easily, or that China is likely to democratize in the near future. Old ways of doing things will die hard, and there will be plenty of new challenges—social protest movements, the spread of popular religion, challenges from national minority—that will persuade many that China cannot afford the "luxury" of democracy in the short term. Indeed, the greatest challenge that China faces over the next decade will be to reconcile the need and demand for political reform in some areas (the southeast coast would appear a good candidate for this role) with the demand to uphold authoritarian rule so as to contain protest from those cast off in the course of reform and globalization.

# 3

# Governance and Civil Service Reform

*John P. Burns*

Since 1980, leaders have sought to increase the capacity and legitimacy of the Chinese state through civil service reform. Attempts to increase accountability, predictability, transparency, participation, and efficiency and effectiveness, all elements of "good governance" (Asian Development Bank, 1995) have gone hand in hand with attempts to make the bureaucracy more meritocratic. Clearly the capacity of the bureaucracy has increased during the reform era. Education levels have risen while the average age of government officials has declined. Still, some features of low administrative capacity systems, especially corruption, continue to characterize China's bureaucracy and undermine its meritocracy. External and internal challenges will make continued adaptation essential. Challenges from China's imminent membership in the WTO and from an increasingly better informed and resourced but impatient public require the state to invest more in strategies for improving the quality of the public service.

This chapter seeks to evaluate the extent to which China's civil service reforms have moved the country closer to a popular paradigm of "good governance." We examine each of the elements of "good governance" in turn.

## SCOPE AND DEFINITIONS

Following standard usage, we define "governance" as "the manner in which power is exercised in the management of a country's economic and social resources for development" (Asian Development Bank, 1995: 3). Governance is neither confined only to governments (nongovernment organizations may also be involved), nor does it exclude partnerships with the private sector.

Many, including belatedly multilateral donors such as the World Bank, the United Nations Development Program (UNDP), and the Asian Development Bank (ADB) have observed that noneconomic factors (or governance factors) have a significant impact on the development process.[1] In this view, "good governance" facilitates development. As the ADB has pointed out, "Without good governance, efforts to reduce poverty will not be effective" (Asian Development Bank, 2000: i). Although different authors have identified different core elements of "good governance," we adopt the following for this chapter: accountability, participation, predictability, transparency, and efficiency and effectiveness (Asian Development Bank, 1995). Our question, then, is to what extent China's civil service reform has made improvements in these areas. To answer the question, we must occasionally stray beyond reforms of the management of the public personnel system to consider public sector reform in China more generally.

Before we begin we need to consider the scope and size of the civil service in China. Generally, public employees may be divided into first, the "core" civil service; second, public employees managed according to the civil service regulations; and third, other public employees (including employees of service units/institutions (*shiye danwei*), state-owned enterprises, and the military) who are not managed according to the regulations. According to the 1993 "Provisional Regulations on Civil Servants" (hereafter, Provisional Regulations) (Ministry of Personnel, 1993), "civil servants" are the managerial, administrative, and professional employees of the "administrative organs of the State" (Article 8).[2] This group may be called the "core" civil service. Unlike the "core" civil services of Western capitalist democracies, included here are the most senior politicians (the premier, vice premier, state councillors, ministers, provincial governors, vice ministers, vice governors, and so forth—the leadership positions (see Article 9)). The "core" civil service staffs the administrative organs of the state at each level down to and including towns and townships (Organization Department, 1997; cited in Ministry of Personnel, 1998: 135–38). According to this definition, in 2001 China employed about 5.4 million "core" civil servants,[3] most of whom worked at the local level.

In addition to the "core" civil service, from 1993 to 1997 the Chinese Communist Party extended the "civil service system" to many other public organizations including the CCP itself and organizations on the Central Committee–controlled *nomenklatura*, such as mass organizations, the legislature, the CPPCC, and the democratic parties.[4] Interviews with mainland judges indicate that the judiciary and the procuratorate are also managed according to the civil service system.[5] If public employees managed according to the civil service system are included, the number of "civil servants" would rise to about 10.8 million (State Statistical Bureau, 2000: 125).

Most public sector employees are excluded from the civil service, such as those who work in the huge service unit or "institutions" sector (*shiye dan-*

*wei)* that includes all teachers, researchers, professionals working in hospitals, and so forth. In 2001 this group numbered about 28 million, almost 13 million of whom were teachers.[6] Employees of state-owned enterprises and the military are similarly excluded.

For our purposes, civil service reform focuses primarily on management reforms of the "core" civil service and indirectly on other public employees managed under the civil service system. Clarity is necessary here because separate rules and regulations have been established for the civil services that do not apply to other public employees.

## BACKGROUND

Reform of the civil service dates from 1980, when Deng Xiaoping put the issue on the Party's agenda (Deng, 1984: 302–325). According to Deng, urgent reforms were needed to rejuvenate the leadership cadre and the system through which it was selected. Reforms included implementing a fixed tenure system that required retirement for most officials at age 60 for men and 55 for women[7] and efforts to improve the quality of China's leadership, especially by recruiting younger, more educated officials. Throughout the 1980s, authorities considered various reforms of the cadre system (Lam and Chan, 1995). In 1987 the then General Secretary Zhao Ziyang announced to the 13th Party Congress that a civil service system would be established for cadres working in government agencies (Zhao, 1987: i–xxvii). Fallout from elite level conflict that surrounded the May and June 1989 street demonstrations in Beijing and other cities delayed the promulgation of new civil service regulations until 1993. Since 1993, the Ministry of Personnel has issued more than a dozen new regulations on civil service management that cover virtually all aspects of the process.[8] In addition to these regulations, officials issued others to reform the cadre/civil service pay system in 1985 and 1993.

Civil service reform has been carried out in the midst of two vigorous attempts to downsize the government (1993 to 1996 and since 1998). Although the first attempt largely failed to achieve its downsizing goals (Burns, 2001), the 1998 campaign has apparently been more effective. As a result, many government agencies have been unable to implement parts of the civil service reforms such as new hiring procedures because based on new staffing levels they are considered to be overstaffed.

To a large extent, reform of the civil service system has been driven by the Party's decisions in 1978 to adopt economic development as its top priority and in 1992 to replace central planning with a market economy (Jiang, 1992: 9–32). In a market economy, a centralized bureaucratic allocation of labor system was no longer appropriate. The specific goals of the Party's civil service reform were first, to improve the quality of the cadre corps so that it could meet the new challenges of economic development, and second, to increase the perceived legitimacy of the selection of cadres which had been tarnished during the Cultural Revolution by such doctrines as the "blood line theory"[9] and since then by favoritism and patronage ("going through the back door") (Bian, 1994).

China's civil service reforms may be analyzed using the "good governance" framework. Accordingly, we examine each of the core elements of governance in turn.


## ACCOUNTABILITY


Following Romzek and Dubnick, we distinguish four types of accountability (meaning taking responsibility or answerability): bureaucratic, political, legal, and professional (Romzek and Dubnick, 1987). Until recently in China, political and bureaucratic accountability (the strongest forms of accountability in most political systems) have been largely the same. That is, subordinates have been accountable to superiors in the administrative hierarchy and all organizations have been accountable to the CCP leadership. The legislature lacked autonomy and played a relatively minor role.


### Bureaucratic Accountability

Civil service reform clearly has reinforced bureaucratic accountability. According to the Provisional Regulations, civil servants must "faithfully discharge their duties . . . and obey orders" (Article 6), and they may not "oppose decisions and orders of superiors" (Article 31). Although civil servants may "criticize or comment on the operation of the administrative organs of the state or the performance of the leaders of those organs" (Article 7), they must "maintain the security, honor, and interests of the state" and "maintain the confidentiality of state and work place secrets" (Article 6). Given the inclusive nature of state secrets as laid down in the Law on the Protection of State Secrets (State Council, 1988 in Burns, 1994: 79–83), American-style "whistle-blowing" is neither officially tolerated nor common.

In a clause added to the draft civil service regulations in 1990, civil servants are explicitly prohibited from: "spreading views which are harmful to the government's reputation, organizing or joining an illegal organization, organizing or joining an anti-government activity such as a meeting, demonstration or show of strength, or organizing or participating in a strike" (Article 31). The need for such a regulation, many senior officials believed, was indicated by the relatively large numbers of civil servants who demonstrated support for students and others occupying Tiananmen Square in Beijing in May–June 1989. The civil service regulations, then, clearly support bureaucratic accountability.

Public sector reforms undertaken in China since the mid-1980s have also strengthened bureaucratic accountability. They include reform of the accounting and auditing systems,[10] contained in amendments to the 1985 Accounting Law and passage of the 1994 Audit Law. In the early 1990s, authorities decided to develop a series of basic and specific accounting standards that were consistent with international accounting practice and would cater to Chinese realities. Since 1992 the Ministry of Finance has issued more than ten such standards (Narayan and Reid, 2000: 4). According to experts who have examined the standards, "with one exception there are no significant differences between the Chinese standards and International Accounting Standards."[11] Governments are required to adopt the standards which improve the bureaucratic accountability. Recent moves by the government for each agency to set up a Treasury Single Account with the People's Bank of China that is supervised by the Ministry of Finance will also help. Pressure on China to fully implement these standards will increase with entry to the WTO.

The ministerial/cadre responsibility system, in existence since at least the early 1980s, has also strengthened bureaucratic accountability.[12] Recent reports of officials firing negligent civil servants in local government who failed to prevent fires and explosions that resulted in the loss of many lives illustrate the resolve of the central government to hold local officials accountable. In 2001 the media reported such cases in Shaanxi (provincial governor), Shijiazhuang (party secretary), and Nanchang (party secretary and mayor) (*South China Morning Post*, May 18 and June 19–20, 2001).

Local governments also use performance contracts to increase bureaucratic accountability. County magistrates sign such contracts with town and township heads in many areas (Edin, 2001). The contracts lay down specific targets that must be fulfilled by the township head and tie his or her remuneration explicitly to target fulfillment. The targets are not just economic, but include the extent to which birth control quotas have been met and "social order" targets have been realized.[13] Similar contracts are signed in many Chinese cities between mayors and bureau chiefs (for example, chiefs of environmental protection bureaus) laying down specific targets for clean air and water to be achieved during a set period of time.[14] Local governments have also instituted a system of performance pledges for public services to increase bureaucratic accountability. In the first experiment with performance pledges in China, Yantai City's Construction Commission required its subordinate agencies to issue performance pledges in 1994 and 1995 (Hu Ningsheng, 1998: 1091–93). So successful were they at improving government services and reducing complaints that the city extended the system to other government departments. Some central government agencies (e.g., the Ministry of Construction and the Ministry of Electric Power) have also jumped on the bandwagon (Burns, 2003: 74–45). As with public sector reforms

overseas, false reporting and goal displacement have probably undermined
the effectiveness of these initiatives.

### Political Accountability

China's monist political system centralizes all formal political power in the
CCP. Although the Constitution describes the National People's Congress
(NPC) as the "highest organ of state power," the NPC exercises its power un-
der the leadership of the CCP.[15] China does not practice a separation of pow-
ers system that would give the NPC equal power with the executive (State
Council) and the judiciary.

The NPC plays several roles in the management of the civil service. First,
it elects the country's most senior civil servants (the premier, vice premier,
and state councillors) and upon the nomination of the premier, endorses the
selection of ministers. Second, the NPC reviews reports of the premier and
other senior officials (the minister of finance, the auditor, and the heads of
the judiciary and the procuratorate) and endorses them. Third, the NPC ap-
proves government policies in the form of laws and plans, such as the Plan
for the Restructuring of the State Council, approved in 1998, and the 10th
Five Year Plan approved in 2001. Through these mechanisms, the NPC su-
pervises the work of the civil service.

As a very high percentage of the NPC delegates are Party members and/or
retired public officials,[16] the NPC has been treated as part of the bureaucracy.
Until March 2003, the chairman of the NPC Standing Committee was retired
premier and Politburo Standing Committee member Li Peng, a bureaucratic
insider.

In recent years, however, the capacity of the NPC and local people's congresses to articulate nonbureaucratic interests has probably increased. First,
although people's congresses continue to elect those candidates nominated
by the party for top (civil service) positions 99 percent of the time, "unexpected results" are not unknown. In the mid-1990s, for example, provincial
people's congresses in Guizhou, Zhejiang, Hubei, and Hainan failed to elect
candidates supported by the party organization.[17] Exercising such independence is very rare, however.

Second, the capacity of the legislature to supervise the civil service has
probably increased in recent years. To the original six standing committees of
the NPC (Nationalities Affairs, Law, Finance and Economics, Education Science Culture and Health, Foreign Affairs, and Overseas Chinese Affairs) have
been added new committees on Internal and Justice Affairs (in 1988), Environmental and Resources Protection (in 1993), and Agriculture and Rural Affairs (in 1998), strengthening the capacity of the NPC to review proposals for
new laws or amendments before they are passed. Although the NPC establishes a Budget Committee when it examines the budget, the committee is not

a standing committee with staff permanently engaged in examining the budget, which seriously undermines the legislature's capacity to review and evaluate public finances (Pu, 1999: 128–129). Committee membership ranges from 15 to 34 members (the Foreign Affairs Committee and the Education Science Culture and Health Committee, respectively). Undoubtedly committee members are highly dependent on papers prepared by the government. Generally speaking, delegates have neither the capacity to generate alternative policy nor to carry out independent investigations. The government is not particularly interested in encouraging developments in this direction.

Delegates have been able to express dissatisfaction with government policy during private discussions of and votes on the work reports prepared by the premier, the minister of finance, the auditor general, the president of the Supreme People's Court, and the procurator general. In recent years, some delegates to both the NPC and provincial people's congresses have voted against the work reports of the procuratorate to protest the government's weak and ineffective handling of corruption.

### Legal Accountability

Legal accountability requires that civil servants regardless of their rank are answerable to the law. Although considerable reform of the legal system has taken place since 1980, China's legal system is more appropriately described as rule by law (and regulation) rather than rule of law. In a rule of law system, the state should be treated like any other actor, which is far from the case in China today.

The capacity of the system to hold civil servants legally accountable depends not only on the quality of the laws and regulations, but on their implementation. This in turn depends on the training and discipline of law enforcement agencies and on the capacity of the judiciary. We will turn to these issues in another section below.

Violations of the law by civil servants are apparently relatively common. Consider the case of corruption. According to Hu Angang, during the latter half of the 1990s, corruption resulted in economic losses of between 13.2 percent to 16.8 percent of gross domestic product (GDP), a staggering amount (Hu, 2001: 34–58). A major component of these losses was tax fraud that from 1994 to 1998 resulted in an estimated loss of between 7.6 percent to 9.1 percent of GDP. Government officials were intimately involved in the most serious cases, such as the case in Shantou City, Guangdong province (*South China Morning Post*, May 15, 2001). The seriousness of corruption in China is revealed in the country's low standing in the Transparency International Corruption Perception Index (58th out of 91 countries rated in 2001).[18] Moreover, from 1993 to 1998 less than half of the corruption cases under investigation led to criminal charges being filed, and only 6.6 percent of these led to corrupt officials being sentenced. According to Hu, "this means that if a person is bribed, there is only a 6.6 percent chance of his being prosecuted." With such a low probability, many officials are undoubtedly willing to take the risk (*South China Morning Post*, March 24, 2001). This helps to explain why even senior officials have been caught. The most senior officials to date include Chen Xitong, former mayor of Beijing; Wang Baoshan, former vice mayor of Beijing; Cheng Kejie, former vice chairman of the NPC; Hu Changqing, former vice governor of Jiangxi province; Qin Changdian, former vice chairman of Chongqing Municipal People's Congress; and Wang Shihui, former vice chairman of the Chongqing Municipal CPPCC. During the year 2000, 21 officials of provincial or ministerial rank were "disciplined" for corruption.[19]

Many corruption cases have revealed that bribery to secure an official position is a serious problem, especially at the local level. For example, the investigation of Cheng Kejie revealed that he accepted bribes when he was Governor of Guangxi province to arrange promotions in the civil service (*Xinhua*, September 14, 2000). Investigations into the former Yunnan Finance Bureau deputy chief revealed that in 1996, when he was head of the party's Organization Department, he accepted *Ren Min Bi* (People's Money) 15,000 to secure the appointment of a county official's son in the procuratorate. He was found to have forged personnel files, adding favorable comments and a fake diploma for the relative of another official in exchange for bribes (*South China Morning Post*, September 9, 2001). By 1996 the practice had become so serious that the *People's Daily* began publishing editorials denouncing it: "Some extremely power-hungry people go all out to bribe organizational and personnel departments. Some subordinates directly bribe their superiors, who are in charge of transfers, deployments, and promotions with bribes worth hundreds of thousands of dollars" (*Renmin Ribao (People's Daily)*, January 17, 1997). In 1997 and 1998 officials were arrested for selling scores of positions in Wenzhou City (Zhejiang), Pizhou County (Jiangsu), Beihai City (Guangxi), Huaibei City (Anhui), Tieling City (Liaoning), Guanfeng County (Jiangxi), and in various places in Heilongjiang province.[20] These cases undoubtedly represent only the tip of the iceberg. The 2001 arrest of the mayor and vice mayor of Shenyang, Mu Suixin and Ma Xiangdong, for taking bribes for, among other things, arranging official promotions indicates that the practice continues to be very serious (*Xinhua*, June 15, 2001; *Liaowang (Outlook)*, June 11, 2001). As the head of the Organization Department, Zeng Qinghong said, "Those who are promoted through improper channels must be brought down and those who buy or sell official positions must be dealt with according to party discipline and state law (*Xinhua*, September 13, 2000). How widespread these practices are is difficult to judge.

Authorities have adopted a variety of strategies for managing or reducing corruption, including law enforcement, education, and so forth. In addition to these more traditional measures, the government has implemented a job rotation system that has seen thousands of officials in sensitive jobs, such as finance and personnel, rotated to new jobs in new geographic areas. Officials have also increased the transparency of the process to reduce corruption, an issue we will discuss below.

## Professional Accountability

The emergence of professional groups in China began only in the 1980s under relatively tight government control and sponsorship. Groups to regulate accountants, lawyers, journalists, and others are now common. These groups have established codes of conduct.

Typical of these developments is the Chinese Institute of Certified Public Accountants (CICPA) set up in 1988 and governed by the Certified Public Accountants Law passed in 1993. The CICPA is charged with, among other things, managing the registration of Certified Public Accounting (CPA) firms, regulating their practices, and developing and monitoring professional standards. According to the law, the CICPA must accept guidance from the Ministry of Finance and the China National Audit Office. The CICPA is financed mostly from membership fees paid by CPA firms, which are required to pay two percent of their revenue to the Institute. The Institute has issued the General Standard on Professional Ethics and the General Standard on Quality Control, both of which came into effect in January 1997. The CICPA carries out inspections of CPA firms to ensure that standards are maintained, and the Ministry of Finance is authorized to impose penalties on members for deviation from the professional standards (Narayan and Reid, 2000: 41–51). Clearly then a framework for ensuring professional accountability exists for accountants in China. Accountants who are also civil servants are bound by both hierarchical (bureaucratic) and professional accountability.

Not surprisingly, when faced with conflicting duties, such as to carry out the instructions of their superiors or to obey professional ethics and enforce accounting standards, many civil servants have put the codes of ethics aside. Evidence of the conflicts is difficult to obtain and mostly circumstantial but has emerged in a few cases. For example, the Liquidation Committee looking into the collapse of the Guangdong International Trust and Investment Corporation, an entity established by the Guangdong provincial government, found gross abuses and reported that the Guangdong International Trust and Investment Corporation's books were in a state of "disarray." Clearly government regulators chose to look the other way rather than enforce the accounting standards laid down by law (Liquidation Committee, 1999: 2). Because the incentives for "whistle-blowing"–type behavior on the part of professionals are so weak, we should not expect dramatic changes here.

Bureaucratic/political accountability is strongest in China as in many other countries. Improving legal and professional accountability still presents challenges to the state.


## PARTICIPATION

"Good governance" also requires that relevant stakeholders are able to participate in policy making. Because of its one party system, civil servants, like other Chinese citizens, may participate in politics (vote, stand for office, and so forth), a matter that we will not consider here. If we narrow the scope of our consideration to participation in the civil service, then clearly during the reform era authorities have expanded the pool of ordinary people who may join the civil service. The civil service has become more inclusive.

First, the initial requirement that only those who are legally residing in Beijing may compete for civil service entry level positions in the central government has been lifted. Although the 1993 Provisional Regulations on Civil Servants simply said that candidates for civil service jobs "should meet the qualifications stipulated by the state" (Article 15), early advertisements for positions in the central government contained the proviso that applicants should be legally residing in Beijing.[21] Excluded from the competition for central government posts, then, were most of the population. Because of China's household registration system, obtaining an urban residency permit is difficult for those born in the countryside. Although the system has been relaxed somewhat,[22] legal residency is still a requirement before a candidate may apply for a civil service job.[23] Since 1997 the government has invited graduates of institutions of higher learning to apply for entry level positions in the central government. Still, in 1997 the Ministry of Personnel continued to require that applicants be legally registered in Beijing.[24] By 1998, however, authorities had arranged examination centers in seven major cities in addition to Beijing for graduates of schools outside the capital to take the entrance examination in (Zhu Qingfang, ed., 2000: 166). These moves and moves to liberalize the household registration system will permit more and more people to participate in the examinations.

Civil service reforms have also encouraged national minorities and women to apply for positions in government. Indeed, the regulations specifically require that local governments in minority areas at all levels give "preference" to applicants from a minority ethnicity in hiring (Article 13). From 1981 to 1998 national minority officials have held a steady seven percent of "cadre" jobs at county level and above (Zhonggong zhongyang zuzhibu [Organization Department], 1999: 3). Still, in provinces with large minority populations, Han Chinese held many leadership positions. In Xinjiang, for example, 53 percent of provincial level leading officials, 39 percent of prefectural level leading officials, and 33 percent of county level leading officials were of minority ethnicity (Zhonggong zhongyang zuzhibu (Organization Department), 1999: 572–575). In most minority provinces, minority officials staffed only about one-third of leading Party positions and up to or more than half of leading government positions.

Although official policy encourages government to hire more women, no affirmative action quotas exist for women as they do for ethnic minorities. As a result, women hold only about 14 percent of leading "cadre" positions nationwide (Zhonggong zhongyang zuzhibu (Organization Department), 1999: 3), of which seven percent are at provincial level, nine percent are at prefectural level, and nearly 15 percent are at county level. In 1996 women were reported to hold only about 19 percent of civil service positions (7.3 percent at ministerial/provincial level, 7.5 percent at bureau chief level, and 11.3 percent at division chief or county level.)[25]

Since 1999 the CCP has adopted new policies of inclusion that acknowledge the contribution of the emerging private sector and private entrepreneurs. In 1999 the NPC amended the state Constitution to recognize new forms of property ownership in addition to state ownership (Zhonghua renmin gongehuo xianfa (Constitution of the People's Republic of China), 1999: 56) Jiang Zemin's "three represents" theory[26] redefines the nature of the CCP and its relationship to society. Moreover, Jiang's announcement on July 1, 2001, that private entrepreneurs could join the CCP is also a step toward more inclusiveness (*Wenhui Bao* [Hong Kong], July 2, 2001). The new policy may permit businessmen and women to join the civil service at intermediate and senior levels. Although government "cadre" positions have long been open to managers of state–owned enterprises, very few ordinary private entrepreneurs have joined the bureaucracy.

These changes present opportunities and dangers for the state. On the one hand, the Party's new policy of inclusiveness may permit the civil service to recruit people with private sector business experience that could lead to new ways of defining and solving community problems. Efficiency could improve. Opening civil service jobs to new groups may thus improve bureaucratic capacity. Certainly this is the argument of "new public management." On the other hand, opening the civil service up to the business community may result in the capture of the civil service. Examples are not difficult to find. According to press reports, in December 2000 private businessmen bribed officials and voters in an effort to elect delegates friendly to themselves to the Hejin county people's congress in Yuncheng, Shanxi province (*South China Morning Post*, September 7, 2001). Businessmen were reported to have bribed up to 60 officials of Yuncheng City to influence the outcome of the election. Due to weaknesses in the legal system, the buying and selling of official positions, already common in some areas, may become even more common. Moreover, civil servants with business connections may be more willing to forego impartiality and make public policy that protects private interests. In so far as corruption is widespread, however, this trend is already well advanced.

Because of the dangers of corruption, civil service reforms have actively encouraged "democratic participation" in personnel decisions, particularly decisions concerning the promotion of leading officials. The Provisional Regulations make it clear that promotion decisions should be based on recommendations by "a combination of leaders and the masses" (Article 41). In recent years the Organization Department has launched campaigns to try to ensure that promotion decisions were not taken by a single leader and that they were more transparent. The "Interim Regulations on the Selection and Appointment of Leading Party and Government Cadres" (1995) make it clear that "one person alone having the say," "forming factions," and "appointing people based on favoritism" are unacceptable (*Liaowang* [*Outlook*], June 11, 2001; *Xinhua*, September 13, 2000). To overcome the practice of "craving for official posts, buying and selling official posts, and obtaining official posts by fraud," authorities have demanded more transparency and that the scope of participation in promotion decisions be widened. "Democratic opinion polls" and "democratic discussions," although not required during the evaluation of officials for leading posts, are specifically provided for in the Provisional Regulations (Article 24). Generally these involve polls of peers and subordinates of the individual official. Promotion decisions are supposed to take into account the results of these activities. The extent to which they do in practice, however, is difficult to gauge.

Formal grievance procedures introduced by the civil service reforms also permit wider participation by civil servants in personnel decision making. According to the Provisional Regulations, if a civil servant disagrees with a personnel decision, he or she may appeal to the body making the decision within 30 days or to the personnel department of the government at the same level (Article 81). Moreover, civil servants may appeal to higher level authorities if they believe that their "legitimate rights and interests" have been infringed by their employer (Article 82). According to the Ministry of Personnel, from 1993 to 2001 there have been only about 300 cases nationwide in which civil servants have used this mechanism.[27]

Finally, we should note that in developed capitalist democracies civil servants participate in personnel decision making through staff associations or trade unions. In some systems, such as Australia, unions play a major role in determining terms and conditions of service for civil servants. Unions represent the interests of civil servants and bargain with the state through elaborate collective bargaining procedures. Although civil servants belong to trade unions in China, they are affiliated with the All-China Federation of Trade Unions, which performs very different roles. Civil servants may not organize or join autonomous unions ("illegal organizations") in China. As a result their interests must be protected either by themselves or by civil service management.

## PREDICTABILITY

Predictability depends on the quality and comprehensiveness of the laws and regulations and the effectiveness of the institutions implementing them. The fair and consistent application of the regulations ("the rule of law") is crucial. As the ADB has observed, "The importance of predictability cannot be overstated since, without it, the orderly existence of citizens and institutions is impossible" (Asian Development Bank, 2001: 7). Civil service reform is designed in part to increase predictability in the management of the cadre corps. New regulations and new institutions (such as the Ministry of Personnel, established in 1988)[28] have contributed to increasing predictability in the management of the civil service. Evidence that the rules are sometimes enforced is not hard to find. From 1995 to 2000, for example, some 10,109 officials were dismissed nationwide for incompetence based on the civil service rules and regulations (366 of them were bureau-level cadres) (*Xinhua*, July 17, 2000). Examining all the changes in this regard is beyond the scope of the chapter.

A particular concern in China has been the failure of officials to consistently implement laws and regulations. In part this is because the incentives motivating personnel in the legal-judicial arena, who are responsible for prosecuting civil servants who violate the law, are either weak or contradictory. First, corruption among the police and judiciary continues to be a serious problem. This is in spite of regulations prohibiting personnel of judicial, procuratorial, and public security departments from engaging in business (*Xinhua*, July 31, 1998). Second, dependent as the judiciary is on local governments for land, buildings, salaries, and local staff, localism is a serious problem in judicial proceedings (*Liaowang* [*Outlook*], February 17, 1998). Judges tend to protect the interests of the jurisdiction in which they are located.

Third, although the Judges Law, passed in 1995, requires that judges have a university degree or equivalent, many judges lack training or education in the law. In 1999, of the country's 240,000 court employees working at "basic level," only 19.1 percent of court presidents or vice presidents had university degrees. Among judges and deputy judges in these courts only 15.4 percent were university graduates (Xiao, 2000: 113). Fourth, like their counterparts in the civil service, judicial and procuratorial officials are relatively poorly paid. Moreover, especially at the local level, the salaries of top judges are significantly lower than those of government executives at the same level. China's administrative system, then, treats the judiciary as just another bureau, like, for example, the grain bureau.

These problems have a negative impact on the predictability of the country's civil service management institutions.


## TRANSPARENCY

Transparency in government decision making reduces uncertainty and helps to inhibit corruption (Asian Development Bank, 1995: 8). More transparent rules, regulations, and procedures also may increase legitimacy. In an arena usually cloaked in secrecy in China, increasing transparency has been a characteristic of civil service reforms. The Provisional Regulations make "openness, fairness, competition, and selection of the best" key priorities for the selection of civil servants (Article 2). In the late 1990s drive to increase transparency in town and township government officials, the CCP specifically identified more transparent personnel management as a target (Zhongyang jiwei bangongting (General Office of the Central Discipline Inspection Commission), ed., 2001). Officials were instructed to make public "matters related to the behavior of officials, matters related to officials' use of entertainment allowances and traveling expenses, and matters related to the transfer, appraisal, rewards, and punishments of local officials" (*Xinhua*, December 25, 2000).

To reduce opportunities for corruption, officials have adopted more open recruitment and appointment processes. These have included publishing the names of candidates for particular positions before they are appointed. When this was done in Jiangsu province for the appointment of more than six thousand officials, popular protests against 203 of them resulted in their appointments being withdrawn (*Xinhua*, July 17, 2001). In Henan province a similar practice resulted in 113 officials having their impending appointments cancelled (two of the 113 were turned over to the police for suspected criminal violations.)

The Ministry of Personnel, while not taking the lead, has followed with its own transparency regulations (Ministry of Personnel, 1999: 72–75). These identify specific items that should be made public, the most important of which are personnel laws, regulations, and policy (See box 3.1). The regulations also identify certain kinds of information that should be publicized to regions and government departments, or made known only within particular departments and agencies. Among the latter are the requirements that internal vacancies be publicized and that the qualifications and procedure for filling the vacancies be made known to everyone within the agency. The principles, requirements, and results of housing allocations should also be published internally. Clearly this regulation was adopted to try to increase the fairness of housing allocations and reduce opportunities for manipulation and underhanded dealing.

---

**Box 3.1. MINISTRY OF PERSONNEL**

Matters to be Made Public

1. Personnel work laws, regulations and policy;
2. The conditions and procedures for examination and hiring of civil servants and examination results;
3. The conditions and procedure for officials to be transferred to and from Beijing, for husbands and wives living in two different places, and for the families of cadres to be transferred from the countryside to the city;
4. Principles and conditions for the arrangements for cadres to be demobilized to civilian jobs;
5. The conditions, process, and results of establishing post-doctoral transfer stations;
6. The conditions and process for evaluating specialist and technical credentials and the conditions process and results for establishing the examination standards for specialist and technical personnel;
7. The conditions, procedures, and results for examinations for the reserve list of people joining international organizations.

(Source: Ministry of Personnel, 1999: 73)

---

The Ministry of Personnel now has its own Web site (www.mop.gov.cn) and since January 1, 2001, has published a monthly gazette (*Zhonghua renmin gongheguo renshibo gongbao*), which replaces a previously internal publication (*Renshi gongzuo zhuankan*) and that includes new regulations, pay scales, speeches of leaders, and so forth. Collections of personnel documents and statistics published either by the Organization Department or by the Ministry of Personnel for the Organization Department continue to be internal.

Traditionally, organization/personnel work has been shrouded in secrecy. With the introduction of a market economy, however, efficient distribution of human resources has required much more public information. The new civil service reforms that require recruitment in a market can only improve the quality of the service, if information about duties, roles, terms and conditions, discipline, and the like is made public.

## EFFICIENCY AND EFFECTIVENESS

A core goal of civil service reform in China has been improving the quality of civil servants. Officials have adopted a variety of policies to achieve this end. First, they have sought to instill competition in personnel selection. Since 1993 candidates for entry or promotion are required to compete for their positions so that only "the best" are hired or promoted. Entry level civil servants must go through a rigorous process that includes both written and oral examinations. The examinations, like those overseas, concentrate not only on basic knowledge, but also on aptitude and problem solving ability. Depending on the position and jurisdiction, candidates for promotion (and/or for redundancy) have to take examinations before they may be considered for a personnel move. As we have seen, however, buying and selling positions continues to be a serious problem, which has undermined the impact of these reforms.

Second, civil service reforms have sought to increase the educational levels of the cadre corps as a whole. Generally, these efforts have been very successful (See figure 3.1). By 1998 bureau chiefs had the highest educational levels, with nearly 90 percent having graduated from university or community college (*dazhuan*). The data hide some variations, however. Although about 80 percent of division chiefs/county–level leaders are graduates of institutions of higher learning, the percentage among officials at division/county level in the far west (especially in Gansu, Ningxia, Qinghai, and Tibet) is much lower (65.5 percent, 69.8 percent, 59.4 percent, and 38.8 percent respectively). There appears to be little difference between party and government leaders in terms of formal educational attainment regardless of administrative level (Zhonggong zhongyang zuzhibu (Organization Department), 1999).

Third, policies to encourage officials to retire have also had a significant impact. From 1981 to 1998, the average age of officials of ministerial or bureau rank fell from 63.6 years to 56.9 years (Zhonggong zhongyang zuzhibu (Organization Department), 1999: 12). In 1980, more than 80 percent of

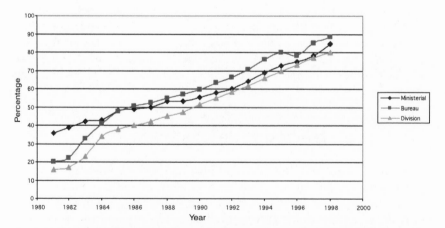

**Figure 3.1.   Leading Cadres in China with University Education, 1981–1998**
(Source: Zhonggong zhongyang zuzhibu (Organization Department), 1999: 5,8,10.)

provincial/ministerial level officials were 60 years of age or older. By 1998 the percentage over the age of 60 had dropped to about 54 percent (Zhong-gong zhongyang zuzhibu (Organization Department), 1999: 6). At bureau level, the number over 60 has dropped from 37 percent to 11 percent, while at county level leaders over the age of 60 are now only about one percent of the total (Zhonggong zhongyang zuzhibu (Organization Department), 1999: 9, 11). These figures provide circumstantial evidence of increased bureaucratic capacity.

An efficient and effective civil service is also highly motivated. Extrinsic rewards like pay and promotion contribute to job satisfaction and higher motivation. Years of paying relatively low salaries compared to those paid in non–civil service jobs[29] have probably lowered morale and enthusiasm among civil servants, especially in China's more developed coastal regions. Low salaries have also probably contributed to an exodus of talent from the service.

Civil service reforms have sought to improve levels of compensation for civil servants and tie rewards more closely to performance to tackle the motivation problem. According to the Provisional Regulations, the state intends to "systematically raise the salary scales of civil servants in accordance with the nation's economic development" (Article 67) and pay civil servants at about the same level as an individual with the same rank in a state-owned enterprise (Article 66). In spite of these policies, visible base salaries remain relatively low (See table 3.1). The top civil servants receive official base salaries of only about RMB 2,900 yuan per month. To this must be added a relatively large invisible income in cash and in kind. Still, the gap between civil service salaries and those outside the service probably remains relatively large, especially in more developed parts of the country. Ministry of Personnel officials conservatively estimate the gap to be between 50 percent to 100 percent in places like Shanghai and Guangzhou. In less developed parts of the country, however, civil service pay may be very appealing. Vertical compression is also marked. If we consider only base salary, the gap between the highest paid and lowest paid is about 1:5.7. If benefits, which tend to be distributed to everyone regardless of rank, are included, officials estimate the gap to fall to about 1:3. Decompressing the salary structure is probably needed to motivate civil servants.

The Provisional Regulations also provide for pay for performance. Yet because most civil servants are able to achieve the threshold for "bonuses," the performance-based component tends to be distributed relatively equally. The Ministry of Personnel reports that less than one percent of appraisees is rated as "basically competent" or "incompetent."[30] From 10 to 15 percent receive the highest rating, and the rest a rating of "competent." Hence, this group, which comprises 85 percent of all appraisees, is eligible for performance-based pay.

Table 3.1: CHINESE CIVIL SERVICE PAY SCALE, 2001

Unit: Yuan/Month

| Position | Post Wage 1 | 2 | 3 | 4 | 5 | 6 | 7 | 8 | 9 | 10 | 11 | 12 | 13 | 14 |
|---|---|---|---|---|---|---|---|---|---|---|---|---|---|---|
| President, Vice President, Premier | 850 | 970 | 1090 | 1210 | 1330 | 1450 | | | | | | | | |
| Vice Premier, State Councillor | 680 | 785 | 890 | 995 | 1100 | 1205 | 1310 | | | | | | | |
| Minister, Provincial Governor | 560 | 650 | 740 | 830 | 920 | 1010 | 1100 | 1190 | | | | | | |
| Vice Minister, Provincial Deputy Governor | 460 | 540 | 620 | 700 | 780 | 860 | 940 | 1020 | 1100 | | | | | |
| Bureau Chief | 365 | 435 | 505 | 575 | 645 | 715 | 785 | 855 | 925 | 995 | | | | |
| Deputy Bureau Chief | 295 | 355 | 415 | 475 | 535 | 595 | 655 | 715 | 775 | 835 | | | | |
| Division Chief, County Magistrate | 240 | 290 | 340 | 390 | 440 | 490 | 540 | 590 | 640 | 690 | 740 | | | |
| Deputy Division Chief, Deputy County Magistrate | 195 | 235 | 275 | 315 | 355 | 395 | 435 | 475 | 515 | 555 | 595 | | | |
| Section Head | 160 | 190 | 220 | 250 | 280 | 310 | 340 | 370 | 400 | 430 | 460 | 490 | | |
| Deputy Section Head | 136 | 158 | 180 | 202 | 224 | 246 | 268 | 290 | 312 | 334 | 356 | 378 | | |
| Section Member | 117 | 133 | 149 | 165 | 181 | 197 | 213 | 229 | 245 | 261 | 277 | 293 | 309 | 325 |
| General Office Personnel | 100 | 113 | 126 | 139 | 152 | 165 | 178 | 191 | 204 | 217 | 230 | 243 | 256 | 269 |

| Grade Wage: Grade | Wage Standard | Basic Wage | Seniority Wage[a] |
|---|---|---|---|
| 1 | 1166 | 230 | |
| 2 | 1030 | 230 | |
| 3 | 903 | 230 | |
| 4 | 790 | 230 | |
| 5 | 686 | 230 | |
| 6 | 586 | 230 | |
| 7 | 490 | 230 | |
| 8 | 408 | 230 | |
| 9 | 340 | 230 | |
| 10 | 281 | 230 | |
| 11 | 231 | 230 | |
| 12 | 190 | 230 | |
| 13 | 158 | 230 | |
| 14 | 133 | 230 | |
| 15 | 115 | 230 | |

Note: [a] One *yuan* for each year of service. *Source:* Ministry of Personnel, Ministry of Finance, "Implementation plan for the adjustment of the wage standard for government employees' [Guanyu diaozheng jiguan gongzuo renyuan gongzi biaojunde shishi fangan] (September 7, 2001) in Ministry of Personnel General Office, *Gazette of the Ministry of Personnel of the People's Republic of China* [Zhonghua renmin gongheguo renshibu gongbao] No. 11, November 15, 2001, 11.

## FUTURE PROSPECTS

Pressure for further reform of the bureaucracy to increase its administrative and policy-making capacity has come from two sources: external and internal. External pressure has come from China's integration with the world economy and the process of accession to the WTO. External pressure has encouraged trends in China toward meritocracy. To negotiate in an increasingly competitive and turbulent external environment, the country needs "the best" officials and civil service reform is designed (in part) to select the most talented people. Increasing the capacity of the state (and non-state actors) to represent the country successfully will continue to be an important challenge. The civil service will play an important role here.

Internal pressure from society will continue to force the pace of bureaucratic reform and is probably more important than external pressure. Because such pressure comes to bear on the entire bureaucracy, and not just those parts that manage external relations, the significance of societal pressure cannot be overestimated. Regional disparities in administrative and policy-making capacity must be addressed to preserve stability and the territorial integrity of the country. They can be addressed through a postings and a job rotation system, which is already in place. But more even economic development is undoubtedly important.

As China develops, ordinary people acquire more resources that can be used to challenge the state if their demands and expectations are not met. Managing China's new private entrepreneurs presents many problems for the state. For the moment the CCP has chosen a mixed strategy of cooptation on the one hand and heightened regulation on the other. Both positive and negative scenarios can be envisaged. On the one hand, the domestic business community, both private and state-owned, may eventually see that the rule of law, in which all players are equal before the law, is in its interest. Pressure to reduce corruption and other forms of power-seeking will then intensify and the civil service should prepare for a new role as a neutral regulator. These trends could push the state in a meritocratic direction. On the other hand, as private business activity expands, more opportunities for the private capture of the state may emerge. A danger is that the civil service retreats from trends toward meritocracy and re-emphasizes political patronage as the government feels more and more under threat.

## NOTES

1. See World Bank, 1994; United Nations Development Program, 1995; United Nations Development Program, 1997.

2. Excluded from the "civil service" are all blue collar employees of the government, including clerks, typists, drivers, janitors, and so forth.

3. Interview, Ministry of Personnel, July 25, 2001.

4. The system was extended to the CCP in 1993, the Youth League, the Women's Federation, the Song Qingling Foundation, the NPC Standing Committee bureaucracy, the CPPCC National Committee bureaucracy, the All-China Federation of Trade Unions, the Science and Technology Association, and the Returned-Overseas Chinese Federation in 1994, the Association of Taiwan Compatriots, the Huangpu Military Academy Alumni Association, the eight democratic parties and the All–China Federation of Industry and Commerce in 1995, the All-China Federation of Literature and Art Circles, the All-China Writers' Association, the All-China Journalists' Association, the All-China Staff and Workers Political Thought Work Research Association, the service units (shiye danwei) of all local party committees, the All-China Legal Studies Association, the All-China Association for Friendship with People's Overseas, the All-China Foreign Affairs Studies Association, the All-China International Trade Promotion Association, the All-China Red Cross in 1996, and the All-China Disabled People's Federation in 1997. See Ministry of Personnel (ed.), Renshi gongzuo wenjian xuanbian (Selection of Personnel Work Documents) (various volumes) (Beijing: Renshi chubanshe, various years).

5. Interviews with Supreme People's Court judges, Hong Kong, May 2001.

6. Interview, State Commission on Public Sector Reform, July 25, 2001.

7. See Manion, 1993.

8. Thirteen regulations are reproduced in Zhu 2000; 249–351 to guide performance appraisal, hiring, appointment and dismissal, reward, retirement, grievance procedures, training, promotion and demotion, conflicts of interest ("avoidance"), and job rotation.

9. See Hong Yung Lee, 1991.

10. See Narayan and Reid, 2000.

11. The exception requires that in China accountants and relevant authorities agree on divergences from regulations and provisions for damaged or obsolete inventories. See Narayan and Reid, 2000: 4.

12. See Ministry of Labor and Personnel, (Laoren (1982) No. 162) in Ministry of Labor and Personnel Policy and Research Office, ed., 1984: 21–22.

13. Social order targets include number of economic crimes over RMB 200 yuan committed during the year, the number of violent incidents resulting in death during the year, the number of demonstrations over 500 people during the year, the number of letters of complaint received, the amount of fire damage, and so forth. See Edin, 2001.

14. Interviews, Environmental Protection Bureau Officials, Ningbo and Changchun, 2000.

15. See Zhonghua renmin gongehuo xianfa (Constitution of the People's Republic of China), 1982.

16. Seventy-one percent of NPC delegates were party members in the 9th NPC, which met for the first time in March 1998. Cadres and military officials made up 33.1 and 8.9 percent of the same NPC accordingly. See Pu Xingzu, 1999: 97.

17. See *Wenhui bao (Hong Kong)*, February 7, 1993 and *Liaowang*, February 23, 1993.

18. See www.transparency.org/documents/cpi2001 (September 7, 2001).

19. See *Wenhui bao*, 1997 and *Xinhua*, 2000.

20. See *Renmin Ribao (People's Daily)*, March 24, 1998; *China Daily*, September 22, 1998; (*Xinhua*), October 29, 1998; *Sing Tao Daily (Sing Tao Jih Pao)*, May 13, 1998; *Ming Pao* (Hong Kong), October 28, 1998; *Liaowang (Outlook)*, March 10, 1997.

21. See *Renmin Ribao (People's Daily)*, August 1, 1994. Included in this group of potential applicants were students of institutions of higher learning located in Beijing and soldiers who were preparing to be demobilized at Beijing.

22. See *Zhongguo qingnian*, January 1997.

23. See the suggestion from an NPC deputy for a Household Registration Law that would lay down a process for rural residents to legally and relatively easily become registered in China's cities in *Xinhua*, March 8, 2001.

24. See Beijing xiwangzhixing wenhua xinxi zixun zhongxin, ed., 1997: 19.

25. Interview, Ministry of Personnel, July 26, 1996. Women staff many more positions (up to a third) in service units/institutions.

26. The Party represents advanced productive forces, advanced culture, and "the fundamental interests of the overwhelming majority of the Chinese people." See *Xinhua*, July 1, 2001.

27. Interview, Ministry of Personnel, July 25, 2001.

28. A government agency to manage personnel work has existed since the early 1950s. The Ministry of Personnel in its 1988 reincarnation was specifically tasked with implementing Organization Department policy on the new civil service system.

29. See the survey conducted in 1993 that compares civil service salaries with state-owned enterprise manager salaries reported in State Statistical Bureau, 1995: 123–24.

30. Interview, Ministry of Personnel, July 26, 1996.

# 4

# Reforming State Institutions: Privatizing the Lawyers' System

*Zhu Sanzhu*

Rapid economic growth and a high demand for legal services in China over the past two decades have helped law become one of the fastest growing professions in the country.[1] It is estimated that there were about 100,000 lawyers and 9,000 law firms in China in the year 2000.[2] Foreign law firms were formally allowed to open representative offices in China in 1992,[3] and at present there are more than 100 foreign law firms that have opened their representative offices in China.[4]

This chapter aims to provide a critical assessment of the reform process of modernizing the lawyers' system in China. Particular attention is given to past changes in governance as related to the administration of lawyers and the future prospects in the light of China's accession to the World Trade Organization (WTO) and the forthcoming 16th Congress of the Chinese Communist Party. The chapter first examines the reforms undertaken by the government to privatize the lawyers' system and the reforms brought about by the 1996 Lawyers Law of the PRC. It then examines respectively the impact of China's accession to the WTO upon the lawyers' system in China and the changing pattern of governance in respect of the administration of the legal profession.

## REFORMING THE STATE INSTITUTIONS: PRIVATIZING THE LAWYERS' SYSTEM

The development of the legal profession in China coincides with China's political, economic, legal, and social changes. In the early 1950s, when the first constitution was enacted and China entered a relatively stable period for legal construction, the legal profession expanded rapidly.[5] However, from the late 1950s when the policy shifted and political movements dominated Chinese society, lawyers became the victims of extreme policies and endless political movements.[6] With the onset of economic reforms and the Open Door policy in 1978, China again embarked upon a stable period of economic and legal development, similar to that of the early 1950s under the 1954 constitution. Lawyers found themselves working in a relatively relaxed and stable environment that allowed them to develop and to flourish. In addition, political, economic, legal, and social changes that had taken place in the previous two decades called for the reestablishment and rapid development of the legal profession in China. It is thus not surprising to find that since 1978 the legal profession in China has developed extensively[7] and has gradually integrated into a society in which lawyers were not traditionally favored.[8]

China's economic reform and Open Door policy entered a new stage in the early 1990s when China embarked on the road toward a so-called socialist market economy. Reforms in the lawyers' system, as with reforms in all other areas, reflected this change. In an important document issued in 1994 regarding further reforms in the lawyers' system, the Ministry of Justice called for changes in four important areas, including the ownership structure of law firms, forms of law firms, status of lawyers, and the way in which lawyers were regulated.[9] Throughout the document the word *boldly* was used several times, which echoed a call from the late Deng Xiaoping during his South China tour for undertaking further economic reforms with a bold spirit[10] and a similar call from the central committee of the Chinese Communist Party in its decision made in November 1993 concerning the reform toward a socialist market economy in China.[11] In the late 1990s, as attention turned increasingly toward China's accession to the WTO, the reform of the lawyers' system became focused on those issues closely related to China's accession to the WTO.

Reform of the lawyers' system is part of a wider program to reform state institutions in China, with the ultimate goal of governing the country more effectively. The main theme and debate running through the lawyers' reform has been how to build an independent and self-regulated legal profession similar to Western models. The reform and changes in the forms of law firms, the status of lawyers, and the way in which lawyers are regulated indicate that, on the one hand, the government is taking steps to privatize the lawyers' system, but, on the other hand, such reform and changes have been limited by China's current administrative arrangement in respect of the regulation of the lawyers' system.

## FROM STATE-OWNED LAW FIRMS TO PRIVATE-OWNED LAW FIRMS

Before reforms began, the lawyers' system was structured as part of the state judicial institutions and was subordinated to the Ministry of Justice and its local bureau. This fundamental feature resulted in a situation in which all lawyers worked for state-owned law firms and provided legal services in their capacities as state legal workers. Lawyers were not allowed to open private offices and engage in private practice. In the late 1980s and early 1990s, when cooperative and partnership law firms began to emerge, this situation changed as state-owned law firms began to lose their dominant position.

The experiment with cooperative law firms and partnership law firms began in 1988 in some provinces and cities,[12] which opened up new forms of law firms in the process of reforming the lawyers' system. In 1996 these two forms of law firms were formally recognized and given statutory status when the Lawyers Law of the PRC was promulgated.[13] The 1996 Lawyers Law of the PRC thus classifies law firms into three types: state-funded law firms, cooperative law firms, and partnership law firms. In accordance with the 1996 Lawyers Law of the PRC, the Ministry of Justice issued three sets of implementation regulations to govern these three forms of law firms.[14]

State-funded law firms are defined as law firms that are set up with state funds by the state judicial administrative authorities, carry out legal business independently, and assume limited liability for the debts of the firm with all its assets.[15] Cooperative law firms are defined as a form of law firm set up by lawyers on a voluntary basis with assets owned equally by all lawyers. A cooperative law firm assumes limited liability for the debts of the firm with all its assets, and all the qualified lawyers working in a cooperative law firm are equal members of the firm.[16] Partnership law firms are defined as a form of law firm set up voluntarily by partners, who participate jointly in the running of the firm; the firm's property belongs to the partners and they bear unlimited and joint liabilities for the debts of the firm.[17] Partnership firms may hire other lawyers to work for them and the relationship between partners and hired lawyers is governed by contracts between them.[18]

Compared with state-funded law firms, cooperative law firms and partnership law firms have greater autonomy and independence. They do not receive any financial support from the state and have to rely on their own work, but they have freedom in many aspects of their day-to-day running of the firm, such as hiring, deciding salaries, dividing profits, and so on. For these and other reasons, there has been a sharp increase in the number of cooperative law firms and partnership law firms. It is estimated that in the year 2000, cooperative law firms and partnership law firms accounted for 15 percent and 25 percent of all law firms in China respectively and they mainly operate in large and developed cities.[19]

## FROM STATE LEGAL WORKERS
## TO PRIVATE LEGAL PRACTITIONERS

In line with the system that the legal profession was part of state judicial institutions, lawyers were defined by the 1980 Provisional Regulations on Lawyers as "legal workers of the state," whose task was to "provide legal assistance to government, enterprises, social associations, and citizens, and to safeguard the interests of the state and collectives and the lawful rights and interests of citizens."[20] The emphasis was on the state and collectives and on the subordinate relationship between lawyers and the state. It was this status that justified strong and direct governmental control over lawyers' professional organizations and their legal practice. Such a status created some contradictions, and questions were subsequently raised, such as how lawyers can act for the defense in a criminal case when they are state legal workers, or how foreigners or a foreign business can employ a state legal worker to defend their interests against Chinese state enterprises.

This status became incompatible with the changes in the late 1980s and early 1990s, when cooperative law firms and partnership law firms began to emerge, which, by definition, were not state-owned law firms. Consequently, the 1996 Lawyers Law of the PRC redefines lawyers as legal practitioners who provide legal services to the public in accordance with the law.[21] This change of definition was regarded as a significant step forward in the reform of the lawyers' system in China for the reason that it paved the way for lawyers to become an independent legal profession and therefore to act in the best interest of their clients in litigations and in other legal services. Now lawyers can, in theory as well as in practice, act in judicial review cases to sue government authorities, in criminal defense cases to argue for defendants, and in cases involving foreigners or foreign business to defend their best interests.

In relation to this change, the 1996 Lawyers Law of the PRC makes changes to the provisions concerning the requirements for lawyers. The 1980 Provisional Regulations on Lawyers, which reflected the more restrictive political thinking at that time, emphasized political requirements, providing that candidates should be those who have the right to vote and be elected under Chinese law and who uphold the socialist system.[22] In contrast, the 1996 Lawyers Law of the PRC requires that persons who uphold the constitution of the PRC may apply for a lawyer's license.[23] It is noticeable that the emphasis has shifted from a political base to a constitutional base. But it is arguable that the change is in fact only in form, not in substance. On the surface the provision has been reworded in order to enlarge the range of candidates, but there is no real change in this respect since "to uphold the socialist system" is one of the four basic principles contained in the current constitution of the PRC.[24] This shows, for example, that the reform and changes intended by the 1996 Lawyers Law of the PRC are limited by the CCP's political and ideological position as represented in the 1982 Constitution of the PRC.

## FROM GOVERNMENT
## REGULATION TO SELF-REGULATION

The relationship between the government and the legal profession is gradually changing in the process of reforming the lawyers' system. When lawyers were treated as state legal workers in the past, the legal profession was subject to strong and direct control by the Ministry of Justice and its local bureaus. All the important matters, such as making rules and regulations concerning the legal profession, issuing licences to lawyers, and disciplining and disqualifying lawyers, were controlled by the Ministry of Justice and its local bureaus. Before 1986 local lawyers' associations were established in some cities, but they exercised only a very limited function.[25] After the establishment of the national All-China Lawyers' Association in 1986, a national self-regulatory system began to emerge. The establishment of the All-China Lawyers' Association indicated that there was both a need for and benefits to having such a national lawyers' association for dealing with certain matters, such as coordinating external relationships with professional bodies of other countries. Compared with the power and functions of the Ministry of Justice and its local bureaus, the All-China Lawyers' Association and local lawyers' associations exercised a limited regulatory function at that time.[26]

Since 1986 local lawyers' associations have been established in provinces and cities directly under the administration of the central government[27] and a more comprehensive nationwide self-regulation system has come into shape. In line with the reform in government administration in recent years, lawyers' associations, like other professional associations, are taking more and more responsibility in the self-regulation of the legal profession.[28] Equally important, more and more lawyers are participating in the self-regulation of lawyers' activities. For example, the Committee for the Protection of Lawyers' Lawful Rights and Interests, one of the six special committees established within the All-China Lawyers' Association, consists of about 70 committee members and advisory members, most of them practising lawyers.[29] It is the largest committee of the All-China Lawyers' Association and plays an increasingly important role in protecting lawyers' rights and interests. As lawyers in China are becoming a private legal profession, the function of lawyers' associations becomes increasingly relevant and important.

But under the current administrative system in China and the arrangement between the Ministry of Justice and the All-China Lawyers' Association in respect of the regulation of lawyers, it is impossible for the All-China Lawyers' Association to be independent and free from control and interference by the Ministry of Justice. This is reflected most clearly in the appointment of the key personnel of the Secretariat of the All-China Lawyers' Association, its executive body responsible for day-to-day work of the association. The secretary-general and three deputy secretaries are all closely linked with the Ministry of Justice: the secretary-general is concurrently holding the post of deputy director of the division in the Ministry of Justice in charge of lawyers and notary public; three deputy secretaries all had worked in the Ministry of Justice and had held various positions before they worked for the All-China Lawyers' Association.[30] By definition, the All-China Lawyers' Association is a nongovernmental and social organization with a legal status and is the self-regulatory body for the legal profession.[31] It is therefore not appropriate for an official from the Ministry of Justice to concurrently hold one of the most important positions in the association. Under such an arrangement it is highly questionable whether the All-China Lawyers' Association possesses a full "self status" and has a proper "self-regulating function."

In general, regulation of lawyers can be classified into three patterns: first, by government regulation and government regulators; second, by self-regulation and self-regulators; and third, by two tiers of regulation and regulators, i.e. government regulation and self-regulation. The regulation of lawyers in China takes the form of the third pattern, combining government regulation with self-regulation but with an emphasis on the government regulation and government regulator. The question as to which pattern is the most suitable pattern for China to build an independent legal profession on is subject to debate, but two tiers of regulation and regulators in China may increase regulatory costs, distort the legal services market to some degree, and lead to excessive interference from the government, a typical phenomenon in China. If it is agreed that self-regulation is the best solution for the legal profession in China in the context that Chinese lawyers are gradually becoming a group of private professionals, then further steps are necessary to reform the current arrangement regarding the relationship between the Ministry of Justice and the All-China Lawyers' Association, and the role of lawyers' associations must be further strengthened.

## CHINA'S ACCESSION TO THE WTO AND ITS IMPACT ON THE LAWYERS' SYSTEM

China's accession to the WTO, which has gone through a long process starting from 1986, has brought about many changes in China in its continuing reform toward a so-called socialist market economy. Not only has China's foreign trade and investment regime been directly affected and changes consequently been made in accordance with the rules and principles of the WTO, but China's economic system, legal system, government administration, and society in certain respects have also been affected directly or indirectly. The legal service market and the lawyers' system are directly affected by China's accession to the WTO. Since 1992, when foreign law firms were admitted into China's legal service market under the 1992 Provisional Regulations on the Establishment of Representative Office in China by Foreign Law Firms, the Chinese legal profession and legal service market have established close links with foreign legal professions. In 1994, in anticipation of China's joining the WTO, the Foreign Trade Law of the PRC was passed, which, among other things, laid down basic provisions concerning the opening up of China's service markets.[32] Since then, the opening up of China's service markets, including the legal service market, has stepped up the process of continuous negotiations with WTO member states.

The impact of China's admittance to the WTO on the lawyers' system has been an issue of great concern for government regulators and lawyers. Various conferences have been held at national and local levels to address the issue and discuss the future development of China's legal profession after China becomes a member of the WTO.[33] In general, the discussion at these conferences has focused on three areas: first, the further opening up of China's legal service market and its consequences; second, the quality of the Chinese legal profession and its ability to compete with foreign law firms; and third, future development of China's legal profession in the context of China's accession to the WTO. A wide range of issues has been discussed, such as the idea of further opening up of China's legal service market, the quality of Chinese law firms and the way to improve them, the standards of legal services and common problems, the impact on the way in which the legal profession is regulated, and the adaptation of foreign and international practices in the development of China's legal profession.

## FURTHER OPENING UP OF CHINA'S LEGAL SERVICE MARKET

The further opening up of China's legal service market is an inevitable consequence of China's accession to the WTO. In line with the growth of foreign trade and investment in the 1990s, China's legal service market was an attractive prospect for foreign law firms and lawyers. Since 1992 the number of representative offices of foreign law firms has increased significantly in China, even though the restrictions stipulated by the 1992 Provisional Regulations on the Establishment of Representative Office in China by Foreign

Law Firms have remained the same. Quantitative restrictions on the number of representative offices a foreign law firm may open and geographic restrictions to the cities where a foreign law firm may locate its representative office have prohibited foreign law firms from setting up more than one office in more than one city.[34] The restrictions on the service that representative offices of foreign law firms may provide to their clients have prohibited foreign law firms from providing legal opinions on Chinese law.[35]

In the negotiations with WTO member states, China agreed to lift some of these restrictions upon China's accession to the WTO. Under the final agreement with the WTO, China has made commitments to eliminate quantitative and geographic restrictions within one year after China's accession to the WTO.[36] In the meantime China maintains its restrictive policies on some other matters concerning the qualifications of foreign lawyers working in representative offices,[37] the business scope of representative offices,[38] and the employment of Chinese lawyers by representative offices of foreign law firms.[39]

Based upon the commitment China has made in the agreement with the WTO, the State Council issued in 2001 the Regulation on the Administration of Representative Offices Set up in China by Foreign Law Firms.[40] Compared with the 1992 Provisional Regulations on the Establishment of Representative Offices by Foreign Law Firms, the 2001 Regulation has enlarged the scope of the service that representative offices may provide. In accordance with Article 15 of the 2001 Regulation, representative offices of foreign law firms are allowed to engage in five kinds of services, which correspond to the commitment China has made in the agreement with the WTO in respect to the business scope of representative offices of foreign law firms.[41] In contrast, foreign representative offices were only allowed to engage in three kinds of services under the 1992 Provisional Regulations on the Establishment of Representative Offices by Foreign Law Firms.[42] As in the past, foreign lawyers are not allowed to represent their clients in court or provide legal opinions or interpretations on Chinese law.[43] Furthermore, foreign law firms must get permission from judicial administrative departments under the State Council before setting up representative offices in China.[44]

This is a step-by-step approach. On the one hand, the legal service market has opened up further by eliminating quantitative and geographic restrictions, but on the other hand, various restrictions are still in place in order to prevent foreign law firms from entering into China's legal service market on a full scale. From the government's point of view, the opening-up should be a step-by-step process that will be adjusted according to the development of the domestic legal service market.[45] In the foreseeable future, even though a large number of foreign law firms are expected to gain access to the legal service market in China, they would still be subject to tight control by the government. They will therefore not be able to form a formidable competitive force to the Chinese legal profession, but rather they will have to cooperate with the Chinese legal profession, which is what the government regulator would like to happen.[46] It is true that the restrictive regulatory rules that foreign representative offices may not recruit Chinese lawyers and that they must appoint Chinese lawyers to handle matters involving Chinese law[47] would protect the business interests of Chinese law firms and thus are good for Chinese lawyers in a sense. However, whether they are sensible rules for the development of the Chinese legal service market and whether they raise the quality of Chinese lawyers in the long term is debatable.

## CHALLENGES AND OPPORTUNITIES FACING THE CHINESE LEGAL PROFESSION

China's joining the WTO and the further opening up of the legal service market has brought about both challenges and opportunities to the Chinese legal profession. This is the view held by the majority of law firms, lawyers, and regulators, although some are more worried about the challenges and related problems in the future development of China's own legal profession. Challenges and opportunities have been recurring themes at conferences and forums held over the past few years in preparing the legal profession and regulators for China's accession to the WTO and its impact on the lawyers' system.[48]

Concerning challenges, competition is considered the primary issue facing the Chinese legal profession upon China's admittance to the WTO. Competition may arise in various areas, including competition in business, in expertise, in management, and in quality. Small scale and a lack of specialization are the two major barriers for local law firms in competing with their overseas counterparts. With regard to opportunities, lawyers and regulators hold the view that China's accession to the WTO and the further opening up of China's legal service market is a historic opportunity for the Chinese legal profession to narrow the gap with their counterparts in developed countries and to bring the lawyers' system in China closer to those of developed countries. The opportunity would lead to the expansion of lawyers' business, improvements in the management system of law firms, an increase in the competitiveness of Chinese law firms, changes to the way in which the lawyers' system is regulated by the government, and a necessary adaptation of experiences of foreign law firms to Chinese law firms.

In the past two decades, the Chinese legal profession has developed rapidly and played an important role in economic reform, the Open Door policy, and the reform toward the socialist market economy. But, as argued by some scholars, the rapid growth of the legal profession presents significant problems, the most serious being competence and professional responsibility.[49] It is expected that after China's accession to the WTO, an open and integrated legal service market in China would help to resolve these problems gradually. In order to compete with foreign law firms, Chinese law firms have to achieve high standards of legal services for their clients and to raise the standards of their professional conduct.

Bringing China's legal profession closer to that of developed countries after China becomes a member of the WTO depends very much upon how successful the changes in the way the government regulates the lawyers' system are. It is argued that the judicial administrative organs of the government still rely on old ideas and means to regulate the lawyers' system, and this creates barriers to the healthy development of the lawyers' system in response to changing circumstances.[50] China's joining the WTO has been seen as providing an opportunity for the government to adjust the relationship between the judicial administrative organs of the government and lawyers on the one hand and the relationship between the judicial administrative organs of the government and self-regulatory associations on the other. So as to improve governmental regulation of the legal profession in response to the changing circumstances under China's entering the WTO, the Ministry of Justice suggested in 2001 and 2002 that the regulation of the lawyers' system in the future should be gradually changed to focus on issues of "licensing (*zhunru*), guidance (*daoxiang*), and supervision (*jianguan*)."[51] The proposed transformation of the role of the government regulator in relation to the legal profession requires the government to strike the right balance between the regulatory functions of the Ministry of Justice and the All-China Lawyers' Association and allow the All-China Lawyers' Association and its local associations to become true self-regulators with proper powers and a genuine independent status.

## RAISING STANDARDS AND THE QUALITY OF THE CHINESE LEGAL PROFESSION

Raising the standards and the quality of the Chinese legal profession has been highlighted as an important task to meet the challenges brought about by foreign lawyers after China's admittance to the WTO. The small scale and the lack of specialization of Chinese law firms, the weak consciousness of individual lawyers of professional ethics, and the low quality of certain groups of lawyers are some of the problems that affect the standards and quality of the Chinese legal profession. In addition, the public's image of the legal profession is not what it should be. People have complained about lawyers for their services and activities, such as high fees and illegal acts. Moreover, there are "underground lawyers," who do not have licenses but engage in legal services in the form of legal consultant companies or some other forms.[52]

These and other problems have caused concern in discussions at the conferences and forums held in the past few years in preparation of the legal profession for the impact of China's accession to the WTO.[53]

Since 1992 the Ministry of Justice has issued a series of regulations and rules concerning professional ethics and discipline in order to raise the level of professional ethics and bring the legal profession under a disciplinary control.[54] In addition, some other relevant government regulators, such as China Securities Regulatory Commission, also issued supplementary rules to raise the standard of professional ethics in relation to particular types of legal services offered by lawyers.[55] Most recently, the Beijing Lawyers' Association, in an effort to bring Beijing local lawyers to a level to meet the challenges brought about by foreign lawyers after China's joining the WTO, issued a code of conduct on a trial basis for Beijing local lawyers, which prescribes the principles of professional ethics and the discipline of lawyers. Some of the provisions and concepts prescribed in this code of conduct are based on rules from developed countries.[56] All these regulatory efforts at both national and local levels are necessary to strengthen the legal profession's self-discipline and ethics standards. Indeed, this is one of the important areas of the lawyers' system that needs considerable improvement in light of China's admittance to the WTO.

Equally important is the continuous training of lawyers. From the All-China Lawyers' Association to local lawyers' associations, the importance of continuous training has been recognized and efforts have been made to bring the training to a higher level. In November 2000 Wu Mingde, secretary-general of the All-China Lawyers' Association, announced plans to provide more opportunities, and even a special school, for up-to-date professional training to meet the challenges brought about by China's accession to the WTO.[57] In previous years, lawyers were sent abroad for training under various cooperative training programs with other countries, which gave lawyers invaluable help in their understanding of the standards of professional ethics and discipline in those countries as well as foreign and international laws and practices.[58] Exchanges and communications with overseas lawyers have been encouraged and have had a profound impact on the quality of Chinese lawyers. As an important part of the training strategy, such training programs will be promoted and will continue to influence the quality of Chinese lawyers profoundly. Local lawyers' associations also promote various training programs to local lawyers to raise their standards. For example, special training will be given to local lawyers in Beijing in an effort to implement more effectively the code of conduct issued recently by the Beijing Lawyers' Association.[59] Without these and other training programs, it is impossible to bring the Chinese legal profession to a level at which lawyers have the necessary foreign language skills, necessary knowledge of WTO rules and principles and related international laws, and proper standards of professional ethics and discipline so that they can meet challenges after China's accession to the WTO.

Starting from the year 2002, a new unified national testing system, "National Judicial Examination," will replace the current lawyers' examination.[60] The new test is designed to provide a high and unified standard for judges and public prosecutors as well as lawyers. Compared with current tests available separately for lawyers, judges, and public prosecutors, the requirements for applicants under the National Judicial Examination are more stringent, and the contents of examination are more comprehensive. It is one of the important judicial reforms in recent years, as it aims at improving the standard and quality of lawyers, judges, and public prosecutors in the light of China's accession to the WTO. In the year 2000, applications for the lawyers' examination reached 200,000, the highest level since 1986.[61] In order to avoid an overheated legal profession and low quality of lawyers by taking in an uncontrolled number of applicants, there has been a proposal that the yearly increase in lawyers will be controlled at 7 percent, which will raise the number of lawyers to 200,000 by the year 2010.[62]

## CONCLUSION

Reforms in the lawyers' system have brought about many changes in the forms of law firms, the status of lawyers, the standards and quality of lawyers, and the way in which lawyers are regulated. The past two decades have witnessed a gradual change from state-owned law firms to private-owned law firms, from state legal workers to private legal practitioners, and from government regulation to self-regulation of the legal profession. The need to modernize the lawyers' system is in line with the transformation of China toward a market economy and the transformation of state institutions toward efficient governance. This modernization process has provided a favorable environment for the legal profession and helped it achieve fast and sustained development. But the reform in the lawyers' system has been carried out not in a vacuum, but in the context of China's overall political, administrative, legal, and social structures. On one hand, the legal profession is becoming a private profession in response to the demand of market forces but, on the other hand, it is still subject to a regulatory regime that was essentially structured in the past, with an emphasis on state control in accordance with the CCP's policy. This shows that the reform in the lawyers' system could not transcend the limitations of China's current political and administrative structures, and the objective to build an independent and self-regulated legal profession similar to Western models has to be fitted into China's own conditions.

The development of the legal profession in China coincides with China's political, economic, legal, and social changes. Lawyers experienced rapid changes immediately before and after the enactment of the 1954 Constitution and again from the late 1970s when economic reforms and the Open Door policy started. However, in the late 1950s and during the ten-year Cultural Revolution, lawyers became the victims of extreme policies and endless political movements. Many changes are taking place in China as a result of China's accession to the WTO, which in turn have a significant impact on China's legal services market and the lawyers' system. The legal services market, like other service sectors, is gradually opening up to foreign law firms and lawyers, which has presented unprecedented challenges and opportunities to the Chinese legal profession.

Whether China's legal profession can begin to approximate that of developed countries in terms of its ability to compete and provide services of a high standard and quality depends to a large extent upon success in changing the way the lawyers' system is regulated by government and how this relates in turn to self-regulation by lawyer's associations. On a more general level, the changing attitude of the CCP toward the rule of law and the consequent constitutional amendment in 1999 have provided an environment in which the legal system in China, including the legal profession, can be expected to encounter fewer barriers in its development. The ideological position of the CCP, which has been modified and redefined from one generation of leadership of the CCP to another, is at the heart of its policy and the way in which it governs the country. In this sense, the resolution of the 16th Congress of the CCP in 2002,[63] together with a new generation of its leadership, will have a profound impact on the legal system and the future development of an independent legal profession in China.

## NOTES

1. The author would like to thank Professor M. Palmer for his invaluable comments.

2. This is based on a figure given in a paper presented by Yu Ning, vice president of the All-China Lawyers' Association, at China-UK Legal Development Seminar, London, April 3, 2000: 1.

3. The Provisional Regulation on the Establishment of Representative Offices in China by Foreign Law Firms, issued jointly by the Ministry of Justice and the State Administration of Industry and Commerce on, and effective from, May 26, 1992.

4. In April 2001, the Ministry of Justice issued licences to another eleven foreign law firms to open representative offices in China. By then 131 foreign law firms had opened their offices in China, including 28 Hong Kong law firms.

5. The Constitution of the PRC was enacted in 1954, marking the beginning of a period, albeit very short, of formal legal construction in China. Between 1954 and 1957,

the newly established legal profession enjoyed a fast and substantial development. It is estimated that there were about 3,000 lawyers and about 800 law firms throughout China before the outbreak of the anti-rightist movement in the middle of 1957.

6. Many lawyers were treated as rightists and sent to the countryside for re-education through labor during the anti-rightist movement. The Ministry of Justice and local bureaus of justice were abolished together with their responsibilities for the regulation of the legal profession in 1959. Over the next two decades, during which the Cultural Revolution (1966-1976) brought China into chaos, there were no legal practitioners in China. For more details about the background of the legal system and the lawyers' system from the late 1950s to the 1970s, see Hung-yee Chen, 1998, especially chapter 3, "The Legal History of Modern China," 20–38; Lubman, 1999: 153–59.

7. Reestablishment of the legal profession began in the late 1970s and early 1980s. In 1979 the Criminal Procedure Law of the PRC was promulgated, which, among other things, lay down the basic provisions (chapter IV, "Defence," articles 26–30) for lawyers to present in criminal defense. In September of the same year, the Ministry of Justice was reestablished to take charge of the administration of the legal profession. In August 1980 the Provisional Regulations on Lawyers was promulgated by the State Council and became the first legislation for the regulation of lawyers. In July 1986 the All-China Lawyers' Association was established, which marked an important step toward the establishment of a self-regulatory system for lawyers in China. In 1986 a national lawyers' examination was set up, first biannually and then annually from 1993. In 1996 the Lawyers Law of the PRC was promulgated, which codified the practices that had been experimented with in the previous years. It thus became the primary legislation to regulate lawyers and their activities, replacing the 1980 Provisional Regulations on Lawyers.

8. It is well known that lawyers were regarded as "litigation tricksters" (*songgun*) traditionally.

9. The Circular of the Ministry of Justice Being Several Issues as to What attention should be paid in the process of deepening reforms on lawyers' work, issued by the Ministry of Justice on March 3, 1994.

10. Speeches made by the late Deng Xiaoping during his south China tour at Wuchang, Shenzhen, Zhuhai, and Shanghai from January 18 to February 21, 1992.

11. The Decision of the Central Committee of the Chinese Communist Party on Several Issues about the Establishment of a Socialist Market Economy System, adopted at the third plenary session of the 14th Congress of the Chinese Communist Party on November 14, 1993.

12. For more details about the experiment of cooperative and partnership law firms in the late 1980s and early 1990s, see Hung-yee Chen, 1998, especially chapter 8, "Legal Institutions: Lawyers, Legal Education and the Ministry of Justice," 128–51.

13. Article 17 of the 1996 Lawyers Law of the PRC: "Lawyers may establish cooperative law firms. Cooperative law firms shall undertake liability for their debts with their entire assets"; Article 18 of the same law: "Lawyers may establish partnership law firms. The partners shall undertake unlimited, and joint and several liability for the debts of the law firm."

14. The Measures on the Administration of State-Funded Law Firms (1996), The Measures on the Administration of Cooperative Law Firms (1996), and The Measures on the Administration of Partnership Law Firms (1996).

15. Articles 2 and 3 of the Measures on the Administration of State-Funded Law Firms (1996).

16. Articles 2 and 8 of the Measures on the Administration of Cooperative Law Firms (1996).

17. Article 2 of the Measures on the Administration of Partnership Law Firms (1996).

18. Article 25 of the Measures on the Administration of Partnership Law Firms (1996).

19. This is based on a figure given in a paper presented by Yu ning, vice president of the All-China Lawyers' Association, at China-UK Legal Development Seminar, London, April 3, 2000, p. 2.

20. Article 1 of the Provisional Regulations of the PRC on Lawyers (1980).

21. Article 2 of the Lawyers Law of the PRC 1996: "For the purpose of this Law, the term 'lawyers' shall refer to practitioners, who have obtained a lawyer's practising certificate and provide legal services to the public in accordance with law."

22. Article 8 of the Provisional Regulations of the PRC on Lawyers (1980).

23. Article 8 of the Lawyers Law of the PRC (1996).

24. The preamble of the Constitution of the PRC (1982).

25. See Hung-yee Chen, 1998, especially chapter 8, "Legal Institutions: Lawyers, Legal Education and the Ministry of Justice," 128-151.

26. They did not have any formal power to participate in setting rules and standards of professional practice and ethics, determining the qualifying conditions for lawyers, or enforcing disciplinary sanctions against members of the profession. See Hung-yee Chen, 1998, especially, chapter 8, "Legal Institutions: Lawyers, Legal Education and the Ministry of Justice," 128–151.

27. Local lawyers' associations have been established in 22 provinces, five autonomous regions, and four cities under the direct administration of the central government, all of which are institutional members of the All-China Lawyers' Association.

28. Article 10 of the Charter of the All-China Lawyers' Association (1999) lists the following responsibilities: (i) support members to practice in accordance with law, protect their lawful rights and interests; (ii) formulate lawyers' code of conduct and oversee their implementation; (iii) responsible for the education, inspection and supervision in respect of lawyers' ethic standards and discipline matters; (iv) review and exchange experiences of lawyers' work, raise the practice standard of the members; (v) organize trainings for lawyers; (vi) deal with complaints concerning members; (vii) formulating procedures regarding members' reward and punishment and oversee their implementation; (viii) organize exchange programs with other countries; (ix) mediate disputes arising in practice among members; (x) participate in legislative activities, voicing suggestions to relevant authorities regarding the construction of the legal system and the lawyers' system; (xi) propagandise lawyers' work and publish lawyers' magazines; (xii) deal with welfare matters for lawyers; (xiii) organize national lawyers' examinations; (xiv) other responsibilities stipulated by laws; (xv) other responsibilities designated by judicial administrative organs and lawyers' association at above levels.

29. See www.lawyers.com.cn/lsxh/zhba/main.htm (in Chinese) (the Web site of the All-China Lawyers' Association), where individual names of these committee members and advisory members are listed.

30. Apart from the secretary-general, who is concurrently holding the post of deputy director of the division in charge of lawyers and notary public in the Ministry of Justice, three deputy secretaries used to hold various posts in the Ministry of Justice: secretary in the general office of the Ministry of Justice; staff in the foreign affairs division of the Ministry of Justice; deputy director and director of the division in charge of lawyers. For more details see the Web site of the All-China Lawyers' Association: www.lawyers.com.cn/lsxh/zhba/main. htm (in Chinese).

31. Article 2 of the Charter of the All-China Lawyers' Association (1999): "The Lawyers' association is a social organization with a legal personality established in accordance with the law; it is the lawyers' self-regulatory organization and exercises the professional regulation of lawyers in accordance with the law."

32. Foreign Trade Law of the PRC, adopted at the Seventh Session of the Standing Committee of the Eighth National People's Congress and promulgated on May 12, 1994, effective from July 1, 1994. Chapter IV, "International Trade in Services" (Articles 22–26), stipulates (Article 23) "China shall grant market access and national treatment with respect to international service trade to concluding or acceding parties in accordance with its commitments made under international treaties or agreements concluded or acceded to."

33. The two most important national conferences were: (1) Chinese Lawyer Millennium Conference, held in Beijing on November 26, 2000, was attended by nearly 1,000 lawyers across the country to discuss the opportunities and challenges in the new millennium and China's impending accession to the WTO, and an important report, "Report on China's Legal Profession," was also submitted to the conference; (2) the First Chinese Lawyers' Forum, held in Kunming city on December 9, 2001, two days before China's accession to the WTO, was attended by 114 Chinese law firms across the country and it passed the "Kunming Declaration" on December 10, 2001.

34. A foreign law firm can only establish one representative office in Beijing, Shanghai, Guangzhou, Shenzhen, Haikou, Dalian, Qingdao, Ningbo, Yantai, Tianjin, Suzhou, Xiamen, Zhuhai, Hanghou, Fuzhou, Wuhan, Chengdu, Shenyang, and Kunming.

35. Article 16 of the 1992 Provisional Regulations on the Establishment of Representative Office in China by Foreign Law Firms stated, "Representative offices and their members of foreign law firms may not engage in the following business activities: (i) represent for Chinese law matters; (ii) interpret Chinese law to their clients; (iii) other business activities that Chinese law does not allow foreigners to engage in."

36. See Annex 9 of the Protocol on the Accession of the People's Republic of China: Schedule of Specific Commitments on Services, List of Article II MFN Exemptions (November 10, 2001).

37. See Annex 9 of the Protocol on the Accession of the People's Republic of China: Schedule of Specific Commitments on Services, List of Article II MFN Exemptions (November 10, 2001). The representatives of a foreign law firm shall be practitioner lawyers, who are members of the bar or law society in a WTO member state and have practised for no fewer than two years outside of China. The chief representative shall be a partner or equivalent (e.g., member of a law firm of a limited liability corporation) of a law firm of a WTO member and have practised for no fewer than three years. All representatives shall be resident in China no fewer than six months each year.

38. See Annex 9 of the Protocol on the Accession of the People's Republic of China: Schedule of Specific Commitments on Services, List of Article II MFN Exemptions (November 10, 2001). Foreign representative offices are allowed: (a) to provide clients with consultancy on the legislation of the country/region where the lawyers of the law firm are permitted to engage in lawyer's professional work, and on international conventions and practices; (b) to handle, when entrusted by clients or Chinese law firms, legal affairs of the country/region where the lawyers of the law firm are permitted to engage in lawyer's professional work; (c) to entrust, on behalf of foreign clients, Chinese law firms to deal with the Chinese legal affairs; (d) to enter into contracts to maintain long-term entrustment relations with Chinese law firms for legal affairs; (e) to provide information on the impact of the Chinese legal environment.

39. See Annex 9 of the Protocol on the Accession of the People's Republic of China: Schedule of Specific Commitments on Services, List of Article II MFN Exemptions (November 10, 2001). The representative office shall not employ Chinese national registered lawyers outside of China.

40. It was issued on December 19, 2001, and came into effect on January 1, 2002. The Regulation contains 35 articles in six chapters, including general principles, establishment, alteration and cancellation of representative offices, business scales and rules, supervision and administration, legal liabilities, and miscellaneous rules.

41. See note 38 for a list of the five kinds of services.

42. These were: (i) to provide clients with consultancy on the legislation of the country where the lawyers of the law firm are permitted to engage in lawyer's professional work, and on international conventions and practices; (ii) to handle, when entrusted by clients or Chinese law firms, legal affairs of the country where the lawyers of the law firm are permitted to engage in lawyer's professional work; (iii) to entrust, on behalf of foreign clients, Chinese law firms to deal with the Chinese legal affairs (Article 15).

43. Article 15 of the Regulation on the Administration of Representative Offices Set up in China by Foreign Law Firms (2001).

44. Article 15 of the Regulation on the Administration of Representative Offices Set up in China by Foreign Law Firms (2001). Article 6.

45. He Min, head of the Administration for China Offices of Foreign Law Firms under the Ministry of Justice, was quoted saying, "The opening-up is a step-by-step process that must be constantly adjusted according to the development of the domestic legal service market." Reported by *China Daily* on December 29, 2001.

46. Wu Mingde, secretary-general of the All-China Lawyers' Association, was quoted saying, "I do not agree with the view that foreign law firms will snatch business opportunities from Chinese lawyers, on the contrary, in the view that foreign firms must cooperate with Chinese lawyers under many circumstances, they bring in a lot of business opportunities. I do not think the business volume of Chinese law firms is going to decline after China enters the WTO." Reported by *China Daily* on November 27, 2000.

47. Article 16 and Article 15 of the Regulation on the Administration of Representative Offices Set up in China by Foreign Law Firms (2001).

48. See note 35 above.

49. Li Yuwen, "Lawyers in China: a 'flourishing' profession in rapidly changing society?" *Asian Legal Briefing* (June 2000): 14–23.

50. For example, even today after several years of reform in the lawyers' system and changes in the status of lawyers, some government officials still regard lawyers as state judicial working personnel, the same as police, judges, and public prosecutors.

51. Speech by Zhang Fusen, Minister of Justice, at a conference attended by heads of Bureaus of Justice at provincial levels, on December 23, 2001; speeches by Zhang Fusen and Duan Zhengkun, deputy Minister of Justice, at a national conference organized by the Ministry of Justice via television and telephone on the Administration of Lawyers on February 28, 2002.

52. It is reported that Shenzhen Bureau of Justice, as part of its preparation for the entry into the WTO, recently cracked down on a group of consultant companies and underground lawyers operating in Shenzhen. It is the first time that such a large scale crackdown has been initiated since the creation of Shenzhen Special Economic Zone more than 20 years ago. Reported by *People's Daily* (in Chinese) on December 25, 2001.

53. See note 36 above.

54. Rules for the Punishment of Lawyers, issued by the Ministry of Justice on October 22, 1992; Provisions Concerning Lawyers' Professional Ethics and Practising Disciplines, issued by the Ministry of Justice on December 27, 1993; Several Provisions Concerning Legal Profession Against Unfair Competition Activities, issued by the Ministry of Justice on February 20, 1995; Circular of the Ministry of Justice on Further Improvement of the System for the Punishment of Lawyers and Strengthening Work on the Punishment of Lawyers', issued on May 20, 1995; Measures on Punishment of Lawyers' Illegal Activities, issued by the Ministry of Justice on January 31, 1997.

55. For example, Circular of the China Securities Regulatory Commission on the Strengthening of Lawyers Engaging in Securities Legal Business, issued on July 3, 1998.

56. Beijing lawyers' code of conduct for practice (trial), by Beijing Lawyers' Association, first brought to light in February 2001 for public consultation and later implemented on a trial basis. There are news reports in Chinese and English about this event and one of them is "New Rules Supervise Lawyers," by *Xinhua News Agency*, on July 4, 2001.

57. Wu Mingde, secretary-general of the All-China Lawyers' Association, reported by *China Daily*, indicated that his association plans to provide more opportunities, even a special school, for up-to-date professional training. Reported by *China Daily* on November 27, 2000. Ref. Note 49 above.

58. Examples include EU-China Legal and Judicial Cooperation Program and the Young Chinese Lawyers' Training Scheme in U.K.

59. See note 56 above.

60. Implementing measure for the National Judicial Examination (trial provisions), issued jointly by the Supreme People's Court, the Supreme People' Procuracy, and the Ministry of Justice on October 31, 2001, and effective as of January 1, 2002.

61. This figure was quoted in reports on the Chinese Lawyers' Millennium Conference held in Beijing on November 26, 2000, at which the "Report on China's Legal Profession" was submitted. Ref. Note 36 above.

62. It was proposed by the "Report on China's Legal Profession" submitted to the Chinese Lawyers' Millennium Conference.

63. In his speech to the 16th Congress of the CCP, Jiang Zemin emphasized the importance of the improvement of governance in accordance with law: "to govern the country according to law" (*yifa zhiguo*). This is in line with the 1999 constitutional amendment and indicates that the CCP will continue to promote further legal reforms and gradually establish rule of law in China.

# 5

# Bringing Culture Back In

*Michael Keane*

China's eventual admittance to the World Trade Organization (WTO) on December 11, 2001, was portrayed by the Chinese state media as a momentous national event as China ascended on to the global economic stage. Despite the fact that its membership has committed China to a progressive liberalization of industry sectors and to a policy normalization advocated by institutions such as the International Monetary Fund (IMF) and the World Bank, the official verdict on the events was "win-win."[1] Although WTO accession had taken fifteen years of protracted negotiations, the Chinese Communist Party proclaimed the accession agreement, initially ratified in Doha, Qatar, on November 11, as a tangible outcome of the economic and social liberalization that had commenced with Deng Xiaoping's Open Door Policy some two decades earlier.

Notwithstanding the euphoria of the biggest consumer market subscribing to the principles of rules-based trade, there has been a paucity of critical analysis directed at the cultural implications of China's membership. In effect, WTO admittance has repositioned China's cultural sector within the remit of global cultural industries, offering the lure of new markets for China's cultural products in return for commitments concerned with audio-visual and information services that provide limited market openings for transnational media corporations. In this new collusion of culture and transnational trade, cultural policy comes directly into the frame of governance.

In this chapter I examine the proposition that the parameters of culture have been refashioned by an interdependent relationship between culture, service industries, and the emerging knowledge-based economy in China. This constitutes the first section of the chapter. The "new" relationships in turn prompt three questions central to the reframing of cultural policy in China. These are dealt with in the following three sections.

The first question concerns the kinds of impact that liberalization, and in particular WTO membership, will have on the development of China's cultural industries. In the second section, we thus examine the benefits and challenges of WTO accession in relation to the uptake of information and communication services in China's cities.

As market liberalization inevitably impacts upon national sovereignty, a third issue concerns the choices confronting China's regulatory bodies in relation to the diffusion of global cultural goods and services via new media technologies. With the disruptive potential of communications sharpened by the forces of convergence, globalization, and digitization, we see a weakening of the authority of central jurisdiction, while autonomy is enhanced for local governments and businesses. This fragmentation of central authority occurs not only in the development of cultural tourism services, but also applies to entertainment and information services, such as television, cable broadband, and Internet service providers. Notwithstanding the fact that central (*zhongyang*) bureaus, such as the Ministry of Culture, the Ministry of Information Industries, and the State Administration of Radio Film and Television, officially confer "landing rights" to foreign media and communications companies, policy fragmentation occurs as sub-state and regional agencies seek to make deals with investors. These often include creative interpretations of central policy to win business. The WTO accession has further clouded the landscape with foreign interests able to utilize the principles of national treatment (Article XVII) to leverage their investments. The fragmentation of sovereignty is captured by the image of arbitrage as footloose multinationals exploit competition between regions for competitive advantage.

The fragmentation of sovereignty and authority in turn leads into the question of how liberalization of cultural markets are linked to issues of civil society, pluralization, and democracy. This key question forms the substance of the fourth section. Does the devolution of state authority diffuse into a more autonomous sphere of social relations supported by more transparent institutions? Does the demand for new cultural services create further liberalization pressures?

These are indeed complicated questions and are not amenable to straightforward answers, particularly given the diffuse understandings of culture among academics, industry, and government. This ambiguity is exacerbated by the reluctance of the Chinese state to engage with issues of cultural diversity and communication rights, issues that are central to civil society organizations worldwide. This is illustrated by China's refusal to participate in the 2003 World Summit on the Information Society, instituted through the International Telecommunication Union in 1998 and endorsed by the United Nations General Assembly in 2001. With the Summit also being targeted by civil society activists operating under a campaign called Communication Rights in the Information Society, China's leaders have decided to boycott the event.[2] The Summit itself has been derailed by uncertainties about just what constitutes culture and information in the twenty-first century. While there are agreements in the international community on what constitutes poverty, environmental degradation, illiteracy, and so on, the relationships between national cultures, communication, and development are less obvious and more contentious.

## CULTURAL POLICY, CREATIVITY, AND KNOWLEDGE ECONOMY

As culture is constantly refashioned in the information age, its application to new emerging forms of governance gains elasticity as well as an expanded provenance. The neologisms *technoculture* and *cyberculture* have found their way into popular currency, particularly among "the digerati"—those who evangelize the benefits of new technology. The former term pertains to technologies that impact upon the shaping of people's lives, from Web portals to short-message services (SMS), while *cyberculture* portends a more libertarian ethos of civil society and grassroots democratization, along with cyber-law, cyber-democracy, and cyber-rights.

The convergence of communications and culture moreover challenges an approach that has artificially separated culture from "the media." In particular, the orientalizing of culture by sinology into particularistic and traditional categories has perpetuated a research tradition that contrasts with the study of contemporary Chinese culture under communism, in which the content of Chinese literature and cinema is examined for evidence of the sovereign individual. "Culture" has been extracted as the essence—something that is expressed within the cracks of state constraints, or which is inherently valuable or exotic, such as the work of new filmmakers, dissident literature, and traditional artifacts. These cultural research traditions have isolated communications, which has been largely framed as propaganda. In the area studies field, traditional culture and dissident culture are accorded an elevated ranking, while the "industrial" output of the commercial culture industries is deemed to be less influential. This is despite the latter utilizing similar indigenous codes of representation and attracting far greater audiences and readerships.

The logic of such sinological separations is undermined by global market research that shows an increasing fragmentation of tastes and a mix of demographics based on income, generation, marital status, and gender. This fragmentation has been aided by the internationalization of cultural industries and new electronic distribution platforms such as satellite television and the Internet that are impervious to national boundaries. Moreover, while high and low cultures exist as critical categories, research into consumption patterns shows that high culture users are increasingly eclectic in their tastes, becoming "cultural omnivores," that is, they consume both commercial and subsidized forms (O'Regan, 2001: 9). Cultural consumption is not confined to the cinema, the museum, or the art gallery. In contrast to a conservative predisposition to argue that there is not enough fine culture, or too much commercial culture, there is a view that culture is ubiquitous and value-adding. In fact, culture is a vital element of economic value chains and it constitutes a way of life. It is also expressed in polyvalent forms from public art to folk festivals, from urban design to the design of Web sites.

The academic fences that have been erected to differentiate culture from media and information present an anomalous representation of real life in which culture is consumed and shared. Rather than elaborating on the debate between aesthetics and populism, however, I want to focus on the fluidity of culture and its contribution to development.

The relationships between cultural policy, governance, and development have not been well established. However, as a response to predicted economic and social benefits of information and entertainment services, multilateral organizations, information policy nongovernmental organizations (NGOs), and national governments now frame development in cultural policy terms. The work of UNESCO through its World Decade for Cultural Development has set the agenda, stressing the importance of the cultural dimension of development, asserting, and enhancing cultural identities, and broadening participation in cultural life (UNESCO, 1996). The 1996 report *Our Creative Diversity* served as a call to arms to link cultural diversity to the "rights to education and freedom of expression, and to the human rights of minorities" (Beale, 2002: 85). This reclamation of culture has in turn led to a movement to view cultural diversity as a resource to be exploited for intellectual property rights. In addition, intergovernmental trade agreements have become part of the rehabilitation and commercialization of culture. The WTO, the international forum responsible for administering international trade agreements negotiated by its members, now incorporates the General Agreement on Trade in Services (GATS) and the Agreement on Trade-Related Intellectual Property Rights (TRIPS). An increasing amount of WTO negotiation is now taken up with disputes over culture.

The World Bank, the Organization for Economic Cooperation and Development (OECD), and the Asia-Pacific Economic Cooperation (APEC) have also published reports linking cultural development and lifelong education with sustainable futures.[3] In short, a return to thinking about cultural policy in Asia has been largely driven by trends in statecraft that are founded on how cultural policy is utilized in providing social frameworks for the negotiation of membership in national societies. In other words, how might cultural programs be developed to encourage populations to be more resourceful and self-regulating? And in a more disciplinary context, how might potentially unruly populations be rendered *governable* in an era of permeable national borders?

To bring this notion of governability into clearer focus we need to link it to governance, which broadly defined refers to "the whole range of institutions involved in the process of governing" including non-state actors and transnational entities (Pierre and Peters, 2000: 1). The remit of cultural policy as an instrument of governance, moreover, extends to increasingly diverse domains of influence, embracing institutions, agencies, and stakeholders affected by policy decisions. The relationship between culture and *governance* thus becomes more enabling at the same time as it retains its capacity to normalize.

The policy shifts from government (as the epitome of sovereignty) to governance inevitably reframe state capacity to administer industrial development, while economic globalization and competition between regions weakens central authority. The concept of "governmentality" provides a useful tool to gauge such shifts and the resultant uneven liberalizations that occur. Derived from the latter work of Foucault (1991), governmentality has been expressed as a "new art of government" in which people are encouraged to be self-regulating rather than dependent on government. Although a feature of liberal forms of statecraft, the concept has been fruitfully applied to describe governmental strategies directed at problem populations to educate and to promote a shift from welfare to prudentialism. The sense is that certain populations are not capable of being self-regulating and thus require a more authoritarian hand to enable them to shift from state dependency. This particular application of governmentality has been described in some detail by Aihwa Ong in her comprehensive study of how new industrializing regimes in southeast Asia evolve systems of "graduated sovereignty" by which citizens enjoy different sets of "civil, political, and economic rights" to placate the requirements of transnational capital (Ong, 1999: 215).[4] Moreover, as Tony Bennett has argued persuasively, the role of culture is central to this process. Culture provides a mechanism by which populations can aspire to improve social capital. Cultural policy, and the legislating of creative and productive environments, is seen as a means by which governments can promote economic prosperity and social harmony (Bennett, 1998: 158–64).

Long considered by national governments as an instrument for shaping distinctive forms of citizenship, cultural policy has been recognized as an instrument for "governing difference" within increasingly multicultural societies. The interdependent relationship between sustainable development and culture forms the basis of the aforementioned *Our Creative Diversity* and the OECD's 2000 report *Towards the Creative Society of the 21st Century*. Culture has become a central theme in many national, regional, and local governmental reform agendas that link creativity, social capital, and development. In this reconsideration of culture, the term "creativity" is linked to capacity-building, not so much in the sense of building vibrant arts and recreational facilities, important as they are, but in linking nations, regions, and localities into the emerging knowledge economy. This kind of cultural development is based on the vision of a future in which national governments deliver basic public services such as telecommunications, health, and education, while facilitating the conditions for value-adding knowledge-based industries based upon sustainable development models.

The rediscovery of culture leads us to speak in terms of the "governmentalization of culture."[5] This refers not to the concentration of cultural policy making within government agencies but rather its democratization. Cultural policy—and thinking about the relations between culture and development—is gradually passed over to a variety of agencies. While cultural policy making is increasingly bundled into converging mega-ministries, it is also developing niche presences within the economic development bureaus of local government.[6] Cultural policy consideration becomes part of economic and new technology development agendas; culture is embedded in trade and diplomatic negotiations; and it functions as an important element of urban development planning and community empowerment programs.[7]

The emerging interrelationship between culture and economic development represents a global policy rethink that is captured in terms such as the new economy, the knowledge-based economy, and the global information society. In these renditions of networked society futures, *transformative* technologies are linked to productivity gains. The Schumpeterian "creative destruction" paradigm views such technological drivers as leading to radical innovation that reshapes political and economic forces (Schumpeter, 1934). This leads to further innovation in goods and services that diffuse within the social fabric. These transformational technologies have shifted the developmental focus from raw material processing and manufacturing to services, or in other words from primary labor (such as processing and assembly) to tertiary (management) and quaternary (knowledge production) labor.

China is currently midstream in the transformation process. It still focuses on resource-intensive development and has the bulk of its workforce located in agriculture, traditional low and medium technology industries, and low-skill services. According to the World Bank report *China and the Knowledge Economy: Seizing the 21st Century*, China's own transformation is progressing simultaneously through four stages. The first is from a rural agricultural-based economy to an urban-industrial economy. The second sees a transition to a services economy, still underdeveloped—which will be the major source of employment growth. This third transformation is represented by the industrial restructuring required to participate in a global economy, while the fourth is the formalization of a private sector (Dahlman and Aubert, eds., 2002: 12–13). As with other developing countries that are attempting to leapfrog into the information age, the knowledge-based economy offers opportunities and directions for policy makers. However, this future is dependent upon framing a new role for government. The report noted "the government must move farther from controller and producer to becoming the architect of a new socialist market and knowledge-based economy" (Dahlman and Aubert, eds., 2002: xix). The relations between flexible production practices, market liberalization, the emerging services economy, and Asian knowledge-based economies were also emphasized at the 2001 APEC meeting in Shanghai, where the new economy was described as a "combination of structural policies and networked information and communication technologies" (APEC, 2002: 11).

The convergence of cultural practices and the governmentalization of culture referred to earlier is manifest in the synergic relations between new media and international entertainment markets. The new media are substantially different from "old" media formats in a number of important ways. The latter are characterized by the fact that they are pre-formed before they are broadcast or disseminated. That is, they are fashioned by writers, journalists, scriptwriters, producers, and directors for a targeted audience or readership. Propaganda is the archetype of the preformed media, disseminated to a supposedly passive audience. With relatively little major structural or technological change in media in China during the latter half of the twentieth century, the propaganda media were able to operate with great efficiency.

The inward-looking focus of China's propaganda industries stands in strong contrast to the internationalization of media markets. During the past decade, there has been a major increase in the share value of global media industries.[8] Much of this activity is generated by a consumer demand for new customized services that can be digitally delivered. While there is understandably a degree of hype associated with the new media (as there is with the new economy), there is, however, widespread agreement that information and communication technologies enable the service economy to operate more efficiently and more globally. The claim of new economy proponents is that people will value goods such as mobile phones for the services they offer, including voicemail, Internet access, and SMS text-messaging. In the future more people will work from home and utilize computers and communications in design, marketing, and public relations. As opposed to the export of commodities, it is important for global service industries to have a presence in foreign markets, whether in the form of direct investment or alliances with domestic businesses.

There is an increasing focus in China on value-added cultural services and professions peripheral to production. With China conducting an increasing amount of business with Taiwan, it is to be expected that China might model its development on Taiwan's service economy, which has outperformed the growth in manufacturing since the mid-1950s (Selya, 1995: 306). Li Conghua argues in *China: The Consumer Revolution* that as the pace of life intensifies in China, more services will be needed to assist in the efficient organization of social and family life (Li Conghua, 1998: 143). The World Bank has estimated that an increase in service industry employment from the current 190 million jobs to more than 270 million will be required during the next decade to offset employment decline in unprofitable formal sectors (Dahlman and Aubert, eds., 2002: 16). While most of these jobs are anticipated to occur in informal service employment and basic infrastructure services such as construction, transport, tourism, retailing, and commerce, many opportunities will be created in small private high-value business services such as marketing, logistics, financial consulting, and management. With an anticipated increase in leisure consumption, the core creative industries of broadcasting, music, advertising, interactive leisure software design, publishing, and multimedia are well placed to expand. With both upstream functions like planning and project management and downstream elements such as distribution, promotion, and marketing increasingly drawing on the creative skills of designers, the cultural environment represents one of the most dynamic areas of the Chinese economy.

## THE WTO: BENEFITS AND CHALLENGES

The 1990s witnessed the establishment of the WTO, a multilateral forum that expanded the existing General Agreement on Tariff and Trade mechanisms to include "trade in services" as a domain of international trade dispute resolution.[9] China's WTO accession offers a mechanism by which reformers are hoping they can deepen systemic reform. While the WTO agreements will have a negative impact upon employment in labor-intensive state-owned enterprises, service industries are a different proposition. These are industries that are subject to internationalization and mergers, and constitute what Danny Quah calls the "Nintendo economy" (Quah, 1996: 20–25). The Chinese Nintendo economy has been rapidly consolidating around China's affluent zones with increased activity in advertising, marketing and promotions, publishing, tourism, digital television, software development, and multimedia. The lure of value-adding cultural service industry development encourages local governments to provide the social and institutional conditions to attract investment and personnel. Emphasis shifts toward growing new economy businesses that operate as second or third-tier enterprises providing creative inputs into mega-enterprises. This global model has been stymied by the problem of duplicate construction (*chongfu jianshe*) within regions, which has meant that it has been difficult for regions to establish a comparative advantage through industrial clustering.

While the relationship of dependency between government and society in China has been broken down by the effects of two decades of reforms, the most dramatic and visible manifestations have occurred in China's cities. Along with increasing rates of property ownership, there has been a great consumer demand for technology-based cultural services. Television is not only used as a means of information access, but it is also a platform for karaoke and computer games, and more recently digital television services. The prospects for development are further underscored by China Telecom's extensive rollout of fat pipe broadband capacity to all provincial capitals. New communications media have been rapidly integrated into Chinese society. Around many of China's universities the standard greeting of *ni chi fan le ma?* (Have you eaten?) is now likely to be *ni shang wang le ma?* (Are you on-line yet?). In 1997 the free e-mail service called Hotmail was launched in America. Hotmail has already become one of the most popular free e-mail services in China and has been replicated by Chinese Internet service providers such as Sina, Sohu, and Netease. Websites include "gaogenxie," a site exclusively tailored for the "modern Chinese woman," and "Dang.dang.com," a Chinese on-line bookstore.

Visitors to China's major urban centers in recent years will have noticed that the presence of the new information age—the *e-shidai*—is ubiquitous. Technology is in your face in China's crowded cities. Streaming video content confronts the casual shopper in city malls like Wangfujing in Beijing and Nanjing Road in Shanghai. Electronic billboards announce the latest Web site with content tailored for Chinese surfers. According to the *Xinhua News Agency*, there were more than 120 million cellular phone subscribers in China as of July 2001 (Li Jialu, 2001). Shanghai has the lowest cellular airtime anywhere in the world (Dahlman and Aubert, eds., 2002: 85). It seems that every taxi driver has a cell phone. WAP-enabled mobile phones are expected to outnumber personal computers as points of Internet access by 2003 (Watts, 2002). From 1995 to 1998, China had the highest growth rate in east Asia and the Pacific of fixed main telephone lines and PCs per 100 inhabitants, 29 percent and 46 percent respectively. China's mobile phones per capita grew at 88 percent a year over the same period, while there were estimated to be 22.5 million Internet users in January 2001 (Dahlman and Aubert, eds., 2002: 84). By the end of 2002, the number of Internet users had increased to 59.1 million, overtaking Japan as the world's second largest on-line nation (CINIC: www.cnnic.net.cn/e-index.shtml). Similarly, China is set to overtake Japan as the world's second biggest computer market outside the U.S. (*BBC News World Edition*: http://news.bbc.co.uk/2/hi/business/2371203.stm). While there is a degree of caution in extrapolating such figures given that most of the growth has already saturated urban markets, there is no doubt that there is an upbeat mood about the benefits of being connected among China's Generation X, the increasingly mobile, educated, and consumer-conscious youth demographic born after 1980. A consumer survey of residents in Beijing, Shanghai, and Guangzhou during September

2002 revealed that more than 75 percent of persons under 35 claimed proficiency at using the Internet, while more than 80 percent of the same cohort aspired to upgrade their tech products (*Far Eastern Economic Review*, December 5, 2002, 62).

The technology boom in Chinese cities can be partly attributed to the comparatively cheap cost of entertainment and leisure goods and the rising affluence and the purchasing power of per capita income. This is calculated by both the IMF and the World Bank to be somewhere between two and five times higher than the official U.S. figure of between $600–700 (Ure and Liang, 2000: 135). An increased demand for cultural consumption has been the catalyst for a growth in marketing services, ranging from electronic monitoring of television viewers by A. C. Neilsen to research by marketing companies into consumer spending patterns. Arif Dirlik has argued that the transfer of corporate consumerism represents the materialization of a fully-fledged Chinese consumer society (Dirlik, 2001: 1–35). Alternatively it can be argued that Western marketing practices constitute a positive "cultural technology transfer" whereby local industries can become more effective in the marketplace (Keane, 2001: 223–36).

## MODELS OF REGULATION
## FOR THE NEW INFORMATION ECONOMY

China's uptake of electronic technology is impressive, even considering the low per capita use of personal computers and the low income of users.[10] Of course, extended optimism about technology uptake is tempered by the reality that development opportunities are dependent on the right kind of industry regulation and a more consistently transparent governance of the information sector. With regard to China's nascent service sector, the targeted areas for compliance with international benchmarks are strengthening the rule of law, the harmonization of international standards, and intellectual property protection. However, the challenges for the government are regulating continually evolving technologies, regulating in a converged sector, and encouraging technological innovation (Dahlman and Aubert, eds., 2002: 88).

Frederick Tipson has provided a useful illustration of the Chinese government's possible responses to the challenge of the information revolution. He argued that China's options can be sorted into three scenarios (Tipson, 1999: 232–33). The first, which he calls "the Singapore approach," is to implement policies that will foster and develop an integrated national information infrastructure that balances economic development and national security. The second is "the Taiwan approach," by which the government opts for a looser control regime, thus allowing the actual booming and contending of "a hundred flowers and a hundred schools of thought." The third scenario is "the

North Korean" approach of attempting to shut down communication development because it is antithetical to authoritarian control.

Of these three scenarios the most likely is the first, the least likely the third. The authoritarian Singapore model has a lot of appeal for China's leadership, nurtured on cultural despotism and convinced that the development of the media and information industries must be carefully controlled and managed by the Chinese Communist Party. However, transplanting the Singapore model into China is not a simple matter of regulating access and monitoring content. Singapore is a small island with an established market economy already nurtured by international finance. Its success in this regard has been due to government-instigated competitive advantages, including union control, and strict adherence to the rule of law. On the other hand, China is a large country with tensions between center and regions. The rule of law, particularly in relation to vexing trade-related issues such as intellectual property, is a huge problem that is not easily resolved.

The second approach, a more pluralistic business environment generated by the need to promote innovation and secure investment, is without doubt the recipe desired by most outside China, and possibly many industry insiders within China. However, the problem for the Chinese leadership is that opening up the cultural sphere is unknown territory. Many within the Chinese Communist Party see foreign direct investment in China's information industries as the thin edge of a Western wedge, one that would undermine the Party's ideological handwork, that is, the "ethical and cultural progress" or "spiritual civilization" (*jingshen wenming*) rhetoric so regularly cranked out by the Chinese Communist Party's propaganda workers.

Moreover, the liberalization of government control over information systems that is desired by transnational enterprises in the name of open trade challenges the traditional preoccupation with order (*zhi*) manifest in deals struck between the Chinese government and international content providers such as News Corporation, the BBC, and AOL-Time Warner to reroute their transmissions via the Chinese Sinosat2 platform (Keane, 2002), and search engines such as www.Google.com to install content-filtering software to prevent Chinese citizens and Web surfers from being exposed to unfiltered information.[11] This concern with protecting cultural sovereignty became even more apparent during 2002 in the wake of TV signal hijacks by members of the banned Falun Gong religious cult, whose hacking of Sinosat's 2A, 3A, and 6A transmissions in 2002 resulted in severe disruptions to five China Educational Television (CETV) services and 25 IP data radio channels (*The China Media Monitor*, 2002: 7, 6).

Surveys of Internet filtering in China conducted by Western-based Internet activists have regularly drawn attention to the Chinese government's penchant for protecting its citizens from information that may be at odds with the national interest. Jonathan Zittrain and Benjamin Edelman of the Berkman

Center for Internet and Society at Harvard University maintain that China's Internet censorship remains amongst the most draconian in the world (Einhorn, 2002). However, while there are civil rights issues attached to such surveillance, it is equally true that a gradient of information accessibility exists based on the perceived benefits and threats to national development and sovereignty. Real-time economic reporting is essentially unrestrained and encouraged, while sexually provocative content or politically sensitive debate is subject to policing with Internet service providers ultimately responsible for the invigilation.

Despite the attendant fear of chaos (*luan*), the approach to communication liberalization over the past two decades has subsequently been a gradual move toward developing information technology hardware within national economic construction plans. As it is for most developing nations, National Information Society policies represent a means to leapfrog from technological backwardness to being a player in the Global Information Society. The "catching up" phase hypothesis suggests that countries with initially low income levels should grow faster because they are able to catch up through transfers of technology and know-how.

The policy drive behind information infrastructure initiatives in China began at the start of the economic reforms in 1978. At the time, information and communications policy was domestic in scope and determined by concerns with national security and the need to rein in unhealthy influences. Content came from a limited archive and was prescriptive. In the best traditions of socialism, it was decided that it was in the national interest for the government to pursue a high-technology development path in order to "overtake the West" (Ure and Liang, 2000: 120). A number of initial programs were started during the 1980s. These were part of several ten-year plans to develop technical infrastructure, best exemplified by the "863 High-Tech Program" (beginning 1986) and the "Torch Program" (1988), both of which were designed to consolidate research and development in broadband as well as electronics and information. As Ure and Liang note, the rationale for policy emphasis on consumer goods and services can be understood by the need to embrace rapidly changing technologies, in particular digital or computer-related technologies (Ure and Liang, 2000: 122).

The consolidation of convergent media industries in China has moved at a rapid pace. With an expected boom in trade in services imminent in the post-WTO new economy, "foreign" telecommunications and media content companies have formed ventures with Chinese partners. Mergers, takeovers, and industry rationalization in the information and communications sector (telecoms, cable TV, Internet service providers) have been frantic. Following the example of the AOL and Time Warner global merger, the Chinese Internet portal Sina.com teamed up with the Hong Kong media "content" company Sun Television Cybernet Holdings and the China-based Stone Group in late 2001 in order to leverage wider markets. In the Internet field, News Corp. set up a joint venture with the *Renmin Ribao* and the Beijing Bidian Xinren Information Technology Co., which is engaged in information technology consulting services. The collaboration produced ChinaByte.com and the portal CSeek.com. At the time of writing, News Corp. also held a 10 percent stake in Netease.com and a 10.2 percent share of Renren.com.[12] A long campaign of lobbying by News Corporation and AOL Time Warner, now owners of the Hong Kong-based company Chinese Entertainment Television, has resulted in "landing rights" being granted in Guangdong Province in south China. This means that these companies are able to broadcast through selected cable television channels in the province. Star TV, the News Corporation Asian flagship broadcaster, now produces a Chinese language entertainment channel called *Starry Sky Satellite Channel (Xingkong weishi)* to complement its Hong Kong-based subsidiary Phoenix satellite channel (*Fenghuang weishi*).

The convergence of delivery platforms combined with digitalization has presented the Chinese government with new kinds of regulatory problems. Creative practices that used to be seen as falling under the umbrella of culture and formally administered by the Ministry of Culture and the State Administration of Radio, Film, and Television now fall into the policy remit of digitally enabled services. The Ministry of Information Industry (MII), formed in 1998, became the super-ministry responsible for overseeing such transformations. It absorbed the functions of the Ministry of Posts and Telecommunications, the Ministry of Electronic Industries, and the network management responsibilities of the Ministry of Radio, Film, and Television. The MII is seen as a response to the convergence (*ronghe*) of telecommunications, broadcasting, information technology, and the need to develop national strategies, policies, and technical standards. It oversees telecommunications and information service licenses and fees, multimedia and broadband developments, broadcasting networks and spectrum allocation, and satellite orbit positioning, as well as monitoring the development of China's Internet and the commercial applications of wireless, fixed line, and satellite networks. Culture thus becomes both a domain of activity that needs to be developed according to industry standards and a space of expression that needs to be monitored according to national security standards.

## CIVIL SOCIETY, PLURALIZATION, AND SERVICE INDUSTRIES

The State Development Planning Commission and the Ministry of Culture are currently increasing efforts to work out a long-term development plan to ensure China's cultural products and industries are competitive while at the same time ensuring that they remain part of the ideological machinery of the Chinese Communist Party. Part of this master plan revolves around modeling "creative industry initiatives" in developed capitalist countries. A dozen major Chinese cities, including Beijing, Shanghai, Shenyang, and Chongqing have enacted a series of regulations and launched a number of new projects to promote "cultural commercialization" (*China Daily*, November 27, 2000). The cosmopolitan leverage of "creative clusters" is becoming evident in China today. This is reflected in plans to make China's cities more dynamic, more creative, and ultimately more attractive to foreign investment. The rationale is that attracting technology transfer and investment will raise the quality of Chinese cultural industries and the creative capacities of its people.

The cluster model is well known to economists and has its Chinese antecedent in the Special Economic Zone activity that has generated higher standards of living for some Chinese while marginalizing those outside the coastal investment belts. As with high-technology parks, the policy approach focuses on developing the physical infrastructure, human capital, and technology base to support expansion and internationalization. These factors are most likely to be achieved in China's big cities, where linkages to multinational enterprises are in abundance. As Peter Nolan notes, "The main goal for the multinational giants will be in the high value-added markets of relatively affluent urban dwellers and international businesses in major cities" (Nolan, 2001: 182). A prime example of new media development is to be found in Beijing, now planning for the 2008 Olympics. Plans are afoot for a new multimedia district, and Beijing's vice mayor Wang Guangtao has announced the intention to build a "digital Beijing information industry" that will draw upon existing broadband capabilities to extend e-government and e-commerce, and "create an environment for innovation in improving the people's living standards through extensive application of IT" (*China Daily, HK Edition*, November 23, 2001).

Underpinning the development of this creative industry activity is the utopian vision of the knowledge economy. However, the knowledge economy—in its increasingly globalized form—is organized along very different lines than the low trust, low responsibility, and highly bureaucratic structures of the propaganda state. It emphasizes partnerships, networking, project-based innovation, and flexible working patterns. It fosters a low hierarchy, high autonomy, high responsibility, and high risk environment. It is recognized from global case studies of multimedia and high-technology enterprises that actors prefer very flexible, loosely coupled, and temporary relations with their contractors, partners, and employees. Moreover, the new economy is calculated to flourish where institutional arrangements are directed toward encouraging entrepreneurship. This, combined with skilled and adaptable workforces, high levels of public investment in education, and cosmopolitan cultural environments, are the prerequisites for development.

The interdependence of actors and institutions, both locally and globally, impacts upon the relationship between culture, services, and knowledge in China. The difference between China's Information Communication Technologies (ICT) sector now and that of more than a decade ago is the increased influence of international actors and institutions, from multilateral forums such as the WTO and the International Telecommunications Union to organizations such as the Motion Pictures Association of America and the Federal Communications Commission. However, the impact from afar is not confined to targeting the central government in Beijing. International business has moved quickly to develop working relations with local government, who can in many instances find ways of helping the foreign partners invest in industries by creatively interpreting guidelines. Municipal and local governments are responding to the challenge of ensuring growth in national knowledge capital through cultural commercialization and regional creative industry strategies, information industry clustering, and the establishment of a new creative milieu to encourage social and intellectual capital. If global trends are any indication, we can expect to see localities and regions pursuing initiatives to capture investment for hard infrastructure at the same time as promoting "soft infrastructure," including better working and living conditions for the techno-elites that work in information technology and creative industries such as software, television, multimedia, and tourism.

Already there is the recognition of the synergies between creativity and the soft infrastructure of creative milieu. An international conference on Business Incubation and Technological Innovation was held in Shanghai in 2001 and drew papers mostly from foreign experts keen to advise on how the Chinese government, and local municipal governments, might act to promote ways to enable China's high-tech parks to partner with venture capital, entrepreneurs, and universities (Watts, 2000). The publicly funded Zhongguancun Science and Technology Park, located near Beijing University and China's leading IT university, Qinghua University, has been allowed to put in place "flexible" regulations pertaining to its management, following a suggestion by the vice premier of the State Council that park officials might like to experiment with organization models that would promote entrepreneurial activity and attract "talented people." Despite its government investment, Zhongguancun's capacity to generate new software applications has been hampered by a lack of entrepreneurship in comparison to the many new incubators (*fuhuaqi*) being set up by young entrepreneurs in China's large cities. Many of these start-ups are staffed by people who have returned from working and studying in the West.

The link between the liberalization of cultural industries and civil society, pluralization, and democracy is compounded by China's WTO accession and a prevailing view among global free traders that there are end-of-ideology consequences. Accession to the WTO extends this paradigm of progress. It introduces an international regime of rules-based trade into China, which is expected to transform China's institutions to international standards. The formalization of China's status as a global trading nation is expected to have pay-offs for foreign commercial enterprises in terms of transparency, market access, and control of intellectual property rights piracy. It is the old liberal argument that markets will provide the momentum for change—but this time the market pressure will come from outside national boundaries. It is also suggested that centralized state authority of key industries will be undermined as civil society activism coalesces around middle-class entrepreneurship. There is a view, however, that both internal change and external pressure arguments are flawed when discussing China. The middle classes and new elites have learnt how to develop vertical connections (*guanxi*) with government officials such that the guarantees provided by legal procedures, including WTO rules-based trade, may be superfluous (Jayasuriya, 1999: 1–27).

## CONCLUDING REMARKS: CULTURE, SERVICES, AND KNOWLEDGE-BASED INDUSTRIES RECONSIDERED

Culture is being refashioned and it is being brought back into the realm of governance. Intellectual property rights devolving from cultural industries are seen as integral to economic development and global trade, while information rights are fundamental to future negotiations in multilateral trade forums. Within China, the drivers of cultural transformation are emerging cultural service industries and the government's desire to establish a knowledge-based economy. These represent the potential ground for the development of a political civil society.

The relations between pluralism and the development of China's content or "creative industries" are indeed significant. There are both challenges and opportunities. The lack of innovation in Chinese cultural industries can be attributed to a number of causes. Excessive politicization and censorship has created a culture of conservatism. The lack of capitalization of industry and the segmentation of markets has encouraged opportunistic cloning of ideas. The challenges lie in enabling an environment more conducive to innovation and experimentation. Innovation and a "risk culture" may well eventuate from increased competition and investment post-WTO. However, what passes for innovation is often revealed to be exploitation of intellectual property rights.

As many of the reports already mentioned in this chapter have indicated, creating a "culture" of innovation is a recipe for a reduced role for government, to move from being the engineer of souls to the animateur of development. Frances Cairncross, the author of *The Death of Distance: How the*

*Communications Revolution Will Change Our Lives,* endorsed by none other than Rupert Murdoch as a must-read book, contends that if countries such as China "liberalize their markets, regulate the inevitable concentration of market power, protect freedom of speech, and promote education and literacy, they will eventually be the biggest beneficiaries of the telecommunications revolution" (Cairncross, 1997: 255). Of course, the talk of democratization and freedom of speech is an oft-repeated mantra by neo-liberal advocates of open markets. In a speech given by U.S. Secretary of State Madleine Albright in January 2000 to the Johns Hopkins School for Advanced International Studies, Albright pointed out that advances in technology and the spread of information were helping American efforts to open the rigid Communist system to free enterprise and political liberty. Albright said, "We are generally pushing in order to open Chinese society. It is all very difficult. However, technology is helping us" (Straits Times Interactive, January 20, 2000).

Technology is also helping the Chinese government. Its modernization imperative is a key element in its five-year planning programs. China's literacy rate of 80 percent is also an asset for a knowledge-based economy (APEC, 2002: 66). There is also cause to be upbeat about the diffusion of many forms of communications media. Despite predictions that computer usage has reached a plateau, applications of new media technology will continue to be taken up rapidly by the middle class and the new generation of consumers. Investment and use of Information Communication Technologies (ICT) is likely to be greatly encouraged by the growth in the market for mobile communications, stimulated by developments in nearby South Korea and Japan. New platforms continue to emerge offering wireless and fixed network connections. The Internet will continue to provide an infrastructure for new forms of electronic business although it is likely to be some time before Chinese consumers place trust in e-commerce. However, while rich multimedia content such as images, audio, video, and virtual reality are being offered to urban audiences, further development of networks and e-commerce will stall if China does not create more bandwidth. With the concept of "broadband" (*guangxian*) sweeping through China, many domestic companies, including China Telecom, China Netcom, and the Great Wall Company, have rushed into the market. Meanwhile the SARFT has instituted its legitimate broadband provider, the China Information Broadcast Network Company, to offset the incursions by competitors.

Nevertheless, the Chinese government's propaganda heralding its broadband network capacity does not disguise the fact that China is still backward in this field. Despite the broadband network being extended to 21 cities, only a small percentage of Chinese households are connected. A major problem is that few residents want to pay the fee, approximately 40 yuan per month, for the newly installed cables, since the majority have been used to networks being supplied free of charge (*The China Media Monitor*, 2001: 6.1).

In addition, a lack of emphasis has been placed on developing the content base that will promote the take-up (informatization) of new media. The key point is that unless there are strong local content industries, China's media and entertainment providers (and consumers) will continue to be drawn to foreign content, whether this content is from "culturally proximate" regions in east Asia or from Western sources.[13] The growth of viable Chinese "content industries" is therefore fundamental to development.

The question of the digital divide provides a reality check for the euphoria associated with techno-determinism. The digital divide exists both between economies and within economies. There are already fragmentations between income, education, culture, and geography. Despite China's impressive uptake of ICTs, basic telephone penetration remains about 10 percent, and less than two percent of people are on-line, compared with on-line rates of up to 50 percent in the U.S. A recent report that averaged research across five measures of policy conditions and preparedness for the new economy ranked China just ahead of Vietnam, Indonesia, and the Russian Federation.[14] And despite the establishment of 53 high-technology parks by 1999, there is little evidence to suggest that the benefits have been diffused into the wider community. Labor productivity with such parks is estimated to be twice that of the overall industrial sector (Zhaoying, 2000, cited in Dahlman and Aubert, eds., 2002: 108).

In conclusion, reframing the relationship between culture, services, and the knowledge-based economy is dependent upon getting the policy right. The establishment of state-run "national champions," highlighted by the agglomeration of the "assets" of the State Administration of Radio, Film, and Television into the China Radio, Film and Television Group, signals a new strategy within China's media and communications sector (*China Daily*, December 7, 2001). It remains to be seen if this signals a new era for creative industry development or simply a recognition that the development of China's media and communications sector is too strategically important to be allowed to devolve into a truly competitive market. As the World Bank report *China and the Knowledge Economy* suggests, for the vision of a knowledge-based future to succeed there needs to be a more enabling and facilitating environment than has existed under tightly controlled political regimes (in Dahlman and Aubert, eds., 2002). In short, while restrictive regulations might work to constrain unruly populations, disciplinary modes of governance are not conducive to new economy growth. Nor is excessive regulation likely to attract the "angels" of the new economy, the entrepreneurs who have returned from the West, in particular from places such as Silicon Valley, where the environment is predicated on government facilitating rather than engineering development. For these ex-patriates, used to the relative autonomy of Western business environments, strong regulation is likely to act as a disincentive to take risks and be innovative.

In addition, central policy needs to reform to provide certainty for foreign investors as much as for local businesses attempting to internationalize. Of the three models mentioned above, the Singaporean model of strong infrastructure and systematic monitoring will be advanced as the best option for China given the sensitivity of information industries. However, for a truly innovative environment to emerge across China's information and entertainment industries, it will be necessary for the government to adopt a more "light touch" regime, to move from an "engineer state" to a facilitator of industry development through indirect support, allowing greater creative autonomy. In this way the technical possibilities of Chinese enterprises will engage with international linkages.

## NOTES

1. For a discussion of the press coverage within China in the lead-up to WTO accession see Zhao Yuezhi, in Chin-Chuan Lee., ed. (forthcoming).

2. The convening organization is the Platform for Communication Rights. For more information see www.itu.int/wsis/about/about_WhatIsWsis_Print.html and Tom O'Regan, www.gu.edu.au./centre/cmp/kcpubs.html.

3. See Dahlman and Aubert, eds., 2002; OECD, 2000a; APEC, 2002.

4. For a discussion of the concept of governmentality in relation to recalcitrant populations, see Hindess, July 13, 2001.

5. For a discussion of this, see Bennett, 1998.

6. In China, the Ministry of Culture used to be the principal organ of decision making in relation to the cultural sector. The commercialization of China's cultural sector and the convergence of media, telephony, and computing has seen an overlap of administrative and regulatory functions among mega-ministries such as the Ministry of Information Industry (MII), the State Administration of Radio, Film, and Television (SARFT), and the State Administration of Press and Publications (SAPP).

7. The United Nations Research Institute for Social Development published a report in 2001 that highlighted the way in which the digital divide is integral to a much broader divide—the development divide. The report drew attention to the potential of ICTs for addressing both divides. The ICT revolution is, in fact, "lending old technologies new relevance." For example, mobile telephones are making radio more interactive and thus relevant, and satellite technology is restricting the ability of governments to control content on television. See Hewitt De Alcantara, 2001, and also Tacchi, September 20–24, 2001.

8. See OECD, Working Party on the Information Economy, 1998.

9. See World Trade Organization Council for Trade in Services, June 15, 1998. GATS clauses concerning Domestic Regulation (Article VI), Subsidies (Article XV), Market Access (Article XVI), and National Treatment (Article XVII) render domestic policy goals contestable through the WTO architecture. For a discussion see Raboy, 1999: 293–310.

10. A report from China's Ministry of Information Industry shows that about half the country's Internet users have an annual income between $750 and $2500, which falls

into the low and middle range of China's income distribution. China's Ministry of Information Industry, 2002.

11. For a discussion of the concepts of order in relation to information control, see Keane (2003). For a discussion of China's Internet filtering, see the report "Real Time Testing of Internet Filtering in China" by Harvard University academics Jonathan Zittrain and Benjamin Edelman available on cyber.law.harvard.edu/filtering/china/. For a wide variety of expert discussion of China's Great Firewall, the Google controversies, and China's policies toward on-line media, cybercafes, and censorship see the Chinese Internet discussion group at chineseinternetresearch@yahoogroups.com

12. See China Online, www.chinaonline.com/topstories/010504/1/B201042413.asp (January 30, 2002).

13. For a discussion of the idea of cultural proximity in relation to media flows, see Straubhaar, 2000: 199–224.

14. The reports were Economic Intelligence Unit/Pyramid E-readiness Ranking, World Economic Forum Current Competitiveness Index, the Global New Economy Index from MetricNet, the World Competitiveness Score from IMD, and the PriceWaterhouseCoopers Opacity Index. See APEC, 2002: 70.

# 6

# Local Governance: Village and Township Direct Elections

*Linda Jakobson*

In early 1999, word spread among China-watchers that a relatively competitive, direct election had been held for the post of township head in Buyun, Sichuan province, in late 1998[1]. Though the Chinese Communist Party branded this historic first an unlawful election, the results of the election were not annulled. No one was punished. This Buyun case gave rise to expectations that decade-long experiments with multicandidate elections for village head were indeed constituting a potential foothold for Chinese democratization, despite widespread cynicism toward grassroots-level political reform.

Optimists viewed the Buyun election as a sign that the first step of introducing electoral reform in villages across China was leading to a crucial second one of initiating genuine electoral reform at the township level.[2] One Chinese researcher, who had been closely involved with the Buyun election, said that the "Buyun experiment was supposed to open the floodgates, and set the stage for nationwide direct township elections in 2001."[3] The optimism was short-lived. In the years following the Buyun election, the upbeat mood among reform-minded Chinese officials and academics advocating political reform soured. Before the next round of elections in China's 45,000 towns and townships in late 2001, the Communist Party leadership made it clear that it would not tolerate genuinely competitive elections for the post of township head. No substantial breakthrough in the election procedures took place, though improvised procedures were experimented with in various locations.

Though leaders of the Chinese Communist Party remain steadfast that they will not adopt the political models of Western countries, they acknowledge the need for political reform. In official Chinese publications in China, it has been commonplace since the 1990s to quote Deng Xiaoping's stance on the symbiotic relationship between economic and political reform.[4] Pressure is mounting among both sections of the populace and local officials to introduce methods that institutionalize accountability and transparency. Direct elections for the position of village head are viewed to be doing just that. When the revised law on villagers' committees was approved in late 1998, the Communist Party abdicated its prerogative to appoint village heads, implicitly conceding that elected ones are more effective. On the one hand, several top Chinese leaders have praised these elections; on the other hand, the leadership's intention is not to democratize China. Village elections were originally promoted as a means to enhance more effective governance and stability in the unruly countryside.

This chapter begins by tracing the formulation of a new law on villagers' committees and the progress in its implementation. It discusses the political rationale underlying the emergence of this new form of village governance and the consequences of several rounds of direct elections in China's rural areas for grassroots political participation and local Party secretaries. It then examines recent attempts to institute competitive, direct elections at the township level. Finally, the broad implications of these changes in local governance for processes of democratization in China is considered.

## THE LAW ON VILLAGERS' COMMITTEES AND ITS IMPLEMENTATION

In November 1987 the Standing Committee of the National People's Congress approved an experimental law stipulating how villages should be governed. Eleven years later, in November 1998, the status of the Organic Law on Villagers' Committees was made permanent. For years intense political debate went on about how much independence villagers' committees should be given to manage village affairs and to what extent villagers should be allowed to choose their leaders.

The law grants villagers' committees relatively broad autonomy, particularly in matters regarding the village economy. The law specifically states that the township government "may guide, help and support village committees, but must not intervene in affairs that are in the purview of the villagers' committee."[5] Multicandidate elections must be held every three years for the post of chair of the villagers' committee, that is the village head, and other positions on the committee. Every adult has one vote. Secret balloting must be ensured. More importantly, there must be more candidates than positions, and candidates need not be members of the Communist Party. Hence, opposing a Party member—by either running against one or openly supporting a non-Party candidate—is no longer a crime. Nor does it carry the stigma of "enemy of the people" as it did twenty years ago. Article 12 stipulates that "any villager over 18 years of age has the right to vote and be elected, regardless of ethnicity, race, gender, occupation, family background, education, financial situation and length of residence, with the exception of those who are deprived of political rights by law."[6]

Upon becoming permanent, the law was revised to specify that "secret voting booths should be set up during the election" and that "candidates should be nominated directly by villagers who are eligible to vote."[7] The method of candidate selection remains controversial among township and county officials. As of late 2002, the so-called *haixuan*-method,[8] allowing villagers to nominate the final candidates, had been adopted in only a fraction of villagers' committee elections. In most village elections, candidates had been put forward either by the villagers' committee, the village representative assembly,[9] or a selection committee made up of the village's Party secretary, villagers' committee members, township officials, and/or members of the village's influential families.

It is impossible to know how many of China's some 930,000 villages have actually had genuinely competitive elections in which villagers have had the right to nominate the final candidates. Estimates vary from ten percent to 60 percent. Reliable statistics about China are difficult to obtain. In the case of village elections, no national data exists. The Ministry of Civil Affairs (MoCA), which is responsible for the grassroots-level governance reform (*jiceng zhengquan gaige*), compiles data based on reports of provincial officials as well as surveys conducted by Chinese and foreign researchers or sponsor organizations. In 2001 several Ministry of Civil Affairs' officials acknowledged that they did not fully trust reports being sent to them from the provincial bureaus, as "officials in China tend to compile statistics in accordance to what they think the central government wants to hear."[10]

Chinese and foreign observers agree that direct elections have been unevenly implemented. The situation can vary even within the same county. A portion of a county's villages may have already held two or three rounds of genuinely open multicandidate elections, while elections in other villages in the county remain reminiscent of the Mao era: the village Party secretary nominates the one and only candidate for village head, after which the villagers are expected to cast their ballots. In some villages no committee elections have been held.

## AN ATTEMPT TO CURB CHAOS IN THE COUNTRYSIDE

Why did an authoritarian government on its own accord set in motion a political process which could, in the long run, undermine its authority? By freeing the peasants from the shackles of the communes, Deng Xiaoping's economic reforms revolutionalized one sector of rural life. Agricultural output soared, as did rural industrial production. Rural residents' incomes increased nearly five-fold between 1978 and 1990.[11] But the disbanding of the communes and the freedom to pursue personal wealth created a new set of problems, including rampant corruption among rural officials and worsening relations between villagers.

Though the authority of village cadres was unclear, they were responsible for enforcing birth control, procuring state grain, and collecting taxes, in other words, doing the central government's "dirty work." They were under intense pressure from their peers in the township governments to carry out these tasks, but found it increasingly difficult to persuade villagers to comply. Average farmers were no longer dependent on village officials, as in the Mao era, when cadres exercised absolute control over peasant labor. Increased autonomy meant a greater unwillingness to obey orders, especially those deemed unreasonable. Extra fees, fines, and service charges levied by village and township officials have been a source of serious contention in the countryside since the disbanding of the communes.[12] As villages receive no public revenues from higher governmental levels, they must raise their own money, not only for taxes which are passed up the ladder to the township, county, and so on, but also for village projects, such as building a new school or road (Choate, 1997: 11).

Simultaneously, economic reform provided cadres at all levels with opportunities to engage in entrepreneurial activities, which in turn led to widespread corruption. Rural residents became increasingly resentful and defiant of cadre power. Especially in villages with collectively-owned factories or enterprises, residents had vested interests in the management of collectively-owned enterprises and the way in which profits were used. Since the mid-1980s, the official Chinese press has reported cases of villagers' retaliation against corrupt leaders for concocting arbitrary levies and unofficial taxes. Village leaders have been beaten and sometimes murdered. Riots have broken out. For example, in 1987, in Shandong province alone, five tax collectors were murdered and over 3,500 wounded (Blecher, 1997: 219). Four years later, the Chinese countryside witnessed 1.7 million cases of resistance, of which 6,230 were so-called disturbances that resulted in severe damage to persons or property. Nationwide, 8,200 township and county officials were injured or killed, 560 county-level offices were ransacked, and 385 public security personnel lost their lives (Perry, 1999: 314–15).

In sum, grassroots political institutions were in disarray. Relations between villagers and village officials were rapidly deteriorating, leading to outbreaks of violence. Rural lawlessness was a serious problem. Arbitrary control by clans and secret societies was on the rise. With good reason, Communist Party leaders feared (and still fear) that rural tensions jeopardized the Party's hold on power. A State Council report in early 1992 warned that 30 percent of the Party cells in the countryside had collapsed. Another 60 percent were extremely weak and disorganized (Wang, 1997: 1433).

From the point of view of the central government, trustworthy and competent officials were vital at the local level, not only to ensure the success of economic reforms, but also to collect grain and taxes and to supervise birth control. But village leaders were increasingly either unwilling or unable to fulfil these obligations. Grassroots political reform was introduced "to cope with the crises of both legitimacy and governability in the countryside" (Wang, 1997: 1433)

## HOW THE UNTHINKABLE BECAME REALITY

Though leaders at all levels were aware that political restructuring in the countryside was necessary to cope with the new problems brought about by decollectivization and establishment of the household responsibility system, there were substantial disagreements over what kind of grassroots reform should be implemented. A prolonged and heated political debate preceded the approval of the experimental villagers' committee law of 1987 (Shi, 1999: 387–88; O'Brien, 1994: 35–41; Li and O'Brien, 1999: 131–37; O'Brien and Li, 2000: 466–68). The essence of this debate continues as officials and researchers promoting direct elections in townships struggle to win over opponents of expanding political reform.

Especially noteworthy was the strong action taken by two so-called conservative Communist Party elders in support of rural self-government and democratic elections. Veteran Communists Peng Zhen and Bo Yibo, known for their conservative stands during other reform-era political debates, believed that cadre-villager relations could be improved, and rural unrest reduced, if villagers were responsible for governing themselves and choosing their own leaders. Those who opposed giving too much autonomy to the villagers argued that township officials would no longer be able to enforce state policies.

Peng Zhen's stance was based on his personal experiences in the Jin-Cha-Ji Border Region where he had experimented with village elections and villagers' councils in the late 1930s and early 1940s. His detailed report to the Politburo in September 1941 took a positive view of the usefulness of popular elections. Peng's report said that "policies such as . . . popular elections had allowed the Party to penetrate into local society and increase its influence" (Saich, ed., 1996: 975). Reinstating Party prestige and making village cadres more accountable to rural residents were precisely what Peng Zhen hoped to achieve with the 1987 law on villagers' committees.[13] He presumed that villagers would be more willing to accept decisions made by elected cadres, which in turn would make carrying out state tasks easier. Peng Zhen also believed that self-governance would lead to the acceptance and cultivation of democratic ideas (Li and O'Brien, 1999: 131). In the 1941 report, he says that "if we conduct popular elections, we should seriously follow democratic principles and the spirit of rule of law in doing so. . . . This will enable the majority of people to understand, from their own personal lives, that democratic politics is far better than authoritarian politics" (Saich, ed., 1996: 1028).[14]

Passage of the experimental law on villagers' committees was but the first step in the long march undertaken by proponents of village self-governance. From the point of view of research on political change and democratization, the struggle over village elections is an enlightening example of how the "unthinkable" was turned into reality against all odds (Shi, 1999: 388). Tianjian Shi has charted the course and tactics of reform-minded officials in the Ministry of Civil Affairs, the main protagonists in implementing the experimental law on villagers' committees, once Peng Zhen had pushed it through the National People's Congress (Shi, 1999: 385–412). These MoCA officials, men in their thirties and forties led by Wang Zhenyao, believed in incremental reform. Wang Zhenyao, a mid-level ministry official, was in charge of implementation of the Organic Law on Villagers' Committees until 1997. He and his colleagues put into practice Huntington's "foot-in-the-door approach of concealing aims, separating reforms from each other, and pushing for only one change at a time" (Shi, 1999: 396). Each step in the gradual process was arranged "to appear to be a natural response to the interaction between the initial reform policy and unforeseen consequences brought about by the previous policy" (Shi, 1999: iii/abstract). To secure the crucial support and cooperation of officials in the provincial bureaus of civil affairs, the Ministry of Civil Affairs created special incentives, including trips abroad.

Knowing full well that any elaboration on the merits of democracy would be used by conservatives as proof of bourgeois liberalization or peaceful evolution,[15] officials at the Ministry of Civil Affairs steered clear of ideological debates, stressing the practical benefits of village self-governance. In interviews and written reports, they stuck to their instrumentalist theme: By encouraging villagers to take part in village affairs and allowing them to choose their own leaders, tensions between cadres and villagers would be eased, which in turn would make villages more governable.[16]

After the experimental law was passed in 1987, the controversy over the pros and cons of village committee elections continued, but it was no longer confined to closed-door meetings. A lively debate took place during the 1990s in Chinese academic and legal journals, in "internal newspapers" with a restricted circulation, as well as in publications put out by the Ministry of Civil Affairs and various Communist Party organs. Numerous articles began with vivid descriptions of murders and robberies or attacks on corrupt officials (Jakobson, 1998: 310/fn 2). Proponents of the experimental law argued that making officials accountable to villagers by introducing direct elections was the most effective way to avoid outright chaos from erupting in the countryside. "The more frequent the peasant uprisings and the more serious the problems become in the countryside, the more willing the higher authorities will be to endorse the village election process," Wang Zhenyao said in 1995 (Jakobson, 1998: 132–33).

As Daniel Kelliher has noted, the "disintegrating order" is "the backdrop alluded to in nearly all writing" on the subject of self-government (Kelliher, 1997: 67). Over the years, officials at the Ministry of Civil Affairs enlisted researchers to conduct surveys in some of the so-called demonstration villages and model counties[17] that they set up across the country. Survey results were distributed to county officials. Glowing accounts were published about improvements in village life after the adoption of electoral reform. Describing the effects of competitive elections for the post of village head in Xinmi county, Henan province, researcher Gao Xinjun writes: "The democratic atmosphere has been lively. . . . Relations between officials and the people have become closer. . . . Society has become more stable. . . . Economic development has been very good. Finally, the fastest rate of growth in collected taxes was recorded in Xinmi in the first half of 1998" (Gao, 1998: 12).[18]

The ingenuity of the tactics employed by Wang Zhenyao and his colleagues cannot be overstated. Opposition to the genuine implementation of the law on villagers' committees was widespread. Incumbent village chiefs were not eager to measure their popularity in open elections; township officials feared that they would no longer hold the same power over elected village officials as they had over appointed ones; county officials worried that elected village leaders would be uncontrollable and would not fulfil their duties to the state. Before 1990, when the Central Committee of the Chinese Communist Party endorsed the experimental law on villagers' committees, some county leaders even threatened officials who contemplated implementation of the law with disciplinary action. A few provincial leaders told Wang Zhenyao that village elections were "too much of a bother." Wang interpreted their words to mean that these leaders were not willing to put their authority on the line to persuade dubious, and in some cases vehemently opposed, county officials to introduce electoral reform.[19]

## FOREIGNERS HAD A ROLE OF THEIR OWN

Foreign journalists, scholars, and foundations have also played a role in the political struggle over village elections. Once pilot projects had been established and a first round of elections was held in demonstration villages, the Ministry of Civil Affairs decided to enlist the support of foreigners for their mammoth project. First and foremost, the ministry needed money to train hundreds of thousands of officials to organize multicandidate elections. Materials explaining the law on villagers' committees had to be printed. Funding was also necessary to arrange conferences to compare the electoral experiences of different provinces. The process of implementing the law on villagers' committees has been—and continues to be—a gigantic educational undertaking.

In 1993, the Ford Foundation provided the first foreign grant. Since then, the Ministry of Civil Affairs has received financial support from the International Republican Institute, Asia Foundation, United Nations Development Program, Carter Center for Democracy, and the European Union, among others. As of 1992, the Ministry of Civil Affairs arranged for foreign observer teams to witness villagers' committee elections.[20] When Wang Zhenyao took to inviting foreign journalists along on his tours to the provinces a few years later, Chinese village elections became a popular subject in newspapers and scholarly journals worldwide.[21] Initially, "village democracy," as the self-government reform has been dubbed in the West, drew approving and cautiously enthusiastic comments.[22]

Financial support was not the only reason the Ministry of Civil Affairs wanted to arouse foreign interest in the electoral reform. Proponents of the villagers' committees law also used the favorable publicity as ammunition in debates with their opponents, claiming that the elections were improving China's international image and useful in countering foreign criticism of China's human rights record.[23] Such claims were not entirely groundless. Accounts of villagers voting corrupt leaders out of office offer a distinctly different kind of image of the goings-on in China than reports of arms proliferation, forced abortions, dissident detentions, and arbitrary justice, to mention a few of the issues which receive attention in Western media coverage of China. Several Western heads of state, including Bill Clinton, have been quoted praising China's elections.

Wang Zhenyao offers another reason why the interest of foreign journalists and scholars was important. Foreigners "did not automatically reject the notion of democratic reform taking place in the countryside."[24] They were willing (and eager) to go to villages and see for themselves. Not only Chinese intellectuals, with their knowledge of political theory, but the vast majority of Chinese urban residents were—and still are—extremely skeptical about peasants being intellectually capable of governing themselves, let alone understanding principles of democracy.[25] As late as 1999, when several top Chinese leaders had endorsed the grassroots-level governance reform in public, a mid-level official affiliated with the National People's Congress retorted at an official lunch, "Teaching democracy to peasants is like playing the piano to cows!"[26]

County and township officials, who seldom have contact with foreigners, were both surprised and honored when foreigners arrived to witness electoral proceedings. In some cases, according to Wang Zhenyao, foreign interest woke local officials to the idea that perhaps elections are worthy and important after all. Similarly, articles published abroad on the subject of village elections evoked interest among hitherto doubtful Chinese researchers.

The way in which village elections were called to the attention of President Jiang Zemin is an illuminating example of how foreigners can be used in political struggles in China. When the Carter Center delegation visited China in 1996, one of the many topics discussed by delegation members and officials at the Ministry of Civil Affairs was the status of the experimental law and the efforts being made to have the law made permanent by the National People's Congress. Ministry officials mentioned that public endorsement of the experimental law by China's top leadership would be beneficial to the cause. At that point, Jiang Zemin had not commented in public on competitive village elections. Ministry officials presumed it possible that he had not been properly briefed about the progress of the grassroots-level governance reform.[27]

Ministry officials let it be known that a statement by the Carter Center's founder, former United States president Jimmy Carter, might be advantageous.[28] When the delegation returned to the United States, Carter wrote a letter on behalf of the center to President Jiang Zemin, praising the delegation's experiences. Jiang Zemin, reportedly taken by surprise, promptly requested a thorough report on the implementation of the experimental law on villagers' committees.[29] On his next trips to the provinces, he inquired about village elections, asking local officials about implementation of the law in their area. According to an official at the Ministry of Civil Affairs, "after that, local leaders had no choice than to start taking the self-government reform seriously."[30] Since then, several Chinese leaders have given their full support to villagers' committee elections. In September 1998 Jiang Zemin praised the self-government as Chinese farmers' "third great invention" (along with the household responsibility system and township and village enterprises) (O'Brien & Li, 2000: 484). Even the conservative Li Peng, upon becoming chairman of the National People's Congress, "started to hold high the banner of village elections."[31] It is evident that the Chinese leadership has also come to realize the public relations value of grassroots democracy in the international arena.

## What Have Been the Consequences of Political Reform at the Village Level?

One direct consequence of political reform at the village level is the increased emphasis on accountability and transparency in village governance. Several sources indicate that elected village cadres are looked upon as more accountable to villagers than appointed cadres (Yue and Zhen, 1997; Kelliher, 1997: 75; Li and O'Brien, 1999: 140–43). Article 22 of the law on villagers' committees requires publicizing financial issues every six months. Hence, the public posting of village finances has become the norm in villages where the grassroots-level governance reform has been implemented. The practice of requiring officials to regularly make public reports on the management of village funds and a whole range of policy measures is becoming institutionalized through local laws and regulations. For example, Article 22 of the law on villagers' committees requires village committees to publicize financial issues every six months.

According to proponents of the villagers' committee election law, elections have also helped to curb corruption. Officials appointed by the township government did not have to worry about what villagers thought about them. Elected ones do. Officials known to demand bribes have been voted out of office. In villages where elections remain a formality, the necessity of going through the electoral process every three years has at least made officials more aware of their public image (White, 1992: 274). Even an unopposed candidate can lose face by receiving a large number of blank ballots.

To the surprise of many doubtful local leaders, elected village chiefs have, on the whole, tried to execute state policies. Many articles provide statistics showing that the governance reform results in higher fulfillment of grain quotas, more taxes, and fewer breaches of the family planning regulations (Kelliher, 1997: 74 fn 46; Rong et al., 1998; Li and O'Brien, 1999: 140–41). No doubt this is one of the main reasons that the central government approved of the experimental law being given permanent status. For example, in Fujian province, a pioneer in villagers' committee elections, 99 percent of 1,200 villages surveyed in 1994 had fulfilled their grain procurement quotas; 92 percent had not exceeded their birth targets; and 82 percent had paid their taxes.[32] It is well to remember that elected village officials have no power to change central government directives. They only have the authority to find the best means possible to implement them. However, elected officials, who rely on villagers' votes, are perceived as less apt to accept demands of extra levies or taxes from bullying township officials. Elected village officials have a greater degree of independence than appointed ones vis-à-vis township officials and have no need to "bow and scrape" before them.[33]

Another clear consequence of self-governance reform is the political activation of rural residents.[34] Initially, most residents in so-called demonstration villages were extremely skeptical about the electoral reform. Only after the first or second round did they realize that they truly were empowered to vote unpopular, incompetent, and corrupt leaders out of office. In many places ordinary villagers took the initiative to draw up more detailed election rules and were quick to lodge complaints with township or county officials about any breaches of the law on villagers' committees.[35] Word of competitive elections spread to other villages, creating a snowball effect.[36] According to officials at the Ministry of Civil Affairs and researchers working on rural affairs, actions taken by ordinary villagers have been a decisive factor in the struggle over village elections. By persistently pressuring higher officials and demanding that elections be carried out according to the law, rural residents have advanced the reform process.

Those who are skeptical about grassroots-level governance reform are quick to point out that the village Party secretary, not the village head, is the most influential person in the village. These claims, in part, are true, though the situation varies greatly from place to place. According to officials at the MoCA, tensions between the village Party secretary and village chief have flared substantially since the experimental law on villagers' committees was given permanent status in late 1998. MoCA officials view this as a sign that meaningful villagers' committee elections have been held since 1999, while previously many elections had been either rigged or held in name only. According to one ministry official, "the contradictions between the Party Secretary and the village chief constitute a healthy sign because it is only natural that a power struggle arises between them."[37]

A much-publicized case of the antagonism between elected villagers' committee officials and the village Party secretary involved a joint letter of complaint to the central government signed in December 2000 by 57 elected village heads in Shandong province. The signatories stated that they were resigning from their posts because the village Party secretary had prevented them from carrying out their duties. In several cases the village Party secretary had not consented to handing over the village seal, a crucial instrument of power needed in all village transactions. In other cases, the Party secretary had not allowed the village head to see the village's bookkeeping records (Li Changhong, 2001; Shou, 2001).

In July 2001, one Shandong village chief, a signatory of the joint letter of complaint, described being brutally beaten up by the village Party secretary and his allies for lodging a complaint to the county authorities (Mykkänen, 2001). In discussions in 2001, MoCA officials in Beijing cited recurring problems deriving from township and county officials siding with village Party secretaries when power struggles emerged between the village Party secretary and the village chief.[38]

The distribution of power between the village chief and Party secretary is not entirely clear. According to Article 3 of the law on villagers' committees, "the rural grassroots unit of the Chinese Communist Party (CCP) should work under the Charter of the CCP and play a core role in leadership."[39] This expression is routinely used when referring to the Party's role in official statements. The Communist Party is not mentioned in any of the other 29 articles, while the rights and responsibilities of the villagers' committee are spelled out in relative detail. Researchers involved with village elections view the ambiguity regarding the power of the local Party as the law's greatest weakness—in the words of one researcher, the top leadership "did not dare undermine the village Party secretary's position."[40]

The Party has not, however, remained immune to the effects of grassroots-level governance reform. The notion of competitive elections with secret balloting is spreading to the Party itself. Though Party secretaries are usually appointed by the township Party branch, Party members in several villages have demanded—and on occasion been granted—the right to choose the village Party secretary by voting among themselves (Jakobson, 1998: 129; Hutzler, 2002). The Shanxi Province Party Organization Department has gone a step further, promoting a two-ballot system with which Party secretaries are elected (Li, 1999: 103–18). In the first round, all villagers—not only Party members—participate in choosing the candidates for the post of Party secretary, after which only Party members vote for the final choice. This is revolutionary because it opens the decision-making process of internal Party matters to participation by non-members. On the other hand, according to Li Lianjiang, who did fieldwork in Shanxi province, township leaders face fewer complaints than they did in the past, and villagers have "secured a measure of control over the key political figure in the village" (Li, 1999: 118).

Lastly, and as far as the political development of the nation is concerned, perhaps the most significant consequence of villagers' committee elections is the demand brewing in townships that the township head should be elected by direct competitive elections. According to researchers involved with political reform and officials working in the Ministry of Civil Affairs and the State Council, the pressure from below is enormous, though the Chinese Communist Party leadership has forbidden direct multicandidate elections at the township level.

## VARIOUS EXPERIMENTS IN TOWNSHIP ELECTIONS

The officials of one township took the law into their own hands in December 1998 and arranged direct, relatively competitive elections for the post of township head. A man by the name of Tan Xiaoqiu became the first township head on the Chinese mainland to be genuinely chosen by the ballots of the township's residents.[41] According to the law, the township people's congress should elect the township head. In practice, the township Party committee often appoints the sole candidate.

The township in question, Buyun, an administrative part of Shizhong district (*qu*) in Suining city (*shi*) in Sichuan province, is small by Chinese standards. There are only 16,000 inhabitants in Buyun, while a large Chinese township can have a population of 100,000. There are altogether 37 townships in Shizhong district with a total population of 1.37 million.[42] The plans for the election were kept secret from higher authorities until a few days before the voting was due to take place. Officials in Suining reportedly gave their quiet consent to the experiment upon being notified.[43] Though several Chinese observers were enthusiastic in their comments about the Buyun election, it is important to note that the primary election was not as open as in villagers' committee elections, in which the *haixuan*-method of nominating candidates is used.

In Buyun the township Party committee was allowed to nominate directly one of the three final candidates. The remaining two finalists were decided by a 163-person selection committee comprised of township officials and the village heads, village assembly chairmen, and three representatives from each of the ten villages under the administration of Buyun. Candidacy was open to one and all, the only prerequisite being a minimum age of 25 and endorsements from 30 residents of Buyun. From the start, there were 15 contenders for the position of township head, including several of the top township leaders. Before the selection committee voted, all of the candidates were asked about their backgrounds and plans to develop the township. Based on the selection committee's vote, a schoolteacher (who was not a Party member) and a village head (who was) were named final candidates. They beat all the so-called township official corps in the primary election. The township Party committee nominated 40-year-old Tan Xiaoqiu, a township official who was Buyun's deputy Party secretary, as their candidate.

During a 15-day campaign period, the three final candidates participated in 13 public debates, answering voters' questions. Two of the debates were held at open air markets in the township center, and ten of them in villages. The campaign activities were reminiscent of "an American election campaign with candidates and their entourages travelling from place to place."[44] On election day (December 30, 1998), 6,236 of the approximately 6,700 registered voters of Buyun cast their ballots in the pouring rain at 17 polling stations, equipped with separate polling booths.[45] The Party's candidate, Tan Xiaoqiu, received a total of 3,130 votes (50.19 percent of votes cast), which was 1,135 more votes than the village head received. According to the rules, if Tan had received 12 votes less, there would have had to be a run-off between him and the village chief.

The Buyun election received widespread attention nationwide two weeks later when a Guangdong newspaper, *Nanfang Zhoumo*, with a circulation of about 200,000, published a conspicuous report of the event.[46] The article, accompanied by photos, explained the electoral process in detail and described the township residents' enthusiasm for direct elections. The central government reacted swiftly. Four days later, the mouthpiece of the Ministry of Justice, *Fazhi Ribao*, published a commentary, "Democracy Should Not Overstep the Law," stating that the Buyun election "violated the Constitution and other laws."[47] Though the commentary's message was clear, its tone was moderate compared to the harsh language used to condemn so-called counterrevolutionaries or other "instigators of instability." It pointed out that laws can be revised and that "there is no need for us to criticize too much the direct election" in Buyun township. The commentary proved to be controversial and led to several articles probing the constitutionality of the Buyun election; among others, a second commentary in *Fazhi Ribao* stated that "history will remember Buyun township for pushing forward direct township elections" (Eckholm, 1999; Li Lianjiang, 2002, 716–18).

Another sign that the Communist Party top leadership was not unanimous on how to deal with the Buyun issue and did not want to—at least publicly— embark on a headlong confrontation with proponents of direct elections, was that the election results in Buyun were not annulled.[48] No one was punished because of the Buyun case, though the initiator of the Buyun election, Zhang Jinming, was later transferred to another position, albeit with the same rank. Zhang, the Party Secretary at the time of Shi Zhong district, is known as an innovative "sharp-minded official in her forties."[49] Daughter of a respected veteran Communist, she had doggedly experimented with direct elections of lower officials before the groundbreaking township head election. According to Zhang, she wanted to find ways to make officials more accountable, pursue more effective means of governance, and deal with problems of corruption. Zhang denies that she wanted Buyun to go down in history as the first place in China to arrange direct township head elections and be remembered in the same way that Xiaogangcun in Anhui province is always mentioned as the village where farmers took the initiative in the late 1970s to start the household-responsibility system on their own.[50] Scholars remain divided as to what degree the central government's adoption of the dramatic economic reforms in the countryside was part of a coherent plan or an inevitable result of pressure from farmers (Bernstein, 1999: 204–07; Zweig, 1997: 153–68).

Despite Zhang Jinming's denial, several observers point out that the personal career ambitions and political aspirations of local Party officials could serve as a driving force to move the township electoral reform process forward (Cheng, 2001; He and Lang, 2001: 12–14; Li Lianjiang, 2002: 722). To be labeled "a historic first" has its own allurement, and it is worth remembering that competition among localities and the desires of local Party leaders to be pioneers have spurred on economic reform since the 1980s.

At least three other townships experimented during the first half of 1999 with direct elections for the post of township head. However, in none of them were citizens given as much power to influence the final outcome as in Buyun. In Zhuoli township, Linyi county, Shanxi province, the local authorities designated three candidates, all of whom were established township officials in leadership positions. Eligible voters were then asked to cast a vote of confidence (a. complete trust/confidence; b. basic confidence; c. do not trust). For an official to be allowed to continue in his position, more than 50 percent of the voters had to have indicated that they trust him (a. or b.) (Li Fan et al., 2000: 73–77).

In Dapeng township near Shenzhen, a double-ballot system was used in April 1999. Citizens aged over age 18 years could only vote in the first round that decided the primary candidates. Anyone who met the following requirements could be put forward as a candidate: a higher education (i.e. university or technical school graduate); under age 50; healthy; "sufficiently revolutionary, young at heart, knowledgeable, and professional"; "reliable and respected"; "and in general be a member of the Communist Party." In the first round, nearly all of the some 5,200 registered voters cast their ballots to determine the most popular candidates among a field of 76 runners. The top six candidates then went on to the second round that began by each person making a speech to a selection committee made up of 1,068 Party members, government officials, and village leaders, as well as representatives from various factories and business groups. In terms of sheer numbers, the selection committee represented approximately one-fifth of the total number of registered voters. The incumbent township head, Li Weiwen, won an overwhelming victory with 813 votes in the second round of voting, in which only members of the selection committee took part. The election outcome still had to be ratified by the township's Party committee and by delegates of the township's People's Congress (Li Fan et al., 2000: 91–96; Huang, 2000).[51]

A group of Chinese researchers, who compiled a book reviewing the experiences from the various experiments in 1998–1999 with direct township elections, evaluated the Buyun model as the one that gave the residents of the township the widest scope of influence. The Dapeng model was praised for giving average citizens the chance to put forward candidates, but it was criticized because the decisive votes were cast by a selection committee that did not necessarily reflect the average citizen (Li Fan et al., 2000: 95–96). It is also noteworthy that Dapeng had a permanent population of 171,000, and a temporary population of over 800,000—yet there were only some 5,200 registered voters (Cheng, 2001). While assessing the importance of elections, the group of Chinese researchers write: "The merit of elections is that elections can solve the problem of official corruption, the contradictory relationship between officials and normal people, and the instability of society, which are some of the critical problems the government is currently encountering" (Li Fan et al., 2000: 177).

In March 1999, a proposed revision of the law on the election of a township head was submitted by the Chinese People's Political Consultative Conference to the National People's Congress's committee on legislative work (*falu gongzuo weiyuanhui*). The proposal was rejected and returned with the comment: "At present, conditions are not yet suitable to revise the law."[52] In June 1999, one of the scholars who drew up the proposal, Bai Gang of the Chinese Academy of Social Sciences, predicted that direct elections of the township head would be permitted in 15 to 20 years.[53] Wang Zhenyao of the MoCA was more optimistic. He believed that within five years the central government would allow experimenting with direct elections in predesignated townships.[54] According to Tony Saich, former director of the Ford Foundation in China, "what is crucial is that everybody believes that it [direct township elections] will take place at some point. The process has already been set in motion."[55]

However, significant political reform will not take place before, at the earliest, the mid-2010s. No major political decisions are expected before Jiang Zemin de facto gives up his grip on power and Hu Jintao secures his position, alongside other CCP leaders who were appointed at the 16th Party Congress in November 2002. After the 16th Party Congress, it became evident that the top leadership of the CCP wanted to shift the focus of grassroots political reform and concentrate on developing a system of checks and balances within the Party rather than allow the village electoral reform process to move up the governmental ladder to the township or county level. After the 16th Party Congress, researchers and mid-level provincial officials in Guangdong predicted that political reform will entail introducing more democratic procedures within the Party, for example, strengthening local Party congresses and making the local Party committee more accountable to Party congresses.[56] The architect of the Buyun township election, Zhang Jinming, once again proved her political agility and determination to promote a more accountable political leadership by organizing the first ever direct election of delegates to the county-level People's Congress in Ya'an, Sichuan province, in December 2002.[57]

The Dapeng "two-ballot" election model is expected to be adopted in Guangdong province's townships during the next round of township head elections in 2004.[58] In line with the years of intense political debate before the law on villagers' committees was granted permanent status in late 1998, officials are reluctant to give a coherent picture of small progress being made on different fronts with regard to township elections. One can conclude that the reform process is piecemeal, and reform-minded officials are intentionally adopting a "foot-in-the-door" approach, as they did during the struggle to win approval for direct and competitive village elections.[59]

From the point of view of the Communist Party, permitting direct elections for the post of the township head would mean forfeiting a substantial portion of genuine power. There are about 45,000 townships in China. Township heads have the authority to make considerably more critical financial decisions than village chiefs. Though the township Party secretary wields more power that the township head, pressure would rapidly mount to change the process of nominating the township Party secretary as well, to make it as open as the election of the township head. It would only be a matter of time before direct elections at the county level would be demanded.

When the Buyun election became public, Jiang Zemin reportedly gave explicit instructions to prohibit any mention of direct township elections in the media and to forbid them in practice.[60] In the words of one Party member working for the State Council, "Jiang and the other top leaders fear that all the Party members would be voted out of office" if such elections were allowed.[61] This assertion, however, might not necessarily hold true. To quote Bai Gang, a well-known scholar at the Chinese Academy of Social Sciences, "ordinary citizens do not distinguish between people on the basis of Party membership when they contemplate who should be a leader. They want fair, honest, and competent people as decision-makers."[62]

In the townships, Party members are often the best educated and the most experienced in administrative work. Also, as Bai Gang and several other researchers point out, even after direct township elections are allowed, the central government will almost certainly restrict the nomination process. The chances for candidates who are not members of the Communist Party to make it to the final round will remain slim. Even in the proposal of Bai Gang and his colleagues, considered progressive in China, a nine to 15 member selection committee would decide which two candidates go to the final round. Though the proposal would have allowed non-Party members to be candidates, it suggested barring anyone who, for example, opposes China's family planning policy.[63]

An even more compelling reason for the top leadership to fear direct township elections is that these elections would encourage political activism on a much larger scale than in villages. Elections cause people to organize, if not into new parties (forbidden by law), then at least into *ad hoc* lobbying groups. Campaigns would inevitably precipitate large-scale gatherings, which could turn into protest meetings.

## LONG-TERM IMPLICATIONS

In the long term, the grassroots governance reform has far-reaching implications. For all its flaws, the reform is institutionalizing a system of checks and balances at the grassroots level. The leadership of the Communist Party has conceded that the most effective weapon in the struggle against despotism and corruption is the ballot box, implicitly acknowledging that leaders chosen directly by the people are more effective than appointed ones. The Party has also accepted that a person who does not belong to the Communist Party is eligible to lead his or her community. These are fundamentally important principles upon which open-minded officials and researchers can base their arguments when pushing for more substantial political reform.

At least 100 million Chinese have now gained personal experience of what direct multicandidate elections entail in practice. Using the most pessimistic estimates, presuming that fair and competitive elections have been arranged in only 10 to 20 percent of China's villages, 86 to 172 million Chinese have already been exposed to the inner workings of a democratic electoral process.[64] Several hundred million more have at least some idea of how meaningful elections should be held. Mechanisms for the implementation of democratic rule are being put into place "to await the day that they are needed."[65] The villagers' committee elections should be viewed as a gigantic educational training ground. Giving villagers a genuine choice is unprecedented in Chinese history.

As Wang Zhenyao of the MoCA points out, "less than ten years ago, running for office (*jingxuan*) was a dirty word, as was 'democracy' (*minzhu*)."[66] He was referring to the repressive political atmosphere following the suppression of the 1989 democracy movement. Today, the pros and cons of elections and democracy are discussed at all levels of the Chinese Communist Party. The notion that rulers need to be made accountable has not only become part of Chinese official discourse; laws are being passed to institutionalize methods that force transparency upon ways of governing. The SARS crisis in the spring of 2003 accelerated this process. Hu Jintao's public admission that the Chinese authorities had not been telling the truth about the numbers of SARS cases unleashed a lively debate in the mainland Chinese media about the significance of transparency and accountability.

The cautious steps taken by the Chinese leadership in recent years to establish a rule of law have increased the pressure from below to open up the political process to mass participation. By passing legions of new laws and then spreading knowledge of their content through the media, the government has promoted the concept of a citizen's rights. As a result—and also because of the flow of information streaming in from abroad—Chinese in both urban and rural areas are more aware of their legal and civil rights than ever before.

Since enforcement of the Administrative Litigation Law in 1990, citizens from all walks of life have seized the opportunity to bring suit against government officials for legal violations and grossly unfair procedures. The media regularly carry reports about ordinary farmers and workers who file legal complaints and seek protection against despotism and arbitrary justice. "Rightful resistance," to use a term coined by Kevin O'Brien, is becoming a legitimate model of behavior when leaders do not follow their own rules (O'Brien, 1996: 33). In 1993, the central government openly encouraged rural residents to resist officials who abuse their power, by clearly stating in the law on agriculture that farmers have the "right to refuse" unauthorized fees and taxes (Bernstein, 1999: 214). According to the law on villagers' committees, one-fifth of a village's residents can jointly file a petition and request a recall of a member of the villagers' committee. After the person being recalled is given a chance to appeal, the villagers should vote on the matter. If more than 50 percent of the village's eligible voters agree with the recall, the villagers' committee member in question loses his or her job.[67] This principle too has profound implications.

The loosening of political control, coupled with a rights consciousness, has led to the emergence of what could be called "sanctioned outspokenness." Against all odds, a growing number of Chinese dare to confront the authorities with the words, "According to the law I have the right to . . ." For decades, repeating the Party line was the safest way to stay out of trouble in the People's Republic. It still is, but because political, economical, and social institutions are in a state of perpetual flux, the boundaries between the permissible and forbidden have become blurred. Armed with texts of official laws, which are unquestionably sanctioned, Chinese are becoming all the more adept at challenging preconceived norms. Only by trial and error can one know with certainty where the boundary line of the forbidden lies in Chinese society today.

Were the main elements of the law on villagers' committees to be applied to all levels of government, the relationship between rulers and citizens in China would be greatly transformed. The Party does not deny this. Commenting on the law of villagers' committees, the mouthpiece of the Chinese Communist Party claims that the "implementation of this democratic supervision system has put an end once and for all to the past practice whereby only cadres could supervise the masses, and has made it possible for the masses to supervise not only themselves but cadres as well. Today, this system has also become a major measure for promoting the building of clean and honest administration in rural areas."[68]

Several scholars of Chinese politics have noted the utilitarian approach that Chinese leaders, from the top down, have towards the concept of democracy.[69] Democratic institutions are not regarded as ends in themselves. Rather, they are weighed by assessing their effectiveness in enhancing China's quest for wealth, power, and stability or dealing with the pressing problems of corruption, lawlessness, and inequality. Corruption is a major cause of the growing protests and a prime threat to the Party's legitimacy. Even the authorities acknowledge that corruption is "worse than at any other period since New China was founded in 1949. It has spread to the Party, government, administration and every part of society, including politics, economy, ideology and culture."[70] Jiang Zemin stated, in his report at the 16th Party Congress (section 10): "If we do not resolutely crack down on corruption . . . the party will be in danger of losing its ruling position, and it is possible the party is headed for self-destruction." So far, competitive elections have been praised in the official media above all as a means of curbing corruption and making leaders more accountable for their actions. For this reason, corruption might well be the catalyst that could entice the top leadership to voluntarily agree to direct township elections. The initiator of the Buyun township election, Zhang Jinming, repeatedly cited corruption problems as one of the main reasons to experiment with various innovative methods in selecting township leaders.[71]

Over the past two decades, the character of Chinese politics has been slowly but steadily transforming. To quote Robert Scalapino, "the most basic political trend in China today is the gradual transformation of Leninism into authoritarian pluralism, not democracy" (Scalapino, 1998: 38). Dramatic social changes and rising official corruption have weakened the state's control. Marxist-Leninist ideology has taken a back seat, having lost its appeal among the populace. As a result, the Chinese system is in a permanent crisis of legitimacy. Violent protests are becoming commonplace.[72] Growing social unrest will, at some point, force the Communist Party leadership to choose between continuing to repress dissent or seeking to bolster the regime's legitimacy by broadening opportunities for political participation. Though using brutal force to control disgruntled citizens is the more likely scenario, village elections have provided ample training ground for increased democracy to be a feasible option.

## NOTES

1. Portions of this chapter are based on my previously published working paper about villagers' committee elections in China (Jakobson, 1999), which I have updated with new research material and interview results following trips to the P.R. China 1999–2002.

2. There are about 930,000 villages (*cun*) in China. On average approximately 20 villages are under the jurisdiction of a township (*xiang*) or town (*zhen*) government, which constitute the lowest level of government in P.R. China. A township or town is administratively under a county (*xian*) or a city district (*qu*). There are in total approximately 45,000 township/town governments and 2,143 county governments, meaning that on average about 22 township/towns belong to one county or city district. (State Statistical Bureau, 1997: 3, 19). For simplicity, "township" is hereafter used to signify both township and town.

3. Interview with Li Fan, director of the World and China Institute (Shijie yu zhongguo yanjiusuo), April 2, 2001.

4. For Deng's views on the need for political reform, see Foreign Languages Press, 1994: 178–81.

5. For an English translation of the law, see www.cartercenter.org/CHINA/dox/laws/organic.html (April 2002).

6. See www.cartercenter.org/CHINA/dox/laws/organic.html.

7. See www.cartercenter.org/CHINA/dox/laws/organic.html.

8. *Haixuan* means "sea election," meaning every villager has the right to nominate a candidate.

9. Villagers' representative assemblies (*cunmin daibiao huiyi*) are made up of villagers who each represent 10–15 households. They were designed to oversee the work of villagers' committees. See Lawrence, 1994: 61–68; O'Brien, 1994: 42–44.

10. Interviews with officials of the Ministry of Civil Affairs, March 28 and 29 and April 3, 2001.

11. Between 1978 and 1990, rural incomes rose from 133 yuan to 629 yuan (White, 1992: 273).

12. See e.g. *Xinhua Domestic Service*, 1997.

13. See Peng Zhen's speeches in Ministry of Civil Affairs, 1990.

14. Peng also states that "the representative body should be the fully empowered representative body. The administrative committees of governments at all levels or their leaders should be elected or removed by the representative bodies. The government has the duty to obey absolutely the decisions of the representative bodies" (Saich, ed., 1996: 1022).

15. Bourgeois liberalization and peaceful evolution are expressions used by conservative ideologues when attacking liberals for deviating from the Marxist Leninist line and being influenced too much by Western values. Bourgeois liberalization is often mentioned as the cause of ills in society that the reforms have brought about. Peaceful evolution—the imperialist Western world's attempt to bring down socialism by infiltrating society with Western values—is cited by the Chinese Communist Party as one of the reasons for Communism unravelling in the Soviet Union and Eastern Europe. See e.g. MacFarquhar, 1997: 340–41, 401–07, 478, 485.

16. See e.g. Research Group on the System of Village Self-government in Rural China and the China Research Society of Basic-Level Governance, 1994; Cao, Guoying, and Zhang, Houan, 1996: 253–57.

17. During the period from 1990 to 1995, 63 counties, 3,917 towns, and 82,266 villages were set up as demonstration sites (Jiang, 1996). In mid-1999 there were over 300 so-called model counties.

18. Xinmi is not a ministry-designated model county. A research project focusing on system of governance was conducted in Xinmi county in 1996 by a team led by Professors Rong Jiben and Cui Zhiyuan with funding from the Ford Foundation.

19. Interview with Wang Zhenyao, January 3, 1997. For more about imperfect policy implementation in China, see O'Brien, 1994: 33; Manion, 1991: 253–79.

20. Individual researchers, e.g. Tyrene White, conducted fieldwork on village elections before 1992.

21. When a group of other Western journalists and I accompanied Wang Zhenyao to Liaoning in March 1995, the foreign visitors' presence made news in the local media. The reason for the trip—villagers' committee elections—was mentioned in passing.

22. See e.g. Gibney, 1993; Kaye, 1995; Mufson, 1995; Spaeth, 1996; *Economist*, 1996.

23. Kelliher points out that the value of village elections as a tool for improving China's international image was not initially a motivation of self-government, but "something proponents stumbled upon" after the experimental law was passed. Kelliher, 1997: 75–77; Shi, 1999: 407.

24. Interview with Wang Zhenyao, September 19, 1998.

25. See e.g. Kelliher, 1997: 80; Li and O'Brien, 1999: 136.

26. Interview on June 18, 1999, with a guest at the lunch, held in Beijing on June 18, 1999.

27. Interview with official at Ministry of Civil Affairs, June 8, 1999. (The interviewee stressed that though top leaders, including Jiang Zemin, had spoken publicly about the importance of strengthening the work of grassroots organizations, they had not specifically mentioned competitive villagers' committee elections.)

28. Interview, June 8, 1999.

29. Interview, June 8, 1999.
30. Interview, June 8, 1999.
31. Interview with Wang Zhenyao, September 19, 1998.
32. Zhongguo dalu yanjiu jiaoxue tongxun, no. 10 (1995): 16.
33. Interviews in Shenyang, Liaoning, March 1995; and in Zibo, Shandong, September 1996.

34. The noticeable increase in villagers' political activation has been pointed out in several interviews related to village elections which I have conducted since 1995, both in Beijing and during the research trips to Liaoning, Shandong, and Fujian provinces. See also Chan, 1998: 519.

35. In Fujian, 4,331 complaints about election irregularities were made following the 1997 elections. Of these complaints, 86.2 percent were dealt with (Bai, 1999: 182).

36. See e.g. Zhongguo shehui chubanshe, 1994: 78–79. The use of the word *snowball* derives from a comment by Wang Zhenyao: "Building democracy is like rolling snowballs" (interview with Wang, January 3, 1997).

37. Interviews with officials at Ministry of Civil Affairs, March 28 and 29, 2001.

38. See also Shi Shuren, 2001, www.peopledaily.com.cn/GB/shizheng/19/20010330/428932. html (April 26, 2002).

39. See www.cartercenter.org/CHINA/dox/laws/organic.html (April 26, 2002).

40. Interview with Li Fan, April 2, 2001.

41. The word *genuine* is used here because 25 days before the Buyun election, on December 5, 1998, voters in Nancheng township in Qingshen county, also in Sichuan province, cast their ballots to select a township head. Therefore Nancheng was technically a historic first. However, in numerous ways the Nancheng election was a "carefully conducted political show" and far less free, fair, and competitive than the Buyun election, resulting in the election in Buyun being widely looked upon, both within and outside of China, as the first real direct election of a township head. See Li Lianjiang, 2002: 709–16.

42. Report on the Buyun township head election compiled by China Elections Watch, in collaboration with the Carter Center for Democracy. See www.gpc.peachnet.edu/~yliu/watch/local.html (April 26, 2002). Buyun consists of ten villages, one neighborhood committee, and 80 villager teams, with nearly the entire population engaged in farming (He and Lang, 2001: 6).

43. Interview with official at the Ministry of Civil Affairs, June 8, 1999. Researchers dealing with the Buyun case remain divided on whether higher authorities were aware of the plans to experiment with direct elections of the township head in Buyun and at what stage they gave their tacit approval. See e.g. Cheng, 2002; He and Lang, 2001: 11–12; Li Lianjiang, 2002: 705, 710–14.

44. Interview with researcher at institute under the Central Committee of the Communist Party, June 14, 1999.

45. Of Buyun's 16,000 inhabitants, 11,349 were eligible to vote, but approximately 4,000 of those were working elsewhere and did not register to vote; hence there were only about 6,700 registered voters, i.e. less than in some of the larger villages in China. (Li Fan et al, 2000: 146).

46. "Zhi xuan xiangzhang," *Nanfang Zhoumo (Southern Weekend)*, January 15, 1999.

47. "Minzhu bu neng chaoyue falu," *Fazhi Ribao (Legal Daily)*, January 19, 1999.

48. A further indication that the degree with which Chinese top leaders opposed

the Buyun election varied was the airing of a 15-minute documentary about the Buyun election on February 26, 1999, by the official China Central Television (CCTV). According to the *South China Morning Post*, "the footage . . . was transmitted four weeks after the State Press and Publication Administration and propaganda departments ordered a media blackout on the [Buyun] election." Though the documentary did not include official comments from any leaders, a researcher of the Legislative Affairs Commission of the National People's Congress was quoted as saying that the election "reflected a positive direction of rural democracy." CCTV officials reportedly consulted the Propaganda and Organization departments of the Central Committee and were given permission to air the program ("Beijing indicates recognition of landmark election," *South China Morning Post*, March 1, 1999).

49. Interview with senior reporter at *Renmin Ribao* (*People's Daily*), June 10, 1999.

50. Discussion with Zhang Jinming in Nanjing, April 3, 2001.

51. Of the six candidates to go to the final round, one was disqualified on the basis of age. See also "Historic township vote in Shenzhen," *South China Morning Post*, April 30, 1999.

52. Interview with researcher at institute affiliated with the National People's Congress, January 7, 2001.

53. Interview with Bai Gang, senior researcher of the Chinese Academy of Social Sciences, June 9, 1999.

54. Interview with Wang Zhenyao of the Ministry of Civil Affairs, June 5, 1999.

55. Interview with Tony Saich, Ford Foundation's China Director, June 10, 1999.

56. Interviews with researchers at Shenzhen University and officials at Guangdong Provincial Government, December 17 and 18, 2002.

57. See e.g. "Zhi Xuan Dang Daibiao" ("Direct election of Party delegates"), *Zhong Guo Xinwen She, Xinwen Zhoukan* (*China News Report, News Weekly*), January 20, 2003.

58. Interview with researcher working on political reform and interview with official working at the Ministry of Civil Affairs, March 28 and 29, 2001.

59. Interview with official working at the Ministry of Civil Affairs, March 28, 2001.

60. Interview with official at the Ministry of Civil Affairs, June 8, 1999. See also "Media blackout ordered on poll," *South China Morning Post*, January 31, 1999.

61. Interview in Beijing with researcher working in organization under the State Council, June 14, 1999.

62. Interview with Bai Gang, June 9, 1999.

63. Interview with Bai Gang.

64. These calculations are based on statistics provided by the State Statistical Bureau, according to which 70.9 percent of the population, i.e. 859 million people, officially resided in the countryside in 1995. Consequently, ten percent of the rural population is roughly 86 million; 20 percent is 172 million (State Statistical Bureau 1997: 69). According to a report published in *Renmin Ribao* on April 9, 2001, 600 million rural residents have taken part in direct elections. "Zhongguo quanmian tuijin nongcun jiceng minzhu," www.peopledaily.com.cn/GB/shizheng/16/200010409/436639.html (April 26, 2002).

65. Interview with social scientist at Peking University (Beijing Daxue), June 4, 1999.

66. Interview with Wang Zhenyao, June 5, 1999.

67. See English translation of the law at www.cartercenter.org/CHINA/dox/laws/organic.html (April 26, 2002).

68. Yue, Yan, and Hai Zhen in *Renmin Ribao*, November 20, 1997 (FBIS-CHI-97-358).

69. Jia Qingguo of Peking University notes that "people want China to change so that we can be equal with the West and discard our second-class citizen status. If Western style procedural democracy does not bring China that longed-for equality, it will not appeal to the Chinese." Interview with Jia in Beijing, June 9, 1999. See also Harding, 1998: 15; He and Lang, 2001: 12–13.

70. Quote by Deputy Procurator-General Liang Guoqing in 1993 (Perry, 1999: 313).

71. Discussion with Zhang Jinming in Nanjing, April 3, 2001. Shizhong was among the first group of ten winners for an award for local government innovation (Saich and Yang, 2002: 5).

72. More than 5,000 protests took place in Chinese cities and the countryside in 1998 ("Beijing's law and order problem," *International Herald Tribune*, January 19, 1999).

# 7

# Neighborhood-Level Governance: The Growing Social Foundation of a Public Sphere

*Zhang Jing*

China's entry into the WTO is not only an economic event, but also a political cal event, which may lead to significant changes in the rules of governance.[1] The government will gradually be forced to follow new principles and new standards. Currently, local governments in China are revising the documents and policies, which might potentially contradict WTO regulations. Also many scholars are concerned with how the government can avoid becoming bogged down in detailed economic affairs which can be regulated by the market, so as to allow the market to play a full role in the allocation of social resources.[2] But the main trend in civil affairs over the past two years has been to strengthen the power of old district organizations, namely the neighborhood committee (*jiedao juweihui*), which is authorized by the government to manage affairs at the neighborhood level. This work has been labeled as "rebuilding city governance at the basic level." Obviously, the working aim of the program is to stabilize and institutionalize relations between citizens and government. However, this is not always in the interests of flat owners, who in the meantime are setting up their own organizations. In doing so, they try to share power with the neighborhood committee so as to govern themselves. This results in power conflicts between the neighborhood committee and these new citizen organizations. Our research revealed that by adopting an equal and contractual approach, these new types of citizen organizations are effectively redefining the framework of social relations. This inevitably constitutes a challenge to the local administrations, which have the authority to manage local affairs. The challenge hinges primarily on the question as to whether communities should be governed from above or whether they should spontaneously manage themselves from below. The distinction between these two perspectives is reflected in turn in issues centering around

121

the entry requirements for conducting public administration, the rights of citizen representatives, and the sources of power of public organizations, their
principles, and codes of conduct. In this chapter we explore the contours of
these challenges through a case study of a dispute in Shanghai.

## NEW RESIDENTS' ORGANIZATIONS
## AND EMERGING CONFLICTS

In an earlier study on communities conducted in 1996 in Beijing, I used the
concepts of individual rights and the rights of an organization to explain the
ineffectiveness of residents' supervision of properties in a small residential
estate in Beijing (Zhang, 1996). My conclusion was that the lack of balance
between the rights of individuals and the rights of an organization hindered
the development of a binding relationship between property owners and
their property company (Zhang, 1996: 94–98). It was a case study of a traditional urban community, a community formed by employees of the same organization where the employees' right of abode was allocated by the employer. Few of the inhabitants had purchased their flats at market prices.
Strictly speaking, therefore, the owner of the property was the employer, not
the inhabitants themselves. Within this community, residents were required
to promote their common interests through "public organizations" authorized by the district government, such as the unit where they worked, the
property management bureau, or the neighborhood committees. To raise
matters of concern, they therefore needed to approach the neighborhood
committee or the owner of the property, that is, their employer, or the district property management bureau. These organizations would then raise issues on behalf of the residents with the property developers, such as requests to preserve more green in front of their apartment blocks, to keep out
smoky restaurants, or to reduce bicycle theft. That was the traditional
method of problem resolution, that is, through a (public) organization. But
that method made a key assumption: that there was no conflict of interest between these organizations and the residents.

In a study of a residential estate in Shanghai several years later, I found a
rather different situation. Not only was there a new form of residents' organization, which had taken upon itself, inter alia, the protection of residents'
rights, but also the emergence of conflict between the authoritative local administration and the new self-organized residents' organizations. We first
outline some of the features of this particular case.

Qing Shui Yuan residential estate in Pudong District was managed by
Chang Yuan Property. Administratively, Chang Yuan Property was under Jin
Qiao Property Development, the developer of Qing Shui Yuan. The residents
elected a property owners' committee of seven members through their repre-

sentatives in accordance with the Administrative Regulations of Residential Properties of Shanghai. Six months later, the Committee found several matters to be unsatisfactory in Chang Yuan Property. First was the issue of illicit renovation. Two to three hundred residents had pulled down weight-bearing walls when renovating their flats, thereby endangering the building. Chang Yuan Property turned a blind eye to this because it had a special relationship with the company that had carried out the renovation. The second matter concerned substandard security. There had been 12 burglaries in just over one year. Third, there were environmental issues, namely, the destruction of large areas of grass and trees by pests. Fourth, there was the matter of overcharging. The property company had overcharged the maintenance fees by six yuan per square meter, or 1,000,000 yuan in total. Furthermore, they had refused to refund the money to the residents. Chang Yuan Property enjoyed the control, and commercial benefits, of the facilities on the estate including the leisure center, roadside commercial properties, garages, and properties occupied by Chang Yuan Property themselves. But it was the residents that paid management and maintenance charges. The maintenance fund for Qing Shui Yuan stood at around 1,200,000 yuan. According to the regulations, the money should have been transferred into the account of the property owners' committee and should be managed by that committee. However, Chang Yuan Property did not effect the transfer. Negotiations did not lead to any resolution of this matter. The Committee then became divided. Most members were in favor of replacing Chang Yuan Property and of "introducing market mechanisms, such as a tender system, to choose a company that would provide better services at better prices."[3] With four in favor and two abstentions, the Committee voted to hire Shang Fang Property. But the local administrative authorities concerned felt that it was too early to allow the practice of choosing one's own property management company. They wanted the property owners' committee to avoid any confrontation. So, Chang Yuan Property refused to hand over the management of the estate. Shang Fang Property wrote back to turn down the deal courteously, after receiving "instructions from administrative authorities higher up."[4] The property owners' committee went to court. The court ruled that as the property owners' committee did not have a formal record of the committee's seal, the case could not be accepted. There are reports that there have been dozens of cases similar to this in Shanghai. Committees of residential estates have often encountered problems with property developers. Indeed, it is rare that the two parties get on.

In this case study the owners were the residents and families living there, who had purchased their properties on the market, and not a situation of all residents working for the same employer. Some residents were colleagues, but these were the exceptions. The residents had happened to have chosen the same estate and had independently purchased their flats there. The organization they worked for was not the owner of the flats. Under these circumstances, their units of employment had no obligation to represent their employees in a dispute with the property developer. As the employer was no longer the owner of the building, there was no ground for the employer to represent the interests of the flat owners. Hence, there was a gap in the organizational structure. The owners in this case ended up being unprotected.

In terms of regulations, neighborhood committees and the district property bureau have always been, and still retain their identity as, the public managers of communities. In reality, particularly in this case, there was little shared interest between these organizations and the residents. Instead, there was conflict. According to an investigation by the property owners' committee of Qing Shui Quan residential estate, the facilities owned by the neighborhood committee were making a profit, but the residents did not know what their share of it was. The property management bureau decided that the dispute was irrelevant to them on the grounds that the issues involved "went beyond their responsibilities." The District Development Office was one of the administrative authorities. However, after numerous complaints and through different channels, it changed its position several times. The directions issued by the District Development Office were contradictory.[5] These administrative authorities understand their role to be only administrative. They are unwilling or unable to represent the interests of residents, let alone take on the responsibility of public management. However, they also have a vested interest in property companies. Some have acquired business opportunities through the use of facilities on an estate. Some depend on the property companies to pay various administrative fees for them. Others have historical links with the predecessors of the property developers. Despite the fact that these offices claim to be looking after residents, their conflicting interests have removed their incentives to do so. As a result, they are reluctant to rein in the property companies. Moreover, their traditional function does not allow them to become the representatives of residents either. Their task has always been to maintain order amongst residents, but not to manage their properties. The qualifications as well as performance of those organizations that have entered the sphere of public management of residential properties have not been defined or evaluated by residents. Nor do these organizations have anything to do with the choices of residents. There is no contractual relationship between them and the residents. Thus the District Development Office's interests cannot be reconciled with the residents' interests through a voluntary contract. Hence, residents had to bypass the local administrative authorities. To quote a member of the Qing Shui Yuan Property Owners' Committee, "They have reported nothing to us." The residents had to promote their shared interests through other channels, such as the property owners' committee. As a result, the property owners' committee became a new kind of organization at the local level, namely, one that represented owners' interests and took on the public function of property manager for the residents.

This case study raises a number of very important issues. What changes have taken place in the nature of these relatively traditional urban communities with the reform of housing? In particular, what changes have taken place in the relationship between the organizations concerned and the members of society? How have these changes affected residents' participation in public affairs? How are they affecting the establishment of a public sphere? What is the impact of these changes on the organizations that used to monopolize the control of entry into such a public sphere? What are the reactions to these changes from existing organizations responsible for public management as well as from the district government? These issues suggest a different approach to understanding and analyzing local governance to that adopted in the past. Such an approach implies understanding the degree of convergence of interests between public organizations and residents; who establishes a public sphere and what are the qualifications for entry; which organizations should allocate resources in public management and what are the principles of allocation; what is the response by the district government when it faces conflicting property-related demands. All these issues reflect changes in the basic structure of society.

## NEW URBAN COMMUNITIES

For a long time, accommodation was allocated by employers to employees, with the exception of a few privately owned properties that had been inherited. Residents were not independent actors in the market. They moved into a property as members of the organization they worked for. On the one hand, accommodation was part of their employment contract or its consequence. There was no direct relationship between the resident and the property. On the other hand, property developers were mostly community development organizations under public (government) administrations. They owned the quasi-rights of properties on behalf of district governments. They were able to control, dispose of, and benefit from the properties. These quasi-governmental organizations were allocated the right to develop and manage properties by district governments. At the same time and to different degrees, they shared some of the social welfare functions of district governments. Some of the fees paid by residents or local organizations, fees for heating and rubbish collection, for example, are symbolic and nominal. Those fees could not cover the real costs of maintaining the service. The real costs had to be met either from subsidies from the district government or the employers of the residents, or even from income from commercial operations on an estate, such as car parks or rent. As a result, property companies saw themselves as the *de facto* administrator, enjoying a status one level above the residents. They were in charge of housing resources in society.

Acting on behalf of district governments, they provided welfare to residents. The rate of occupancy did not affect their survival and their income did not depend on fees and charges. Moreover, their costs were covered by the government. However, if property companies stopped functioning, then there would be a huge impact on residents. In the eyes of the property companies, residents were quasi-beneficiaries of social welfare, people that needed to be managed. In short, it was the residents who depended on property companies, not vice versa. Residents had no way of influencing the behavior of property companies.

In this relationship, there were no corresponding rights, responsibilities, and obligations. However, there was an established structure, namely, a kind of collective, organizationally-shared property right. In other words, the organization the residents worked for (that is, the work unit) shared the property rights with the property management organizations. But this structure had an exclusive definition of the concept of "public." In this definition, only specifically authorized organizations were considered "public." It recognized only the relationship between those organizations as "public to public." Members of the public, residents, and individuals would have difficulty finding a solution to a problem, unless they could inflate the situation into an issue between two organizations, a "public to public" matter. An issue between two organizations was a "public to public" dispute. It would be resolved "public to public." If necessary, the district government would intervene to mediate. In this structure, a resident was defined as a "private individual." She/he did not have the same status or rights as an organization. "We only handle matters concerning a public organization," "we don't work for individuals," "one shouldn't do such and such a thing on one's own"—all these refrains have become part of the official vocabulary that residents have become accustomed to. This relationship defines the status and rights of members of the public and residents as individuals. It illustrates the monopoly the above-mentioned organizations enjoy in the sphere of public affairs. Members of the public have no established route to public affairs. They have to rely on one of those organizations.

However, the Shanghai case study points to very different emerging relations in the new residential estates. The most fundamental difference is the change in relationship between residents and the ownership of property. The ownership now belongs to the individual or the family by virtue of a purchase. Employers, the property administration bureau, or developers are no longer the owners. The new owners are the groups or individuals who have purchased the property. There thus emerge two opposite sides of a market relationship. The residents, as owners, pay fees for security, landscaping, and rubbish collection services from the property company. In return for fees, the property company provides these services. In this market relationship, parties to the transaction—the property company and the property owners—have become two opposite ends of an equation. To be more precise, this is an arrangement in which parties have corresponding rights and responsibilities. It is a corresponding relationship because the property company now depends on choice by the market as well as on management fees for survival. This has increased the power of the party that makes the choice, that is, the consumer or the property owner.

If we take property management as a market commodity, then refusing to purchase substandard services, or choosing to buy property management services from an alternative company through competitive tendering, is inevitable in the market. The owner's right to choose is legalized by the Administrative Regulations of Residential Estates of Shanghai. The Regulations clearly recognize the right of the owners' committee, duly elected by representatives of the owners, to choose property management companies through a contractual agreement. This right to choose by the residents represents a relationship between them and the property companies different from the one in the past. The two parties are the two sides of a transaction bonded by a contract. It means the property company has changed from a quasi-governmental administrator with power and responsibilities in public affairs to an ordinary enterprise providing management services. If the company depends on providing services for revenue, it will in effect be losing its traditional "public" character. It will become a commercial entity that earns income by providing services, not by collecting fees. Obviously, we are talking about two different sources of income. Fees are controlled by the collectors, who only need to maintain their status as the administrator to safeguard this source of revenue. Providing services gives consumers the choice to select the provider. Whether the property company can maintain its income stream depends on its competitiveness in the market. Hence, the property company as fee-collecting administrator and as profit-earning market actor are two different entities with different social statuses, the former being a public organization and the latter a nonpublic organization.

This change in status symbolizes the emergence of a new social relationship. The status of many quasi-governmental organizations is changing as they move from officialdom into society and transform from administrators over and above their subjects to social entities with corresponding rights and obligations bounded by contract through choice. The reason the residents and the property companies need each other is that they can satisfy their respective needs, namely, promoting their respective interests, through cooperation, that is by providing the work required by the other party. This change also means that, along with the new relationship in property rights, the rule of allocation as well as parties to the allocation of some of the scarce social values, resources, commodities, and labor, have changed too. More specifically, the change in "the rule" is that property companies now have to compete for management functions. The criterion in this competition is the quality of services provided, not one's official position, nor one's status in, nor proximity to district governments. The changes in the allocation of management functions include the shifting of some of the tasks of public administration to residents. Previously, these management functions used to be the sole responsibility of local government, the property administration bureau, employers, or property developers. Now they have become mainly the responsibility of the residents. However, residents are willing to entrust the responsibilities of management to property companies for reasons of cost, time, and expertise. The allocation of market resources in property management used to be carried out by the government. It is now carried out by owners of the property in that residents select a management company through competitive tendering. This in turn leads to a change in the system of accountability. Property companies used to be accountable to their administrative superiors. They are now accountable to residents. Property companies have become agents for the residents, instead of being the agents for their superiors. The owners' organization, namely, the property owners' committee, has become the organization for mediating property owners' interests. In this way the property owners' committee begins to enter the public sphere.

## NEW CITIZEN ORGANIZATION

Understanding the nature of the property owners' organization, that is, the property owners' committee, is important in understanding changes in society in China. The property owners' committees have entered the public sphere as active entities. Their behavior demonstrates new principles that cannot be found in previous forms of public organization.

The property owners' committees represent residents. They attempt to participate in the allocation of priced commodities such as management resources and service provision, in other words, the allocation of value, through their right to select service providers on a competitive basis. As the resources and services allocated are to meet the needs of the public, they have become (quasi-) public products. Prior to this, such allocation was done entirely by administrative organizations. In the Shanghai case study, the administrative organization of the previous system still remains. The administrative authorities continue to maintain their status as the ones who allocate property management resources. These administrative organizations continue to have a monopoly over determining who is eligible to participate in public affairs. They alone define the scope of public affairs, that is, what does and what does not constitute public affairs. They decide which organizations are qualified to manage public affairs. For example, they decide which organizations can be a public organization and who is qualified to be a public manager. Individual citizens and groups are not included in this process of definition. In fact, they are defined as belonging to the "private" sphere. They are not considered qualified to represent the public interest, or to participate in public activities.

However, though this system continues to exist in Shanghai, the emergence of the property owners' committee is an indication of change. Residents' communal affairs once handled by appointed public organizations are now instead starting to be handled by residents' organizations. This indicates that the organization of society is moving from the private sphere to the public sphere. Although the move is slow as well as uncertain, the power of separate individuals has begun to congregate on an experimental basis. A society of multipolemic, nonofficial entities composed of unrelated private individuals is moving toward becoming a society of autonomous citizens in alliance, an entity in the public sphere. These organizations participate in public affairs and work together with some of the public organizations under district governments. They share the responsibility of management and also handle issues concerning public affairs.

Of particular significance are the characteristics of these new public organizations of residents, including the issues they handle, they way they are authorized and established, their internal structure, and the grounds upon which they exercise their rights. These characteristics are not seen in existing public organizations. It is through these new organizations that residents have developed not only a close relationship with district governments, legal bodies, and commercial companies in the market, but also between residents themselves, one that is based on shared interest. We examine each of these facets in turn.

## ISSUES HANDLED BY PROPERTY OWNERS' COMMITTEES

Some of the most common issues handled by property owners' committees on new estates include securing a green belt in public areas and the concomitant demand to reduce profit-making facilities; environmental protection and particularly the banning of catering businesses in the vicinity to avoid oily smoke; noise pollution; hygiene, specifically timely rubbish collection; property maintenance and maintenance of street lighting; and security, especially ensuring that all manholes are properly covered and perimeter walls are maintained. Another common issue is property-related charges: how to decide the level of management fees, collect payment, use the fund, decide how much should be charged for maintenance, manage the requirement to report budgets to residents' representatives, and, more specifically, calculate communal areas and prove to residents' representatives that the calculation is free of error. These are all typical public issues in a community. They relate to the interests of not just one family or household, but the whole community. The basic responsibility of a property owners' committee is to safeguard the owners' interests by holding agency organizations accountable so that they cannot evade their responsibilities. These issues used to be the responsibility of governmental organizations or their agencies such as employers, residents' committees, and the property management bureau. Now, citizens' organizations have taken on the responsibility of supervision. The shift in responsibility is in part the result of a growing awareness of citizens' rights and responsibilities,[6] and in part a response to low efficiency in existing public organizations.

## AUTHORIZATION AND PROCEDURE OF ESTABLISHMENT

The property owners' committee of an estate is formed through election by a meeting of the owners or owners' representative assembly. There is a specific term of office. In the Qing Shui Yuan case study, the procedure was as follows: those who wished to serve the community volunteered themselves as candidates. All 16 volunteers automatically became candidates. There was one representative elected from every five entry doors. If a building had more than five entry doors, there would be two representatives elected from that building. The candidate's list was publicized for two weeks for consultation. After mediation, five of the candidates withdrew, having been informed that these posts were unpaid. These candidates had recently been made redundant and had hoped to find new employment through these positions. Three to four meetings were held among the representatives. Seven of these emerged as the final candidates. The list was submitted to Office No. 6 of the property bureau.[7] Property owners' committee members were elected on the basis of having the time required for the post, a sense of responsibility, knowledge including specialist knowledge in legal and property related affairs, and the ability to represent owners' interests. Members were basically volunteers working part-time and were not paid a salary. Sometimes they even had to cover some of the expenses such as travel.[8] The terms of reference were decided by the owners. Committee members could not take on matters beyond their authorization, even if such matters concerned the owners. For example, in Qing Shui Yuan, the cost of decoration for the committee's office was questioned. The committee had to justify it in a written report.[9] This shows that members would not be able to stay in their post if they acted without permission from, or refused to be controlled by, the residents.

## GROUNDS FOR EXERCISING RIGHTS

During the dispute at Qing Shui Yuan, there were many instances in which the law was applied. These included the legality of the property owners' committee's stamp on official records; whether the Neighborhood Committee was entitled to call an assembly of owners' representatives; the conflict of interest of one property owners' committee member who was both a member of the committee and a staff member of Shang Fang Property; and whether competitive tendering should be subject to authorization from the owner representatives' assembly. It can be seen from all of the above that property owners' committee members were using the law as grounds for exercising their rights. In other words, influence and authority from their rights and the exercise of their rights were not the result of administrative allocation, but granted by law. When dealing with these matters and in their daily routine, property owners' committee members had to study relevant legal documents, and familiarize themselves with and be guided by the Regulations on Residential Estates, Environmental Law, Restrictions on Noise regulations, and so on. When they dealt with an issue, they would follow regulations, be it the calculation of quantity, the criteria for property purveyance, or finding precedence in the press or from similar cases in other residential areas. Organizations that members often went to for assistance included legal bodies, lawyers, government environmental protection departments, administrations of industry and commerce, and media, including newspapers and television stations. Members also invited the neighborhood committee to the owners' representatives' assembly and to witness voting in competitive tendering.

## PUBLIC RESPONSIBILITY

In some estates in Shanghai, the property owners' committees also have the authority to approve the use of funds for large-scale maintenance and construction. In these cases property companies require approval from the property owners' committee at the planning stage, particularly for investment in maintenance. This prevents wasteful services, and thereby keeps under control any charges to owners. To do that, the property owners' committee needs to control the budget for the estate according to the relevant laws on finance, accounting, and borrowing.[10] Thus, this citizens' organization is now taking on the responsibility of budget supervision, whereby, indirectly, it also plays a supervisory role in the development of public facilities within the estate.

The property owners' committee has also formulated an "owners' convention" for residents to regulate their own behavior. The convention comes into effect after being passed at the owners' assembly. It stipulates that the use of property and the transaction of its ownership must be conducted in accordance with the law; that residents must cooperate with the management of the estate by the property company; that residents must pay the charges and fees and must not occupy communal areas, climb over the perimeter walls, park at will, draw graffiti, set up stalls, or leave litter; and that residents are liable for personal injury to others and damage to other people's properties. This is a rational step in the development of public facilities and budget management. It is also indicative of citizens' autonomy according to the law.

## INTERNAL STRUCTURE AND ACTIVITIES

The property owners' committee usually consists of five to seven members, all of whom are residents on the estate. The director of the property owners' committee does not have any more power than members. The director's function is to call meetings. His personal view cannot influence the way members vote. In the case of Qing Shui Yuan, the main members of the property owners' committee were divided on the issue of competitive tendering. In the end, some members withdrew for the rest to cast their votes. The activities of the property owners' committee are mainly to gather views, communicate information, negotiate problems, liaise with relevant organizations, and discuss action plans.

From this we can observe that first, the property owners' committee is a public organization in a community. As such, it is driven by the "public" interest of the residents. Its actions follow different social regulations. These are self-autonomy, choice, matching rights with responsibilities, participation, public authorization, citizens' responsibility, and actions in accordance with the law. This distinguishes the property owners' committee from "private" organizations and administratively appointed "public" organizations. Property owners' committees are changing the principles upon which society is organized and to which people have become accustomed. Second, the emergence of this type of community public organization in cities, as well as their efforts to enter the public domain and to manage public affairs, has given rise to a new sphere of public activity. This sphere integrates the shared interests of the citizens, and also promotes cooperation, strengthens autonomy, encourages participation, and reinforces the trust, supervision, and self-control that is based on agreement among citizens. Third, community citizens' organizations mediate between governmental organizations and individuals. They link up citizens with the government. They promote the need for law and its dissemination. They help to improve the organization of society according to law. Fourth, this development is also creating new social capital,[11] social cooperation, trust, and a new social identity as citizens. It in turn fosters a new kind of social relationship between individuals and the public, amongst social organizations, and between society and state organizations. The development is also giving rise to public policies concerning citizens' own interests as well as fostering spontaneous and important independent organizations that are recognized by the public.

At the core of this transformation in social relations is the notion that parties are bound by agreement. This means that the relationship between managers and the managed has become one in which both parties to an agreement have corresponding rights and responsibilities, each able to hold the other to account. Clearly, this is a restructuring as well as a transfer of social rights.

## REACTIONS FROM THE NEIGHBORHOOD
## COMMITTEE AND THE CONSEQUENCES

Despite the mandate given by the Administrative Regulations of Residential Properties of Shanghai, the property owners' committee challenged the authority of existing community public organizations such as the Qing Shui Yuan Neighborhood Committee, the District Property Bureau, the Street Affairs Office, and the District Land Planning Bureau, all of which had mandates from the district government. Thus, the conflict between the property owners' committee and the property management company became in effect a conflict between the property owners' committee and the abovementioned organizations over the power of public management. During the conflict, the property company received strong support from the existing public organizations. The Street Affairs Office instructed the property company not to "transfer maintenance fees to the property owners' committee's account" so as to stop the property owners' committee from controlling the finances.[12] Senior officials of the Office issued three instructions so as to interfere with the property owners' committee's meeting on competitive tendering. These were first, to let the property company apologize to the property owners' committee for any inappropriate actions; second, to heed the advice of the Party Branch at the Street Affairs Office that the property owners' committee should unite with the neighborhood committee; and third, to suspend competitive tendering.[13] Neither the Street Affairs Office nor the neighborhood committee would tolerate a property owners' committee "mis-positioning itself."

From the point of view of some property owners' committees, they are the sole authority in the residential estates. Externally, they consider themselves a social group with no one above them and no one to control them. Internally, they have every say. Everything within the estate has to be decided by them, no matter how big or small the matter is. Property companies must do what they say. Nobody has the right to object.[14]

Thus, the power struggle between the property owners' committee and the Street Affairs Office and the neighborhood committee is a dispute about who rules when it comes to regulating social order. Management organizations at the grassroots, such as the Street Affairs Office and the neighborhood committee, are authorized by local governments to maintain social order. Thus, they believe their authority to govern comes from their authorization through administrative channels in the form of documents from higher authorities and by virtue of their authoritative position, which is recognized by higher authorities. Consequently, the neighborhood committee issued several documents carrying its stamp to instruct the property company what to do. When the property owners' committee demanded that the property company transfer the maintenance fund to the property owners' committee account in accordance with the Regulations,[15] the neighborhood committee instructed the company, "you cannot transfer the property maintenance fund to the property owners' committee's account at your own will".[16] After the property owners' committee voted to switch to a new management company, the neighborhood committee instructed the current one as follows, "we require your company to continue managing the property within the estate and to not hand any documents or maintenance funds over to anybody else." These instructions required the property company to act under the guidance of the neighborhood committee instead of at the request of the property owners' committee. As a result, the property owners' committee's request to the property company was ineffective.

However, the property owners' committee's authority came from the owners' assembly and statutes. There were 67 eligible representatives. Over 50 percent of them signed a statement supporting the property owners' committee. The property owners' committee sought advice from lawyers regarding the legality of the neighborhood committee calling an owners' assembly. The law firm, Xu Yi Zhu in Shanghai, issued a statement "Disputing The Illegally Called Owners' Assembly and Statement to All Owners' Representatives."[17] However, neither the statement signed by owners' representatives nor the statement by the lawyers were sufficiently authoritative. The focus was now on the views of the owners' representatives, who were divided on the issue of who had the right to call an assembly. As there was no clear definition as to who was entitled to call an assembly, each side tried to call an assembly in order to pass a resolution in their favor. In its notice of an owners' assembly, the Street Affairs Office said:

"The agenda for the assembly is a vote on the following matters related to Qing Shui Wan Residential Estate. 1. Shouldn't we cancel the management contract that the property owners' committee has signed with Shang Fang [the new property company]? 2. In view of the increased number of residents on the estate, shouldn't we increase the number of property owners' committee members, or hold a fresh election? The format of the conference: there will be no debate, just a vote on the motions."[18]

The property owners' committee, on the other hand, wanted to get the assembly to approve the new contract. In their view, the notice from the Street Affairs Office to reform the property owners' committee was a "decision by the Land Planning Bureau and the Street Affairs Office to elbow aside the property owners' committee, although it was not within their power to make such a decision." In the property owners' committee's view, these bodies "wanted to see a new property owners' committee formed by people they approved of." The property owners' committee decided "to take legal action."[19] As the two parties had made conflicting proposals, and there was total confusion about rights and responsibilities, each party ended up trying to stop the other from calling a meeting. Suing and countersuing continue to date.[20] The dispute led to extreme actions. Failing to switch to a new company through competitive tendering, the property owners' committee tried to increase the pressure by starting a boycott of fee payment. They felt that there was no other means of containing the property company. As peaceful and open competitive tendering was not respected, rumors about certain members were rampant. Owners could not get accurate information. They split into two extreme groups, vehemently supporting their own side with no hope of a compromise. Several assemblies later, there was still no agreement. As we can see, there was a powerful organizational force at play that wanted the grassroots to be governed within the existing power structure. It wanted to make sure that if the property owners' committee ignored this structure, it would have no place in it. On the other hand, the property owners' committee felt "The Sixth office, the Street Office, the Neighborhood Committee, the Land Planning Bureau and Open Commerce have all sided with the property company. Thus, the property owners' committee is isolated and without support."[21]

As a result, there was no way of negotiating a solution to the conflict. The dispute was passed back to the existing power structure to be resolved by orders from higher authorities in the government. Administrative measures were taken to request Shang Fang Property Company to withdraw their bid for the contract. It was made clear to them that their relationship with Qing Yuan Property was that of "brotherhood." In other words, to enter into conflict with Qing Yuan Property was inappropriate, inconvenient, and should not have been considered in the first place. At the same time, the property owners' committee failed to bypass the district government administration to seek rights relief from a third party, the court, although they continued to try. This is because to become a legal party to the proceedings, the plaintiff needed them to submit their "administrative seal for official records." In this case, although the property owners' committee had followed the standard procedure of the Public Security Bureau with regards to their seal, it had not submitted the report on "Stamp Submitted For Official Record" to the District Comprehensive Planning and Land Bureau. Therefore, the property owners' committee could not use that stamp for legal purposes. It could not be a plaintiff. The case of the property owners' committee versus the property company regarding the latter refusing to hand over property management to the new company was thrown out by the court.[22] Thus, the property owners' committee does not have the legal right to bring a case to court prior to approval from the administrations concerned. Its dispute with the property company cannot be resolved through legal channels. The final solution lies in administrative, and not legal, means.

Although the ownership of property has changed, that is, owners have evidence to prove their ownership, they still cannot acquire the right to manage the properties. For example, owners still cannot choose or decide what companies to use to manage their properties. There is no fundamental difference here between this case and the power structure on a residential estate in Beijing described at the beginning of the chapter. When previous owners, such as employers, have lost their influence, new owners emerge in place of them with a new property ownership relationship. But the balance between rights and responsibilities has not changed accordingly. It remains strongly supported by the power of the administrative system that remains. In that power system, the relationship between the new owner and the property company is perceived by the administrative authorities to be the same as the one on traditional residential estates. The property company is still the manager with a monopoly and special protection. At a macrolevel, the structure of this relationship does not recognize the owner and the property company as autonomous entities with corresponding rights and responsibilities that therefore can hold the other party to account through a contractual agreement. It still resorts to a traditional method for conflict resolution, namely, administrative orders.

## DISCUSSION

By attempting to hire a property company through competitive tendering, Qing Shui Yuan Property Owners' Committee was in effect developing a new system. At the surface level, it was just about making property companies compete for management contracts. Yet compared with what had happened before, there were major differences. First, property companies had to compete for a market share instead of being allocated business and protected. This rationale should stimulate companies to improve the quality of services instead of simply hunting for rents. Even for Qing Yuan Property, such a system was still fair, even though it might have resulted in their contract not being renewed. It was possible that Qing Yuan would improve its services, reduce costs, and go on to win contracts in future rounds. Second, more opportunities to win contracts would lead to better quality property services. This would satisfy owners and the government alike, and be consistent with the public interest of society. Third, the new contractual relationship between property companies and owners was necessary for a self-regulated and self-managed society so that cooperation between members of the society could be organized through a contractual agreement between them. But this process was abruptly halted as higher authorities in the administrative structure put a stop to competitive tendering. This in effect protected Qing Yuan Property's exclusive right in the management of the estate. The argument for protecting Qing Yuan Property was perhaps that Qing Shui Yuan estate was developed by Qing Yuan Property's parent organization. Therefore, Qing Yuan Property had the first right of refusal and permanent ownership of the management resources. Although Qing Yuan Property had been devolved from its parent company, and has since become an independent commercial enterprise, at critical moments of competition, its parent company still considers itself to have the power to allocate management resources. In other words, devolvement has not eliminated the protection of one's subordinates. This thus enables Qing Yuan Property to acquire quasi-ownership of property resources. Even if someone else provides better services at lower costs, they are not entitled to any part of the business. Nor are the consumers and owners/residents allowed to choose and decide.

There are thus two competing perspectives. The property owners' committee felt that the property right rested with the owners, not with the property company. The property owners' committee wanted to define the standards of accountability themselves and wanted to replace companies that did not meet the standards. In their view, the power to decide on the management of the property derived from their ownership. Qing Yuan Property felt that they had an indisputable, de facto right to manage the estate for historical reasons. It was they who had carried out land acquisition, development, construction, and investment. The property owners' committee's argument thus infringed upon their right. The reaction from the district government was to support Qing Yuan Property through administrative control. Administrative control in this case meant that it impeded the development of a contractual relationship between social members according to their own will, a contractual relationship that was the basis of cooperation and mutual reliance between social members. The benefit of such a contractual relationship lies in the fact that when a transaction is taking place between social entities, be it individuals, organizations, or institutions, all terms and conditions will be negotiated between the parties involved. "Unless all parties believe that they will benefit from the transaction, they will not be able to reach an agreement" (Friedman and Friedman, 1979 [Chinese Translation, Shangwu Press, 1998: 55]) In social interaction, if there is an agreement to protect rights, to specify the obligations for the parties concerned, then it follows that there will be self-regulatory responsibility; there will be a relationship, whereby both parties will be able to monitor the other; there will be a relationship of mutual reliance so that the advance of one party's interests depends on cooperation from the other. This will encourage widespread cooperation. The interests of all parties will be controlled and coordinated in society. In this case study, such a relationship was being developed between Qing Shui Yuan Property Owners' Committee and the property company bidding for the management contract. The opportunity for such a development was stifled by administrative interference.

The property owners' committee is a kind of citizens' organization. It wants to share some social rights. Its purpose lies in the management of social property. It aims to protect property by aggregating as well as representing the interest of owners (residents). The emergence of this kind of citizens' organization comes hand in hand with social change. To some degree, it replaces the function of employers that previously represented residents. The difference is that this kind of citizens' organization attempted to enter the territory of public management, to take on the responsibility of citizens' property management, which had always been the responsibility of appointed organizations such as neighborhood committees and the property management bureau. The appointed organizations are the products of existing systems. Once property ownership changes, their true nature is revealed. They compete with residents in terms of rights and interests. They separate the interests of administrative bodies at the grassroots from the interests of residents. Administrative control reinforces this negative structure, preventing the formation of a new contractual relationship. As such, it has a negative effect on the overall development of society, for it reinforces social structures that heighten conflicts. This is precisely what causes community disputes.

Owners expressed their discontent with Qing Yuan Property by seeking an alternative provider. The company failed to keep residents satisfied, failed to manage their property well, and failed to use the management fees efficiently. This cannot be said to promote the public interest. On the contrary, owners have the right to demand benefits to society. Every citizen is an actual or potential owner. Citizens' duty to manage, citizens' demand for quality social services, and citizens' supervision over irresponsible behavior will benefit all citizens. If there is a better arrangement such as competitive selection of a property company, the benefit will in principle extend to all citizens. In that sense, one can say that such an arrangement benefits the public. What is more important is that the principle of "competitive tendering" has wider applications than the principle of "historical precedence." The substandard service provided by Qing Yuan Property meant that they were not competitive. What was also unfair was that instead of improving the quality of services, they requested administrative protection of their monopoly of resources. The beneficiaries of their action were themselves, not the members of the public. Compared with the public interest of the urban communities, that is, the owners, their interests were the particularistic interests of one group. Ethically, it was also not fair. If a property company is not able to provide satisfactory services to the public, why should they retain the perpetual right to manage resources? Clearly, the outcome of the case in this study was unfair. It protected the party that failed to serve the public interest and protected low efficiency.

The development of social contractual relationships is related to the development of a range of systems. These systems will mean that evading responsibilities bears costs. When owners have the right to choose, evading responsibilities will lead to serious consequences for the property company. It will lose its position in the management market, which is a very high cost. The potential consequences for the company thus could be enormous. But if the owners do not have the right to choose, the property company will not have to pay a high cost, even if they are evading serious responsibilities. Not only that, the government will have to spend a considerable amount of time and energy to get the company to improve its services. Developing owners' civil rights can change the circumstances under which the government has to interfere. It will substantially increase citizens' opportunities to exercise their duties in social supervision, therefore reducing the need to chase rents. This case shows that administrative interference in the owners' right to choose can create social costs: the protection of a property company that did not want to improve services and the protection of their dominance in this particular management resources market; an increased burden on the government to mediate a settlement and maintain social order; frequent conflicts in the community; no progress in the development of citizens' rights to decide on the management of their private property; overreliance on governmental organizations; one-sided overburdening of government with rights and responsibilities in public management, and its inability to transfer these rights and responsibilities to citizens; insufficient social pressure on the property company to improve management; and ineffective control of attempts to evade responsibility in public service and management.

If government interference makes a difference, all property companies will do everything they can through administrative channels so as to gain advantage. Qing Yuan Property did just that—they went one level up in the administrative structure to seek protection. If this were to continue, private organizations, enterprises, social groups, and special interest groups would compete with each other to establish relations with administrative organizations. This could develop into disputes between administrative bodies, between different levels of an administration, or between administrations across industries. If the dispute took place between a government body and a social organization, it could lead to a situation of "state versus society." Clearly, if a dispute develops, spreads, and escalates, it not only damages administrative authority and efficiency, but also has a negative effect on the establishment of social cooperation. It encourages reliance by social organizations on the government, instead of on society, and thus hinders society developing its own self-reliance, self-regulation, control, and the ability to supervise. Such a development is clearly not conducive to social order.

Property owners' committees want to control the service and costs of property management by demanding their right to choose. That is a natural development in citizens' rights and responsibilities. From the government's point of view, this is also an opportunity for administrative bodies to transfer some of the duties of social management. To do that, one needs to weaken administrative allocation and monopoly through protection so as to introduce a completely different relationship between these bodies and the owners. If Qing Yuan Property wishes to maintain its control of the management resources, it will have to change from being a quasi-administrative body to an enterprise operating according to market principles. It will have to put itself on similar terms to the owners in terms of rights and responsibilities, and place itself within the restrictions of a contract. In this way the public sphere can provide checks and balances against a monopoly of market rights. But this change in relationship cannot be consolidated, unless there is support from a wider, more comprehensive system. That is, the way rights are allocated needs to be changed. In this particular case, it would require owners' autonomy. It would depend on the representatives of the citizens, that is, the property owners' committee, being allowed to participate in management, so that they could exercise power of control over the property company through their choice of manager to ensure value for money. For society as a whole, by changing the way rights are allocated, one will be able to establish a binding relationship between parties. The final outcome will be that all parties will be moving in the direction of better and more rational behavior that is consistent with the public interest in society. This is a form of social integration at lower cost and higher efficiency. It is also a way for members of society to maintain social order through self-regulation.

To summarize, the social changes apparent in the Qing Shui Yuan case point to a demand in society for the establishment of some fundamental principles of citizenship. These include the establishment of citizens' responsibility to participate in social management; the improvement of social trust and supervision; the development of a social relationship with corresponding rights and responsibilities; and the observation of "impersonalism" as the norm for social relationships rather than the particularism of highly personalized relations and transactions. Meanwhile, some citizen's organizations are already practicing these principles. This represents a transition toward a society ruled by law, the basis of which is the impersonalized social relationship. Clearly, this is an improvement that meets citizens' needs in a broader context, a "public improvement" (Rawls, 1997 (Chinese Translation, 1999)). It is consistent with the principle of "fair exchange," as opposed to "fair allocation" (Hayek, 1978). The value embodied in this improvement can well be shared with other public organizations and be consistent with the objectives of the government.

## FUTURE PROSPECTS FOR GOVERNANCE AT THE GRASSROOTS

This case study of the Qing Shui Yuan dispute is a challenge for governance at the grassroots. The key question is whether it is a matter of citizens' governing themselves or being ruled from above by government. The differences between the two revolve around the qualifications for entry into the public sphere, the rights of public representatives, the mandate of the public management organizations, and their terms of reference, as well as the basic principles they embody. China is at a crossroads. Should it strengthen the powers and functions of traditional public organizations at the grassroots? If so, China will need to resolve the problem of how public interest is to be represented. Failing to do so means that there will be frequent conflicts at the grassroots as members of the public are compelled to find alternative channels of representation to defend their rights. The ever-increasing number of community disputes in Beijing and Shanghai are testimony to such a trend. Or should China strengthen the role of new, public organizations in establishing social order, such as self-regulating property owners' committees? If so, China will need to resolve, amongst other system-related issues, the matter of how to devolve the power of public management. If this latter route is followed, then it raises a number of issues around the nature of public organizations, specialization in public management, and nonpolitical staffing of public institutions. Though changes in government regulations and laws as a result of WTO entry are aimed at further integrating the national economy into the global economy, increasing economic liberalization and the extension of property rights will also require a basic redefinition of how civil affairs are governed.

## NOTES

1. I would like to thank the Foundation of Chinese Youth that awarded me a research grant for the year 2000–2001. This chapter draws upon the work of Juergen Habermas on the public sphere. It uses the concept of public sphere as presented in his chapter "The Public Sphere," in Chen, 1998.

2. Chen Xian. "WTO entry prompts government reform." *China Daily*, January 4, 2002, 4(N).

3. Source: records from visits by Zhang Lei, Sociology Department, Beijing University, 2001, 1 (unpublished).

4. Source: records from visits by Zhang Lei, Sociology Department, Beijing University, 2001, 1 (unpublished).

5. See documents about the dispute issued by the district development office (unpublished).

6. On citizenship see the works of Barbalet, 1991; Turner, 1993; Bendix, 1964; and Marshall, 1964.

7. Interview record, a member of the neighborhood committee, 2001: 1.

8. Interview record, a member of the property owners' committee, 2001: 1.

9. Source: "answer letter" response to public opinion by property owners' committee, 2001, 1 (unpublished).

10. Source: *Yezhu Gongyue* (the Property Owners' Agreement), 2000, 7 (unpublished).

11. A term used by R. D. Putnam, "The prosperous community: Social capital and public life," *American Prospect* 13 (1993): 35–42.

12. Source: A letter from street affairs office to Chang Yuan property management company (unpublished).

13. Interview record: A member of the neighborhood commitee, 2001, 1 (unpublished).

14. Source: A working report by the district property bureau (unpublished).

15. Source: A letter from the neighborhood committee to the property management company, 2000, 4, 29 (unpublished).

16. Source: A letter from the neighborhood committee to the property management company, 2000, 8, 25 (unpublished).

17. Source: A working report, by the local government, no. 13–14 (unpublished).

18. Source: A notice about the meeting of the property owner's deputy, by the Street Affairs Office, 2000, 8, 4 (unpublished).

19. Source: A working report about the dispute, by the property owners' committee, 2000, 8, 10 (unpublished).

20. See "Memo on the dispute," by Zhanglei (unpublished).

21. Interview record: head of the property owners' committee, 2001, 1, 18.

22. Interview record: head of the property owners' committee, 2001, 1, 18.

# 8

# New Directions in Civil Society: Organizing around Marginalized Interests

*Jude Howell*

Governance in China has often been described as totalitarian or authoritarian, or conversely as nonliberal and nondemocratic. This is mirrored in the very limited space available for autonomous association and the narrow, constricted nature of political society in the first three decades after Liberation. With the relaxation of political controls in the reform period, the space for intellectual debate and for associational life has opened up and widened out. The proliferation of independent organizations in the late 1980s led scholars to talk in terms of an emerging civil society in China that might be the engine of democratic regime change.[1] Such normative aspirations were shattered by the events of 1989. The usefulness and applicability of civil society began to be contested and alternative concepts and theories such as public sphere and corporatism entered the discourse of China scholars.[2] Subsequent studies of China's social organizations underlined their deep links with the Party/state and the stunting effects of the corporatist regulatory framework.

Yet from the early 1990s onward, the development of an intermediary sphere of relatively independent organizing has entered a new phase that has been little analyzed or documented. This phase is characterized, first, by the emergence of a new stratum of organizations concerned with the interests of marginalized groups in society, and second, by the proliferation of institutional forms shaped to circumvent onerous state restrictions on association. The sphere of more independent association in China is no longer the abode of those with much to gain from the reform process, such as intellectuals, professionals, and businesspeople, but also of interests that are marginalized or losing out in the process of reform.

The purpose of this chapter is twofold: first, to describe and explain the emergence of, character of, and policy influence of a stratum of social organizations concerned with marginalized interests in the 1990s; second, to consider the implications of these cases for how we set about theorizing governance processes and civil society in China. The chapter is divided into three sections. In the first section, we focus on the emergence of a new stratum of organizations in the 1990s that are concerned with the interests of marginalized groups in society. We then look closely at the process of societal organization in three specific fields, namely, HIV/AIDS, labor rights, and gender in the workplace. In the third part we move on to explore the extent to which these specific organizations are characteristic of corporatist or civil society-type organizations, and constitute part of a public sphere. Finally, we consider the implications of these findings for understanding and conceptualizing processes of governance in China.

## A NEW WIND IN CIVIL SOCIETY: ORGANIZING AROUND MARGINALIZED INTERESTS

In response to the turmoil of June 1989, the Committee of the State Council issued in October of that year the Management Regulations on the Registration of Social Organizations, replacing the 1950 regulations. These required organizations to affiliate to a supervisory body (*guakao danwei*), which was responsible for overseeing the day-to-day affairs of its dependent associations, and to register with the Division of the Supervision of Social Organizations in the Ministry of Civil Affairs, in effect a form of corporatist licensing.[3] The 1989 regulations heralded a truce between the Party/state and civil society organizations, whereby the Party/state defined anew the boundaries of permissible associational activity, but did not push these back to the highly constricted frontiers of the pre-reform period. This is not least because it also recognizes the many positive functions that more autonomous social organizations can perform in the context of rapid economic and social change, such as serving as new channels for the dissemination of Party policy, delivering specialized services, coordinating sectoral policy, mediating disputes, and welfare and advisory services. On the grounds of financial and administrative irregularities in some social organizations,[4] the Ministry of Civil Affairs sought to reassert its authority by revising the regulations in November 1998, rendering the registration process even more stringent.[5] As some social organizations were disbanded and others cautioned, a new truce was drawn, tilting the balance of power further toward the Party/state. The tightening of regulations marked, on the one hand, an attempt to reassert control, but, on the other hand, a realization that the expansion of social organizations was crucial for the reform of both state institutions and enterprises.[6]

Yet, truces and boundaries are never congealed for eternity. Since the early 1990s, dynamic actors in China, located in informal networks, associations, salons, clubs, and projects, have continued to chip away at the frayed edges of state authority, thereby contesting and redefining the borders of the associational sphere. It is within this context of contested boundaries and an uncertain truce that the development of a new phase of civil society from the early to mid-1990s onward becomes particularly interesting. The two outstanding characteristics of this new phase are, first, the more rapid growth of associations concerned with providing services on behalf of and/or representing the interests of groups marginalized in the reform process; and second, the flourishing of new forms of association such as networks, centers, user groups, projects, and third or fourth-level associations, which bypass the need to register as social organizations. We explore each of these features in turn and analyze the combination of variables facilitating the emergence of this new stratum of associations.

Since market reforms began, social organizations have operated in a range of domains, such as academia, professional interests, trade, business, culture, arts, services, charitable work, religion, friendship, and recreation. But in the 1980s and early 1990s, the majority of social organizations have been located in the fields of academe, professions, business, and trades. Pei's study of a sample of social organizations finds that in 1978, 50 percent of all registered national associations were concerned with natural sciences, technology, and engineering (1998: 292). With the increasing diversification of civil society, by 1992 such organizations accounted for 17.5 percent of all registered associations. However, with the growth of registered academic associations for the social sciences, humanities, and management studies from 13 in 1978 to 224 in 1992, the total percentage of associations accounted for by academic interests remained high at 46 percent. Similarly business and trade organizations grew dramatically in the 1980s, from three in 1978 to 212 in 1992, accounting for 27 percent of all registered national social organizations. These tendencies of diversification and the uneven growth of social organizations in different domains is also repeated at lower levels.

The rapid proliferation of business, trade, professional, and academic organizations in the 1980s and early 1990s reflects both the changing nature of the economy and the Party/state's recognition of the need to liberalize spaces for association to facilitate the development of the market. In 1988 the renowned Chinese economist Xue Muqiao argued that social organizations in the economic sphere could "serve as a bridge between the state and enterprises" in a new form of indirect regulation, avoiding both the deficiencies of state planning and the potential anarchy of the market (Xue, 1988). By encouraging the growth of professional associations, trades, and business associations, the Party/state could realize the desire to move away from direct regulation toward a more hands-off, indirect management of the economy. This allowed business and trades people to establish horizontal networks of interest, communication, and information, thereby enhancing information flows about market changes. It also enabled relevant industrial, agricultural, and commercial governmental departments to shift some of their functions onto these associations, thereby contributing in the long run toward a more streamlined state concerned with macroplanning rather than microregulation. In promoting the development of academic organizations, the Party/state hoped to unleash intellectual creativity and dynamism, which it deemed essential for modernizing China's economy and maximizing the absorption of new foreign technologies and processes. The members of the academic, professional, business, and trades organizations were also precisely those that were benefiting from the process of economic reform and had much to gain from the new economic direction. The rapid growth of these organizations during the 1980s and early 1990s reflects the dual imperatives of, on the one hand, the market, and, on the other hand, the Party/state. Fostering the development of social organizations is thus a key element in the Party/state's strategy to create a "small government and big society."[7]

In contrast, charitable organizations concerned with the interests of vulnerable and marginalized groups experienced only very modest growth in the 1980s. Pei's study reveals that the number of national-level charitable groups and foundations increased from two in 1978 to only 16 in 1992, accounting for only two percent of all registered national social organizations, a pattern that is mirrored at lower levels (1998: 292). Similarly, public affairs organizations, such as consumer societies, environmental groups, and children's affairs groups, grew from zero in 1978 to only eight in 1992. The very modest growth of charitable organizations in the 1980s reflects in part the continuing responsibility of urban state and collective enterprises for the welfare of their employees along with expectations that the state should be the key provider of welfare services. It also relates to the lack of a private sector or services sector that could act as an alternative provider, and the absence of significant sources of private wealth that might be used philanthropically.

From the early 1990s onward, this trend began to change as a new stratum of associations concerned with societal groups that are marginalized and vulnerable in the process of reform emerged, marking a new phase in the development of civil society. These new organizations include women's groups; legal counselling centers for women, children, and workers; prisoners' wives groups; rural development centers and organizations; associations for people living with HIV/AIDs; self-help cancer groups; poverty alleviation associations; disabled groups; and charitable foundations.

The exact number of these organizations is difficult to quantify,[8] not least because of the rudimentary nature of data collection at county and district levels and the avoidance by many of these associations of the registration process.[9] Information thus has to be gleaned from a variety of organizations such as the Ministry of Civil Affairs, international donor agencies, Chinese publications on nongovernmental organizations (NGOs) and social organizations, the China Non-Profit Organizations Information Network, the NGO Center at Tsinghua University, and relevant journals such as the *China Brief*, which regularly monitors the development of associations concerned with social issues. In 2001 the *China Brief* produced a directory of 250 NGOs operating in the fields of health, environment, education, gender, arts and culture, urban welfare, rural development, and poverty. Even though access to information and funding constraints prevented the investigators from tracking down every relevant organization in every province and county in China, it is nevertheless striking how many social organizations are engaged in welfare and charitable work compared with the 1980s.[10] Some specific organizations such as women's organizations have been relatively well documented in both Chinese and English scholarly work.[11]

Though the development of organizations concerned with marginalized interests has grown in the 1990s, the numbers are still limited, particularly for those marginalized interests such as people living with HIV/AIDs or sex workers, who encounter considerable social prejudice, or those interests which the Party/state perceives to threaten social stability, such as workers' rights organizations. Moreover, amongst registered social organizations, academic, professional, and trades organizations continue to dominate. Of the 9,190 new social organizations approved in 1999, 5,748, that is 62 percent, fell into this category (Ministry of Civil Affairs, 2000: 132–133). By the end of 1999, academic, professional, and trades associations accounted for almost two-thirds of all social organizations (Ministry of Civil Affairs, 2000: 134–135).

What then accounts for the expansion of organizations concerned with marginalized and vulnerable groups in the 1990s? Why did this development not occur earlier in the 1980s? The reasons are complex, involving both domestic and external factors. On the domestic side, the key factors include the deepening of economic reform following Deng Xiaoping's southern trip in 1992, the continuing reform of the state, the formulation of a new strategy for social security and protection, and indeed the second characteristic of the new phase, namely, the ingenuity of social actors in evading restrictive registration requirements by establishing associations by other means. On the external side, the salient variables are the Fourth World Conference on Women held in 1995 and the growth of external aid to China in the 1990s.

In the wake of Deng Xiaoping's tour of southern China in 1992, the process of economic reform deepened as the reformers embarked upon some of the more tricky and contentious aspects of restructuring. Of particular relevance is the acceleration of state enterprise reform from the mid-1990s onward, which led to the closure of many enterprises and to the retrenchment of well over 33 million workers, according to official statistics.[12] The need to provide a safety net for the laid-off (*xiagang*) and unemployed as a result of state enterprise reform was a prime stimulus to the redesign of the welfare system, which had in the past relied in urban areas primarily upon state enterprise and in cases of dire need upon the Ministry of Civil Affairs. Given that the Party/state sought to minimize its role in the micromanagement of the economy and social welfare, it began to develop alternative systems of protection, such as medical and social insurance schemes involving contributions from employers, employees, and local government; private provision of health care; community development schemes that provided employment to laid-off workers and inspired local self-help initiatives; charitable initiatives such as child sponsorship, the highly popular Project Hope being a case in point; and social organizations that provided services to vulnerable and marginalized groups such as the disabled, elderly, children, women, and the sick. These initiatives in turn are set against a broader background of restructuring and downsizing of state organs, which has gathered pace since 1997.[13]

Systemic pressures were thus a key variable underpinning the growth of associations addressing the needs of marginalized and vulnerable groups. The deepening of state enterprise reform could not be achieved unless alternative systems of social protection were set in place. The development of a services sector would also provide an additional source of employment, which could absorb the laid-off and unemployed. Furthermore, as market reforms deepened in the 1990s, the negative dimensions of economic restructuring intensified, reflected in new forms of urban poverty, unemployment, and increased income disparities. For the political elite, maintaining social stability in a context of minimal political reform was paramount. Hence, the creation of a new architecture of intermediary organizations to deal with welfare issues was one way of alleviating poverty and reducing discontent.

As for the rapid growth of women's organizations from the early 1990s, a key factor was the hosting by China of the Fourth World Conference on Women in Beijing in 1995 (Howell, 1997). Though some earlier independent women's organizations and research centers had emerged in the late 1980s, women's organizations mushroomed in number in the run-up to the 1995 Conference. The changes within the All-China Women's Federation, and in particular the recognition that it could not address the diverse needs of an increasingly differentiated constituency of women, contributed to the development of a space where women could organize more autonomously. As the NGO Forum would also be held in Beijing, it was politically important, particularly in the light of Tiananmen, that China could display a contingent of active, nongovernmental women's organizations. The preparatory process for this grand international event exposed cadres from the All-China Women's Federation, activists, and scholars to the role of women's nongovernmental organizations in other countries, thereby creating a climate of openness toward the development of such organizations. Women across China seized this moment to gather in salons to discuss women's issues, to set up self-help groups for divorced women and single mothers, to raise sensitive issues such as domestic violence, and to establish organizations providing services to female migrants, rural women, and women seeking divorce. It was a moment of opening, a moment of intellectual and organizational dynamism, and the beginnings of a public sphere where the discussion of gender issues was no longer confined to Party/state institutions.

International aid agencies and foundations played a key role not only in facilitating preparations for the 1995 Conference on women but also in stimulating the emergence of organizations concerned with social issues. In the 1990s international aid agencies expanded their programs in China, whilst at the same time the activities of international NGOs grew. Support from these international agencies has catalyzed the development of a number of associations and centers, such as the Yunnan Reproductive Health Association, the Yunnan Participatory Rural Appraisal Network, the Center for Integrated Agricultural Development in Beijing, the Shenzhen Women's Migrant Workers' Center, and the Center for Biodiversity and Indigenous Knowledge in Yunnan province.

The second key feature in the development of civil society since the 1990s, namely, the continuing bypassing of the registration process, has also contributed to the emergence of this new stratum of organizations concerned with marginalized interests.[14] Though the 1989 and 1998 regulations on social organizations proved to be a powerful mechanism for stunting the growth of registered intermediary forms of association,[15] they did not succeed in hemming in associational activity. Finding the conditions for registering a social organization too onerous, social actors have responded with ingenuity to find alternative ways of associating, such as affiliating to established associations; setting up research institutes and centers under the protective umbrella of more liberal university environments; forming networks, salons, clubs and informal, loose groups; and organizing through projects.[16] In this way they have recaptured associational space, pushed back the boundaries set by the Party/state, and thereby redefined the truces staked out in both 1989 and 1998. The practice of affiliating to a registered association as a second or third or even fourth-level association obviates the need to register with the relevant department of the Ministry of Civil Affairs. Affiliated associations are only required to submit a file to higher authorities. Similarly, by forming a network, members not only avoid having to register, but also are able to establish relations across the country. The current regulatory framework prohibits registered organizations from setting up branches in other provinces for fear that they might give rise to multiple and competing concentrations of power.[17] Setting up as a network, salon, or informal grouping avoids the administrative baggage of councils and board members that associations tend to have.

Nevertheless, whether a particular group of people can succeed in by-passing the registration process and deflecting the attention of the Party/state depends not least on how threatening their activities appear to local and/or central authorities. The boundaries of this space are thus fragile, insecure, and subject to repression. This is most evident in cases of organizations attempting to address the needs and interests of laid-off workers, in which most initiatives are quickly banned and forced underground, or in the case of spiritual groups such as the Falun Gong, whose capacity to penetrate and mobilize society took the CCP by surprise, unleashing a fierce response.[18]

In brief, a new layer of associations concerned with the interests of those marginalized or losing out in the reform process has emerged in the 1990s, adding another sediment in the complex archaeology of associational life in reformist China. Addressing the problems of marginalization, poverty, and equity, this stratum confronts head-on some of the social consequences of rapid economic change. As such, it is potentially disturbing for the Chinese Communist Party, which increasingly stakes its legitimacy upon its success in promoting economic growth. By dealing with thorny issues such as unemployment, discrimination, HIV/AIDS, and gender inequalities, such associations threaten and inevitably serve to test out the solidity of the boundaries marked out in the truces of 1989 and 1998.

In the next section I examine more closely a subsection of this stratum, namely, organizations and individuals operating in the fields of HIV/AIDS, labor rights, and gender in the workplace. All three fields are concerned with issues that are marginalized, either because they are deemed to be highly sensitive politically as with labor rights, or because they invoke social taboos as with HIV/AIDS, or because they concern social groups with low status such as female migrant workers and female laid-off workers. Moreover, these fields overlap to some extent, as issues of labor rights include issues of gender discrimination and HIV/AIDS impinges on employment and gender relations. We draw upon 70 semistructured interviews with Chinese networks, associations, social organizations, projects, and international development agencies in Beijing, Kunming, and Xishuangbanna in Yunnan province, Shenzhen, Xian in Shaanxi province, and Hong Kong during two field visits in autumn 2000 and spring 2001.[19]

## WORKING AT THE MARGINS

Most organizations in the fields of HIV/AIDS, labor rights, and gender in the workplace have not registered as social organizations, but have adopted forms that maintain a greater distance from the state. In most cases they operate under the wing of a host organization such as a registered association or research institute so as to gain status, legitimacy, and protection and also to access potentially important government links. Or they operate out of existing associations or through the mechanism of international donor projects. Aware of the sensitivity of the issues they are dealing with, most calculate that registering as a social organization would not succeed in any case and so do not even attempt this route. Indeed, in two cases, organizations were informally advised by relevant government officials to avoid registering as a social organization and to take another form such as a project or affiliated association on the grounds that this would be less laborious, less time-consuming, and less likely to attract unnecessary government attention. As the head of one association related to me, "We tried to register with the local Civil Affairs Bureau but there is a long way to go if you go directly there. It is a complicated process to register and we are very busy. One of our members works in the Civil Affairs Bureau. He is the author of the first draft of our documents. He said the process of registration was too complicated. It takes too much time. He did not recommend us to go this route." [20] Like potential applicants, local government officials find the regulations tedious and frustrating and are ready to cast a blind eye to people who they judge as safe and as pursuing activities of mutual benefit.[21]

All this has led to a new multitiered configuration of organizing, reaching from registered social organizations at the top to substrata of affiliated centers, networks, groups, and projects. For example, the Yunnan Reproductive Health Association is affiliated to the Yunnan Women's Theoretical Research Association, which in turn is affiliated to the Yunnan Women's Federation. The Yunnan PRA Network is based at the Rural Development Research Center, which in turn falls under the Institute of Geography. Under the PRA Network is a Gender and Development Network. The Yun-Man Development Institute, whose goal is to assist poor and marginalized people, is an independent organization approved under the Science and Technology Commission as a "people's run science and technology group" (*minban keji zuzhi*). The Center for Women's Law Studies and Services in Shaanxi is a project under the Shaanxi Provincial Research Association for Women and Family, which in turn is affiliated to the Women's Federation. The China Aids Network is a second-level association under the China Foundation for the Prevention of STD/AIDS. Other forms of organization "float" within the system, unattached to any particular center, association, or institute, the national gender network being a case in point. The complex, multilayered institutional arrangements distinguish this stratum from professional and business organizations and is crucially related to the marginalized, yet politically sensitive nature of the issues at stake. Within this stratum there are also differences in the ease of organizing around issues, with HIV/AIDS, labor rights, and gender in the workplace being considerably more problematic because of social taboos and political sensitivities than, say, organizing around cancer, the elderly, or the disabled.

( Taboos and social norms around sexuality and sexual behavior )as well as legal and regulatory prohibitions on drug use and sex work underpin the marginalization of people living with HIV/AIDS and relatedly drug addicts and sex workers, and similarly the difficulties in organizing around these issues. Furthermore, the willingness of provincial and local government authorities to address the spread of HIV/AIDS influences considerably the range of governmental and nongovernmental interventions and the space available to discuss and engage critically with government policy. Yunnan province, for example, which is perhaps the most open province in this respect, has collaborated closely with international donor agencies to conduct research, experiment with new practical approaches to prevention and treatment, and develop new policies.[22] These initiatives, which have involved local professional and research associations, have opened up spaces, albeit limited, for the discussion of HIV/AIDS and related government policy. In contrast, Henan province, where unhygienic blood collection led to the spread of HIV/AIDS in several rural areas, has suppressed public discussion of the issue.

Nevertheless there are few registered nongovernmental organizations focusing specifically on HIV/AIDS, not only because of the social taboos surrounding the disease but also because organizing would increase the visibility of drug addiction and sex work, both of which are supposed to be illegal. The key organizations in the field of HIV/AIDS are the China AIDS Network, an interdisciplinary national network of professionals engaged in action research, health awareness, and advisory work, founded in 1994;[23] Beijing Aizhi, an Internet group that played a key role in exposing the spread of HIV/AIDS through a blood plasma factory in Henan, established in 1994;[24] and the China Foundation for the Prevention of STDs and AIDS, a registered foundation of public health professionals involved in research, public education, and intervention, started in 1988.[25]

Social taboos and legal constraints likewise make it difficult for people living with HIV/AIDS, drug addicts, or sex workers, or for their carers, to organize themselves. In 1994, a group of researchers and activists in Yunnan set up the Yunnan HIV/AIDS Care Network (*yunnan guanhai HIV/AIDS gongzuo wangluo*). The group published four newsletters and held three meetings, but due to a lack of money and time the network folded after two years.[26] In 2001 there was only one self-help group for people living with HIV/AIDS, namely, one linked to the Loving Heart Home (*Aixin Jiayuan*), an HIV/AIDS ward in You'an Hospital in Beijing. In March 2002 Mangrove Support Group, a self-support group, was set up in Beijing by a person living with HIV/AIDS.[27] The Loving Heart Home in practice rarely meets and functions at the most as a contact mechanism between outpatients and inpatients, whilst Mangrove plays a more active role as a support group for people living with HIV/AIDS.[28] Other self-help groups have also emerged in

Sichuan, Yunnan, Shanxi, and Xinjiang provinces,[29] and Guangzhou and Shanghai[30].

Aware of the limitations of organizing around HIV/AIDS and sex workers, medical professionals and social science researchers use the openings provided by international donor projects and membership associations such as Yunnan PRA Network and Yunnan Reproductive Health Association to gain experience, sharpen their practical and intellectual tools, and learn about international practices. Existing associations thus provide a springboard for engaging with sensitive issues and also act as a protective shield because of their contacts with government and prestige. In this way they can work in the crevices of a space shaped by restrictive regulatory and legal frameworks and social norms.

The project mechanism has provided a way of organizing around the health needs of sex workers, who constitute one of the growing transmission routes for HIV/AIDS. With the support of international donor funds, the China AIDS Network has piloted a center in Hainan island to provide advice and counselling on HIV/AIDS to sex workers. The only other nongovernmental organizations so far that have tried to address the interests of sex workers, or advocated around their social and economic rights, are some of the legal aid centers for women, which have defended sex workers in court against pimps and taken up cases of enforced prostitution.[31] The Hong Kong sex worker concern group *Ziteng* has also organized workshops and conferences in China and other Asian countries to promote the self-organization of sex workers, involving sex workers from China and other countries.[32] For some, involvement in projects is a strategic step toward setting up a nongovernmental organization. As one researcher in Kunming stated: "My vision is to do a range of projects on social issues so that the government recognizes these issues and your work and then on this basis to set up an NGO."[33] So, in a context where establishing a registered social organization in the domain of HIV/AIDS and sex work is highly constricted, donor-supported projects serve as a training ground for potential NGO leaders and initiators.

Making an issue a public issue is an important part in the shaping of public spheres, and more broadly, in the development of the organizational building blocks of civil society. In contexts where the ruling government dominates the determination of public issues through its control over the media, research agendas, and political activity, the actions of individuals who draw attention to issues that are marginalized, repressed, and held invisible is particularly important in the development of public spheres and civil society. Salient examples here are Dr. Gao Yaojie of Henan province, who has highlighted the plight of poor farmers infected with HIV after selling their blood, and the HIV/AIDS activist Wan Yanhai, who set up Beijing Aizhi. Though the local authorities have responded with hostility to their work, as it is perceived as bringing public shame upon the area, both have persisted against the odds. In July 2002 the offices of Aizhi were shut down and the following month Wan Yanhai was detained by the police for distributing an internal document on the Internet concerning the Henan blood-collection scandal. He was released in the autumn and the organization he established, namely, Beijing Aizhi Xindong Yanjiusuo, was finally granted permission to register. This about-turn by the central government reflected not only a concern with the international attention provoked by Wan Yanhai's detention, but also the effects of growing international pressure upon China to recognize the scale of HIV/AIDS and to take serious measures to prevent its further spread.[34] Though such initiatives by individuals do not constitute collective action, by claiming issues from the narrow realm of public authority, they do create a critical, public sphere around the issue of HIV/AIDS, which can be both a precursor to as well as an outcome of associational processes.

Whilst social taboos, legal restrictions, and the politics of face make organizing around HIV/AIDS difficult, issues of social stability and regime threat make working openly in the field of employment to address workers' rights particularly challenging. Cases of labor disputes, including those centering on women workers, are usually dealt with in labor arbitration committees and the courts. However, attempts so far to establish specialized, nongovernmental counseling and legal advice centers for workers have been stymied by the authorities, who view these matters as too sensitive and potentially destabilizing for nonstate bodies to pursue.[35] When intellectuals or workers have distributed pamphlets informing employees of their labor rights, exposed grievances, and violations, or attempted to establish autonomous trade unions or organizations of laid-off workers, they have been rapidly clamped down upon by public security agencies. There are, however, a few examples of nongovernmental initiatives to support workers. For example, the renowned labor lawyer Zhou Litai has boldly exposed the plight of workers injured and maimed in industrial accidents and fought through the law courts for compensation. A nongovernmental agency in Hong Kong has established an advice center for migrant workers in Guangzhou, using a small shop as its base.[36] In the Panyu suburb of Guangzhou in 1998, a former government lawyer set up a Migrant Workers' Document Handling Service Center. This not only provides legal advice to migrant workers but also offers training for workers and support for injured workers. [37]

In contrast, activists concerned with the interests of women workers, whether laid-off, migrant, or victims of labor rights' violations, have met with greater success in establishing organizations to address their needs, not least because of the spaces and more open climate created through the 1995 Fourth World Conference on Women. These organizations have generally taken the form of nongovernmental legal aid centers for women, of which there are eight altogether in China. Some of these focus specifically on women workers, such as the Shenzhen Women Workers' Center and Fudan University Women's Legal Counselling Center, whilst others address other gender issues such as domestic violence, rape, and divorce, as with the Shaanxi Women's Legal Counselling Center and Beijing University Women's Legal Counselling Center. The Shenzhen center is unusual in that it sets out to empower female workers by providing them with skills to organize themselves and negotiate in the workplace. It also facilitates the setting up of mutual support groups, distributes information on workers' rights through its mobile bus, and organizes discussion groups amongst female migrant workers. In conjunction with a local hospital, it has set up a center for victims of industrial accidents and occupational diseases, providing training and advice.[38] In general, organizing around women workers has been easier than around labor rights. This relates, on the one hand, to the historical construction of women by the Chinese Communist Party as a vulnerable category in need of special protection, and, on the other hand, to the tendency for associations in this field to focus on realizing legal rights rather than making broader demands for change in the political system. Apart from nongovernmental legal aid centers, there are also other localized initiatives such as the Female Migrant Workers' Club in Beijing. This serves as a meeting point for female migrant workers, provides information about the rights of workers, and offers support to female migrants engaged in disputes with their employers.

## CORPORATIST OR CIVIL SOCIETY ENTITIES?

To what extent does this new stratum point to the consolidation of a corporatist system of intermediary relations[39] or to the flourishing of a more autonomous, diverse, and even critical civil society? Are they autonomous organizations, defining their own agenda and relying on their own resources? Or are they creations of the Party/state, prioritizing its interests and oriented to directives from above? To what extent do they engage critically with the Party/state to bring about policy and social change to the benefit of their constituents? In order to understand whether these new organizations point to the consolidation of a corporatist pattern of state-society relations or an expanding civil society, we need to look closely at their relationship to the Party/state and in particular their degree of independence. Of interest, therefore, are the funding basis of the organizations, the involvement of the Party/state in the establishment and management of the organization, whether the organization is licensed to have a monopoly of representation, and whether the organization sets its own priorities and determines its own activities.

## SOURCES OF FUNDING

Most of the new organizations working around marginalized interests in the fields of HIV/AIDS, labor rights, and gender in the workplace rely upon international donor funding rather than state funding. For example, the Ford Foundation and Novib have supported the infrastructure and activities of the China AIDS Network; Oxfam Hong Kong has contributed to the funding of the Shenzhen Working Women's Center, the Shaanxi Women's Legal Counselling Center, and the Center for Victims of Industrial Accidents; and Ford Foundation support catalyzed the development of the Yunnan Reproductive Health Association and the Yunnan Participatory Rural Appraisal Network. Reliance on donor funding arises not only because of a desire to minimize any government interference, but also because of the difficulties in securing funds from other sources, be it from local governments, companies, or from the general public. Without funding, these organizations cannot easily provide services or perform other activities. Local government has at the most provided free office space or permitted the seconding of salaried staff. Secondment can sometimes serve as a way for local governments to keep a watchful eye on an organization, as with the union cadres assigned to work in the Shenzhen Migrant Workers' Center, or as a way of streamlining staff and government functions, as with the Xishuangbanna Women and Children's Psychological and Legal Counselling Center, where the director, driver, and accountant are all formally employed in the Justice Bureau.

## STATE INVOLVEMENT IN THE ESTABLISHMENT AND MANAGEMENT OF ORGANIZATIONS

All of the organizations interviewed were founded by concerned individuals "from below" rather than by government departments "from above." The idea for the Shenzhen Women Workers' Center arose out of discussions amongst female scholars and activists in Hong Kong who were concerned about the treatment of female migrant workers in China. The head of the Xishuangbanna Women and Children's Psychological and Legal Counselling Center had for a long time wanted to work more closely with disadvantaged women. Similarly, the Yunnan Reproductive Health Association and the Yunnan Participatory Rural Appraisal Network originated upon the initiative of people who had participated in a training program on participatory rural appraisal. The national Gender Network was started by women scholars and activists at a nationwide conference in Xian in 2000. The China Aids Network and Beijing Aizhi both grew out of the initiatives of highly committed individuals.

Although all the organizations interviewed were started voluntarily from below, some also involved government leaders in their activities by inviting them to sit on the leading councils of associations. In this way they could access resources, amass contacts, enhance the prestige of the organization, and gain protection.[40] However, this also runs the risk that such officials intervene too much in the affairs of the organization. This was the case with one nongovernmental legal counselling center, which encountered excessive intervention from a quasi-governmental agency, distracting the center from its goals. As the interviewee put it, "At first I approached this agency about this [establishing the center] and they wanted to cooperate. But I found the relationship with the agency more and more unsatisfactory. At first they let me do things. Then as the center began to get funding, they wanted to get more involved. . . . I found a lot of time was taken up with the administrative processes of the agency. I felt that as a people's organization I was supposed to serve the people and not spend all my time dealing with leaders." [41] So as to reestablish the goal of meeting clients' needs and provide a counterweight to this local agency, the leading council was expanded to include five rather than only two government departments.

While recognizing the potential benefits of links with government agencies, some associations nevertheless tried to minimize their role so as to preserve their autonomy. Finding the right supervisory organization, with sufficient confidence in the work of the affiliated organization to take a hands-off approach, is crucial to its operational independence. In practice it may take some time before the sponsoring agency gains this level of trust. In some instances the supervisory department may never feel able to, or want to, let go of the reins. The Yunnan Reproductive Health Association reflected carefully on the various options for supervisory bodies so as to preserve its independence. For example, they decided not to affiliate to a prestigious, local professional association for fear that it would try to control them and "give them tasks from above." [42] In opting finally for the Yunnan Women's Theoretical Research Association, they carefully secured their independence by offering their publications in return for a hands-off approach. In the words of the president, "We don't want our supervisory department to behave like a mother-in-law towards us. We wanted them to promise that they would not interfere in our work. Initially they were suspicious but then they found we were good people and they now leave us alone. They want us to say that our publications are theirs. So we carry the name of their society on our publications as they don't have any publications themselves. That's the deal." [43]

In brief, all organizations in the sample studied were founded from below. Most tried to limit state involvement in their activities by choosing carefully their host or supervisory agency or organizing themselves in a way that avoided registration. The few that had significant numbers of government officials on their leading councils were able eventually to minimize their role, thereby enhancing their own autonomy.

## LICENSING

Granting an organization a monopoly of representation is a key feature of a corporatist pattern of state-society relations. It is apparent from this investigation that this monopoly is constantly subverted through the creation of associational forms that bypass the registration procedures. In entering new fields of activity, an existing association or network extends its scope of work beyond its original remit, and thereby undermines the monopoly another organization might claim. For example, though there is only one Women's Federation representing "women" as a generic category, there are many different local and national organizations addressing specific gender issues, including those of women in the workplace. Similarly, although there is only one China AIDS Network, other organizations such as the Yunnan Reproductive Health Association or the Yunnan PRA Network also are engaged in HIV/AIDS prevention work in cooperation with local governments. In this way, social actors weaken the corporatist framework and redefine the terms of association. At the same time, cooperation between local governments and these other associational types further strengthens the opening up of spaces for association around marginalized interests. The attempt through licensing to restrict the space and range of organizational activity has thus turned into a facade of monopoly.

## PRIORITY SETTING

A key test for the degree of autonomy of an organization relates to whether it is able to set its own priorities, devise its own strategies, and implement the projects and activities it considers relevant. An organization that responds primarily to instructions issued from above by state authorities has only minimal autonomy. Past research reveals that registered social organizations in China vary considerably with regard to how much they determine their own priorities and activities. At one pole there are those social organizations that government departments have set up as part of a broader strategy to reduce the size of the state and/or to raise external sources of funding. Their activities are driven by the needs of the state rather than those of their clients. Then there are semigovernmental social organizations which have dual functions. On the one hand, they perform tasks on behalf of the state; on the other hand, they provide services for their members and articulate their interests. At the other pole are those social organizations which primarily determine their own aims and activities, taking their members' or clients' interests as their starting point.

In the case of the organizations investigated in this research, all started from the perceived needs of their clients or members. They set their own goals and determined their own activities. Even when registered social organizations were assigned tasks from above, they asserted the priority of their clients' needs, as illustrated in the case of the Xishuangbanna Women and Children's Psychological and Legal Counselling Center. Taking clients' needs as the starting point does not mean that these organizations perceive themselves as in opposition to the state. Several interviewees stressed the point that the government welcomed a client-focussed approach, especially when dealing with HIV/AIDS, because it did not have the capacity to work at such a microlevel. While the women worker's center in Shenzhen clearly prioritized the interests of its target group, it also took advantage of opportunities to work with local authorities so that it could increase its outreach.[44] Cooperation with government departments thus came about not in response to commands issued from above but through a mutual recognition of comparative advantage. Associations and networks need the support of government departments and mass organizations such as the Women's Federation as an entry point into rural areas, while government agencies require the assistance of associations, centers, and networks to implement international projects and gain access to international donor funds. In the words of an interviewee from the Yunnan Reproductive Health Association, "We need a government network, like the Women's Federation, for this makes our work convenient. It helps us to organize a focus group discussion or visit households. So there is a cooperative relationship. If you go to a local place, the government can support us." [45]

However, though the organizations investigated gave priority to their clients' interests and sought the support of government bodies to carry out their work, they also recognized the boundaries of what was possible and in some instances even set the boundaries themselves in anticipation of the government's reaction. In the early 1990s, Yunnan provincial government was reluctant to address the issue of HIV/AIDS, believing that this discredited the image of the province and deterred potential domestic and foreign investors and traders from conducting business there. Though it allowed pioneers, such as the well-known psychologist Li Jianhua, to work with drug users and sex workers and experiment with therapeutic rehabilitation, they had to keep their work low-profile. As Li Jianhua related, "In 1988 I was already allowed to do this work with drug users and commercial sex workers but I was told to keep quiet about it and not talk about it."[46] A member of the Yunnan Reproductive Health Association described to me the precarious line that researchers and activists had to tread in a terrain where the boundaries of the possible were fluid and unpredictable, "You can do difficult things but you have to be careful. You need the government's approval so there is a limit. It depends on timing as to what you can't do or you can do but if you do it, you mustn't do it too much."[47]

To sum up, the organizations operating in the fields of HIV/AIDS, labor rights, and gender in the workplace are relatively independent entities that have been formed from below and set their own priorities and initiate their own activities. The majority have not registered as social organizations, not least because they anticipate excessive state intervention and take instead the form of centers, networks, projects, or affiliated associations. Those organizations that have registered have managed to minimize intervention by government officials in their daily activities and prioritize the interests of clients over directives from above. International donor funding has been crucial in the development of this stratum of organizations.

The question remains as to whether this layer of organizing has created or constitutes part of a public sphere concerned with marginalized interests. We can conceptualize a public sphere as an arena where societal actors come together to engage in rational-critical debate about public affairs that have otherwise been the prerogative of the Party/state.[48] This public sphere gains political salience once actors use their opinions, ideas, and knowledge to bring about change in society and government policy. In this way they become part of political society, which in the case of China has been limited to a small number of incorporated mass organizations.

The participation of registered social organizations generally in policy processes takes the form of invited consultation and comment on policy changes, including the drafting and amendments of relevant regulations and laws. Participation is initiated from above rather than from below. To be invited for consultation not only endows an organization with prestige but also is in the first place contingent upon an organization enjoying status, legitimacy in the eyes of government officials, and connections to government. Organizations can enhance their prestige by fostering ties with government leaders, such as by inviting them to be council members, as was done effectively by the Yunnan Reproductive Health Association, by establishing links with the media, and by implementing government and/or international projects.

The organizations interviewed tried to influence government policy and the attitudes of government officials through research dissemination, the demonstration of alternative models, and by conducting training courses for government leaders.[49] Carrying out detailed field research with marginalized groups such as poor people, sex workers, people living with HIV/AIDS, migrant workers, and drug addicts, and then presenting the results, analysis, and policy recommendations to government officials and in the media is a key strategy used by researchers, who can draw upon the prestige of their associations and institutes, to influence policy.[50] Individual activists and civil society organizations attempted to influence government thinking by developing alternative models and practices. For example, the pioneer psychologist Li Jianhua introduced and adapted the therapeutic community model of drug rehabilitation in Yunnan.[51] In his words, "In China we have a policy and then we do something. But according to my experience, I want to use a model to change policy. Ours is the first therapeutic model in China. It is very successful. More and more people realize that you should rehabilitate people in this way."[52] Similarly, training was seen as a route for influencing the attitudes of government officials and, indirectly, policy. In discussing their training work on reproductive health and health reform, the head of the Yunnan Reproductive Health Association highlighted the links between training and policy influence: "We hope to influence policy this way, even though we are far from Beijing. Training is national so through this we hope to change attitudes so people don't look down on weak people." [53]

Though individual activists and associations adopted a number of strategies to influence government policy and the attitudes of officials toward marginalized groups, their influence is at best indirect and at most episodic. There are no institutionalized channels of participation by nongovernmental organizations, apart from the traditional mass organizations, in policy-making processes.[54] Though some individuals and associations are consulted and invited onto experts' consultation commissions, they have not sought to systematize their participation, or to create formal channels for marginalized groups to consult directly with government, or to assist the poor to organize themselves. Hence, though the activities of these organizations have opened up debates around gender and to a lesser extent HIV/AIDS and labor rights in academic and policy circles, and also in society through the media, they have not significantly influenced policy processes. Nor have they made a political case for the defense and promotion of the interests of people living with HIV/AIDS or female migrant workers.

The emergence of a public sphere around these issues remains embryonic, tentative, and precarious. What we have is a protopublic sphere, whose contours and features are evolving in a context of uncertain political boundaries. When the Party/state interprets recommendations as criticisms and critique as counterrevolution, it uses its repressive agencies to curtail the autonomy of individuals to organize, to reflect, and to debate, the detention of the HIV/AIDS activist Wan Yanhai in August 2002 being a salient example. In the case of HIV/AIDS and labor rights, the Party/state continues to limit open discussion and reflection, thereby conserving "the public" in the public sphere as belonging to the Party/state. At the most it has allowed the extension of this public to include a select group of technical experts. But this is far removed from the public sphere envisaged by Habermas, where social differences were bracketed and a broad range of societal actors could partake in the discussion of public affairs. In the case of gender (see chapter 9 by Du Jie) and environmental issues, the Aladdin's cave of critical debate and reflection has been opened further, though the door can always be closed if necessary.[55]

There is thus a multiplicity of protopublic spheres that are occupied by technical and intellectual elites, that are evolving separately and unevenly, and, because of their uncertain and episodic relation with the Party/state, are both transient and fragile.

## CONCLUDING REFLECTIONS

What then does this investigation of a new stratum of organizations in the fields of HIV/AIDS, labor rights, and gender in the workplace tell us about processes of governance in China? Has the Chinese Communist Party consolidated its control over society through corporatist regulation, or has the space for autonomous organization become increasingly plural, diverse, and wider? Have societal actors begun to carve out a public sphere that allows critical debate around issues that were otherwise regarded as only a matter for the Party/state? Is governance becoming more plural, more democratic, more negotiated than before?

First, the Party/state's attempt to regulate society through a corporatist framework appears to be failing. The ingenuity of social actors in organizing through means that evade the tortuous and constrictive registration processes has weakened the potency of the corporatist framework. Even those organizations registered as social organizations have managed to keep at bay any unwanted state intervention. The picture that the corporatist frame is trying to encompass turns out to be larger than it can contain, and ever-expanding. Decentralization and the streamlining of state agencies down to county level have left government and governance processes fragmented and sclerotic, unable to pursue a corporatist agenda, let alone keep track of, or contain, the proliferation of societal groups and activities.

In turn, the increasingly complex landscape of associational forms that are successfully circumnavigating regulatory restrictions testifies to the ongoing seizure of crevices and spaces by societal actors and the continuing diversification of interests in the arena of civil society. Yet the occupation of spaces is never certain, never complete. Once boundaries are overrun, once the Party/state perceives debate as critique and organization as destabilizing, then the agencies of repression set in. The Party/state and society are caught in an undercurrent of contestation, each struggling to ride the wave. The ebb of dialogue and open reflection is hurled back in a flow of repression. Political liberalization in China remains tentative, fragile, and unpredictable.

As long as organizations, centers, or networks confine themselves to service delivery, then local governments are prepared to tolerate their activities. Autonomy gained is politics lost. In this sense this new stratum of organizations resembles the kind of public sphere described by Rankin (1993) in late imperial China, where extrabureaucratic activity is encouraged, provided it does not take on a political purpose. In contemporary terms, the introduction of the concept "nonprofit sector" by Chinese scholars in the late 1990s echoes this rendering of the public sphere.[56] Such a public sphere that evades political society and politics, and underplays voice, individual rights, interests, and widening reflective participation in public affairs, amounts to a depoliticizing of civil society.

However, there is a tension in contemporary China between the emergence of a depoliticized public sphere concerned with philanthropy, service, and public goods, and a politicized public sphere that resonates more closely with liberal-democratic versions of civil society as the site for promoting individual rights and checking state power and critical traditions of protest in China. The latter kind of public sphere is episodic, brittle, and embryonic. What we see emerging are protopublic spheres of rational-critical debate. These emerge as researchers and activists push open the spaces for critical reflection by tackling complex and sensitive issues in their research, by linking up with sympathetic media workers, and by influencing government officials through training. Governance processes thus appear to be more plural than before reforms began but participation remains limited to an intellectual and technical elite with patronage links to Party/state officials. The protopublic spheres in the area of marginalized interests are similarly occupied by intellectual and technical elites who claim to speak on behalf of others. More open governance is not necessarily more inclusive or democratic, though the opening up of debate and critical reflection may be an important step in this direction. But once individuals overshoot the boundaries of political acceptability, then the public sphere of critical debate shrinks and reverts to its lesser form of service delivery. The "public" in public sphere thus remains contested.

Second, governance processes in China are increasingly fragmented, localized, and messy, despite continuing attempts by the central Party/state to exercise some macrocontrol, impose unitary regulations and legislation, and maintain a central control. The restructuring of state organizations in the late 1990s (see Burns chapter 3 in this volume) has reduced the capacity of officials to monitor social organizations, while local officials are prepared to be lax about the implementation of regulations where the activities of nonregistered groups benefit local development. It is thus no longer appropriate to think in terms of a single civil society or public sphere, or a unified, predictable process of governance. The corporatist framework fails in part because it is a unitary response to an increasingly diverse and differentiated reality, a modernist response to a postmodern reality. The complex relations with the Party/state guided by contradictory impulses of mutual advantage, self-protection, and preservation of autonomy defy a simplistic, generalized statement about the character of civil society. In practice there are multiple civil societies and multiple emerging public spheres that are localized and specific, forming a tapestry of association and, on occasions, voices that local governments sometimes encourage, sometimes ignore, sometimes contain, and sometimes repress. The diverse civil societies do not constitute an overarching, self-conscious civil society that speaks in the liberal-democratic image of civil society with a collective voice to check the state and protect individual rights. Yet the growth of networks suggests that this is a direction that civil society may be moving towards, a direction that is risky.

Third, associational life is becoming not only more complex and diverse, but also more differentiated and potentially contentious. The space for organizing autonomously in China is now being grasped by those concerned with the marginalized and the losers in the reform process. As China becomes increasingly subject to the vacillations of the global economy and as economic inequalities sharpen, we can expect contestation to be played out as much vis-à-vis the Party/state as within civil society. For researchers this requires moving beyond a fixation with an assumed conflictual dichotomy between the Party/state and civil society to analyze also the societal divisions and cracks that puncture civil society and shape its relations with the Party/state.

Fourth, scholars' attempts to capture the rapid changes in state-society relations in China using the theoretical and conceptual armory of corporatism, civil society, and the public sphere have greatly enriched the study of state-society relations and associational life in contemporary China. However, their application has also highlighted their limits in describing and explaining an increasingly complex and fluid social reality. In questioning the adequacy of these frameworks, some scholars have turned to other concepts to frame their investigations. Ding (1994), for example, makes a forceful argument against applying a conception of "civil society versus the state" to explain the collapse of communist systems. In its place he proffers the notion of "institutional amphibiousness" to describe the way apparently autonomous institutions are parasitic upon the state and how social groups located in state institutions use their positions to manipulate and convert those state institutions to antistate ends. However, the concept of institutional amphibiousness does not allow the researcher to capture the varying degrees of autonomy of social organizations, as described by this and other studies, nor the complexity of relations between state agencies and different associational forms. Whilst it highlights the indeterminacy of state-society boundaries and, therefore, the weaknesses of regime-centered and society-centered accounts of transition, it cannot explain why more autonomous forms of association have flourished in the reform period of communist history, nor why the new phase discussed in this chapter evolved.[57] Though Brook (1997: 19–45) does not seek to evaluate the applicability of the concept of civil society to China, his focus on the concept of "auto-organization," that is "the voluntary, autonomous organization of social life" (22), enables him to free his analysis and discussion from the normative and ideological interpretation of civil society as in opposition to the state.[58] In different ways the endeavours of both Ding and Brook indirectly point to the need to disentangle the normative from the empirical, a fusion which has done much to obfuscate the discussion and application of the concept of civil society.[59]

The limited explanatory powers of corporatist, civil society, and public sphere theories inevitably open up the thorny question of the applicability of Western social science to non-Western settings, a refrain which is oft rehearsed in relation to China. The argument that "Western" social science is redundant in "other" contexts because it is irretrievably implicated in a particular history and culture not only fails to problematize the notion of "Western" but also falls prey to its own logic of essentialism. No theories or concepts are value-free. Hence, the importance of reflexivity in the social sciences, which compels the researcher to question how their values, norms, and structural position in the research setting and society impact upon the way they frame questions and interpret reality. Such reflexivity also requires the researcher to question why particular theories and concepts gain currency at particular historical moments, and how and by whom such theories and concepts are deployed for normative and ideological ends.[60] Given that social science theories rest upon contested, value-laden ontological, and epistemological premises, their adequacy in describing and explaining reality should form the basis for judging their relative merits, rather than any essential cultural source.

Finally, external agencies have played a much greater role in the nurturing of civil society and public spheres than has been previously understood in China. Though international development aid to China is relatively miniscule in relation to its GDP,[61] in certain key sectors and regions donors bring significant resources that benefit both cash-strapped local governments and also nongovernmental associations, networks, and centers. This raises important issues around the dependence of an organization on donor funding that can end up prioritizing the interests of donor agencies over its original purposes, as well as questions about the long-term sustainability of such organizations. Such issues apply not only to China but also to other aid-recipient contexts (Howell and Pearce, 2001). The role of donors in supporting civil society also implies that to understand associational life in China it is no longer sufficient to confine analysis to domestic forces; in the context of increasing global integration, external variables become a key piece in the jigsaw of civil society. As China becomes more embedded in the global economy, the impact of international development agencies, social movements, and global civil society on Chinese civil society is likely to increase. This has implications not only for the future trajectory of civil society, but also for the direction of politics and governance. Given the deepening fissures within society and the potential for social discontent and protest, the importance of fashioning robust, predictable, and legitimate arrangements for the articulation and intermediation of diverse and conflicting interests cannot be underestimated.

# NOTES

1. The concept of civil society has been defined in numerous ways. It has often been appropriated for diverse ideological purposes, muddying both its normative and empirical content. In this chapter we use the term civil society to refer to an intermediary

sphere of voluntary association, comprising a range of organizations, groups, networks, and associational forms, that is situated between the state and the family, and that has some degree of autonomy from the state. In doing so we do not impute to civil society a predetermined normative meaning or agenda of democratization.

2. See, for example, White, Howell, and Shang, 1996; Howell, 1998a; Brook and Frolic, 1997; Madsen, 1993; Rankin, 1993; Strand, 1990; Unger and Chan, 1996; and Wakeman, 1993. In an attempt to resolve some of the difficulties in applying Habermas's notion of the public sphere to China, Huang (1993) proposes an alternative concept of the "third realm."

3. Similarly, the stipulation in the regulations that there can be only one organization for one particular interest or constituency is a classic corporatist feature.

4. An additional factor affecting the revision of the regulations was the emergence of the China Democracy Party in 1998. The emergence and subsequent prohibition of this party fed into the revisions of the regulations in 1998 in the clause banning former political prisoners from leading nonprofit organizations (Wright, 2002: 913).

5. For example, a required floor of 50 individual or 30 institutional members was set. National level organizations had to have a minimum of RMB 100,000 for their activities and have a fixed location. Apart from the Regulations for the Registration and Administration of Social Organizations, two other sets of regulations were introduced in 1998, namely, the Provisional Regulations for the Registration and Administration of Private Non-commercial Institutions and the Provisional Regulations for the Registration and Administration of State-Owned Non-Commercial Institutions.

6. In particular both Jiang Zemin, in his speech to the 15th Party Congress and Luo Gan, secretary general of the State Council, in his speech on the plan to restructure the State Council, underlined the significance of social organizations in the reform of the state and economy. See Saich (2000: 128–31) for further details of this. Woodman (1999: 18) notes that the revision of the administrative regulations in 1998 rather than the passing of a law on social organizations (which remains a draft) strengthens the hand of the Party-state by limiting the extent of any debate on social organizations.

7. For a very detailed discussion of "small government and big society," see Ru, ed., 1998.

8. Pei's study, for example, draws upon a sourcebook produced by the Ministry of Civil Affairs in 1995 and a sourcebook published for Shanghai. Since then the Ministry of Civil Affairs has not published such a detailed study of social organizations.

9. Other reasons include the time required to collect and analyze information at the national level, the method of categorization of organizations, the lack of accessibility of information, and, in particular, the very general categories used in the Ministry of Civil Affair's Statistical Yearbook.

10. In 2002 the NGO Center at Qinghua University published a survey of 500 NGOs in China.

11. See, for example, Howell, 1997; 2000; Hsiung et al., 2001; Li, 1993; Li, 1990; and Liu, 1995.

12. It should be noted that the official figures are underestimates, not least because they are calculated according to the number of laid-off registered with the neighborhood committees. Other estimates place the total between 45 and 60 million. Furthermore, millions have also been retrenched from collective-owned enterprises.

13. For further details of these reforms, see chapter 3 by Burns in this volume.

14. Saich (2000: 133–36) similarly identifies strategies of circumvention, including registering as a business operation, setting up a subsidiary organization, functioning as an unregistered, informal group, and using personal connections. This study points in addition to the multilevel process of affiliation (that is, not just a secondary level process) and to the appropriation of the "project" vehicle.

15. In October 1993 there were reportedly over 1,460 registered national social organizations, 19,600 branch and local organizations registered at the provincial level, and 160,000 social organizations registered with county authorities, a total of 181,060 (Interview, Ministry of Civil Affairs, October 1993). By the end of 1998, this had fallen to 162,887 registered social organizations (Ministry of Civil Affairs, 2000: 132). In the year 1999 alone, the registration of 35,236 social organizations had been cancelled. By the end of 1999, there were only 136,841 registered social organizations in China, a considerable decline since 1998, leaving the total well below that of 1993 (Ministry of Civil Affairs, 2000: 134).

16. In rural areas, the reemergence of religious belief groups, clan-based organizations, temple associations, and other informal groups has not only deepened horizontal social ties but also added to the growing complexity of associational life, which lies beyond, and flourishes in spite of, adminstrative controls.

17. This was one reason why the CCP clamped down so fiercely on the Falun Gong, which had succeeded in establishing a vast network across China. See Østergaard's chapter 11 in this book for further details.

18. For a detailed discussion of the Falun Gong, see Østergaard's chapter 11 in this volume.

19. I am extremely grateful to the Department for International Development UK, which provided me with an ESCOR small grant to carry out this research. Despite the fact that many of the organizations were located in different parts of China, most of the organizations working in the fields of HIV/AIDS, labor rights, and gender in the workplace could be interviewed. However, due to a lack of resources, only five out of the eight nongovernmental women's legal counselling centers could be interviewed. Where organizations could not be directly interviewed, secondary information was used to gain a picture of their organization and activities. The chapter also draws upon research carried out on laid-off workers in 1999 and 2000. I am grateful to the Leverhulme Trust for providing a grant for this research. I am also grateful to the invaluable research assistance provided by He Xiaopei in the spring of 2001.

20. Interview, E31, December 2000.

21. Saich (2000: 134–35), too, recounts a similar case in Wuhan, where the local Civil Affairs Department recommended affiliating to a university as an easier route to setting up a center than registering as a social organization.

22. UNAIDS, the UK Save the Children Fund, OXFAM Hong Kong, MSF-Holland, the Australian Red Cross in collaboration with the Yunnan Red Cross, the Salvation Army, and Project Grace International have sponsored a range of projects in Yunnan, such as public education about HIV/AIDS, peer education in schools, and interventions targeted at vulnerable groups such as drug users, sex workers, migrants, and lorry-drivers.

23. In addition, this organizes national conferences on HIV/AIDS, informs professionals of the latest medical findings, provides opportunities for researchers outside of Beijing to make international contacts, and advises the government. It has carried

out action research amongst commercial sex workers, truck drivers, hotel staff, and taxi drivers in various provinces in China.

24. This started out under the Beijing Modern Management College in 1994, but after becoming independent later that year, encountered difficulties in registering and as a result has operated since 1997 as an Internet group, thereby bypassing the need to register (*China Development Brief*, 2001: 76).

25. To my knowledge these are the only specialized HIV/AIDS organizations in China. There is also a monthly publication called *Friend*, published under Qingdao University Hospital, that addresses issues of concern to the gay and lesbian community, including awareness of HIV/AIDS.

26. Interview, E32, December 2000.

27. Mangrove was set up in March 2002 in Beijing with the support of the Ford Foundation (see *China Development Brief*, autumn 2002: 21 for a profile of Mangrove). Marie Stopes China is engaged in a one-year capacity-building program for Mangrove, involving skills training and strengthening communication. Mangrove is also involved in the editing of a magazine called *Hand in Hand*, written for and by people living with HIV. I am grateful to Susie Jolly, He Xiaopei, Billy Stewart (DFID Beijing), and Kate Mills (Mary Stopes China) for providing information about this self-help group.

28. According to the interviewee (E50, March 2001), the self-help group of the Loving Heart Home is not very active because patients do not live near to each other, so it mainly takes the form of the hospital requesting help from an outpatient for an inpatient.

29. I am grateful to He Xiaopei for bringing these groups to my attention. See also the profile of Mangrove in *China Development Brief*, autumn 2002: 21, which refers to support networks not formally established in Guangdong, Henan, Sichuan, Xinjiang, and Yunnan. The group in Sichuan comprises mainly people who contracted HIV through selling blood at the county hospital. As part of its £15 million China-UK HIV/AIDS Prevention and Care Project, the Department for International Development (UK) has, since 2002, been encouraging the formation of self-help groups for people living with HIV/AIDS in the two project provinces of Yunnan and Sichuan. Such groups currently exist but are not formally registered. The project aims to make these more sustainable. These groups provide mutual support such as child care and develop income-generating activities such as a charcoal briquette factory in Zizhong County, Sichuan province. I am grateful to Billy Stewart (DFID Beijing) for information about this project.

30. I am grateful to Kate Mills (Mary Stopes China) for information about their work with HIV/AIDS support groups in Shanghai and Guangzhou.

31. Interview, E49, March 2001.

32. It should be noted that *Ziteng* describes itself in its materials as a "sex worker concern group" (see *Ziteng* newsletter, September 1999, issue 9). It was founded in 1997 and hosted a conference on sex workers in East and South East Asia in mainland China in 2000, with the support of NOVIB (Ziteng/Asia Monitor Resource Center, 2000).

33. Interview, E16, December 2000.

34. In June 2002, a UN report entitled "HIV/AIDS. China's Titanic Peril" drew considerable attention, suggesting that China was on the brink of an HIV/AIDS epidemic. In-

dicative of the growing priority given to HIV/AIDS by the central government is the phenomenal increase in central government investment in HIV/AIDS prevention and control from RMB 15 million in 2000 to RMB 100 million in 2002. It is against this background that the release of Wan Yanhai and the approval of his organization has to be situated.

35. An interesting case is the negative response of the central government and ACFTU to the creation of a village-level and municipal migrant workers' association in Zhejiang province (See Xie, 2002 and Pan, 2002 for further details). Formally established in April 2002, the association was prohibited in July 2002 on the grounds that only the ACFTU had the legal authority to protect workers' rights. According to the ACFTU, the migrant workers' association in question was a "second trade union," that is, a union outside the ACFTU and therefore outside the law.

36. Interviews, October and November 2002, Hong Kong.

37. For further details see Weldon, 2001–2002: 25–27.

38. Interview, October 2002, Hong Kong.

39. Schmitter (1974: 93–94) describes the key characteristics of corporatism as follows: "Corporatism can be defined as a system of interest representation in which the constituent units are organised into a limited number of singular, compulsory, noncompetitive, hierarchically ordered and functionally differentiated categories, recognised or licensed (if not created) by the state and granted a deliberate monopoly within their respective categories in exchange for observing certain controls on their selection of leaders and articulation of demands and supports."

40. For example, the Yunnan Reproductive Health Association invited three government officials to sit on its council of 40 members. The remainder are from various research units, universities, and academies. The president and four directors of the association are all academics.

41. Interview, E39, March 2001. For reasons of sensitivity, the name of the center and quasi-government agency are not revealed.

42. Interview, E30, December 2000.

43. Interview, E20, December 2000.

44. When the Guangzhou Women's Federation, Labor Bureau, and Health Bureau organized an event for women on March 8th in Zhongshan district, the Shenzhen Women Workers' Center also participated. Indeed it claimed that its activities were more popular than those of the Women's Federation: "Actually lots of people came to our bus and they preferred our stalls to those of the Women's Federation" (Interview, E37, March 2001).

45. Interview, E32, December 2000.

46. Interview, E22, December 2000.

47. Interview, E32, December 2000. Similarly, as the head of the China Aids Network stated, "It's our policy to work subtly. I know how to manage things . . . do a little ahead but not too showy" (Interview, E48, March 2001).

48. This conceptualization of public sphere draws upon the seminal work of Jürgen Habermas (1992). In a special issue of *Modern China* in 1993, social historians such as Frederic Wakeman Jr., William Rowe, Mary Bacus Rankin, and David Strand deployed the concepts of public sphere and civil society to analyze the texture of associational life in the late Qing and early Republican periods.

49. It should be noted that not all the organizations were interested in influencing government policy, and none operated solely as advocacy groups. The Shenzhen

Women Workers' Center, for example, focused on female migrant workers and had no desire to engage with government. As a representative of the center stated, "Our focus is on the workers rather than trying to influence government. When we attend conferences, for example of NGOs, then we explain the situation of workers, but otherwise we don't do much advocacy work" (Interview, E37, March 2001).

50. The Yunnan Reproductive Health Association regularly passes research reports to the Ministry of Health, the Women's Federation, and the China Family Planning Association with the goal of influencing their ideas (Interview, E20, December 2000). Likewise, the China AIDS Network successfully promoted the use of condoms, leading to a change in government policy on condom distribution. Similarly, the head of the Rural Development Research Center in the Yunnan Academy of Social Sciences related to me that by reporting the research results on poor farmers to local and central government, publicizing them in local newspapers, and organizing dialogues with government officials, they could bring both the problem and proposed solutions to the attention of leaders (Interview, E29, December 2000). Similarly the Beijing University Women's Legal Services Center published books on women's rights and interests, including case studies, so as to raise these issues in the public domain (Interview, E14, December 2000).

51. Saich (2000: 136–37) notes the example of the China Family Planning Association in influencing government policy through innovative pilot schemes.

52. Interview, E22, December 2000. A similar view was expressed by a member of the PRA Network engaged on a project on community trafficking, involving county officials, local communities, and the Save the Children Fund, UK. In her view, "We try to influence local government through our model. The ACWF is an advocacy organization and can influence Jiang Zemin through its words. We can't influence central government because we are in Kunming but we can use a model" (Interview, E27, December 2000).

53. Interview, E20, December 2000.

54. For a discussion of the influence of the All-China Federation of Women on policy-making processes, see Howell, 2003.

55. Environmental organizations in China such as Friends of Nature and Global Village have skillfully used the media and personal connections to Party officials to raise environmental awareness and critique the negative environmental effects of economic policies, bringing about changes in local and national policies.

56. The term "nonprofit sector" or "Third Sector" is adopted from the ongoing research of Lester Salamon at Princeton University on the growth of private, nonprofit, voluntary organizations. The term became influential in China following an international conference on the Non-Profit Sector and Development held at Tsinghua University in Beijing in July 1999. For a collection of works on the non-profit sector, see Zhao and Irving, eds., 2001 and Zhao Liqing, 2001; Zhao, 1998; and Hong and Kang, 2001.

57. There is a tension in Ding's article between "institutional amphibiousness" as an outcome of processes of change and as a causal variable in processes of change. Moreover, in his conclusion, he suggests that "eventually the civil society model will become relevant to China" (316), falling into the same teleological trap of those he initially critiques, namely, those deploying the dichotomous, antagonistic view of civil society as in opposition to the state. However, he later suggests that given the pervasiveness of east Asian states, institutional amphibiousness would still likely

characterize postcommunist countries such as China, but without clarifying why such amphibiousness might be regime-weakening or regime-strengthening at particular historical moments.

58. This then allows Brook to argue that such auto-organization is a stabilizing rather than a destabilizing factor, the reverse of a position which places civil society and the state in opposition to one another.

59. For a more detailed discussion of this point and the way in which this conceptualization of state-civil society relations pervades donor agencies' programs to support civil society, see Howell and Pearce, 2001.

60. Hence the need to situate the usage of civil society in particular political contexts. The dominance of the "civil society versus state" interpretation of civil society theory occurs at a particular historical juncture of regime collapse in east European Leninist states and the concomitant celebration of the apparent end of ideology and the inevitability of liberal democracy. Similarly, Des Forges (1997: 68–95) provides a fascinating account of the historical antecedents of three types of civil society concepts and realities in China and how rulers appropriate and deploy these versions for particular political and ideological ends.

61. In 2000 China received U.S. $1,735 million in net disbursements of official development assistance, accounting for 0.2 percent of GDP. This compares with 13.3 percent for Uganda and 11.6 percent for Tanzania (UNDP, 2002: 203–206).

# 9

# Gender and Governance: The Rise of New Women's Organizations

*Du Jie*

The concept of civil society has been increasingly used to explain and understand the emergence of new forms of autonomous organization during the reform period (White, Howell, and Shang, 1996; Howell, 1998a and b; Gold, 1990; Wakeman, 1993; Madsen, 1993; Brook and Frolic, 1997).[1] Civil society can be defined as "an intermediate associational realm situated between the state on the one side and the basic building blocks of society on the other (individuals, families, and firms), populated by social organizations which are separate, and enjoy some degree of autonomy from the state and are formed voluntarily by members of society to protect or extend their interests or values" (White, Howell, and Shang, 1996: 3). Interest in civil society in general and in China in particular has been centrally concerned with processes of democratization. This arises not least because there is an implicit assumption that the emergence of civil society and democratization are positively correlated, but also because, in the case of China, there is an aspiration that civil society promises the route to democratic change.

Civil society is not a homogeneous entity but a collection of institutions and actors with different interests. In China detailed studies of civil society have focused on professional organizations, trade and business associations, and nongovernmental organizations (Unger and Chan, 1995; White, Howell, and Shang, 1996). Though there is a limited, but growing, collection of studies on more independent women's organizations, the gendered nature of civil society in general has received little attention in China.[2] Yet women's organizations are an important component of most contemporary civil societies.

In the reform period, and especially under the impetus of the UN Fourth World Conference on Women, women's organizations in China underwent considerable change. On the one hand, new types of women's organizations have emerged, breaking the monopoly of the state-built women's organizations. On the other hand, the long established women's organizations like the ACWF initiated a process of internal reform so as to adapt to the rapidly changing socioeconomic context and the concomitant changing matrix of gender needs and issues.

In China, women's organizations are now one of the most dynamic elements of civil society. Women's organizations comprise those institutions, collectivities, and networks that are organized around gender issues. In the pre-reform period, the ACWF and the Women Workers' Department (*nu gongbu*) in the All-China Federation of Trade Unions (ACFTU) were the only legitimate women's organizations.[3] Established by the Party/state, these two women's organizations were part of the Party/state system and enjoyed little autonomy. The ACWF has played a crucial role in promoting gender equality in China. Since 1978 new forms of women's organizations have begun to emerge. Their growth and development began to take off from the late 1980s and accelerated in particular in the run-up to the Fourth World Conference on Women held in Beijing in 1995. These new women's organizations vary in their degree of autonomy from the state, with some blatantly founded from above and others maintaining an independent distance from the state. Many of them have played an active role in serving women's interests.

The purpose of this chapter is to examine the development of women's organizations in China and explore their impact on gender policies. The term *gender* refers to the socially and culturally constructed perceptions of differences between men and women as well as socially and culturally shaped attributes and behaviors ascribed to being male and female (Hom and Xin, 1995). The gender concept was first introduced to China in the 1980s, but the term began to be used more frequently during the preparations for the Fourth World Conference on Women in 1995. The concept of gender has been translated into Chinese as *shehui xingbie* (social sex), meaning that society constructs the behavior of men and women based upon their biological sex. The chapter first outlines Molyneux's classification of women's organizations as a framework for situating Chinese women's organizations. It then examines changes in women's organizations during the reform period (1978–2003), looking at both reform within the ACWF and the emergence of new, more autonomous women's organizations. The chapter then goes on to explore the strategies that women's organizations adopt to negotiate changes in gender relations and policies. Finally it considers the challenges and prospects for women's organizations in the context of globalization.

## WOMEN'S ORGANIZATIONS: INDEPENDENT MOVEMENTS, ASSOCIATIONAL LINKAGES, AND DIRECTED MOBILIZATION

To understand the relation between these women's organizations and the Party-state in the pre-reform and reform periods, it is first necessary to outline the potential nature of such relations. In doing so, we draw upon Molyneux's (1998) classification. She identifies three types of women's organizations in terms of their degree of autonomy or dependence. She distinguishes, first, "independent movements," in which women organize autonomously and set their own goals. Second are "associational linkages," whereby these autonomous women's organizations form alliances with other political organizations, some of whose objectives they share. Molyneux argues that this kind of linkage avoids the dilemma of autonomy or integration and the danger of co-optation. The third type is "directed mobilization," which is where authority and initiative clearly come from the outside, so that "there is little, if any room for genuine negotiation over goals." The third type can take different forms. In some cases women are mobilized, for instance by a nationalist movement, to help achieve a general goal, with no specific commitment toward furthering their interests, or even at the risk of losing some of their already existing rights. Alternatively, "women's interests" may form part of the overriding objectives, but as defined by external leaders, as in some socialist or communist movements.

In the case of the ACWF, during the period of state economic planning, we can see that the relation between the ACWF and the CCP was one of directed mobilization. The ACWF was subject to the higher (institutional) authority of the CCP and was typically under the control of the Party/state. This subordination could be seen in relation to the overall goals of the organization, the administrative system, and the roles of the ACWF. By directing the goals and activities of women's organizations, the Party/state was able to subordinate women's interests to those of the Party. On the one hand, the Party/state subsumed women's interests under its broader political goals and thus gave women's interests legitimacy.[4] On the other hand, it demanded that women's organizations prioritize the Party/state's goals over those of women's movements and organizations. In terms of the administrative system, the ACWF and the Women Workers' Department in the ACFTU have extensive networks through their branches that are established within the Party/state system. This administrative structure has ensured that the ACWF has the authority and resources to implement state policy on women and to mobilize and represent Chinese women, and yet has reduced its autonomy and weakened its effectiveness at lower levels.[5] The roles of the ACWF have been contradictory, torn not only between implementing Party/state instructions and advocating women's rights but also between emphasizing the importance of women's productive and reproductive roles. In the reform period, new types of organizations have emerged, which correspond more closely to Molyneux's first category of independent movements.

## DEVELOPMENT OF WOMEN'S ORGANIZATIONS IN THE REFORM PERIOD (1978-2003)

Women's organizations have expanded rapidly in the reform period. On the one hand, the ACWF initiated a process of internal reform and expanded its domain of activities to meet the changing needs of women in the context of economic reform. On the other hand, new types of women's organizations began to emerge, especially in the run-up to the Fourth World Conference on Women held in Beijing in 1995. Both these old and new women's organizations have enjoyed greater autonomy from the Party/state and participated more actively in state affairs than during the period of central planning. In this section we examine, first, the changes in the ACWF and second, the development of new, more autonomous women's organizations.

### REFORM WITHIN THE ACWF

After the introduction of reforms in 1978, the ACWF reestablished itself in several ways. First, it resurrected its network throughout the country, having ceased to operate during the Cultural Revolution period. It strengthened its capacity to function by reestablishing branches at all levels. By 1994 there were 55,303 branches and over 86,053 full-time cadres appointed and paid for by the Party-state (The Women's Studies Institute of China, 1998).

Second, the ACWF made considerable efforts to expand its traditional working areas to appeal to an increasingly diverse constituency of women. Traditionally, the working domains of the ACWF were the neighborhood committee and the countryside. After the reform, however, the ACWF made deliberate efforts to set up women's professional and occupational associations in the economic, technical, cultural, and educational spheres so as to extend its working areas beyond its traditional reach. For example, the ACWF initiated the establishment of the Women Entrepreneurs' Associations, Women Lawyers' Associations, Women Judges' Associations, China Women Mayors' Association, Female Professors' Association, and so on, so as to create a body of women's NGOs for the Fourth World Conference on Women. Many of these associations later became group members of the ACWF.

Third, the ACWF began to reform its functions and activities so as to increase its autonomy from the Party/state. In the early reform years in the 1980s, there was an internal debate on the functions of the ACWF. Some cadres criticized its top-down structure and its subordination to the

Party/state and called for greater space for independent activities. In 1988, at the Sixth Annual Congress of the ACWF, the debate about the relationship of the ACWF to the CCP reached a peak. As Zhang Guoying, then vice-president of the ACWF and first secretary of the Secretariat of the ACWF stated in her working report:

> For a long time, due to the influence of weaknesses in the political system, such as a lack of separation between the function of the Party and state, a lack of separation between Party organizations and mass organizations, in some aspects, it is hard to distinguish the ACWF from a working unit of the Party committee or functional agency of the government. The characteristics of a mass of organization are not distinct. To a great degree the ACWF has an official colour and bureaucratic tendencies. It issues demands from the top down more than it reflects the voices of the masses. There is insufficient articulation and protection of women's interests. It has separated itself from the female masses to a certain degree. As a result, the link between the Party/state and women has weakened (ACWF, 1988b: 23).

Fourth, the ACWF has renegotiated its position and space by seeking economic independence. The ACWF has sought to gain more autonomy by raising funds from abroad and establishing enterprises to lessen its financial dependence on the Party, thus giving it potentially the material conditions for prioritizing women's interests (Howell, 1998b). For instance, donor agencies such as the United Nations Family Planning Association, the World Bank, the United Nations Development Program (UNDP), the Canadian International Development Agency, and the Ford Foundation contributed over Rmb 40 million in 2000 to development programs and projects for women and children. These efforts occur within the broader context of the Party/state's promotion of the socialization of mass organizations (*shehui zuzhi shehui hua*), aimed at making them less bureaucratic than in the planned economy. This in turn is part of a broader attempt to reconfigure state-society relations in the direction of a "small government, big society" (*xiao zhengfu, da shehui*).

Nevertheless, the Party/state has still played a crucial role in directing women's organizations. Jiang Zemin, the top-ranking CCP leader, delivered a speech at the commemorative meeting of the 80th anniversary of International Women's Day on March 8th, 1990. He said, "without the leadership of the Chinese Communist Party, without the guarantee of a socialist system, there will be no liberation of Chinese women. Adhering to the leadership of the Chinese Communist Party is both the historical choice of the Chinese people and the essential and inevitable approach for Chinese women's liberation" (Jiang, 1990: 5).

Furthermore, the Party/state continues to define the role of women's organizations in a gendered way. Party/state leaders require women's organizations to "attach great importance to family planning, building up the country through thrift and hard work, managing a household industriously and thriftly" (ACWF, 1994: 13). Even though family planning is an essential national policy, the Party/state calls only upon women's organizations to attach importance to this issue, instead of making the same demand on other mass organizations, such as the ACFTU and the Communist Youth League (CYL).[6]

## EMERGENCE OF NEW TYPES OF WOMEN'S ORGANIZATIONS

Several factors have contributed to the proliferation of women's organizations. First, the Party/state has decentralized some of its power to lower levels of government and attempted to separate out government and Party functions. Decentralization has given local governments greater leeway in a range of economic domains and has contributed to the expansion of a space within which social organizations, like women's groups, can operate.

Second, the Party/state has slowly loosened its control over social organizations and encouraged their formation and development to address emerging needs that it is unable to meet. As part of its structural reforms, the Party/state has reduced social services such as local child care services that it had previously provided. As a result, full-time working parents encounter problems in taking care of their children and/or elderly relatives. In order to tackle these problems, the Party/state has promoted service-oriented social organizations to take over these services. This has prompted the emergence of women's organizations that focus mainly on social services.

Third, the process of preparing for and hosting the Fourth World Conference on Women in 1995 has had a significant impact on the development of women's organizations. The Party/state actively encouraged the development of women's organizations for this event. Since the Tiananmen tragedy in 1989, the Party/state has overhauled and rectified social organizations. Yet the Party/state has shown tolerance toward women's organizations. In 1992 the Chinese government set up a national preparatory working committee that included a special working committee on the NGO forum for Chinese women. This committee served as the counterpart of the UN preparatory organization. Promoting a Chinese women's NGO forum and enhancing Chinese women's development were a key part of the national preparatory work (Huang Qizao, 2000).

Fourth, during the preparations for the Fourth World Conference on Women, women's organizations and individual women in China became familiar with and participated extensively in the activities of international NGOs (Liu, 2001). Never before had Chinese women had so many opportunities to participate in international women's affairs. Over 5,000 Chinese participants attended the 1995 NGO Forum on Women held in Huairou, Bejing, August 30–September 8, 1995. Before the conference and the 1995 NGO Forum, many women's organizations or individuals had had opportunities to go abroad to attend international forums and conferences (Huang Qizao, 2000). Through these activities and occasions, Chinese participants became exposed to the international women's movement and acquired valuable skills in organizing NGOs.

By the end of 1999, there were more than 7,300 women's organizations that had registered with the relevant department of the Ministry of Civil Affairs. There were four types of new women's organizations, namely, service-oriented, occupational-based, research-oriented, and project-based organizations.

Service-oriented women's organizations provided services that the state could not provide. For example, one women's group created in January 1993 a national monthly magazine with the title of *Rural Women Knowing All*, which provided a diversity of services to rural women in China such as a Migrant Women Workers' Club in Beijing, a Rural Women's Practical Skills School, literacy classes, and microfinance training projects (*China Development Brief*, 2001). Similarly, the Women's Hotline, initiated by the Women's Research Institute, opened in Beijing in September 1992, offering counselling services to women to help them to improve the quality of their lives.

Occupational organizations provided information and opportunities for career development among female professionals. Some of these are national-level organizations, such as the China Women Mayors' Association and the Chinese Women's Association for Science and Technology, whilst others are based in local areas, such as the Capital Women Journalists' Association and the Shanghai Women Engineers' Federation. This type of organization has been criticized by some feminist writers for prioritizing production over the reproductive concerns of women, such as childcare, maternity leave, and associated benefits (Moser, 1993: 202).

Research-oriented organizations, centers, and institutes have been established in universities, the ACWF, the social science research academies, and in women's NGOs. The first women's studies center in China was set up by Li Xiaojiang in Zhengzhou University in 1987. By the end of 1999, there were 36 women's studies centers in universities and colleges. These have played an important role in developing women's studies courses and establishing the academic field of Chinese women's studies. Particularly well known are the women's studies centers in Zhengzhou University, Hangzhou University, Peking University, Tianjin Normal University, and the Central Party School. Women's federations at different levels have also been involved in developing their capacity in women's studies. In 1991 the ACWF set up the Women's Studies Institute of China, which is primarily concerned with theoretical research. There are also women's studies institutes at the provincial level, such as Heilongjiang Women's Studies Institute (1986), Jiangsu Women's Studies Institute (1990), and Sichuan Women's Studies Institute (1994). These institutes focus on key policy issues affecting women. Apart from universities and the ACWF, many social science academies at different levels have also set up institutes or centers on women and development studies. For example, the social science academies of Sichuan (1994), Yunnan (1994), Hebei (1995), Shanghai (1995), Jiangsu (1997), Beijing (1999), and the China Academy of Social Sciences (1995) have all set up institutions on women's studies. Finally, in order to bring together these different institutional strands, in December 1999 the Women's Studies Institute of China set up the China Women's Studies Association as an extensive network of institutions and organizations devoted to women's and gender studies. By 2001 more than 40 universities and colleges and ten social sciences academies had set up women's or gender research centers.

Project-based networks are based on plans that seek to promote gender equality. The Project of Combating Domestic Violence, initiated in 2000, is a case in point. Cosponsored by international agencies such as the Ford Foundation, NOVIB, SIDA, and the Oslo University Human Rights Center, this venture established a network under the China Law Society to facilitate communication between women's organizations and government around issues of domestic violence. In this way, many women's organizations or groups concerned with combating violence against women, such as the ACWF, Gender and Development Coordinators' Working Group, Maple Leaf Women's Psychological Counselling Center, and Media Monitor Network for Women, have come together to form an effective network in their fight against domestic violence.

## WOMEN'S ORGANIZATIONS' STRATEGIES FOR NEGOTIATING GENDER

Women's organizations, be they large or small, have different starting points and adopt different strategies to negotiate around gender issues with the state and the civil society. I examine first the ACWF's efforts to bring about gender change through legislation and policy. I then explore the initiatives of new women's organizations in addressing the needs of women at the grassroots, in the field of research, in gender planning, and in raising sensitive issues.

## THE ALL-CHINA WOMEN'S FEDERATION

The starting principle of the ACWF in promoting gender equality is "equality between men and women" (*nan nu ping deng*). The meaning of "equality between men and women" stems from the Party/state's Marxist approach to women's liberation. In 1990 President Jiang Zemin made an important speech at the 80th anniversary of the March 8th International Women's Day, which laid out the parameters of a Marxist women's perspective in China. He raised five important issues: first, private property and class oppression are the fundamental causes of women's subordination; second, women's liberation will come true only when all the oppressed are liberated; third, entering social production is a precondition of women's liberation; fourth, socialism provides an essential guarantee for equality between men and women— though translating equality in law into reality is a hard task since the process of women's liberation is a long and arduous one; and fifth, women are a crucial human resource in creating civilization and promoting social development, and contribute to both production and reproduction. Valuing and protecting women is a symbol of social progress (Jiang, 1990). At the welcome ceremony of the Chinese government for the Fourth World Conference on Women in 1995, Jiang re-iterated that "equality between men and women" is a basic state policy (Jiang, 1995).

The ACWF in general embraces the idea of "equality between men and women" as their guiding principle rather than "gender equality." The difference here is that by emphasising "equality between men and women," the ACWF takes men as the normative yardstick and standard of equality and identifies the women's "poor quality" (*suzhi di*) as the main reason for their disadvantages, and thus overlooks the patriarchal structure of society. With its focus on women, it resembles in some respects the "women in development" strategy common in development institutions in the 1980s, which aims to enhance women's participation in economic development In contrast, a "gender equality" approach emphasizes the need to change unequal gender relations between men and women. This in turn resembles more the gender strategy adopted in the late 1980s and 1990s by many development institutions, which stressed mainstreaming of gender issues and getting institutions right for women. The "equality between men and women" approach is evident in the speech "Strengthening Research on Women's Studies, Enhancing Women's Development" given by Peng Peiyun, the president of the ACWF, at the National Women's Studies Forum convened by the ACWF in December 1999 in Beijing. When addressing the importance of adhering to the Marxist principle of women's liberation, Peng (2000) even cast doubt upon the concept of gender:

> Recently, many scholars and academies have translated and introduced the concept of gender and theory of gender from abroad. Gender theory is an important analytical framework of Western feminism. It may be helpful to observe the differences between women and men and to raise awareness of equality between men and women. However, our state has been used to the concept of "equality between men and women." Moreover, the government has made "equality between men and women" a basic state policy. So we should earnestly comprehend, publicize, and implement it. As for Western

gender theory, personally I think several aspects need to be explored: first, has it revealed the fundamental cause of gender inequality?; second, is it able to explain the causes of all kinds of women's problems existing contemporarily?; third, is it able to define the conditions and ways of women's liberation? (Peng, 2000)

The reason that the top leader of the ACWF adheres to the principle of "equality between men and women" and avoids even using the concept of gender deserves further exploration. Is it because the ACWF has to obey the Party's direction and maintain unity with the state, and so uses "equality between men and women" as a strategy to localize the concept of gender so as to fit in with existing institutions? Or is it because the ACWF in general is not quite clear about the concept of gender, so in using the principle of "equality between men and women," it reveals its gender blindness and its lack of awareness about the shortcomings of Marxist gender analysis?

Whatever the reasons may be, the ACWF has pursued the issue of gender equality both with the Party/state and in Chinese society. In principle, the ACWF takes an equity approach, that is, it seeks to achieve equity for women in the development process. It has placed considerable emphasis on women's economic development through access to employment and the marketplace. Women's economic participation in the development process has been seen as synonymous with equity.

The equity approach that the ACWF embraces emphasizes "top-down" legislative and other measures at the macrolevel. This approach is reflected in several respects: first, it has played an important role in facilitating a national machinery for enhancing women's status. In response to a proposal from the ACWF, the Chinese government set up in 1995, and has continued to strengthen, the National Women and Children Working Committee (NWCWC). Serving as a link between governmental organizations and nongovernmental organizations, the NWCWC has increased its membership from 20 in 1990 to 29 in 2002. Of these, 24 are government departments and five are nongovernmental organizations, including the ACWF. Its office is located in the building of the ACWF in Beijing.

The inclusion of the ACWF into the national policy machinery is highly significant. In this way the ACWF has developed links to national policy makers and has been able to exert greater influence in gender planning. For example, the ACWF has promoted and participated in the process of drafting "The Program for the Development of Chinese Women." As a member of the NWCWC, the ACWF also participated in the implementation, supervision, and evaluation of this program. Since 2000 the ACWF has made a significant contribution in the preparations of the Program for the Development of Chinese Women (2001–2010), which the State Council finally endorsed on April 20, 2001. Moreover, this program has been integrated into the Tenth

Five-Year Plan for National Economic and Social Development (2001–2005), reflecting the significance the Party/state attaches to this work.

Second, the equity approach is reflected in the efforts of the ACWF to engender legislation, particularly in relation to women's rights and interests. The issuing of the "The Law of the People's Republic of China on the Protection of the Rights and Interests of Women" on October 1, 1992, illustrates well the crucial role of women's organizations in engendering legislation. It was the ACWF that first initiated a proposal to formulate a special law for women to combat effectively the barriers to women's development in the transition toward a market economy. As of 2003, the ACWF is initiating a proposal for presentation to the National People's Congress to amend the 1992 law on the Protection of the Rights and Interests of Women. The ACWF has also brought gender equity into the newly promulgated Marriage Law. It organized several workshops and studies and put forward a proposal, namely, the "Five Suggestions Regarding Revision of Marriage Law," which targeted phenomena such as domestic violence, extramarital relationships, bigamy, and concubinage (Peng, 2001a). Many issues put forward by the ACWF and other women's organizations were adopted in the final draft, domestic violence being a noteworthy case.

Third, the ACWF has attempted to integrate gender equality into national policy. In the process of market reform, some state policies have not taken into account gender relations in China and have therefore reinforced gender inequalities. For instance, the decollectivization of agriculture realized in part through the introduction of the household responsibility system ignores gender inequalities in intrahousehold decision making, resource distribution, the allocation of labor and income, and welfare. In 1998 the Chinese government passed the Land Management Law, which not only extended the right to use land from 15 years to 30 years, but also stipulated that the land would remain stable regardless of population changes in the village, that is, the exit of a daughter upon marriage or the entry of a wife into a marriage. In response, the ACWF drafted a paper entitled "Pay Attention to and Safeguard Women's Legal Rights and Interests in Rural Land Contract System" (2001), based upon their investigations into these issues. They succeeded in getting this suggestion promulgated by the General Office of the Central Party Committee.

Another example concerns numerous appeals to women by some scholars, journalists, and National People's Congress delegates and government officials to give up waged work to enhance the prospects of men gaining employment. Wang Xiancai, member of the National Committee of the Chinese People's Political Consultative Conference (CPPCC), argued at the session of the National People's Congress and CPPCC in October 2000 that women should "return home to take care of the family" and "give up their working posts for young people to gain employment" (Jiang, 2001: 28).

These appeals in turn influenced policies on women's employment. The idea of "phased employment" (*jieduan jiuye*) was included in the Proposal for Drafting the Tenth Five-Year Plan (2001–05). This meant that female employees would be encouraged to leave their work for a period to undertake vocational training or for reasons of pregnancy, without payment and welfare. The ACWF and other women's organizations strongly resisted this proposal. They argued that in a context of surplus labor it was unlikely that women who choose to stay at home for a period for reasons of pregnancy and child care would be able to resume the same job, due to increasing competition in the labor market. Furthermore, the idea of phased employment reinforces the notions that women should have prime responsibility for social reproduction; that social reproduction is the private responsibility of the household, and specifically women, rather than the public responsibility of the enterprise and state; and that reproductive work is not valuable, hence should not be rewarded through a wage.

During the open discussion on the Proposal for Drafting the Tenth Five-Year Plan (2001–2005), the ACWF put forward a proposal to omit the term "phased employment." It lobbied many female and male representatives of the National People's Congress and the Chinese People's Political Consultative Conference to sign its proposal and raise this issue at the conference. In the final draft of the national plan, the idea "phased employment" was omitted. This revision is highly significant, as it ensured a sound policy environment for women's participation in economic development.[7] In both these examples, the ACWF used its official positions in the National People's Congress and the CCP Central Committee to influence successfully the decision-making process.[8]

Even though the national ACWF employed its resources and connections with policy makers at the top level, its efforts at the grassroots level are less ambitious and innovative. At the grassroots level, the ACWF has organized a campaign for rural women to acquire literacy and learn technical skills, and to emulate each other for higher achievements and contributions. This campaign is called the "Double Learning and Double Emulation." The ACWF has also called upon women in urban areas to work hard and strive for achievements in their work, this campaign being referred to as "Women's Achievement in Their Work." All these activities and campaigns focus on women's roles in production and therefore prioritize the Party/state's overall goals in economic development over women's interests.

Similarly, the ACWF continues to call upon women to contribute more in social moral and family affairs. From the point of view of the Party/state, an important role of the ACWF is to safeguard moral purity and stability. This is in the speech of President Jiang Zemin at his meeting with newly promoted top leaders of the ACWF on September 10, 1998, when he stated that the ACWF should mobilize Chinese women to manage the household thriftily, to ensure moral standards in the family, to show filial piety to the old, and to take care of the young. He especially addressed the role of women as mothers in educating young people and in safeguarding the morals of the nation and the good tradition of the party (ACWF, 2000). In order to answer the Party/state's call, the ACWF continued with the campaign of "Five Good Civilized Families."[9]

In brief, the ACWF has used its channels of access and resources to negotiate gender with state policy at the macrolevel. It has succeeded in bringing issues of gender equity into some national policies. It has put forward proposals for decision-making bodies in critical areas of concern, such as women's rights to contract land, amendments to the Marriage Law, reproductive insurance for women, and the prohibition of trafficking in women and children. However, its affiliation to the Party/state and its top-down method has constrained it in representing women and meeting women's needs at the grassroots level.

## NEW WOMEN'S ORGANIZATIONS

In contrast to the ACWF, most of the new registered and unregistered women's organizations, which have emerged in the reform period and especially since the mid-1990s, have made gender equality their starting point, rather than the "equality between men and women" approach typical of the ACWF.

First, it was women academics, who first introduced the concept of gender into China in the 1980s. Initially, some scholars, such as Qi Wenying, a historian at Beijing University who had been exposed to women's studies in universities abroad, opened up women's studies and gender issues as new arenas of study for academics and paved the way for developing similar programs in China. It was not until preparations began for the Fourth World Conference on Women that the concept of gender became more popular with Chinese academics and activists. They found a gender perspective appealing, not only as a theory for research, but also as a basis for personal change. In 1993 the Overseas China Women's Studies Society collaborated with the Tianjin Normal University to hold the "First Session of the Symposium on Women and Development in China," in which the concept of gender was formally introduced for the first time. For many participants, this introduction to the concept of gender was a watershed in their academic careers as well as their personal lives (Wang, 2000). From then on, under the influence of the Fourth World Conference on Women and the promotional activities of international donor agencies, the concept and theory of gender have spread amongst women's organizations. Women's organizations in Beijing and Tianjin municipalities, Xian in Shanxi province, and Kunming in Yunnan province have been the most active in China in promoting gender issues (Wang, 2000).

Second, unlike the ACWF that has more access to the Party/state and so is better equipped to negotiate gender issues at the top level, the newly formed women's organizations or groups are usually small in size and have less access to the top echelons of the Party/state hierarchy. For this reason the latter focus their efforts on Chinese society, and in particular on meeting the needs of grassroots women, conducting research, promoting gender planning, and raising gender sensitive issues.

## MEETING THE GENDER NEEDS OF GRASSROOTS WOMEN

New women's organizations have developed new ways of reaching women by setting up hotlines, clubs, salons, and counseling centers outside of the state. For example, the women's group based on the monthly magazine *Rural Women Knowing All* provides information, training, health, law, and technology services to rural women in China. Its popularity continues to grow, its circulation reaching 150,000 copies in less than two years. Similarly, the Women's Hotline offers free consultation services to women on many issues. These organizations, whether urban-based or rural-based, are popular amongst women because they provide particular services needed by the women.

According to Moser (1993: 1999), service-oriented organizations tend to adopt a welfarist approach, their objective being to augment the role of social welfare agencies by meeting the practical gender needs of poor women relating to health, education, and other services. They generally have no clear theoretical understanding of gender subordination or its links to other forms of oppression. However, this type of women's organization is urgently needed by women and has played an important role in empowering women. For women who lack economic resources, the welfarist approach can help them address immediate needs and gain economic empowerment. In the context of economic reform in China, the increasing numbers of retrenched, female workers, and state cuts in health and education budgets, more and more women have encountered economic hardship. Services provided by these new women's organizations can meet women's diverse needs and empower them economically. However, from the point of view of the Party/state, these new service-oriented women's organizations can play an important role in dealing with economic crisis and sustaining social stability.

## MAKING RESEARCH AN IMPORTANT BASIS FOR
## THE DEVELOPMENT OF GENDER SENSITIVE POLICIES

Stimulated by the preparations for the Fourth World Conference on Women, the new women's centers, institutions, and organizations have formed a new academic community concerned with gender issues. They have made a significant contribution to the construction of gender issues, catalyzing research on gender and introducing the concept of gender. They have pushed the establishment and development of women's studies units and courses in several universities. In doing so, they challenged the existing theory on women's liberation. For example, women's groups, such as East Meets West Feminist Translation Group, and women's studies centers, such as the Women's Studies Center in Tianjin Normal University, have translated Western feminist literature into the Chinese language. Some of the articles they have translated, such as Hartmann's "The Unhappy Marriage of Marxism and Feminism" (1986) and Rubin's "The Traffic in Women" (1975), challenge the orthodox Marxist interpretation of the oppression of women.

Apart from developing women's studies and introducing the concept of gender and alternative theories of gender oppression into China, these research institutions have also conducted detailed research into women or gender and development. They have addressed specific problems facing Chinese women in a highly practical way and presented a number of policy proposals to the government. For example, the women's studies center in the China Academy of Social Sciences holds forums every year and then turns the suggestions from participants into policy proposals to submit to relevant governmental departments. One such draft proposal is "Policy Suggestions on Chinese Women's Reproductive Health," which scholars, activists, and women's reproductive health organizations developed in 1998. This proposal sought to promote women's access to reproductive health services and enhance their participation in reproductive health decision-making processes. This proposal wielded considerable influence in society. The process of making research an important basis for the development of gender-sensitive policies was later named after its coordinator[10] as the "Qiu Renzong's phenomenon" (Yi Ying, 2000).

However, research institutions cannot directly empower women. Research organizations need to develop structures and methods of accountability in relation to both action organizations and the subjects of their research. Only then can they avoid the development of rifts between themselves and other groups, as has happened in other contexts (Moser, 1993: 203).

## PROMOTING GENDER PLANNING

In the past few years, many programs, especially antipoverty ones, have been implemented in poverty-stricken areas or among vulnerable populations. However, the design and implementation of these plans often do not start with a gender analysis, as some program officers are often not aware of gender analysis. Also, in many of these plans, women are usually passive beneficiaries, playing only a minor role in the implementation of programs.

In order to bring a gender perspective into development plans, women's organizations advocate a gender perspective in programs such as micro-credit in rural areas and incubator projects in urban areas.[11] The Gender Training Group[12] based in Beijing has run several training courses that have proved effective in raising gender awareness amongst project managers. Participants include rural women, women cadres in the Women's Federations at different levels, government officials, policemen, judges, and people from various walks of life.

## RAISING GENDER SENSITIVE ISSUES

Some of the women's organizations have adopted a different position to the government when speaking out on issues. In August 1998, the Chinese government remained silent after the anti-Chinese riots and reports of sexual abuse and rape in Indonesia. The Media Monitor Network For Women, an association of women journalists, organized a public meeting of women to condemn the Indonesian government. Women from other organizations and groups, such as the East Meets West Group, participated in a public meeting with international publicity (Ge, 1999). The Capital Association of Women Journalists, the first of its kind in the country, has monitored the media in gender issues and given training to employees in the media industry. Their work has positively influenced the mass media. They have helped to initiate discussions on many gender-sensitive issues, such as women's rights in land tenure and domestic violence against women, in the journal the *China Women's News*, which is affiliated to the ACWF.[13]

Project-based women's networking has also proved to be an effective means of raising gender-sensitive issues. For example, "the Network Against Domestic Violence in China: Research, Intervention and Prevention" is one of the most influential networks in Chinese society. It played an important role in raising the issue of domestic violence and collaborated with other women's organizations and groups, such as the ACWF and the Gender Training Group, to place this issue into the Marriage Law and to make people aware of this issue through gender training. It was able to exert influence by operating under the umbrella of the Chinese Law Society, which has access to the National People's Congress and whose membership includes eminent scholars such as Chen Minxia, also coordinator of the network, and by establishing a constructive relationship with the ACWF, which was also a member of the network.

In brief, new women's organizations have used diverse means to gradually raise the profile of gender issues, such as addressing women's needs, developing women's or gender studies, running training courses to promote gender planning, and raising gender sensitive issues. However, these women's organizations lack access to the Party/state and so are limited in the degree to which they can influence policy making at the macrolevel.

## CHALLENGES AND PROSPECTS
## FOR WOMEN'S ORGANIZATIONS

Though much attention has been paid by policy makers and scholars to the potential impact of globalization, and particularly WTO entry, on China's economy, there are very few analyses that consider the effect of increasing globalization on women and gender relations. Many officials and academics (both male and female) are optimistic about China's entry into the WTO, highlighting the opportunities. However, critics of globalization argue that it can also widen inequalities and global injustice. Moreover, without explicit consideration of gender issues, women's needs will continue to be ignored. As Afshar put it: "If the underlying issues of female subordination are not addressed, then globalization and development policies are unlikely to result in practical measures that meet gender needs" (Afshar ed., 1999: 14). Research carried out by the ACWF suggests that gender inequalities in education, employment, income, and time devoted to household chores have been worsening since the reforms began in 1978 (ACWF and China Statistics Bureau, 2001).

Some scholars have warned that WTO entry will intensify this trend (Li Xiaoyun, 2000). Given that in many parts of China, women have been left with the farm work as men migrate to the cities, then the potential negative impact of cheap agricultural imports on farmers and their working conditions will fall harder on rural women. As rural households have to purchase health and education services, then those unable to compete with cheap global agricultural imports will likely reduce their purchases of such services, with a disproportionately negative impact on young girls. Similarly, as state enterprises prove increasingly unable to compete in the global market, then women will continue to be laid-off, particularly those aged 40 and over with minimal skills. As export-oriented enterprises strive to compete globally by reducing benefits, then women may lose entitlements such as maternity leave. Furthermore, domestic legislation aimed at protecting women's interests may be interpreted as a non-tariff barrier or hindrance to competitiveness and so effectively overlooked. What then are the challenges for the ACWF and new women's organizations in responding effectively in the future to gendered processes of economic and social change?

## THE ACWF

There are several challenges for the ACWF. The first challenge relates to its overall goal. Peng Peiyun, president of the ACWF, called on cadres of the ACWF at all levels to prioritize women's interests. In her words,

How to represent women's interests conscientiously, and to deal with people's overall interests and protect women's particular interests precisely is a problem facing the Women's Federation. At the same time, we have to see that there is an increasing diversity of social organizations and a rapid development of various spontaneous women's organizations, due to complex and profound changes in our society. It is crucial to get women's organizations and women's masses to identify with the functions and work of the Women's Federation, if we intend to give them direction and services. This is another important issue ahead of us. (Peng, 2001a: 5)

Peng raised the issue of the representation of women's interests in order to gain the support of women's organizations and the mass of women. However, what are women's interests? Which women's interests should the ACWF represent and which should it put on the agenda? These are challenging issues for the ACWF, given the context of increasing social differentiation, widening inequalities, and social injustice. For example, as the material and social differences between women have been increasing, the ACWF finds it increasingly difficult to organize unified activities to unite women nationwide (Gu, 2001). A one-size-fits-all approach is no longer effective.

In prioritizing women's interests, the ACWF may also come into conflict with the interests of the Party/state. In the past the ACWF has tended to prioritize the interests of the Party/state over those of women (Zhang, 1994). If it is to give greater priority to the interests of women, then the ACWF needs to change its top-down way of working and develop equal and cooperative ways of working with new women's organizations (Liu, 2001). How far the ACWF can distance itself from the Party will depend not least upon the broader political climate (Howell, 1998b; 2000).

As for the "particular" groups of women's interests, for example, the rights and interests of lesbians, the ACWF has so far remained silent, or even excluded these groups from the right to protection. The Beijing Lesbian Group meets informally in bars and restaurants in order to avoid the attention of the police (He, 1999). It is unable to choose whether to cooperate with or to confront the state, since the state does not tolerate gay and lesbian organizations. Not only does the ACWF not protect the interests of lesbians, but it also does not stand up for sex workers. The CCP has condemned sex workers as representing an erosion of socialist morals and the ACWF has tended to blame the victims, namely, the sex workers, rather than their male customers. Tang Shengli, an 18-year-old girl, refused to provide sexual services, jumped off a building, and was later paralyzed. She was highly praised by society, including the Women's Federation, as a saint, brave enough to protect her purity. For the ACWF sex workers are treated as degenerate persons in need of rescue. Their rights as women and as workers are excluded from the agenda of the ACWF at all levels as well as other women's organizations.

A second key challenge for the ACWF is in its management structures and operational capacity. With the downsizing of the state at county level, the positions of cadres responsible for women's work have been reduced, or their area of work has been sidelined. In many counties, cadres responsible for women's work usually have several tasks to fulfil, and so carry out women's work as they can. They are thus unable to devote much energy to protecting women's interests (Li Xiaoyun, 2000). At the village level, the participation of cadres responsible for women's work in village committees since the introduction of village elections has continued to remain low, and in some villages, even to decline. For example, the percentage of female members in village committees declined by 19 percent in the sixth round of elections in Qingdao, Shandong province, in March 1999 (Qingdao Women's Federation, 2000). In urban areas women's work in neighborhood committees is also likely to weaken further, as the ACWF concentrates its future work at the higher level of the community. All these factors challenge the ACWF's capacity to influence and network at the local level.

## NEW WOMEN'S ORGANIZATIONS

It is often assumed that WTO entry will make China more open to the world and more exposed to processes of democratization. This more open environment is likely to keep open and expand the space of civil society, a process which will also benefit women's organizations. However, there are some constraints affecting women's participation in civil society and the development of new women's organizations. First, statistics indicate that women spend more time on household chores than men, exceeding men on average by 2.7 hours per day (ACWF and China Statistics Bureau, 2001). Bearing prime responsibility for child care, care of the elderly, and many household tasks, women tend to have less time than men to participate in public activities. Furthermore, poor women on the whole tend to have less time and resources to set up organizations for themselves than middle-class women. Most of the new women's organizations are run by highly educated, elite women in urban areas.

Second, WTO entry will not make it easier for some women's organizations to survive. Some organizations, such as the Beijing Lesbian Group, will continue to face difficulties. Unless state policy becomes more tolerant toward differences in sexual orientation, it is unlikely that lesbian groups will be able to function openly.

Third, women's organizations also face challenges in administration and management. These include the reproduction of existing hierarchical structures, and finding mechanisms of internal transparency and democracy within the organizations. A further challenge relates to how new women's organizations should mobilize women. Given increasing social stratification in China and the interfaces between gender and class identities, how should new women's organizations mobilize around gender and class? How can a women's movement be shaped when women's identities and interests are increasingly diverse?

To conclude, both the ACWF and new women's organizations face challenges in the context of continuing economic reform, globalization, and economic liberalization. Though the Party/state has been able to define the priorities of work of the ACWF, the organization is not totally subordinate and passive. The ACWF is an agency for change, as demonstrated in its impact on policy making and its efforts to use existing spaces and contacts to negotiate around gender equity. Women's organizations are a key element in the expanding landscape of social organizations in China, representing one of the most dynamic parts of civil society. They have brought issues of gender to public attention and developed new ways of organizing around women's needs.

A key challenge for the future will be how the ACWF and the new stratum of women's organizations can work together effectively to promote gender equity. Both the ACWF and the new women's organizations, both registered and unregistered, have their strengths and weaknesses. By further sharing of information and resources through joint projects and more collaboration around gender and development issues, the ACWF and new women's organizations could together have a much greater impact on making governance systems and processes in China work well for women.

## NOTES

1. Paper for Forum on Governance in China, IDS, University of Sussex, UK, September 11–13, 2001.

2. This is the case more generally. Theories of and empirical studies of civil society do not in general deal with the gender dimensions of civil society. However, there is a small but growing body of literature that is beginning to address the gender contours of civil society. These include Fraser (1997) and Howell and Mulligan's (2003) special issue on gender and civil society.

3. At the local level the ACFTU set up Women Workers' Committees (*nu zhi gong weiyuanhui*).

4. For details of Party leaders' commitment to women's interests in the late 1940s and early 1950s, see ACWF, 1988a.

5. This is because it is the local Party committees and local governments rather than the ACWF that deal with staff recruitment, budget, and organizational priorities for local level Women's Federations. The national ACWF provides only instructions on guidelines and activities to lower levels.

6. In its mission statement, the ACFTU, for instance, states its social functions as: "1) Safeguard the economic interests and democratic rights of workers; 2) Mobilize

and organize workers to participate in economic construction and reforms in order to achieve the targets for economic and social development; 3) Represent and organize workers in the administration of the state and social affairs and the democratic management of enterprises; and 4) Educate workers to constantly improve their ideological and ethical awareness and their scientific and cultural competence" (ACFTU, 2000: 2–3). There is no mention here of family planning, even though it is one of the basic state policies.

7. For further information on this issue, see Cai, 1999 and Peng, 2001b.

8. In particular, Peng Peiyun, president of the ACWF, is also vice-president of the Standing Committee of the National People's Congress and the vice-president of the ACWF, Gu Xiulian, is also a member of the CCP Central Committee.

9. The following are the criteria for a model family: loving the motherland, abiding by the laws and working for the public good; studying diligently, working hard and being enthusiastic and responsible for the work; promoting equality between women and men, respecting the old and loving the young; changing unhealthy habits and customs; performing family planning; managing the household economically and thriftily; and protecting the environment.

10. Professor Qiu Renzong in the Philosophy Institute of the China Academy of Social Sciences was the coordinator of such activities. He assembled many researchers in women's studies

11. Incubator project refers to microcredit projects for laid-off female workers, a key example being Tianjin Women's Federation's incubator project established in 1999.

12. The Gender Training Group was established following a "Gender and Development" train-the-trainers program in Beijing in 1999. The program was organized by the six Chinese authors of a "Gender and Development Training Manual" sponsored by UNDP China. The aim of the program was to promote increased gender awareness in development projects and government policies by organizing participatory gender awareness training activities.

13. Readers of the *China Women's News* include women cadres, scholars, and activists in the field of gender and women's issues.

# 10

# The Working Class and Governance

*Marc Blecher*

Two commonplaces of Chinese politics today are that the working class has fallen hard and fast, and that the leadership is profoundly concerned about the political implications of proletarian discontent. Indeed, such anxieties are often adduced as a key explanation for the persistence of hardliners' domination at the peak of the Chinese state—which has lasted half a decade from the end of 1998 until this writing in mid-2003, a rather long turn in the cyclical wheel of reformist politics in China, and one that shows little sign of abating despite the economic decrescendo that hardline policies generally bring in tow. The leadership's worries about its workers are understandable: in the Maoist period, the Chinese proletariat was both pampered and yet also capable of generating significant radical politics at key moments.[1] Those anxieties may be reflected in the timing of the June 4, 1989, crackdown, just a week after the Beijing Autonomous Workers' Federation had put in its appearance. Since that time, deep price and labor market reforms have only increased the pressure on this beleaguered, crestfallen, and potentially radical class. Protests by workers who are mistreated on the job, who are owed their wage or benefit arrears, who are laid off and demand their jobs back or at least their meager benefits paid, or who are retired and have not been given their pensions have become endemic, forcing local leaders to scurry around town in panicky damage-control mode.

Yet just how panicked should they be? Over two decades into the Dengist and, now, post-Dengist period, the state has accomplished the very hardest structural reforms—price and labor market liberalization—which have involved the most formidable difficulties, the deepest pain, and greatest political risks, especially with respect to the working class. It has survived the protests of 1989, which have not been repeated, though there were good

reasons to expect them to be, and a number of the kinds of political opportunities that can occasion such social movements[2] (such as the collapse of
state socialism in Russia and Eastern Europe and the death and succession of
Deng Xiaoping). Just what sort of governance problem, then, does the Chinese working class really pose for the state after all?

This chapter begins by asking how large or small the problem is—i.e., by
adducing the factors that amplify or diminish the pressure that the working
class may put on the state. The subsequent section proceeds more qualita-
tively, inquiring into the kinds of governance problem that China's proletariat poses. Next, the chapter takes up very briefly the strategic and policy
implications flowing from these analyses, including the prospects for "good
governance"-based solutions. It concludes by ruminating on the prospects
for the state's capacity to govern the working class specifically, and to govern China in light of the working class's response to social movements or
crises emanating from outside it, such as significant rural protests, an economic collapse, an international crisis, or a serious imbroglio in the top leadership.

## HOW SERIOUS IS THE
## WORKING-CLASS THREAT TO GOVERNANCE?

Both immiseration and relative deprivation theories would predict that the
declining material, social, and political position of the Chinese working class
would raise their anger, frustration, or desperation, as well as their propen-
sity to act upon such feelings. In absolute terms, life for much of the proletariat has, in important respects, gotten harder, meaner, and more humiliat-
ing. Gone are the days of guaranteed employment, economic and social
security, exalted social and political status, and the capacity to stand up to
management. The working class has declined even more markedly in relative terms. Gone too are the days when it made sense for a bright young secondary graduate to choose a factory job over a university seat because being
an intellectual was "too much trouble" (*tai mafan*) while being an industrial
worker was prestigious.[3] When such a massive, geographically concentrated
class with a definite history of radicalism suffers so precipitous an absolute
and relative decline in its material conditions, social status, and political and
ideological position, the state has a governance problem.

Unemployment poses structural difficulties for the state distinct from
workers' unhappiness and grievances about it. As workers lose their affilia-
tions with state-run enterprises, the government loses its capacity to monitor
and regulate their activities. Residents' committees, which lack the funding,
the administrative infrastructure, and the political clout wielded by "work
units" (*danwei*), cannot possibly take up these tasks, which, if anything,

have only grown more urgent as workers have both more grievances and more free time and private space to think about them, discuss them with each other, and perhaps begin to act on them. In addition, in the new administrative environment that places workers in a more attenuated relationship to the state, it is becoming more difficult for the government to provide benefits to unemployed workers. Enterprises that have laid off workers often lack the funds to pay out the small but frequently important allowances to which the laid-off are entitled. Workers whose firms have actually closed can only be provided for through the budgets and offices of local governments, in which funding arrangements and administrative relationships and responsibilities toward the local unemployed are likely to be murkier than was the case with the enterprises that employed them. The monies intended to palliate the ex-workers may be hard for cash-strapped local governments to allocate. Or these funds may be even more likely to leak, as the officials meant to dispense the funds may prove less responsible in or capable of discharging this responsibility. Or workers may be less likely to be able to find the relevant office or produce the required documents. Such outcomes are themselves one kind of governance problem. Moreover, insofar as they only alienate and anger workers even more, they can only, of course, produce another, more dangerous challenge for governance.

Many of the strikes and workers' protests that have become endemic in urban China in recent years revolve around precisely such issues. These protests themselves form a significant governance problem for the state. Local authorities with little training or experience in handling such matters have had to face new and difficult challenges. They have to quell often large, often angry phalanxes of aggrieved workers in ways that neither give in too much nor too little, either of which could encourage further protests. They must mobilize police and security forces, secure political backing from superiors, coordinate with relevant parallel organs, and obtain funding—all in all, a thorny governance problem. And at a deeper level, of course, strikes and demonstrations, which are illegal, represent a public challenge to the government.

Critics of welfare in Western capitalist states have long argued that such schemes are in fact efforts to govern the poor.[4] Similar arguments could be made for the embryonic welfare plans of the Chinese government. Rationalized retirement, medical, unemployment, and re-employment schemes are surely organized in significant part because of the state's interest in them: in the social peace they promise, and in the capacity they impart to the state to keep track of, regulate, and keep dependent—i.e., to govern—workers. The literature on Chinese welfare schemes is replete with analyses of the administrative, financial, and political difficulties involved.[5] Most Chinese social insurance and benefit schemes are, of course, underfunded. They involve bureaucratic complexities which workers have trouble navigating. Generally, the workers who are in most need of welfare support hail from precisely those enterprises that are least capable of contributing to social insurance funds, which means that those impoverished (ex-)employees usually do not qualify. Yet the very existence of state-run (as opposed to enterprise-run) welfare programs may run the risk of making the state a lightning rod for the anger and protests of poor, beleaguered workers, by bringing together around a newly shared complaint proletarians who might otherwise not find a way to connect with each other. Indeed, shortfalls in the payment of pension benefits have been a major focus of working-class protest (Hurst and O'Brien, 2002). All in all, state-run welfare plans, intended to enhance the state's ability to govern the working class, also run the risk of making that task more nettlesome and risky.

Finally, the state's difficulties in creating an environment of enforceable labor standards present a serious challenge to governance. The efforts put into drafting and promulgating the 1995 Labor Law demonstrate the state's understanding of this issue. Yet most workers I interviewed in Tianjin over subsequent years had not heard of the law, or if they had they were unaware of its provisions and the remedies it offered.[6] The few who had heard of or even experienced collective contracting—a key provision—said it was a mere formality that had little if any consequence for them. Not a single worker I have interviewed thought that the official labor union, which is given responsibility for negotiating, monitoring, and enforcing the contracts, did anything significant to improve their working lives. Moreover, and especially with the decline of the old state sector and the rise of private and joint-venture firms, labor conditions in many new plants are deteriorating. Some American multinationals may be able to claim with some justification that pay and working conditions in their plants are better than the norm. But for every such plant, many others engage in the highly exploitative and draconian practices that create the very norm which the better new plants can so easily surpass.[7] While such practices are, unfortunately, all too frequently tolerated by desperate, submissive workers, they are also the very places in which wildcat strikes and spontaneous protests, however infrequent, do occur. Such outbursts have proven manageable for the state thus far. As we shall discuss further below, though, they are the sparks that, in a different context less favorable to economic growth and political stability, could prove explosive.

Yet this inventory of factors that make the Chinese working class a governance problem is offset by another that actually works in the state's favor. The first is the fragmentation of the Chinese proletariat. Against a simplistic homogenization thesis, Elizabeth Perry has, to be sure, developed the intriguing and persuasive argument that the internal stratification of the working class has provided bases for affiliation that have promoted collective action at several key moments in recent Chinese history, from the 1930s to the

1960s (Perry, 1993; Perry, 1994; Perry and Li, 1997). It seems reasonable to hypothesize, however, that that differentiation has helped prevent such strike waves and radicalism from spreading into a more coherent, resilient, and truly national labor movement. In modern-day Tianjin, all the workers I have interviewed since 1995—many of whom were laid off and most of whom were in pretty dire straits—knew about the protests by fellow Tianjin workers that have become almost daily fare. However, they dismissed them as the work of just a handful of people with whom they had little in common. This response is typical:

> Very few workers go down to government offices to make a fuss (*naoshi*). Those who do generally are either retired workers who are not getting their pensions, or else workers with special problems such as illness, injury, or some special problem in their family's livelihood. There are several hundred thousand laid-off workers in Tianjin now, but only a few dozen engage in this sort of thing; it's a tiny percentage.

> The people who protest down at City Hall are just old workers who are not receiving their pensions and who have no other way out.[9]

> [Only] those with special problems made a fuss.[10]

In late 1990s Tianjin, generation was a major cleavage rending the working class. In interviews, younger workers, that is those in their late teens through their 20s, were more optimistic about the labor market—and justifiably so, since their employment prospects were reasonably good. They were, therefore, less worried about job security (a major concern for older workers) as well as housing, health insurance, and welfare issues, and readier to accept despotic management and oppressive labor processes. "Some younger workers actually like to be laid off [since it frees them to find other work while still providing them a small allowance], but the older ones don't."[11] Likewise, skilled and unskilled workers felt they had little in common with each other. For example, the skilled were opposed to strengthened labor contracts (favored by unskilled workers), which, they correctly felt, deprived them of the labor market flexibility from which they stood only to gain. No male worker I interviewed evinced the slightest concern about labor issues affecting women specifically. Place has always been a deep source of cleavage in the Chinese working class.[12] All the workers I interviewed—young and old, skilled and unskilled, male and female—took as their universe their home city. Not a single Tianjin worker expressed the merest concern for the dire situation in the Northeast, for example, or worried that the severe crisis of China's deep rustbelt could spread to their town. Even competition between the employed and unemployed weakens the working class.

Workers all know that they are workers and that that's all they are; that they have no way to become anything else; that they are in the same boat, with the same fate (*mingyun*). This often involves competing for the same jobs, which they understand too. This weakens them as a class.[13]

All this fragmentation strengthens the ability of the state to govern the working class. It probably helps explain the state's perhaps somewhat surprising success in the vast majority of cases in preventing the plethora of small strikes and protests from linking up and spreading even within the same city, much less across different localities.

The various coping strategies available to workers also strengthen the prospects for successful governance. The availability of informal labor markets and employment—even in only moderately prosperous places like Tianjin[14]—helps take the sting out of unemployment.

> At first, most of us were afraid of being laid off. But then after it happened most found out that it wasn't so bad; that they could make do in various ways. Many people are better off now.[15]

The existence of even just a moderately active labor market also focuses unemployed or immiserated workers on finding work rather than finding allies for protest.

> Most workers in my old plant found some way to make a living. You have to eat, after all. Some go into small business, some find jobs on the labor market.[16]

This applies both to those who can find such work but also to many others who have not, but who can, nonetheless, live in hope of doing so.

> Yes, of course it's unfair [that some workers have better pay or job security than others just because they happen to be employed in firms that are doing better (a point to which we shall return)]. But most workers think that the way to deal with the inequality is to try to make more money for themselves.[17]

Families provide an important resource, both in the job market and out. In surveys done in Shanghai and Wuhan in the mid 1990s, 48 percent and 40 percent of unemployed workers respectively said that they found new work through family connections (Solinger, 2000). Those unable to find work usually rely on their families to sustain them in the meantime.

> I am the second child in my household. I have younger and older sisters, and I have a five-year-old daughter who starts school this year. My wife is laid off, and right now runs a very small food and drink stand. Business is not very good. My father is a worker, and my mother is retired. They both have income, and they

get reimbursements from their units when they are sick. But for this, things would be even more difficult.[18]

If you're laid off and you can't find other work, you can only rely on your parents and relatives.[19]

For some laid-off workers, such dependence is actually an attraction.

If older workers have sons and daughters who are earning a good living, then they just want to stay home rather than go to work.[20]

Governance of the working class is also eased by the positive predisposition to the reform project in the broadest sense that is evinced by so much of the working class, including many workers who are themselves suffering from it. The results of a survey I conducted in 1997 and 1998, using Q-analysis,[21] a methodology intended to penetrate below mere opinions to probe the deep structure of workers' world views, revealed four identifiable ideological proclivities: dubious but resigned acceptance, ongoing though latent and pessimistic commitment to collectivism, critical though noticeably enthusiastic acceptance of the market as a new and ineluctable reality, and alienated individualism. Each of these outlooks involved a complex and textured admixture of positive and negative postures toward various aspects of China's structural reforms. Each is coherent, suggesting that workers have found ways to make sense of their rapidly changing world. None of the four outlooks is firmly or fundamentally oppositional. To take the most potentially explosive issue, concerns about unemployment were real, but they were tempered by a sense that the levels were tolerable, that other issues (especially wages) were more important, and/or that there were ways, as we have seen, to cope (Blecher, 1998).

Interviews I conducted with dozens of Tianjin workers from 1995–1999 reveal the depth with which the market and the state exercise hegemony over workers' thinking. Even those who were faring poorly in the new market environment believed nonetheless that competition and market allocation of employment and income were both right in a normative sense and were more effective than the planned economy, even though many had done well under the latter. They all accepted without much thought, not to mention indignation, the sea change that occurred from the late 1980s onward, under which workers' incomes and job security came to depend on the economic condition of their particular enterprise—essentially subjecting them to the luck of the draw—rather than, as before, depending on the state. They generally did not hold the state responsible either for this profound change or for taking care of its negative effects. They tended to blame their problems on their own enterprise's management, on local officials, or on dumb luck.

The fact that many workers responded to their economic difficulties by try-ing to help their enterprises' production and sales efforts is clear evidence of the hegemony of the market (Blecher, 2002). And the fact that they have ac-cepted so fully the separation that the state has effected between itself and the enterprises both absolves the state from responsibility for their welfare in most workers' minds and helps insulate it from such anger and protest as do develop (Blecher, 1999).

As Deng Xiaoping intended, economic growth itself is undoubtedly a ma-jor boon to the state's project of governing the working class. Even most workers who are suffering from despotic management, declining incomes, or layoffs and unemployment evince a clear appreciation for the vast mate-rial progress that the reforms have brought in tow, even though they are not sharing in the wealth. Most of my interlocutors viewed China's glittering new prosperity not just as a sign that the policies are correct, but also with some hopeful anticipation that sooner or later some of it is bound to trickle down to them or their children. Economic growth also fragments the working class further by region, sector, ownership form, skill level, age and gender, mak-ing it far more governable.

Finally, the state's impressive, monopolistic organizational apparatus is a major boon in its project of governing the working class. Officials of the All-China Federation of Trade Unions (ACFTU) admitted candidly in private that their major work now focuses on "stabilization" (*wending*).[23] The union does so through close monitoring of potential protest in enterprises, dispute medi-ation, judicious application of subsidies and assistance to those in particularly difficult situations, research into workers' attitudes and material situations, and some contract negotiations and Labor Law enforcement work. Together with the state's security apparatus, it works to prevent the development of any independent unions. When spontaneous strikes and protests break out, vari-ous state agencies work in what by now appears to be a well-practiced col-laboration to provide some combination of an eye to identify the protesters, an ear to grasp and record the source of the problem, a hand to provide some material relief, and a fist to mete out punishment to unruly ringleaders.

All in all, then, the magnitude of the governance problem posed by the working class appears neither overwhelming nor minuscule. Material diffi-culties, the eroding capacity of the state to monitor workers once they are unemployed, the daily drumbeat of protest, the slow and uneven uptake of welfare schemes, and the difficulty of regulating increasingly despotic man-agement all make governance of the working class more difficult. On the other hand, growing working class fragmentation, the availability of multiple coping strategies, the hegemonic ideology of the market and the state, the structural separation of the state from the enterprises, economic growth, and the state's vast, multistranded, and monopolistic organization all facilitate such governance.

## WHAT KIND OF GOVERNANCE
## PROBLEM DOES THE WORKING CLASS POSE?

Governing the working class involves a number of *political* challenges. The state must maintain the monopolistic organizational capacity, and the commitment to use it, that have served it so well through the difficult reforms of the 1980s and especially the 1990s.[24] This task is growing more difficult every day, of course, as the working class becomes more complex and heterogeneous, as it gradually moves out of state-run housing (where it was easier to find and watch), as protest continues to occur, and as the work of economic development and the attractions of business divert the attention and energies of state officials. The government must remain willing to use force as necessary, and adroit in doing so. It must work hard to prevent the appearance of political opportunities that can catalyze social movements (Tarrow, 1998). This last task involves preventing the kind of open leadership splits that in 1988 helped create the conditions for the 1989 protests, and avoiding domestic and international setbacks or crises that could cause either doubts about the state's capacity to govern or popular disappointment or anger at the way it governs. All that will grow more difficult in coming years as China moves toward ever more unalloyed capitalism (which poses a number of controversial issues within the leadership) and toward more complex and intensive international relations (including participation in the WTO and the Olympics, or the SARS crisis, all of which subject China to close scrutiny and direct contact with, and intervention by, foreign economic, social, and political forces). The state must also work to maintain the hegemony that it has established, both directly and via the market, over the terms of debate and proletarian predispositions. That involves not only or even mainly ideological interpellation, but, probably more importantly, maintenance of the underlying conditions of such hegemony that influence workers much more, including, most prominently, economic growth, political stability, and a modicum of administrative efficiency or at least coherence.

Governance of the working class also has several *social* dimensions that pose challenges for the state. Fragmentation cuts both ways: on the one hand, it undermines the working class's capacity for unified collective action, while on the other, it makes the political task of monitoring and regulating the working class more difficult. A similar problem arises with respect to residential structure: the diversification of working class housing arrangements makes it more difficult to monitor and regulate workers, but it also facilitates governance by fragmenting them further and, if Ira Katznelson's theory is applicable, potentially undermining the proletarian content of their politics in favor of concerns more focused on neighborhoods.[25] Finally, there is a generational dynamic that also has its own contradictions. On the one hand, older workers appear to evince a firmer commitment than younger ones to the Maoist period values of proletarian dignity and equality that have come under such assault over the past two decades. On the other, though, the traumatic experiences of the Cultural Revolution may well have exercised a restraining influence on collective action among older workers; younger workers might, under some circumstances (to be discussed further below) be less restrained from joining in radical activity for the very reason that they have not experienced its dark side.

There are, naturally, a number of economic and *work-related* dimensions to the problem of governance of the working class. The state faces a problem of being able to enforce policies on labor—including wages, working conditions, hours, benefits, and various abuses of workers by management, all stipulated in the Labor Law—and also on corruption, a major focus of many angry workers and labor disputes. In addition, there are serious policy and financial dimensions involved in providing welfare payments to ameliorate the worst effects of marketization. It must not only provide an adequate level of benefits, but also take account of the danger that its failure to do so could focus discontent and protest on the state rather than on enterprises, where protest can be more easily dissipated, and which provide a useful buffer between the working class and the state. Finally, and most fundamentally, governance of the working class provides the state with the challenge of maintaining economic equilibrium and preventing a serious recession or a depression, the political effects of which could be profound.

In short, the challenge of the People's Republic of China in governing its working class during a period of radical structural transformation is multifaceted. Moreover, it involves the delicate task of dealing with a number of processes with potentially contradictory effects that could make governance both more and less difficult. The job will require much sophisticated statespersonship and a generous dose of good fortune.

## WHAT IS TO BE DONE?

What indeed? To what specific measures might the state try to attend in its efforts to govern its working class?

*Politically,* it is continuing to support its official labor unions and neighborhood committees, two of the most valuable institutions in its program to monitor and regulate workers. It might like to strengthen "work unit" (*danwei*) organization in similar ways, but that is much less likely to succeed in the face of marketizing reforms that undermine such forms of unitary organization. It should, of course, persevere in its stated goals of becoming ever more serious about promoting "good governance" measures, such as attacking corruption, promoting greater enterprise transparency, and developing the rule of law. There is probably some room for progress here even in the absence of the development of political organization of civil society, to which the state remains deeply opposed. But there are also severe limits, including the state's declining capacity to influence enterprises and the continued preeminence of the party, which precludes significant structural autonomy of various state institutions (such as the labor federation or the judiciary). Invigoration of the labor unions, which would necessarily involve some democratization, would be both wise for the state and welcome to the workers. This will be difficult to achieve, however, in the face of the deeply entrenched Leninist habits of party control and the state's institutional coadunation, not to mention the low capacity of ACFTU to organize itself even along its present lines within the burgeoning private sector. Likewise, more robust labor-management relations—even along lines of the modest corporatist proposals already being mooted in China (such as elections of labor representatives to enterprise boards of directors) (Cui, 2001)—would help. That, however, is even less likely to succeed so long as the shortcomings of the ACFTU persist. The leadership seems all too well aware of the need to maintain iron discipline and unity so as not to create a political opportunity for a movement of angry workers or other opponents whose mobilization could in turn catalyze the proletariat. It also seems cognizant of the need to prevent political opportunities for social movements by handling international confrontations—with Taiwan and the US most prominently—in a way that maintains its high stature at home but avoids a potentially dangerous donnybrook that could end in disaster. Most prominently at the moment of this writing, it is continuing to develop and deploy its security and repressive apparatus, and to assign to its "mass organizations" such as the ACFTU the task of monitoring workers' attitudes and political activity and preempting political protest (rather than providing genuine social organization and representation).[26]

In terms of *social and economic policies*, the state has to find the proper balance in a number of arenas. It can continue to promote or at least tolerate further fragmentation of the working class—about which it has little choice anyway given the realities of the market economy—so long as it is able to maintain sufficient capacity to monitor and regulate both work and the working class. That will prove quite a challenge, and will require significantly increased resources and power for the Ministry of Labor, the ACFTU, or the Ministry of Civil Affairs and local government agencies working at the neighborhood and street committee levels. The government might try simply to muddle through for another decade or so, until the older generation of workers, who are as a whole less favorably predisposed to the reforms, has passed from the scene. In this connection, it could make efforts to divert working class concerns from the workplace to neighborhoods as part of a strategy to dig Gramscian trenches against working class radicalism (Katznelson, 1981). This could involve democratizing or at least encouraging participation in grassroots neighborhood organs. In terms of welfare and employment, far more elaborated, rationalized, comprehensive, and well-financed welfare and re-employment programs can probably only help pacify the working class, though the state must be careful not to raise expectations too much lest it create programs that are viewed as inadequate and that would serve as a focus for unhappiness and possible protest. Finally, the state will have to continue to pay attention to effective macroeconomic management in order to avoid a serious crisis.

## CONCLUSIONS

The working class presents the state with two distinct though related kinds of governance problems. First, the state must govern the working class itself. In view of the balance of forces, some making China's proletariat harder to manage and some making it easier, the goal itself does not appear unattainable. The tactics and strategies to reach it will be complex, requiring that it attend to a diverse range of factors, that it balance contradictory forces and possibilities, and that winds favorable to the state blow. The state must prevent a dynamic in which even a small, radicalized section of the working class mobilizes in ways that can catalyze much wider protest. In so complex and precariously perched a situation, above all the state must avoid a major economic or political crisis that would undermine the coping strategies that the working class has developed for itself, that would have the potential to unify the working class against the state, that could subvert the ideological hegemony that rests upon the basic health of the market reformist project and the essential effectiveness of the government, and that in general can create opportunities for social movements to develop.

Second, the working class figures prominently in the wider problem of governance generally. Social, economic, and political powderkegs abound in China. A pattern observed by Barrington Moore, in which a broad rural uprising creates a political opportunity for mobilization by radicalized sections of the working class (Moore, 1966),[27] remains a distinct possibility in China that in turn could spread rapidly, given the fragility of the state's capacity to govern the working class. It must prevent links or chain reactions between disgruntled workers and other causes such as environmental, national, or religious or spiritual movements—an imperative that no doubt drove its crackdown on dissident movements that made environmental or pro-worker claims in late 1998, ushering in the subsequent period of hardline dominance. It must not allow a serious public cleavage in the leadership, much less permit the working class to take sides in it.

Looking back over the past 23 years, one cannot but be impressed (even if one is in part depressed) by the success of the Dengist and post-Dengist leadership in knocking the working class off its Maoist-era pedestal, in overcoming a dangerous threat to its power in 1989, and in pushing through soon thereafter the hardest economic reforms—of prices and the labor market. Perhaps the most daunting tasks of governing the working class have been achieved already. In some respects the state acts as if it thinks so, i.e., in the boldness with which it continues to pursue the most radical and, some would say, callous policies on the labor market and enterprise reform, and in its far more half-hearted approach to welfare development. But as we have seen, the state's continuing efforts to monitor, regulate, and, where necessary, to suppress the working class show it does not believe it is yet out of the woods. And as a politically savvy Communist party that has already chalked up profound political successes in a period of deep transformation, it ought to know.

## NOTES

1. On the latter point, see Perry, 1994: 1–27; Perry and Li Xun, 1997.
2. On political opportunity theory, see Tarrow, 1998.
3. Interview, Hong Kong, December 1975. This interview was carried out with the late Professor Gordon White as part of a joint research project on micropolitics. The findings of this research appear in Blecher and White, 1979.
4. The *locus classicus* is Fox Piven and Cloward, 1971.
5. One of the best summaries of the problems is White's chapter in Goodman, White, and Huck-ju Kwon, 1998: chapter 8.
6. During field trips in 1995, 1996, 1997, and 1999 I have interviewed 45 workers, mostly in Tianjin but also in Beijing and Kunming, in connection with research for several articles and a book tentatively entitled *A World to Lose: Workers' Politics and the Chinese State*.
7. For a stunning catalogue, see Chan, 2001.
8. Interview, June 7, 1999.
9. Interview (2), May 25, 1999.
10. Interview (2), June 8, 1999.
11. Interview, May 28, 1999.
12. See, for example, Hershatter, 1986; Honig, 1986; Perry, 1993.
13. Interview (1), June 8, 1999.
14. From 1991 to 1999, gross value of industrial output in Tianjin grew 14.2 percent per year, compared with 10.9 percent nationally. It is more difficult to find consistent time-series data on household income over this period, but the following may provide a rough guide: in 1999, urban "real income" (*shiji shouru*) in Tianjin was 7,671 yuan, which was 368 percent higher than the average urban "cash income" (*xianjin shouru*) of 2,087 yuan in 1991. Comparable national figures are 5,889 yuan and 1,996 yuan, a 295 percent increase. Tianjin's average urban real income in 1999 was significantly below that of Shanghai (10,989 yuan), Guangdong (9,206 yuan [n.b., this is not Guangzhou, which would surely be higher]), and Beijing (9,239 yuan). (*Zhongguo tongji nianjian (China Statistical Yearbook)*, 2000: 319; *Zhongguo tongji nianjian (China Statistical Yearbook)*, 1992: 288.)

15. Interview, June 7, 1999.
16. Interview, June 7, 1999.
17. Interview, June 7, 1999.
18. Interview (2), May 25, 1999.
19. Interview, May 28, 1999.
20. Interview, May 28, 1999.
21. For a description of Q-analysis as well as the findings, see Blecher, 1998. The 29 workers, who were surveyed in depth in 1998 in connection with the research forthcoming in *World to Lose*, all hailed from Tianjin.
22. See, for example, Khan and Riskin, 2001; Riskin, Zhao, and Li, eds., 2000.
23. Interview, May 23, 1999.
24. The collapse of the USSR and the state socialist regimes of Eastern Europe may suggest that the state needs not just a vast, monopolistic organizational apparatus but also the political will to use it, which seemed to evaporate at the end.
25. Katznelson has argued that the separation of workplace and home provides a Gramscian hegemonic "trench" that undermines class-based politics (Katznelson, 1981).
26. In 1999 central ACFTU officials described their organization's main task as promoting "stability." Interview, May 1999, Beijing.
27. See, in particular, chapter 2.

# 11

# Governance and the Political Challenge of the Falun Gong

*Clemens Stubbe Østergaard*

After seven years of toleration and two years of sharp conflict, the societal phenomenon of the Falun Gong had run its course, at least within China itself. From the point of view of governance, there are, however, still many things to be learned by analyzing the organization, the state's unsophisticated handling of it, and the societal forces and interests remaining. It is rare to have as our laboratory a crisis involving a cross-regional, cross-class formation, though some regions and some strata do dominate.[1] The typical Falun Gong follower was a middle-aged, female, poorly-educated city dweller in the rustbelt, while core members seem to be either younger males or retired cadres in the same locations.[2] An important, though smaller, group was made up of educated people, marginalized by their work units, or previously influential people now stripped of power, including PLA-officers (Leung[3], 2001: 7; Vermander, 2001: 9).

It is, of course, no surprise that socioeconomic change at the pace China has seen over the last decades creates anomie and turbulence. Perhaps the surprise is that societal conflict has not been sharper, and one might look for the "stabilizers" at work. After all, we have seen a telescoping of developments, which Europe had centuries to accommodate. In the light of this, the chapter takes up the theme of state-society conflict, focusing on the case of the Falun Gong and the state policies employed. The problem is how to explain the variations in government policy over time. It is argued that the Falun Gong was a new kind of popular fundamentalism, characterized by strong organization and modern management technology, which, in interaction with officialdom, turned into a political interest group organization, leading to a collision with the Party-state.

Here I shall not attempt to deal with the categorization-debate, that is, whether the Falun Gong is a *xiejiao* (heretical sect), cult, sect, religion, or new religious movement; nor the international ramifications of the Falun Gong and its development in Taiwan and Hong Kong; nor with the obvious and well-covered human rights aspects of the campaign against the Falun Gong. Instead, I will proceed by first looking at the interests, sometimes the yearnings, of the large body of people "ready" for recruitment. Next I will argue that the popular fundamentalisms found in Chinese history cater precisely to this syndrome, though often the anomie and turbulence were created by natural disasters or impoverishment rather than by dynamic societal change. The Falun Gong differs, in my view, from these. I depict it as a new popular fundamentalism by describing its very strong organization and its deft use of modern technology and modern marketing methods. I go on to argue that minor irritations experienced by the Falun Gong between 1996 and 1999 were responded to in a fashion that gradually turned it into an interest group acting politically. This leads directly to the acute state-society conflict, initiated when one authoritarian leader finally brought his "troops" to the very headquarters of other authoritarian leaders. The chapter then looks at the motives and the means employed by the Party/state in managing this expression of interests. A brief attempt is made to explain the defeat of Li, leader of the Falun Gong, in terms of miscalculation. Finally, I reflect upon what this tells us about state, society, and the political system, what the consequences of confrontation have been, and what other options were open to the government.


## POPULAR ISSUES OF DISCONTENT IN THE 1990S

A number of factors have interacted to create a large body of people in China with a desire for alternatives to the public health system, a growing discontent with public and private morality, and a spiritual vacuum alongside the hope to redeem somehow a life spent on a discarded ideology. A yearning for something to participate in, other than the political system, also seems evident.

The PRC health sector was relatively successful, providing reasonable medical services for free or at a very small fee (Lampton, 1977). After the reforms the sector has lagged behind, been partly privatized, and become increasingly based on fees. At the same time, pensions stagnated and the real income of middle-aged people fell, while the previously common system of family support for the elderly has also been eroded. A survey in 1997–1998 showed that the two most important concerns for ordinary people were unemployment and medical costs (Xu Xin, ed., 1999, quoted in Leung, 2001: 12). *Qigong*, with its breathing and physical exercises, has been seen as a way to improve health and reduce medical expenses. It was promoted as health-improving in the 1950s, and again from the start of the reforms, and has even enjoyed popularity amongst the top political leadership. Discontent with decaying morality is widespread. The corruption in official life, *guandao*, is particularly noxious and was a main factor behind the Tiananmen demonstrations (Østergaard, 1989). For the middle-aged and elderly, many other developments in society are abhorrent and alienating, such as prostitution, street crime, triads, female emancipation, divorce, breakdown of family values, lack of respect for the old, strange youth cultures, homosexuality, and so on. Fierce competition in the market economy promotes a materialism foreign to many in this age group, intensifying their anxiety over the direction society is taking. Many were formerly privileged urban workers, nostalgic for parts of the past. Some retired cadres nurse grudges against the ideological and behavioral "deviations" of the Communist Party and feel powerless in the face of reforms. Surveys show a sharp rise in the belief that the pace of reform is too fast (Tang and Parish, 2000: 111).

With the Party's unravelling of socialist ideology has come a spiritual vacuum. No rival ideas were able to grow in the shadow of the Chinese Communist Party's control of information and communication. What now can explain the world and the individual's role in it? No alternative moral vision has arisen. Nationalism is certainly not sufficient, nor does the "science worship," spread first by May Fourth intellectuals and today by the engineers leading China, appeal to those with a failed education, who perhaps cannot distinguish it from Li's parascience (*Nanfang Zhoumo*, 1999). The retreat from Maoism and the realization that one's life has been spent on a discarded ideology can lead to materialism and cynicism, and thus to corruption, but obviously also to increased idealism and a wish to redeem the past.

Finally, with the end of many collective units, such as the work unit (*danwei*), communes, study groups, and grassroots Party activities, there is an unsatisfied demand for an "apolitical" collective movement based on the individual. Something to participate in, to enable one to keep a role in society—even after retirement.[4] This need is particularly strong for those too old or too unskilled to participate in the new collective mission: going into business, xiahai (literally "jump into the sea"). The post-Mao equation of national progress with scientific modernization and entrepreneurial wealth creation leaves little imaginative space for nonscientists and nonentrepreneurs to contribute (Kipnis, 2001: 10).

## POPULAR FUNDAMENTALISM: THE ANSWER?

The old Chinese popular fundamentalism, described by David Ownby, caters to most of the syndrome described above (Ownby, 2000: 3). Folk Buddhism often had millenarian elements and could, as happened with the

White Lotus movement, impact on political life, inspiring rebellion leading to a change of dynasty. The state has suppressed movements similar to the Falun Gong hundreds of times in Chinese history. As late as 1911–1949, among the huge religious presence embracing tens of millions of people in China, were many groups of cultivators,[5] who repackaged the original White Lotus cosmology, retaining the ideas of the end of the world and the possibility that moral behavior could save them—and possibly even the world. They were suppressed in the years from 1950 to 1954, but "there were dozens, perhaps a couple of hundred, rebellions between 1955 and the beginning of the Cultural Revolution that were organized by these same religious groups" (Ownby, 2000: 6). For a while, Maoist communism then became a religious phenomenon that replaced all religions (Wong and Liu, 1999: 48). When verdicts were changed and labels removed after 1978, many left prison with nothing to sell but their religious practices. The biggest comeback was the "Qigong craze," limiting itself to bodily techniques and supported by the government for ten to 15 years as a Chinese science and a boon to popular health.

Popular fundamentalism has five characteristics.[6] First, it has a body-oriented discourse, encompassing everything from health and healing to superhuman powers. In the Falun Gong's case, the simplified exercises seem very healthy for older people, while sickness is due to karma. "Medicine or various treatments . . . will bring about new sickness-karma and lead to different kinds of sicknesses. Surgery can only remove the flesh in the superficial physical dimension" (Li, 2001a: 29). Even the critical journalist Dai Qing is convinced that Master Li Hongzhi possesses the healing skills and supernatural abilities that many ancient doctors had (Dai Qing, 2000: 8). He is able to promise people who persevere immortality, eternal youth, a third eye, the absence of illness, and a number of the ten thousand supernatural abilities known to him. Everything achieved is lost at once, if you leave the movement (Heberer, 2001: 6–8).

Second, it has a discourse of morality. Physical transformation is achieved mostly through moral practice. For some groups morality is very central. This is the case for the Falun Gong. Li fulminated against "degenerate influences" like homosexuality, television, sexual freedom, rock 'n roll, women's liberation, and also the aliens that are taking over humanity via cloning (Li, 2001b: 232).

Third, there is a larger structure characterized by a discourse of exile and return. The world has become a bad place and we should go back to where we once were (Ownby, 2000: 8). This links up with millenarian beliefs and apocalyptic notions, which have their roots in Buddhism (Palmer, 2001: 16–18). For Li Hongzhi, we are "in the time of the last Havoc" (Li, 2001a: 26). Civilization was already destroyed 81 times and rebuilt by a few survivors. The successful followers will make it through the apocalypse (Li Hongzhi,

1998: 20; Heberer, 2001: 6). As to "exile and return," Li is explicit: "You fell here from a holy, pure and incomparably splendid world . . . go back in a hurry" (Li, 2001a: 6, 55, 98).

Fourth, the unregulated creation of scriptural truth is another common trait of these groups. The scripture is syncretistic and may offer models of the cosmos and the place of humans in it, as well as models for acting in that cosmos (Kipnis, 2001). It also criticizes everyone else as heterodox. The Falun Gong certainly has its own all-encompassing scriptures, seven books in seven years, written and jealously guarded by Li, which undertake to explain not only this world, but the entire universe through eternity—complete with extraterrestrials and parascientific cosmological speculation.[7] The Falun Gong tends to monism and all other belief systems are rejected (Li, 2001a: 25).

Fifth, they are communities, offering the social joys of participation in a symbolic community, the chance to volunteer and to show loyalty to the unquestioned leader. There are easy parallels to Maoism or the early Chinese Communist Party. In the Falun Gong, exercises must be done publicly in a group and followers have been organized in groups of ten (Li, 2001a: 91). The leader must be obeyed: "You should never do what I don't allow you to" (Li, 2001a: 81). Past actions may be redeemed by good deeds. Becoming a martyr for the movement in the struggle against evil can be a shortcut to higher levels of existence and thus to the final Consummation which provides supernatural powers and godlike status. This is indeed a collective movement based on the salvation of the individual, and one which allows former Red Guards to expiate their sins and reduce their heavy karma. For higher cadres, too, it presents a way to cleanse themselves.

We have seen the several motivations for participation and their fulfilment in the Falun Gong: the desire for healing, through exercises and moral purification expelling sickness karma; the concern about morality and search for moral guidance, fully covered by the founder's conservative fulminating over real and imagined social ills and the individuals' "cultivation"; the filling of a spiritual and ideological vacuum, through the creation of an arena of symbolic participation, concerned about providing models of and for a general order of existence, world-ordering models that accommodate mass participation; and finally, the need for increased social solidarity, through community formation around the organization (Kipnis, 2001: 46).

China is not the only country to have this kind of movement and to have age-old beliefs, and behaviors seize control of the popular imagination (Perry, 1999: 326). The spectacular growth of the Falun Gong over a few years remains puzzling, however. In the next section I go on to characterize the phenomena, which set it apart from other popular fundamentalisms and from everything else on offer in the religious supermarket in China of the mid-1990s, namely strong organization and modern management technology.

## NEW POPULAR FUNDAMENTALISM?
## MODERN MARKETING AND STRONG ORGANIZATION

The Falun Gong grew explosively at a time when less *savvy qigong* movements declined.[8] I ascribe this to the skilled way that Li and the Falun Gong leadership used available modern methods of communication, management, and marketing and built a strong and flexible organization as a vehicle for spreading the doctrine and the movement.

The use of the fax, mobile phones, and later the Internet gave a strength of communications never before available to an organization in China. With the liberalization of this sector in the 1990s, as well as technological progress and increasing affluence, the hierarchical organization in the process of construction could be turned into an efficient command structure. What the railway workers were for the early Chinese Communist Party, the Internet has been for the Falun Gong. The Internet, encrypted e-mail, and the flourishing Internet cafes in Chinese cities made it possible for the top leadership to remain in control, even after it left China for the U.S. in 1996 (Smith, 2001a). The efficient use of the possibilities of the World Wide Web also gave the movement the option of establishing a strong global propaganda presence.

Modern marketing methods have also helped make the Falun Gong a highly modern phenomenon, an antimodernity movement using postmodern methods. As shown, market demand existed. To begin, Li simplified the complicated *qigong* exercises, making them ready for mass consumption. He also undertook product development when he, after a few years as an "ordinary" *qigong*-master, started publishing his scriptures. The timing was good—he was able to take over many confused qigong practitioners looking for spiritual guidance, some from associations dissolved by the government (Palmer, 2001: 21). The product, the doctrine, and the exercises now promised speedy salvation, with consummation in as little as two years (Li, 2001b: 57), and catered to both textual and nontextual adherents. It was kept highly uniform and standardized over time, and great efforts were made to prevent pirating—a lingering death awaited these people (Li, 2001a). Acquisition of supernatural powers was made into a strong "sales point," and so was the "cultural revitalization" side, stressing the glories of Chinese civilization.

The continually expanding market found in China through proselytizing (Li, 2001a: 46, 61), and repeated admonitions to study and learn by heart, was further developed by "merchandising."[9] Based on the best-selling books, audiocassettes, videos, and VCDs, it progressed into, for instance, pads, special clothing, and gilt-framed pictures of Li. Dai Qing mentions a friend who "bought copy after copy of Zhuan Falun and supplementary materials and replaced Mao's picture with Li" (Dai Qing, 2000). At times complete sets were sold at 300 yuan. Letting donations to exercise classes be voluntary is also a kind of price differentiation, which is helpful for reaching consumers at varying income levels.[10] When the time came to expand the market by "going global," Li did this by means of world lecture tours, interviews, and finally by the move to New York, making the Falun Gong a "transnational corporation." The scriptures are now translated into ten to fifteen languages.

Whether Li segmented his potential market remains unclear,[11] but his demand that exercises be done in public, and the many "events" created by followers from 1996 onward certainly have helped sales, as has the books' reputation for magic properties. Production of publications seems to have been undertaken by people close to, but not identical with, the leadership of the organization in those provinces where it is strongest.[12] Until 1996 official publishing houses published the works, a number of which belonged to the military. After they were banned, production and sales continued uninterrupted but through less official channels. This is why followers maintain they do not buy the books and other items (Amnesty International, 2000: 15–18).

Apart from marketing skills, public relations have been run highly professionally. Since the move to New York, the firm Rachlin Management and Media Group has provided an official spokesman (thereby limiting media access to an erratic Li), press releases, video materials, and a huge system of well-run Web sites, as well as shortwave transmissions beaming to China. The human rights theme has been used to the point of stealing the show from the relevant NGOs, accusations of being a cult have been countered, and those areas of the U.S. most liable to New Religious Movements have been saturation bombed.

Another important respect in which the Falun Gong differs from old popular fundamentalism is in its organizational structure.[13] It is/was a resilient, hierarchical, cell-type organization. At the top, but beneath Li, was the Falun Dafa Research Society in central Beijing, the administrative headquarters; in provincial capitals were central bureaus (General Instruction Stations or in recent translations General Assistance Centers); and in lesser population centers were 1,900 sub-bureaus (Assistance Centers), each in charge of activities in a prefecture or municipal city. At the grassroots were 28,000 Practice Stations penetrating into various sectors of society.[14] Linked to these were "monitors" responsible for overseeing the teaching of newcomers. Mass rallies—*sharing conferences*—were also a feature. At a later stage preparations were made to set up second, even third echelons of leadership at the various levels to replace possible arrests (*Renmin Ribao*, 1999a).

In this structure, important processes were found. One centers on the personnel network, the core network of coordinators and assistant coordinators. Leaders at province-level were trained at headquarters before being appointed by Li. Leaders at lower levels have to go through similar vetting and appointment from above. "The assistance centers, general assistance centers in different regions, and the Research society have the right to replace any assistant or person in charge of a branch . . . practitioners' speeches [at rallies] must be approved by the assistance centers" (Li, 2001a: 46–47). Most were volunteer workers, though some of the leaders were being rewarded. Another important process lies in the continuing correction of errors in work methods used by the organization. Li's admonitions at times read exactly like old CCP documents on work methods, criticizing commandism, bureaucratism, careerism, deviations, splittism, eight-legged essays, and so on.

In some respects the organization was indeed reminiscent of the CCP in the 1920s or 1930s, with its central committee and its thousands of local cells linked through leaders, who may only know each other by e–mail address. Expansion could be horizontally; when the membership of a group increased to a certain number, ten according to Heberer, a new *qigong* group was formed under new leadership. A movement that expands horizontally can grow fast and is more difficult for the state to suppress (Leung, 2001: 8; Heberer, 2001: 4).

The main characteristics of the organization are several. It is nationwide. It is divided into a core network and a mass of followers, who are generally wholly loyal and dedicated to the man in absolute authority, the former military man in complete control of the hierarchy. Transparency has never been a feature. The Falun Gong presents the same challenges to research as the Chinese Communist Party.

The Falun Gong thus differs from the old popular fundamentalism in two important respects, which are mutually supportive. It has a very strong organization, making it highly centralistic and uniform. It also employs modern technology and marketing methods. These two factors, and Li's charismatic power, made it easier for Li to change the nature of the organization when required.

## TOWARDS ACUTE STATE-SOCIETY CONFLICT

In this section I first describe the various knocks received by the Falun Gong as it began to grow rapidly and then chart the responses of the Falun Gong. I then argue that all this gradually transforms the Falun Gong into an interest group, acting politically. In doing so the Falun Gong, for reasons to be discussed, crosses boundaries still maintained by the Party/state, evoking various fears, leading to the drastic policy change in June–July 1999.

From the beginning of the 1990s, the state started to grow wary of the slide in some *qigong* circles from bodily techniques to quasi-religious cultivation. Some *qigong*-groups were dissolved because they were too large and their leaders too charismatic. There were gradually more attacks on superstition and pseudoscience. From 1995 an antisuperstition (*mi xin*) campaign was conducted and there was an attempt to clean up "the *Qigong* Party"

(Amnesty International, 2000; Heberer, 2001: 21). This was the year when the Falun Gong started to grow rapidly, following the publication of the first volume of *Zhuan Falun* in January. There was no media criticism of the Falun Gong until an article appeared in *Guangming Ribao* on June 17, 1996, which took the *Zhuan Falun* as an example of the growing number of publications since 1992 that could be described as "feudal superstition" (*fengjian mixin*) and "pseudoscience" (*wei kexue*). The article touched on a number of the points used against the Falun Gong three years later. There was also a document from the *News Publication Department* prohibiting publication of *Zhuan Falun* and three other books. Apart from this, it seems individual "investigative" reporters were set in motion by deaths or dramatic events (e.g. *Nanfang Zhoumo*, 1999; Li, 2001a: 21). Beginning in 1996, Buddhist organizations found it necessary to distance themselves from the Falun Gong in local publications and soon developed a more systematic criticism, comparing it to dangerous cults like Aum Shinrikyo (Holbig, 2000: 139).[15] In November, the national Qigong Research Association excluded Li, based on his posing as a god, spreading feudal superstition, and fabricating political rumors. But in the words of Dai Qing: "By 1997, Li Hongzhi . . . was earning an annual income of more than RMB 10 million. From this we can infer that the organization had been quite leniently regulated" (Dai Qing, 2000: 4).

Li Hongzhi did not take the same relaxed view of things. The Falun Gong response was right from the start "contentious politics," while Li himself left for the U.S. Li wrote in 1997: "From the incident with the *Guangming Daily* (1996) until now, every Dafa disciple has played a role . . . some wrote without reservation to the authorities for the sake of *Dafa's* reputation; some spoke out against the injustice done by the irresponsible report" (Li, 2001a: 58). Over the next three years, there would be 78 incidents involving more than 300 followers. Usually the target would be various media offices or provincial and city governments. Writing of the month-long demonstrations leading to a Beijing TV journalist being sacked in 1998 after an interview with physics professor He Zuoxiu,[16] Li said:

A few scoundrels from literary, scientific, and qigong circles, who have been hoping to become famous through opposing qigong, have been constantly causing trouble. . . . Some newspapers, radio stations and TV stations in various parts of the country have directly resorted to these propaganda tools to harm our Dafa, having a very bad impact on the public. This was deliberately harming Dafa and cannot be ignored. Under these very special circumstances, Dafa disciples in Beijing adopted a special approach to ask those people to stop— this actually was not wrong. This is only to be done in extremely restricted situations (Li, 2001a: 93).

But it happened again and again to "uninformed and irresponsible media agencies." Thus Li gradually turned the Falun Gong into an interest group,[17]

asking his followers to take part in "collectively presenting the facts to someone" (what others would call harassment or intimidation), "clarifying *Dafa*,"
"appealing to higher levels (*shangfang*)," demanding the sacking of a TV
journalist, and holding 18 large demonstrations between April 1998 and April
1999, as well as write-ins, sit-ins, musical barrages, petitioning, and so on.
"The masses of trainees have always gone benevolently to offer explanations
to the relevant people. Even when they have gone in large numbers, they
have maintained perfect order."

It is obvious that there was opposition in the organization to this turn of
events:

> There are some who have engaged in divisive activities, making the current sit-
> uation more complicated. Some even stopped cultivating, others circulated ru-
> mours. . . . A number of key contact persons in different regions analyzed *Dafa's*
> situation with the unhealthy habit of observing social trends, a habit developed
> over years of political struggle. By relating isolated problems that arose in dif-
> ferent regions, *they concluded that some social trends were unfolding* and so
> they communicated this to practitioners . . . could anything damage the Fa more
> seriously? . . . Only at the critical time can we see a persons heart. . . . Expose
> those who undermine the Fa in a disguised way. (Li, 2001a: 58, see also 93–94)

The interests or ideas articulated before April 25, 1999, and the demands
communicated to targets such as local authorities, media organizations, and
central Party and government organs may be summed up in five points: first,
the right to have a nationwide "theocratic" organization; second, the right to
have no interference or criticism from media or authorities; third, demands
for improved morality and for a replacement of a "dirty political system" with
one composed of Falun Gong practitioners (Li, 2001a: 37); fourth, less materialism, rush for profit, and money, in effect leading to a slower pace of reform avoiding the economic and social externalities; and fifth, equal status
for para-science and modern science and medicine (Li, 2001a: 29). No special authority to "so-called 'scientists.'"

The Falun Gong could be viewed as a grouping of reform-losers and otherwise socially or politically frustrated people, set to form a societal counter-
movement to show that the material, money-oriented sphere is not all, and
that there is also a spiritual realm unsatisfied by the state's administration of
society. They demonstratively negated politics and the political system, but
could be mobilized even to the point of sacrificing their well-being or their
lives (Li, 2001a: 63 et passim; *Xinhua*, 2001a). The group's resources as an interest group were notably its numbers, the strong financial basis, its organizational skills, its cohesion, and the international support it could rely on in a
time of Sino-American tension (Xu, 2001). Though interest groups are often
oligarchic, this one had so little voice for rank-and-file members in group political activity that it cannot be regarded as a harbinger of democracy.

## GOVERNANCE VERSUS EXPRESSION OF INTERESTS, POLICY MOTIVES, INSTRUMENTS, AND LIMITATIONS

In ending its policy of inaction, and breaking the normal 1990s pattern of "as long as it is not a movement, anything goes" (Wasserstrom, 2000: 4), what were the state's motives, the policy instruments and their costs, and the key variables conditioning the state's room for maneuver?

When Li's confrontational strategy culminated on April 25, 1999, with the surprise surrounding of Zhongnanhai by 10,000 followers for 13 hours, an invisible boundary was evidently crossed, from the state's point of view.[18] The policy up to then had been one of low-profile appeasement. According to Dai Qing (2000: 4), it was "Four Nos": No propaganda. No reporting. No criticism. No organizational affiliation. Over the next three months, the Falun Gong was first researched by experts and the decision was then made to ban the organization and employ a very wide range of policy instruments in a war of attrition. The context of decision making was anti-American student demonstrations after the May 7 NATO-missile bombing of the Chinese embassy in Yugoslavia, president Lee Teng-hui's provocative call for state-to-state relations with Taiwan, big government efforts to fight severe floods in Central China, and the approaching tenth anniversary of Tiananmen.

The Party/state had at least five interacting reasons for undertaking the costly conflict with society implicit in the policy change of June–July 1999. First was the aim of maintaining a monopoly on nationwide organization (*People's Daily* overseas edition, July 23, 1999). The main concern was to avoid a spillover to other organizations. The Falun Gong's example could set in motion other forces, opening up the public sphere for autonomous organizations and associations. This would upset state corporatism (Chan and Unger, 1996: 95; Ding, 1998: 67–8). Second, Li overstepped the limits at a particularly sensitive and very tense time, potentially jeopardizing social stability.[19] This helped unite a leadership otherwise divided on the issue (Luo, 1999). The third reason was preventing a mass "exit" from the political system. These were people who, in Hirschmann's terms, had given up "voice" and exhausted "loyalty." Yet now they could be mobilized by an authoritarian leader abroad. Attracting a following as big as Li's provides a basis for pursuing larger social, political, or economic goals. Symbolic participation can always be seen as both an end in itself and as a means to other ends (Kipnis, 2001: 10).[20] Fourth, clearly the reform-minded leadership had an interest in defending reforms, past and future, against criticism from organized antimodernity reform-losers. Palliative measures adopted toward the typical categories of followers support this interpretation. Fifth, there was a strong element of hegemonic struggle over political legitimacy.[21] The belief system of the Falun Gong was directly contrary to the remaining Party ideology and to national modernization goals. The glorifying of tradition implicitly questioned the justification of the very existence of the Chinese Communist Party over the last 80 years, and the Falun Gong could also become a dangerous challenger to the mantle of nationalism, a remaining source of political legitimacy (Ownby, 2001: 13). Finally, Jiang Zemin felt his power and deep beliefs in science affronted by the "encirclement" and took a personal interest. The Falun Gong duly singled him out for direct verbal and symbolic attacks, thus strengthening this factor.

If these were the main motives for policy change, what then were the policy instruments deployed by the state after July 1999? There were legal, political, administrative, and economic measures.[22] The counterattack was first of all turned into a legal issue. People's Republic of China (PRC) laws require all social organizations, including religious groups, to register with the government and impose restrictions on religious practice in the name of social stability. Since the organization was not officially recognized, it was illegal. All activities organized by an illegal organization are ipso facto illegal[23] (*China Daily*, 2001). The crackdown on an organization not registered in accordance with PRC laws would potentially be consistent with the rule of law, but the way in which the crackdown was conducted, particularly illegal detention and other procedural violations, violates any credible interpretation of the rule of law. On the basis of this, a large number of arrests of Falun Gong leaders were made. Other legal instruments were bans against state employees being *Dafa* practitioners (*Xinhua*, 2000a: 26). On the same date, Party and Youth League members were similarly forbidden to participate in the Falun Gong. The international "costs" of the legal attack have primarily been caused by the death in police custody of one to two hundred practitioners over the subsequent two years, the administrative use of re-education camps and annulments of the rights of those arrested to sue the government.

The next move was the largest political propaganda campaign since 1989. The main issues were health and science, including suicides and "*qigong* psychotic reaction" syndromes, seemingly confirmed by Li as early as December 1995 (Li, 2001a: 21; *Xinhua*, 2001); the cult issue, depicting the struggle as part of the legitimate efforts of states everywhere against dangerous cults (Fouchereau, 2001: 10; *Xinhua*, 2001e); the issue of foreign influence, with Li singled out as a Western agent (He Chong, 2001); and the depiction of Li as a predatory trickster with an inflated ego (*Xinhua*, 2001c). Modeled on the campaigns of yesteryear, it was heavily TV-oriented, involved other media, countless meetings at all levels, public destruction of materials, creation of *ad hoc* anti-Falun Gong organizations, an effort resulting in 1.5 million signatures, and so on (Perry, 2000). The "costs" of the campaign instrument are mainly internal. It is wearing and expensive, distracts from other work, and thus can only be used occasionally. Furthermore, there is the risk that in a large campaign local officials may go too far.

Administrative means have been central to the effort against the Falun Gong. These include the creation of a special office under the State Council, the Office for the Handling of the Evil Cult, the conduct of electronic war on Falun Gong communications, and the establishment of a task force in public security, the 610-office (established June 10th), right down to local authorities and re-education camps and deprogramming centers (*Chengdu*, 2001; *Xinhua*, 2001g). To get around problems of local implementation, quotas were employed and a variant of the traditional *bao jia* method[24] was used, that is, local governments would be held personally responsible for every protester that reached Beijing. The fines were then passed down even to mayors and county heads, ending with the individual police officer looking at financial ruin if he could not prevent "his" Falun Gong followers from reaching Beijing. This is the background to some of those deaths in police custody which were not due to suicide or illness (Johnson, 2000).

Implementation problems were severe. With the surprise element of the Zhongnanhai-demonstration, the policy-process started at the very top, leaving little time for traditional means of managing the implementation process (Sutton, 1999). Key stakeholders did not participate, and local authorities implemented central guidelines with varying zeal and understanding. It became necessary for the General Offices of the Central Committee and the State Council to issue a joint circular stressing the need to differentiate among followers, to be patient, and to avoid oversimplification. It pointed out the need to help solve the practical difficulties of former practitioners and to create more cultural life and more sports activities (General Office, 1999).

Apart from this, a number of wider policy measures undertaken after April 1999 can be seen as responses to the challenge of the Falun Gong, and thus as successes for the interest group. In February 2001 the government announced a new health care system for the rural areas. In March 2000 pensions were increased by 30 percent, and later a five-year plan for the care of the elderly was produced. New attempts at popularizing science have been undertaken, and in the field of education the idea of introducing the Confucian classics into primary school education is under discussion. Confucianism incarnates the traditional state skepticism toward religion as being equivalent to superstition and possibly sedition.

The key variables conditioning and limiting the state's room for maneuver, apart from all the fears and motives outlined above, are as follows. First, the lack of internal consensus and discipline in the Party leadership, among center and localities and in grassroots organs of the party, have constrained the actions of the state; second, the Party's relative lack of experience in dealing with a movement of this kind; third, the Falun Gong's strong use of an international audience, particularly in the U.S. The extensive use of human rights appeals does, however, not seem to have had any effect in China, though the aspiration to the rule of law has influenced the course of the counterattack. Fourth, the state has wanted to avoid attacking established religious freedom, such as it is, and as a consequence has pursued a united front strategy.

The final variables are the lack of innovative thinking and a basic sense of the need for state-society negotiation and bargaining.

## EXPLAINING THE OUTCOME: LI'S MISCALCULATIONS?

The state seems, contrary to some expectations, to have won the conflict against the Falun Gong.[25] Though there is support in the struggle against the Falun Gong from many parts of society, such as scientists, journalists,[26] reform supporters, the private sector, the sunbelt (*Nanfang*, 1999), and established religions, to name a few, there seems to be two overwhelming explanations for the government's success. One is found in Li Hongzhi's miscalculations, the other in a basic dilemma of his organization.

Perhaps due to the many Party-members among followers, Li underestimated the reaction and the capacity of "the opponent" to use state power as described above. This became obvious, first, in the way he politicized his organization, and second, in how he organized the Zhongnanhai "siege." The argument has been made that this kind of organization always ends up politicized. "All prophetic protest-movements sooner or later move from religious to economic and political goals, only the timing and the intensity of this 'reversal' varies" (Lee Jin-woo, 1987 in Heberer, 2001). Kipnis explains the politicization in the following way:

> Ironically, the state requirement that these activities keep their distance from "politics" creates the potential for politicization. As the institutional boundaries of "religion" and 'science' are continually policed and renegotiated, the practitioners of these "apolitical activities," in China as well as in liberal, secular democracies, are compelled to focus on their relation to the state (Kipnis, 2001: 9).

Yet Li could have chosen a different strategy and kept a lower profile. He may simply have overplayed his hand because he was proactively relying on government reactions to provide vivid proof of the manichean world view in his scriptures and as "tests" of his followers. His greatest gift to the state was the Jingwen, issued on New Year's Day 2001, which some followers interpreted as asking for an escalation of the struggle against the state, including the supreme sacrifice. The self-immolations on Tiananmen in January 2001 in retrospect were a turning point, ending most domestic sympathy for what began to look rather more like a fanatical cult.

Surrounding Zhongnanhai with a sit-in was a major miscalculation. How did it come about? One interpretation goes as follows: First, since 1989 the CCP had been careful about confronting social forces head on. There is a price for using force, and the state needed time to recover after conducting a major operation against social protest. This is why the Falun Gong and many other unregistered mass organizations were able to flourish. At the same time, there was tolerance toward localized interest-based protest in the 1990s. This tolerance may have been interpreted as weakness, but the soft approach of the state does not mean that it lacks the means to deal with social resistance like the Zhongnanhai adventure.

Miscalculations or not (Dai Qing, 2000: 5), there was also a basic dilemma for Li, which is likely to have led to the Falun Gong members' problems from 1996 onward. Members had simply gotten more than they bargained for (and less). On the one hand, he was clearly promising practitioners a way out of the world, while on the other, he was leading them directly into the thick of it, into the world they knew all too well. Trying to construe the conflict as a transcendent, metaphysical one, or protesting repeatedly that he was completely uninterested in politics, in the long run could not resolve this dilemma (Li, 2001a: 52, 63, 111, 114).

## STATE AND SOCIETY—
## THE CONSEQUENCES OF CONFRONTATION

For a party directing reforms, there is a difficult balance between relaxing control in order to stimulate social vigor for economic growth and exercising state authority in order to extract social compliance (You Ji, 1999: 3). The long period of ignoring the Falun Gong and many other expressions of protest reflects one side of this balancing process. The ongoing neglect of this increasingly powerful organization, which masqueraded as a wholly spiritual movement, was linked in turn to the state's lack of the requisite management skills and the political system's lack of sufficient channels for interest-articulation and political participation. When a confrontation became more or less unavoidable, the Party regressed to well-known political rituals—campaign and coercion—though it is worth noting that the need for the rule of law and wider policy change was recognized. The rituals may have won the day (Smith, 2001b), but they are costly and have not improved respect for the Party—and this begins to matter since public opinion has emerged as a political force in contemporary China (Whyte, 2000: 147).

China's history, and the many economic and political uncertainties of the summer of 1999, may have caused a real fear in the leadership of the potential for a sectarian-based movement to head a rebellion of discontent, leading directly to the loss of Heaven's mandate (Perry, 2001). Changing the role of the Party to that of the social-democratic parties in European history, reducing corruption, expanding political participation, and establishing a vision-enriched timetable for further political reform is well overdue (White, 1994; Li Nian-ting, 2001). The rise of the Falun Gong may, paradoxically, have been one of the factors stopping the fertile discussion of political reform in late 1998. The confrontation has certainly led to a tightening of controls on society and repercussions for other sects.

What other options were open to the government? Not many, if we accept that, given its size and assertiveness, the Falun Gong did represent a domestic threat to Chinese Communist Party control—and an externally encouraged one at that. The "soft option" of ignoring the problem and hoping it would go away was tried for a while, but failed. Co-opting the movement was not possible, given its tight hierarchical organization and its millennial character. Draconian measures could not be used: how can one jail millions?

What does this mean for governance in the future? The main lessons, at least for perceptive younger leaders, are likely to be fourfold: first, to be more aware of social developments and their costs and to do more to help structure society, perhaps in a way similar to Singapore, or perhaps by letting acceptable civil society grow stronger; second, to improve the channels of communication between state and society, in the final analysis by means of a more consultative or democratic political system; third, to improve opinion surveys and intelligence work as well as government decision-making structures so as to be able to strike preemptively; and finally, to focus on the long-term improvement of health, education, care for the elderly, social security, and social ethics.

There are parallels here to the Chinese government's attitude to the problems of terrorism: military measures really only treat symptoms; what is important is to get to the root causes of political, economic, and social inequity. Mitigating the desperation of losers in the development process will dry up the flow of willing recruits.

Should a similar problem arise again, China's steadily increasing recourse to the rule of law and greater integration in the global economy will demand greater finesse and a stricter adherence to legal rules. However, with the worldwide assault on civil rights in the wake of September 11, 2001, it may now be possible to get away with more, particularly against a movement that uses violence and can conveniently be labelled as terrorist.[27]

The Falun Gong from 2001 spun into a discourse of retribution,[28] worldwide all-out attacks on the Chinese government, and much talk of elimination of its opponents (*Jingwen*, June 3 and 4 and July 27, 2001, and numerous reports on www.clearwisdom.net, July 2001). For its activities in China, it relied for a long time on foreigners, for instance assigning a Californian the task of interrupting satellite feeds, attempting to replace CCTV programs with Falun Gong transmissions from Taiwan. In its propaganda in the West, it has focused on human rights to a degree that it almost seemed to want to raise its profile in the West by riding on the back of popular sympathy for the plight of its "pawns" in China. However, with the Sino-US rapprochement after September 11, American congressmen no longer needed the Falun Gong to pressure China.[29] It is the end game in China, but Li has a certain American and Taiwanese following and there will no doubt remain pockets of underground followers in some Chinese cities, waiting for apocalyptic events (*Xinhua*, 2001b).

## NOTES

1. I thank Anne Wedell-Wedellsborg, Peter Henriksen, an anonymous referee, and several Chinese scholars for pertinent comments. Among sources used have been the Falun Gong Web sites, the *World News Connection* documentation, *China Daily*, the *New York Times* archives, China Aktuell, Summary of World Broadcasts, and the works and the *jingwen* of Li Hongzhi.

2. An unpublished report from *China's Academy of Sciences* placed the average age of Falun Gong followers over 40 years. The majority were low and low-middle income and over 60 percent were female. (Leung, 2001: 7).

3. Leung's paper first appeared as a mimeo in 2001 and a later version of the paper, "China and Falun Gong: Party and society relations in modern era," was published in *Journal of Contemporary China*, volume 11, number 33, November 2002: 761–84.

4. This category is well covered in Hurst and O'Brien (2002).

5. *Cultivators* is a technical term referring to people following movements similar in character to the Falun Gong.

6. Ownby, 2000, for the first four.

7. Like Mao Zedong, Li Hongzhi is much more outspoken in his lectures and interviews. In a rare talk in 2002 he took credit for averting the otherwise predicted destruction of the earth by a comet and World War III.

8. Though not before many of them had already, in the words of Ownby (2000: 7), "made a ton of money."

9. In the early years of the organization, before the books, the main income was simply from admission fees to lectures and courses. Holbig (2000: 137) mentions a fee of 53 yuan for a lecture in Harbin or of 40 yuan for a training course lasting more than one day. Voluntary donations are continually being made.

10. "Falun Gong members purchased numerous copies of Zhuanfalun, a variety of pictures of Li (framed or unframed, goldplated or not goldplated, etc) and made voluntary donations to their exercise classes." Dai Qing (2000: 4).

11. An indication of this may be found in Li, 2001b: 48, discussing target groups.

12. Many details on this can be found in "Police crack Falungong illicit publication cases," *Xinhua*, October 21, 1999a, FBIS-CHI-1999-1021, and in "Using Falun Gong," *Xinhua*, 1999b.

13. Just as Li Hongzhi and the Falun Gong regularly deny selling anything, taking donations, or being involved in politics in any way, they also strenuously deny having an organization at all. A recent, very cautious contribution is James Tong, "An organizational analysis of the Falun Gong: Structure, communications, financing," *China Quarterly* 171. September 2002: 636–60.

14. Much of the following is based on a close reading of Li Hongzhi, 2001a. For details, see also *People's Daily*, August 20, 1999b: 2; *People's Daily*, November 1, 1999a:

4; Wong and Liu, 1999: 25; *People's Daily*, overseas edition, July 23, 1999: 1 (Doc. 17 in CLG 1999).

15. The *Zhongguo fojiao xiehui* (China Buddhist Association) called the Falun Gong a heretical doctrine, a syncretistic hodgepodge, which under cover of Buddhism damaged its followers. A strong and elaborated condemnation, comparing the Falun Gong to the Solar Temple Order and Aum Shinrikyo, and using the dreaded expression *xiejiao* (twisted learning, heretical sect), came as early as the January 1998 meeting of the China Buddhist Association.

16. Beijing Television interviewed the famous physicist, and atheist, one of whose students was hospitalized after Falun Gong meditation, on May 11. Followers invaded He's house, then demonstrated outside Beijing TV every day for a month. Up to 2,000 strong, they forced the station to air a sympathetic portrayal of the group and fire an editor. This happened to 14 other media outlets. The China Press and Publication Administration's policy was "three nots": media should not be for it, not be against it, and should not label it good or bad. He, a famous academician, decided to attack the policy, wrote in vain to Jiang Zemin, and tried to publish critical articles. "The government was mostly supportive of us," says a Falun Gong spokesman in New York in 1998 (Johnson, 2000).

17. Defined as a collectivity of individuals who either formally or informally cooperate to protect or promote some common, similar, identical, or shared interest or goal (Kolb, 1978: 165.) The Falun Gong constitutes a borderline case between Gabriel Almond's "non-associational groups" and "institutional groups" occasionally active in the political processes, similar to the Buddhist hierarchy in some Asian states. Actions entail some degree of potential or actual violence, protest marches, demonstrations, sit-ins, possibly spontaneous anomic outbreaks, but more likely decided by Li and the leadership of the Falun Gong. Its articulation functions communicate to the government the general and specific needs, problems, and opinions of the group and demand government action to promote their interests.

18. It was well-prepared from the point of view of public relations in the U.S. Some weeks before the demonstration, the unknown Li offered *Time* magazine an interview (*Time*, 1999), and on the day of the demonstration a close associate called the magazine and told it in advance of the size and target of the demonstration. Previous to the demonstration there had not been a single article on the Falun Gong in, for instance, the *New York Times*.

19. There were a number of meaningful anniversaries in 1999. At the same time, the economic outlook was dim after the Asian crisis.

20. On January 31, 2001, 16 followers tried to cover the portrait of Mao Zedong facing Tiananmen with a giant portrait of Li Hongzhi.

21. Vivienne Shue has treated this in one of several papers discussing the Falun Gong, "State Legitimation in China: The challenge of popular religion," given at the 2001 Annual Meeting of the American Political Studies Association in San Francisco.

22. A useful collection of documents is found in Ming Xia and Shiping Hua, eds., 1999.

23. Other laws allegedly violated were articles 20 and 24 of the Constitution, the Criminal Law on assembly and demonstrations, the Criminal Law on spreading superstition, and publication laws requiring approval for the publication of books.

24. This refers to a system of local administration and control in Imperial China using subdivisions of a thousand, a hundred, and ten households. Members of each unit were held responsible for each others' behavior.

25. Cf. Robert Weller in *Time* magazine, July 1, 2001, and *Xinhua* 2001d.

26. In a remarkable article published March 1999, the independent-minded *Nanfang Zhoumo* (*Southern Weekend*), in Guangzhou, covered the Falun Gong organization in Hangzhou in a highly critical manner, stressing many of the points raised in the subsequent political campaign (*Nanfang*, 1999).

27. Notably, the Falun Gong has not publicly been described as a terrorist organization, even though Hong Kong magazines have linked it to bomb incidents in China.

28. Numerous articles on Falun Gong Web sites describe the retribution received by China, and often addresses and telephone numbers of cadres said to be persecuting Falun Gong are posted on the net.

29. The Falun Gong was no longer a subject at the 16th CCP Congress, but one notes that Wu Guanzheng, who defeated the Falun Gong in one of its strongholds, Shandong, became a member of the CPPCC Standing Committee.

# 12

# Getting to the Roots: Governance Pathologies and Future Prospects

*Jude Howell*

China seems to be a paradox: on the one hand, it has a thriving capitalist economy; on the other hand, the catalyst behind its phenomenal growth has been none other than the Chinese Communist Party. Economic liberalization and socialist authoritarianism have marched hand in hand. Unlike many ailing post-Soviet states with weakly institutionalized democratic structures and fragile economies, the Chinese Communist Party has unleashed a tide of economic entrepreneurialism, raising living standards and making China a major economic global player, while at the same time maintaining territorial power. However, by the mid-1990s the stresses and strains of this paradox were becoming increasingly apparent, both to scholars within China and to external observers. At the turn of the millennium, Chinese scholars resurrected, albeit cautiously, the spectre of political reform, warning that without further political liberalization and democratization, it would be difficult to move ahead with economic reform.[1] International development and financial institutions, which had played a key role in advising government leaders on the direction of market reform, began from the mid-1990s to take on board more systematically the institutional dimensions of governance reform, providing programmatic and project support to civil service reform, legal reform, auditing, and accounts. Thus governance began to capture the attention of scholars and policy makers as an important variable in the sustenance of China's economic achievements and the prospects for deepening economic reform.

This book has highlighted some key dimensions of the governance challenge in China. In particular it has drawn attention to the need for political reform (Fewsmith); the necessity of processes of institution-building such as strengthening state capacity, introducing effective systems of regulation, and improving the legal framework (Burns, Zhu, Keane); the need to enhance regime legitimacy through power sharing at the local level and the opening up of spaces for association and public debate (Jakobson, Zhang, Howell, Du); and the importance of managing social discontent (Blecher, Østergaard). Inevitably it is not possible within the space of one volume to cover all the dimensions of governance that affect a given context. The social, political, and environmental consequences of the Three Gorges Dam, the desert landscapes carved out through deforestation, and the gross pollution of air and water through unbridled industrial production all create enormous challenges for a government bent on rapid economic development at any cost. Yet how the environment is governed has generational consequences and global ramifications that pay little respect for territorial borders. The cross-border character of many environmental problems in turn requires the negotiation of international treaties and agreements, drawing China further into processes of global governance.

Similarly, corruption is a major concern of many urban and rural dwellers in China. Indeed it was a prime factor behind the swelling of demonstrations during the turbulent year of 1989 and continues to be a key cause underlying rural collective action and urban discontent. Citizenship and rights, too, merit further attention, particularly given the virtual denial of multiple entitlements such as schooling, health care, and housing to millions of migrant workers in China, an issue that Solinger (1999) addresses in fine detail. How the Chinese Communist Party maintains its territorial integrity, particularly in the face of the impassioned ethnonationalist struggles in Xinjiang and Tibet, and how it maneuvers to achieve reunification with Taiwan are likewise important aspects of governance.

This volume has teased out some of the key governance weaknesses afflicting China's regime, whether these become manifest in the legal system, civil service, environmental protection, national unity, citizenship, or gender issues. These deficits include not least the pervasiveness of clientelistic state-society relations and corruption; the continuing weakness of the rule of law and the concomitant prevalence of rule by man; the fusion of the Party/state and the subsequent subordination of state officials to political power; the erosion of the legitimacy and authority of the Chinese Communist Party; the lack of effective channels for participation and representation; weak systems of accountability and transparency; the disjuncture between ideology and practice; and the weak capacity of the central state to raise revenue and enforce national policy. The effects of these governance deficits are momentous: mass alienation from politics, low levels of trust in Party/state officials, increasing social unrest, environmental degradation, and the inability of the central state to redistribute resources for the purposes of reducing poverty and addressing income, interregional, and intraregional disparities.

Most significantly, these governance problems make it increasingly difficult for the Party to deepen economic reforms, a move that is essential if China is to compete globally and at the same time maintain social stability. With social tensions running high and with few outlets for the expression of grievances, it will be hard for the Party to gain popular support for hard-reaching reforms, particularly those which lead to redundancies and material hardship.[2] Such a situation is exacerbated by the lack of any persuasive ideology, which marries theory to practice and can build a consensus around common perceptions and aspirations. The lack of conflict-resolution mechanisms, the restrictions on the media, and the limits on autonomous organization leave the Party locked in a destructive cycle of spontaneous bursts of collective action met with increasing repression, which in turn only adds to general disenchantment and alienation from the Party and politics. Unable to redistribute resources effectively because of corruption, the declining authority of the center over localities, and the lack of an effective taxation system, the Party/state cannot establish a comprehensive, functioning welfare system to serve as a stabilizing valve for discontented and impoverished rural and urban dwellers. Moreover, corruption, patronage, and local developmentalism mean that the state cannot regulate capital for the purposes of guaranteeing decent employment conditions, protecting the environment, or safeguarding the interests of consumers, making it difficult again for the Party to gain support for further economic reforms.

## WHAT THEN LIES BEHIND
## CHINA'S GOVERNANCE PROBLEMS?

The roots of China's governance deficits lie in a combination of political, institutional, and economic factors. The key *political* factor is the deep-seated  drive of the Chinese Communist Party to retain a monopoly of power. For any party that has held the reins for over half a century, it is not surprising that there is a reluctance to shed power, authority, and the resources these generate. This reluctance is reflected in the piecemeal results of attempts to separate the Party from government and the Party from the enterprise; in the contradictory approach of the state towards social organizations, which are on the one hand encouraged, but on the other hand periodically scrutinized, regulated, and prohibited; in the reluctance of the mass organizations to recognize more autonomous groups and organizations; and in the continuing efforts of the Party to incorporate increasingly powerful interests, such as private entrepreneurs, rather than expand the space for self-organization and expression.

The Chinese Communist Party's drive to retain power is in turn related to its declining authority and legitimacy, a process of erosion that had already set in following the disastrous decade of the Cultural Revolution. The more Party leaders are aware of growing distrust toward Party members and state officials, the more they struggle to hold on to power. The more the Party over-reacts to perceived opposition, as happened with the Falun Gong movement, the more it declines in stature. Repression belongs to the armory of the weak rather than the strong. Yet the contradictions in an ideology, which now up-holds both the working class and capitalists as advanced forces, and the gap between such an ideology and a set of policies, which reduce the power and prestige of workers and peasants while glorifying the capacity to "get rich quick," only exacerbates the Party's claim to rule. Moreover, tagging legiti-macy on to promises of rising living standards is inherently dangerous. In times of boom and prosperity, it can work wonders; but in times of recession and hardship, such frail promises only undermine the authority to rule.

Despite its declining legitimacy and authority, the Party has still been able to maintain and even increase its membership. As of 2002, Party members numbered 66.4 million, with membership growing by ten percent since 1997. To achieve this it has opened up membership to otherwise excluded groups, beginning with intellectuals in the early 1980s and private entrepreneurs in 2001. Furthermore, whenever non-Party members have been elected on to village committees, the Party has speedily co-opted popular leaders, thereby enhancing their local legitimacy. It has also tried, though with less success, to establish Party cells in private enterprises and social organizations. By giving priority to technical competence, entrepreneurship, and knowledge rather than revolutionary credentials, military performance, or class background, the Chinese Communist Party hopes to develop a modern Party, or, as Jiang Zemin stated in his speech in July 2001, a "ruling Party" rather than a revolu-tionary Party. Such a party would draw on technical expertise, scientific knowledge, and also political loyalty to develop China's economy. This at-tempt at modernization and technicization may be the saving grace for the Party. However, the continuing failure to discipline corrupt Party/state offi-cials is a strong counterforce undermining these efforts to overhaul the image and reputation of the Party. This in turn relates to the persistence of deeply embedded personal relations of obligation and loyalty, which permeate Party life and bind state and society. Thus the Party's drive to retain power in the face of its eroding legitimacy is a major factor underpinning current gover-nance problems in China and the prospects for the future.

The sclerosis and fracturing of Leninist institutions, their pathological weaknesses, and the concomitant absence of legitimate, stable, institutional alternatives have likewise contributed to China's governance problems. The sclerosis and fracturing of Leninist institutions have roots in the growing dis-juncture between the material basis of institutions and their set of functions, operational methods, and practices. The Leninist architecture of vertically or-ganized state institutions, overlaid by a similarly vertically layered Party structure, operating according to principles of democratic centralism, is premised on a particular material foundation. This material basis consists of a state-planned economy made up of state and collective enterprises in urban areas and communes in rural areas. It is through these building blocks that the Party/state not only controlled production but also mobilized participation and consent.

The diversification of ownership systems has gradually undermined this material basis of the Party/state. The main damage inflicted here has been on the capacity of the Party/state to mobilize support, to persuade, and to maintain authority at the microlevel. In particular this is related to the decline of the rural commune as a node of social and political community and to the demise of the work unit as a site of ideological reproduction and political mobilization. Furthermore, it has weakened the capacity of the central state to levy resources from richer regions to send to poorer areas. Coupled with decentralization, this has in turn aggravated regional inequalities.

Against this context of the market-driven sclerosis of Leninist institutions, certain pathologies, which were crucial for maintaining the predominance of the state under the command economy, now hinder both the ability of institutions to adapt and change and the emergence of alternative legitimate institutional forms. These pathologies include the incentive structure governing bureaucrats' behavior and performance, the tendency to protect institutional interests and resist the sharing of resources, power, and authority, the pathology of elitism, and the politicization of the state. The Leninist system of incentives rewarded the fulfilment of targets, upward compliance within the framework of tightly compartmentalized, vertical systems, and political loyalty (Lieberthal, 1995: 171–72). "Thinking vertically" and "looking up" the hierarchy for approval are the way to progress, or at least to safeguard one's interests, in Leninist institutions. However, the pressures of global competition demand a market-facilitating state architecture, which regulates at the macrolevel rather than at the microlevel, and which is staffed by competent technocrats, independent of politics. The need to assess policy alternatives rather than merely implement orders from above, and the need to listen to and analyze demands from diverse constituencies, require a different matrix of skills, motivations, and energy to those encouraged in the Leninist state architecture.

The fragmented authority of the Chinese state encouraged a politics of bargaining between and within institutions at all levels (Lieberthal, 1995). This in turn motivated bureaucratic leaders to strengthen and expand their departments and to protect departmental interests. This institutional tendency to protect vested departmental and/or local interests, often referred to respectively as "departmentalism" and "localism," continues to hinder the resolution of fundamental cross-cutting issues such as the environment, poverty, and HIV/AIDS, which require interagency cooperation. Similarly, it has hindered the development of a joined-up approach to policy making that bridges institutional divides and seeks holistic solutions rather than fragmented, departmental responses. The tendency for local institutions to introduce economic regulations to strengthen their own powers rather than to clarify boundaries and processes, likewise, blocks the effective and consistent regulation of markets (Asian Development Bank, 2002: xi, 61).

Just as departmentalism thwarts holistic problem-solving, so too the pathology of elitism inhibits reformist efforts to devolve state functions to society. The notion of a revolutionary vanguard elite, with advanced levels of consciousness and knowledge, is characteristic of Leninist political parties. Such a concept could be grafted with some ease onto the Chinese context, which claimed a long tradition of elitist governance with highly limited avenues of citizen participation. Though the Chinese Communist Party used the methods of mass campaigns to enhance the participation of non-elites, this took the form of subordinated mobilization rather than active, citizen-inspired, voluntary action. The notion of a legitimate elite with advanced consciousness and knowledge similarly pervades state practices, as over 80 percent of civil servants are Party members (Asian Development Bank, 2002: 35). There is thus a deeply rooted distrust toward the idea of citizen participation in political affairs. Both the chapters by Du and Zhang draw attention to the reluctance of local institutions, the neighborhood committee, and the Women's Federation respectively to share power with local, more independent groups.

Institutional resistance to change, fed by pathologies of departmentalism and elitism, and by a perception that change will undermine the power base of bureaucrats and political leaders, have hindered the development of citizen-led alternatives. Illustrative of this is the failure to create effective institutions of representation and participation, particularly for those new socioeconomic groups such as migrant workers, unemployed, laid-off workers, self-employed, and private entrepreneurs, and new professional groups such as lawyers, accountants, and managers in foreign enterprises. Without effective channels for relaying the concerns and views of new socioeconomic groups upward, the Party/state becomes not only increasingly out of touch with the changing needs of society but also unable to negotiate and balance an increasingly diverse range of interests. The institutional vacuum thus weakens state capacity and eats away at the bare threads of legitimacy.

Finally the pathology of Party domination over the state undermines governance reforms. In his article on the *bianzhi* system, Brodsgaard (2002) singles out the Party's need to maintain control as a key constraint on administrative reforms, particularly when these involve downsizing. Efforts to enhance the capacity of bureaucrats through introducing open competition based on meritocratic criteria are compromised by the politicization of the civil service. This sets up a potential tension between political motivation and professional judgement. Similar dilemmas have long bedevilled the mass organizations of the All-China Federation of Trade Unions and the All-China Federation of Women when certain economic policies such as state enterprise reform or family planning intensify the contradiction of having to represent simultaneously the dual interests of their constituents and the Party. The culture of secrecy within the Party, with its roots in the history of revolutionary struggle and the Cold War, has combined with departmentalism to stymie efforts to enhance the transparency of regulations, thereby hindering the development of the private sector. Though WTO entry, increasing access to the Internet and the media, and requirements to bring Chinese regulations and law in line with international practice will foster greater openness, the overlap between the Party and the state will be a constant constraint upon this. The lack of state autonomy is complicated further by the web of personalized, clientelistic relations which pervade relations both within the Party/state and between the Party/state and society.

China's governance conundrum has an *economic* as well as a political and institutional logic. Paramount here are the contradictions amongst economic reforms and the disjuncture between institutional reform and economic reform. Decentralization, for example, has galvanized economic entrepreneurship and growth at local levels, but has also made it increasingly difficult for the central state to impose its will over regions, whether for redistribution through taxation, social control, or other purposes. The liberalization of prices, diversification of ownership systems, and decollectivization of agriculture have similarly disrupted the tax system, leading to almost two decades of decline in budgetary revenue. Though tax-sharing system reform was introduced in 1994, the budget accounted for only 15 percent of GDP in 1996 compared to 35 percent in 1978 (Asian Development Bank, 2002: 18). The special privileges and incentives in trade and foreign investment given to coastal regions during the 1980s unleashed enormous local energy to attract foreign companies, leading to booming exports and a concentration of foreign investment in these parts. However, the regional bias of these privileges during the 1980s contributed to the widening of a regional gap between the East and West.[3] With local governments bearing responsibility for education, health, and infrastructural development, the stark differences in the financial capacity of county and township governments in poor areas and rich areas has likewise intensified the unevenness of development across the country. Similarly, the reform of state enterprises will not only enhance economic efficiency and China's global competitiveness, but also will lead to rising unemployment.

The social consequences of rapid economic development have highlighted vividly the disjuncture between economic and institutional reforms. The gap between the rich and poor has risen substantially in the reform period, with China's gini coefficient, a standard measurement of inequality standing at 40.3 in 2001, higher than India at 37.8 and almost as high as the USA at 40.8 (UNDP, 2002: 194–97).[4] For any government, addressing poverty poses fundamental questions around the appropriate role of the market, state, and society. In the case of China, however, the old institutional channels for welfare provision, such as the commune and urban work unit, are dissolving rapidly and a new institutional system of welfare provision is only partially established. Without an effective social security system, retrenched state workers and the unemployed will encounter increased hardship, aggravating resentment against the already rising income gap in urban areas and contributing to social tension. Similarly rapid economic development in the coastal areas has provided employment opportunities for millions of rural migrants, but without the development of an institutional infrastructure to support their welfare needs. Rural migrants find themselves discriminated against in these urban havens, deprived of the rights of schooling for their children, access to housing, or health care. Such discrimination fosters a sense of social alienation and discontent, which along with unemployment amongst retrenched state workers is a powderkeg for social protest.

Though economic reforms have generated a new cast of losers, it has also created new socioeconomic groups that have benefited from the new market opportunities. These include rich farmers, private entrepreneurs, professionals such as lawyers, accountants, computer experts, intellectuals moonlighting as consultants, and managers in foreign-invested enterprises. Though these *nouveaux riches* may be content with luxury consumables and private villas, there will be some who will begin to demand at least greater accountability from the state, if not a greater role in public affairs. Given that there are still considerable regulatory and legal blockages to the private sector (Asian Development Bank, 2002: 72–74), increasing frustration is likely to lead private entrepreneurs and managers to seek institutional channels to articulate their needs. This will put pressure on the new trade, professional, and private associations to become more forceful agencies of interest representation, demanding accountability from the state and attention to their immediate interests.

## TO WHAT EXTENT THEN ARE CHINA'S PROBLEMS UNIQUE?

With the end of the Cold War, international development agencies, financial institutions, and Northern governments began to place governance issues squarely on the aid agenda. The normative aspiration was for consolidated liberal democracies across the globe, ensuring respect for human rights, the dominance of the rule of law, and efficient and clean public administrations. As stated in the introduction, international agencies such as the World Bank took a narrow managerial approach to governance issues, focusing on the public administration, the legal system particularly as it relates to economic governance, and auditing. Bilateral donors and some multilateral agencies interpreted governance more broadly to develop programs and projects on electoral reform, human rights, the judiciary, political parties, and building democratic and accountable institutions.

Governance in China, too, has drawn the attention of multilateral institutions and bilateral development agencies. The UNDP, Asian Development Bank, World Bank, Ford Foundation, Asia Foundation, Canadian International Development Agency (CIDA), and European Union have all established various specialized programs and projects to address key governance problems. Most of these have focused on policy development, and to a lesser extent on the legislative framework, public sector training, and the corporate sector. Between 1995 and 1997, donor agencies reported U.S. $2.5 billion in assistance to governance programs, out of a total development assistance of U.S. $4.2 billion. Over three-fourths of this amount was allocated to policy development and implementation, which accounted for 90 out of a total of 234 governance programs[5] (UNDP, 1998: 22). The UNDP, Germany, and the Canadian International Development Agency provided the bulk of assistance in the legislative framework, whilst the World Bank and the Asian Development Bank were the main donors for policy development and implementation programs. UNICEF accounted for 77 percent of donor assistance to decentralization and local governance programs, amounting to U.S. $62 million.[6]

Several agencies have provided support for quasi-nongovernmental agencies to prepare for and attend international fora such as women's groups for the Fourth World Conference on Women in 1995 or environmental groups for the World Summit on Sustainable Development in Johannesburg in 2002. International nongovernmental agencies such as the Save the Children Fund U.K. have supported human rights awareness through a focus on children's rights.[7] Nongovernmental democratic institutions such as the Carter Center for Democracy and the National Republican Institute, foundations such as the Asia Foundation and the Ford Foundation, multilateral agencies such as the EU, and some bilateral donors have supported the promotion of village elections across China through training programs, international exposure visits, and research projects. The Canadian International Development Agency is the only agency to have set up a special fund to support civil society, though other donors such as the Ford Foundation and the Asia Foundation work closely with non-state and/or quasi-state agencies.

China's governance problems are not unique. Like many countries in the South and transitional contexts such as the former Soviet Union, China faces similar governance deficits such as a weakly institutionalized legal system; a lack of transparency and accountability; an unclean, inefficient public administration; a lack of respect for civil and political human rights; weak institutions of interest representation and participation; and restrictions on the media. It also confronts a similar array of challenges such as an increasingly competitive global environment, social upheaval and alienation arising from rapid economic change, environmental degradation, the rapid spread of HIV/AIDS, and secessionist demands from minority groups.

Moreover, some of the underlying causes of China's governance deficits can also be found in other contexts. The former Soviet Union shared with China a similar Leninist institutional infrastructure, characterized by vertically insulated ministries and agencies, overlapping Party and government structures, and a narrow array of mass organizations serving as transmission belts between society and the Party. This generated similar pathologies of governance, such as the lack of autonomous government institutions, a constricted civil society, limited channels of participation and representation, violations of civil and political rights, and sharp restrictions on the private sector, greater in China than in the Soviet Union. The clientelistic ties between the Party, government, and society in China have also lain behind the weaknesses of postcolonial state formation processes in many African countries, such as Kenya, Malawi, and Zaire. A lack of mechanisms and institutions of transparency and accountability have similarly created a fertile soil for corruption in China, Cote d'Ivoire, Peru, Kenya, Zimbabwe, and India. The politicization of the public administration has reduced the autonomy of the state not only in China but also in Kenya under Kenyatta and Moi, Côte D'Ivoire under Houphouet-Boigny (Medard, 1991), or Ethiopia under the Workers' Party (Clapham, 1991). Weakening state institutions and the absence of legitimate, regular institutional alternatives underpin not only some of China's governance problems but also those of transitional regimes such as Russia, Vietnam, Poland, and Romania.

Though China shares symptoms and causes of governance malaise with other transitional and Southern countries, its starting point for remedying these is more robust for a number of reasons. First, China has enjoyed over two decades of rapid economic growth, becoming a major global economic producer, a key player in global trade, and a highly attractive destination for foreign direct investment. It does not suffer the severe economic stagnation of the former Soviet republics, nor the "undevelopment" of many sub-Saharan African countries, which have witnessed declining growth rates in the last decades of the twentieth century. Though economic performance does not necessarily correspond directly with effective governance, it does, however, create a potentially strong material base for bolstering state capacity.

Second, despite the problems of corruption, fragmentation of authority, and unevenness of governance reforms, the Chinese state is relatively strong compared with states like Mozambique, Burkina Faso, Bangladesh, and Nepal. With its long history of state administration, China does not face the same challenges of state capacity-building as in the new postsocialist states of Kyrgyzstan,

Belarus, or Ukraine or postcolonial states such as Congo, Kenya, Namibia, and Mozambique. China is not a failed state like Liberia. Moreover, China's political elite, despite the problems of corruption, has a developmental agenda centered on economic growth, raising living standards, and reducing poverty, unlike many countries in sub-Saharan Africa, or the Philippines under Marcos, or Nepal[8].

Third, with its large domestic economy, sustained high economic growth rates, and growing significance in world trade, China is not aid-dependent, unlike Mozambique, Bangladesh, and Ethiopia. Official development assistance to China in 2000 accounted for 0.2 percent of GDP, compared with 13.3 percent for Uganda, 11.6 percent for Tanzania, and 0.3 per cent for India (UNDP, 2002: 202–06).[9] China ranks 24th out of 90 countries on the Human Development Index, enjoying relatively high literacy, life expectancy, and low mortality rates compared to countries such as Tanzania, Bangladesh, India, Mozambique, Peru, and Bolivia. In terms of human development, China has done significantly better than many countries in the South over the last two decades, with a human development index value of 0.718 in 2001, compared to 0.564 for South Asia and 0.467 for sub-Saharan Africa (Asian Development Bank, 2002: 2). China is thus better positioned than many countries in the South or transitional economies to define its own agenda for governance reform.

Finally, compared to conflict-ridden countries such as Liberia, Angola, Sierra Leone, Sri Lanka, Afghanistan, and Tajikistan, China enjoys relative political stability, despite the independence struggles in the border provinces of Xinjiang and Tibet. The recent succession at the 16th Party Congress in November 2002 proceeded smoothly. Apart from its brief invasion of Vietnam in the late 1970s and its militaristic posturing against Taiwan, China has not been engaged in war with other states, nor has it been riven by civil war for over half a century.

Whilst these factors create a more favorable context for improvements in governance, compared with many postsocialist states and countries in the South, maintaining economic growth and addressing issues of redistribution will be central to regime maintenance and political stability in China. The international governance agenda assumes that democracy and economic development go hand in hand, contrary to modernization theory in the 1950s, which made democracy conditional upon economic development.[10] For Chinese leaders the examples of postsocialist states, with their fragile economies and weakly institutionalized democracies, or the many newly democratic regimes in the South, do not appeal as models for development or improved governance. Instead, Chinese leaders have preferred to look towards nearby east Asian states such as Singapore and South Korea, which have combined authoritarianism with rapid economic growth.[11] Though some China scholars have begun to call for political reform, arguing that authoritarianism eventually becomes dysfunctional for economic development, as witnessed in Taiwan and South Korea, Chinese leaders have over the last decade opted for minimal changes in the political system. Since the repression of the democracy movement in the summer of 1989, there has been no nationwide challenge by workers, students, or others for democratic regime change. Moreover the recent attempts by the China Democracy Party to establish an alternative party were easily quashed (Wright, 2002). The Chinese Communist Party does not yet face the same degree of organized resistance that pushed political liberalization and democratization in South Korea and Taiwan in the 1980s.

## What Then Are the Prospects for Governance in China?

Our earlier analysis pointed to the combination of political, institutional, and economic variables lying at the heart of China's governance deficits. The likelihood of regime change is slim in the short term. Substantive political reform requires champions, visions, and constituencies of support. Though the theme of political reform was reignited in the late 1990s, anticipation of the 16th Party Congress in 2002 cast a shadow over this debate. With a new cast of leaders in the expanded Politburo and old rival protectors steering from behind the bamboo scenes, it is unlikely that political reform will take center stage in the next five years. As the new leaders jockey for position, they are unlikely to jeopardize their ranking by embracing such a hot and divisive topic. In the short term, therefore, we can expect little movement on the political reform front.

Given the appeal of authoritarian rule to Chinese leaders and intellectuals on both the right and left, and given the past success stories of authoritarian regimes such as nearby South Korea, Singapore, and Taiwan, there is little incentive for the Party to pursue a more democratic type of regime based on multiparty politics. At first sight it may seem that *"plus ça change, plus c'est le même."* China will remain authoritarian. However, this will no longer be on behalf of the working class and peasantry, but in the interests of domestic and global capital. With a thriving economy motored by capital, local governments have been quick to foster productive alliances with domestic and foreign capital.[12] At the national level, Jiang Zemin's speech in July 2001, which opened the doors of the Party to private entrepreneurs, marks another move in this direction. However, the gap between ideology and practice may become too great to sustain, triggering yet further disenchantment and unrest. As long as the carrot of economic prosperity has some meaning, then the stick of repression will be tolerated. However, once the economy falters, social unrest is likely to mount, undermining stability and deterring potential foreign investors.

In the long term, maintaining legitimacy, promoting clean government, and improving the image of the Party will be key goals of the Party over the next decade. The CCP's preference will be, like that of the World Bank, to concentrate on the narrow managerial aspects of governance. In this vein we can expect the Party to continue to promote more competitive forms of election for political positions at township and county levels, but it is unlikely that it will tolerate multiparty competition. This would be too great a threat to its power base. Liberal democracy is not on the agenda. The Party will continue to attempt to incorporate competent and popular leaders at all levels as a strategy to reproduce itself and improve its legitimacy and authority. However, much of this depends on the performance of the domestic and global economies, for once economic recession sets in, then maintaining legitimacy, which has as its prime source economic performance, will be hard to sustain.

Deeper global economic integration will subject China further to pressures to reform its institutions, laws, and regulations in the direction of greater transparency and predictability. Demands for accountability will no longer be confined to domestic forces but also extend to transnational companies, foreign governments, and international institutions. A salient example is the World Health Organization's public criticism in April 2003 of China's handling of the outbreak of Severe Acute Respiratory Syndrome (SARS) and its demand that China present open and accurate reports on the number of suspected and confirmed cases. International development agencies, both governmental and nongovernmental, will influence, in some regions more than others, the shape and trajectory of the spaces for autonomous organization and action. However, the dominance of the Party will continue to constrain progress in governance reforms such as public administration, developing effective institutional channels for representation and participation, transparency, and accountability. The Party's drive for power will hinder China from achieving the kind of state autonomy that underpinned South Korea's economic success. Moreover, unless Chinese leaders address firmly the issue of corruption, the erosion of Party/state authority and legitimacy will continue to bedevil the Party's determination to retain power.

The privatization of public services and goods such as housing, medical care, and schooling will continue to generate conflicts of interest between individuals, local authorities, and private service companies. The boundaries of public authority will continue to be contested, and without predictable rules and principles for their resolution, governance will remain localized, uneven, and fragmented. The negative impact of WTO on some parts of the economy and society will likely lead to further social discontent and alienation, intensifying the cracks and weaknesses in the institutions and processes of governance. A reliance on repression may solve the immediate crisis, but is not a long-term solution. There is some room for optimism, but also much reason for pessimism. What remains clear is that governance processes in China will increasingly command the attention of political leaders in China. They ignore them at their peril.

## NOTES

1. For example, in August 2000, Hu Angang and other scholars put forward a comprehensive plan for reform of the Party, a shortened version of which appeared in 2001 in an edited volume *China's Strategic Vision* (Lawrence, 2002a: 37).

2. In its report on development management, the Asian Development Bank (2002: 15) notes that even though there are some mechanisms of participation such as legislative hearings, these apply only to limited areas such as pricing, are not required by law, and are unevenly implemented.

3. For more details on regional inequalities, see Zhang, 2001.

4. The Gini index measures inequality over the entire distribution of income or consumption. A zero score represents perfect equality and 100 represents perfect inequality. China's gini index has increased substantially over the past two decades from 0.29 in 1981 to 0.39 in 1995 (World Bank, 1997) and 0.43 in 2001, a 50 percent rise in 20 years. According to the UNDP poverty index, China ranks 24th out of 90 countries, with 18.5 per cent of the population, that is 250 million, living off less than one dollar per day (UNDP, 2002: 157).

5. It should be noted that the UNDP includes general public service training within this category because of the difficulty in distinguishing a policy development program from a general training program. Thus policy development includes a significant element of training.

6. The EU was the second highest donor in this category, accounting for 14 percent of total support, or about U.S. $11.5 million. In terms of program numbers, UNICEF and the Ford Foundation were the largest donors (UNDP, 1998: 25).

7. Similarly, the Ford Foundation has supported women's rights work as well as legal reform, and the development of legal counselling centers.

8. Even within countries there can be vast differences in the developmental agendas of political elites. While Andhra Pradesh state in India has a dynamic political leadership focused on economic and social development, Orissa state's leadership, in contrast, lacks a pro-poor elite that can develop an agenda of poverty reduction and growth.

9. Official development assistance to China in 2000 accounted for 0.2 percent of GDP, compared with 13.3 percent for Uganda, 11.6 percent for Tanzania, and 0.3 percent for India. Per capita official development assistance in 2000 amounted to U.S. $1.4 for China, compared to $35.2 for Uganda, $29.7 for Tanzania, and $1.5 for India. In terms of net official development assistance disbursed in 2000, China accounted for a larger absolute sum of $1,735 million, than $1,487.2 million for India, $819.4 million for Uganda, and $1,044.6 for Tanzania (UNDP, 2002: 203–06).

10. For a classic work on the preconditions for democracy, see Lipset, 1959.

11. There is a debate as to whether Singapore is best described as a semidemocracy or one-party state, though there is agreement that Singapore displays a number of authoritarian traits (Brooker, 2000: 249–52).

12. An interesting illustration of such alliances is the growing pressure on journal and magazine editors to avoid criticizing the practices of companies investing in particular localities and the complicity of local judiciaries in protecting local economic interests against media exposure of fraudulent company practices. The financial magazine *Caijing* lost a lawsuit taken by a Shenzhen real estate firm on the grounds of defamation in June 2002 and had to pay RMB 300,000 in damages. See Lawrence (2002b) for further cases.

# References

Afshar, H., ed. 1999. *Women, Globalization and Fragmentation in the Developing World*. London: Macmillan.

All-China Federation of Trade Unions. 2000. *Introduction of All-China Federation of Trade Unions*. Beijing: ACFTU.

All-China Lawyers' Association. 1999. *Charter of the All-China Lawyers' Association* (in Chinese). www.lawyers.com.cn/lsxh/zhba/main

All-China Women's Federation. 2001. *Chinese Women's Movement* 8. Beijing.

———. ed. 2000.. *Selected Documents of Work on Women and Children 1998–1999*. Beijing: China Women's Press.

———. 1994. *Selected Documents of Work on Women and Children since the Sixth Congress*. Beijing: China Women's Press.

———. 1988a. *Mao Zedong, Liu Shaoqi, Zhou Enlai, and Zhu De on Women's Liberation*. Beijing: The People's Publishing House.

———. 1988b. *Self-Respect, Self-Confident, Self-Dependent, Self-Strengthening in Order to Make Achievements in Reforms: Collection of Documents of the 6th National Women's Congress*. Beijing: Chinese Women's Publishing House.

The All-China Women's Federation and The Statistics Bureau of China. 2001. *The Report on the Social Status of Women in China (The Second Issues)*. Beijing.

Amnesty International. 2000. "PRC: The crackdown on Falun Gong and other so-called 'heretical organizations.'" March 23.

Asian Development Bank. 2002. *Development Management: Progress and Challenges in the People's Republic of China*. Manila: ADB.

———. 2000. *Promoting Good Governance*. Manila: ADB.

———. 1995. *Governance: Sound Development Management*. Manila: ADB.

Asia-Pacific Economic Cooperation (APEC). 2002. *The New Economy and APEC*. January 30. www.apecsec.org.sg.

Bai Gang. 1999. "1998–1999: Zhongguo cunmin zizhi buru guifanhua fazhan xin jue-duan." In *Shehui lanpinshu: 1999 Zhongguo shehui xingshi fenxi yu yuce* (Blue Book of Society: 1999. Analysis and Forecast of the State of Chinese Society). Bei-jing: Shehui kexue wenxian chunbanshe.

Barbalet, J. M. 1991. *Citizenship*. Chinese translation version: *Gongmin Zige*. Taibei Guiguan Book.

Beale, Alison. 2002. "Identifying a policy hierarchy: Communication policy, media in-dustries and globalization." In *Global Culture: Media, Arts, Policy, and Globaliza-tion*, edited by Diane Crane, Nobuko Kawashima, and Ken'ichi Kawasaki. Lon-don: Routledge.

Beijing xiwangzhixing wenhua xinxi zixun zhongxin, ed. 1997. "Guojia gongwuyuan luyong kaoshi zuixin jingshenji baokao yinshi zhinan (State civil service appoint-ment examination: Latest guide for applicants)." Beijing: Zhongguo dangan chubanshe.

Bendix, Reinhard. 1964. *Nation-Building and Citizenship: Studies of Our Changing Social Order*. London: John Wiley and Sons.

Bennett, Tony. 1998. *Culture: A Reformer's Science*. Sydney: Allen and Unwin.

Bernstein, Thomas. 1999. "Farmer discontent and regime responses." In *The Paradox of China's Post-Mao Reforms*, edited by Merle Goldman and Roderick MacFarquhar. Cambridge, Mass.: Harvard University Press.

Bian Yanjie. 1994. *Work and Inequality in Urban China*. Albany, N.Y.: State Univer-sity of New York Press.

Blecher, Marc. 2002. "Hegemony and workers' politics in China." *China Quarterly* 170 (June): 283–303.

———. 1999. "Strategies of Chinese state legitimation among the working class." Pa-per presented at the Workshop on Strategies of State Legitimation in Contemporary China. Center for Chinese Studies, University of California at Berkeley. May 7–9.

———. 1998. "What are Chinese workers thinking?" Paper presented at the annual meeting of the Association for Asian Studies. Washington, D.C.

———. 1997. *China against the Tide*. London: Pinter.

Blecher, Marc, and Gordon White. 1979. *Micro-politics in Contemporary China: A Technical Unit During and After the Cultural Revolution*. London: Macmillan; White Plains, N.Y.: M. E. Sharpe.

British Broadcasting Corporation. 2001. "China plans massive health shake-up." Feb-ruary 16. www.bbc.co.uk.

Brodsgaard, Kjeld Erik. 2002. "Institutional reform and the *Bianzhi* system in China." *China Quarterly* 170 (June): 361–86.

Brook, Timothy. 1997. "Auto-organization in Chinese society." In *Civil Society in China*, edited by Timothy Brook and Michael B. Frolic. Armonk, N.Y.: M. E. Sharpe.

Brook, Timothy, and Michael B. Frolic, eds. 1997. *Civil Society in China*. Armonk, N.Y.: M. E. Sharpe.

Brooker, Paul. 2000. *Non-Democratic Regimes: Theory, Government and Politics*. New York: St. Martin's Press.

Burns, J. P. 2003. "Governance and public sector reform in the People's Republic of China." In *Governance and Public Sector Reform in Asia: Paradigm Shift or Busi-ness as Usual?*, edited by I. Scott and A. B. L. Cheung. London: RoutledgeCurzon.

———. 2001. "Downsizing the Chinese state: Retrenching the government in the 1990s." Unpublished paper.

Cairncross, Frances. 1997. *The Death of Distance: How the Communications Revolution Will Change Our Lives.* London: Orion Publishing Group Ltd.

Cai Yiping. 1999. "An unfinished debate: Equality in employment—conclusion of the discussion on equal employment between men and women." *China Women's News.* September 28.

Cao, Guoying, and Houan Zhang. 1996. "The villagers' self-government in Lishu county, Jilin province of the People's Republic of China." In *Village Elections: Democracy inRural China. Commentaries,* edited by the Ministry of Civil Affairs. Beijing: Ministry of Civil Affairs.

Carter, Colin. 2001. "China's trade integration and impacts on factor markets." In *China's Agriculture in the International Trading System,* edited by OECD.

Carter Center. 2002. "English translation of organic law on villagers' committees." April 26. www.cartercenter.org.

———.Reports on the Village Election System. www.cartercenter.org

Chan, Anita. 2001. *China's Workers Under Assault.* Armonk, N.Y.: M. E. Sharpe.

———. 1993. "Revolution or corporatism? Workers and trade unions in post-Mao China." *Australian Journal of Chinese Affairs* 28 (January): 31–61.

Chan, Anita, and Jonathan Unger. 1996. "Corporatism in China. A developmental state in an East-Asian context." In *China after Socialism. In the Footsteps of Eastern Europe or East Asia?,* edited by Barrett L. McCormick and Jonathan Unger. London: M. E. Sharpe.

Chan, Sylvia. 1998. "Research notes on villagers' committee election: Chinese-style democracy." *Journal of Contemporary China* 7, 19: 507–21.

Cheng, Joseph Y.S. 2001. "Direct elections of town and township heads in China: The Dapeng and Buyun experiments." *China Information* XV, 1: 104–37.

*Chengdu Sichuan Ribao.* Li Binglin. "Chengdu brings into play advantage of ideological and political work and makes a success of transformation of Falun Gong followers." FBIS-CHI-2001–0131. January 30, 2001.

Chen Qingtai. 2002. "Jingji quanqiuhua xia de zhengfu gaige (Reform of the government under economic globalization)." *Neibu canyue* 10. March 15: 2–6.

Chen Xian. 2002. "WTO entry prompts government reform." *China Daily.* January 4.

*China Daily.* December 7, 2001; November 27, 2000; September 22, 1998.

*China Daily* in *South China Morning Post.* 2001. "Judicial justness, efficiency top agenda." March 10.

*China Daily HK Edition.* 2001. November 23.

*China Development Brief.* 2002. "Civil society in the making: 41 NGO profiles." Autumn: 7–26.

*China Development Brief.* 2001. "250 Chinese NGOs: A special report from *China Brief.*" Beijing.

China Elections Watch (in collaboration with the Carter Center for Democracy). 2002. *Report on the Buyun Township Head Election.* April 26. www.gpc.peachnet.edu/~yliu/watch/local.html

China Media Monitor Intelligence (CMM-I). 2002. *The China Media Monitor* 6, 7. September 29.

———. 2001. "China's broadband industry at crossroads." *The China Media Monitor* 6, 1 (December).

China Online. 2002. www.chinaonline.com/topstories (accessed January 30, 2002).

Choate, Allen. 1997. "Local Governance in China." Talk at seminar "Asian Perspectives: Focus on China." Arranged by Asia Foundation. Washington, D.C., March 20.

Clapham, Christopher. 1999. "State, society and political institutions in revolutionary Ethiopia." In *Rethinking Third World Politics*, edited by James Manor. London and New York: Longman.

*Clearwisdom.net.* 2001. Reports on the Chinese Government's response to Falun Gong from 2001. www.clearwisdom.net.

Cui Zhiyuan. 2001. "Whither China: The discourse and practice of property rights and corporategovernance reform in China." Paper presented to the Forum on Governance in China. Institute of Development Studies, University of Sussex. September 11–13.

Dahlman, Carl J., and Jean-Eric Aubert, eds. 2002. *China and the Knowledge Economy: Seizing the 21st Century.* Washington, D.C.: WBI Development Studies. January 16. www.worldbank.org

Dai Qing. 2000. "Members of Falungong in an autocratic society." *Harvard Asia Quarterly* 4, 3. (Summer): 1–7.

*Dangjian yanjiu conghengtan (State Reform Commission survey).* 1998. Dangjian Duwu Chubanshe.

Davin, D. 1976. *Women-Work: Women and the Party in Revolution China.* Oxford: Clarendon Press.

Deng Xiaoping. 1993. "Zai Wuchang, Shenzhen, Zhuhai, Shanghai dengde de tanhua yaodian (Essential points from talks in Wuchang, Shenzhen, Zhuhai, and Shanghai)." *Deng Xiaoping wenxuan* 3. Beijing: Renmin Chubanshe.

———. 1984. *Selected Works of Deng Xiaoping.* Beijing: Foreign Languages Press.

Des Forges, Roger V. 1997. "States, societies and civil societies in Chinese history." In *Civil Society in China*, edited by Timothy Brook and Michael B. Frolic. Armonk, N.Y.: M. E. Sharpe.

Ding Xue Liang. 1994. "Institutional amphibiousness and the transition from communism: The case of China." *The British Journal of Political Science* 24: 293–318.

Ding Yijian. 1998. "Corporatism and civil society in China: An overview of the debate in recent years." *China Information* 12, 4 (Spring): 44–68.

Dirlik, Arif. 2001. "Markets, culture, power: the making of a 'second' cultural revolution in China." *Asian Studies Review* 25, 1: 1–35.

Di Yinqing and Guan Gang. 1999. "Meiguo wei shenma jiyu yu Zhongguo chongkai ruguan tanpan." *Gaige neican* (Internal Reference on Reform) 8. April 20: 39–42.

Eckholm, Eric. 1999. "Beijing asks that an electoral 'first' also be a last." *International Herald Tribune.* January 27.

*Economist.* 1996. "China's grassroots democracy." November 2.

Edin, Maria. 2001. "The cadre responsibility system: CCP governance over township leading cadres." Unpublished paper.

Einhorn, Bruce. 2002. "Is your Web site available in China?" *BusinessWeek Online.* September 16. www.businessweek.com.

Fang Ning, Wang Xiaodong, and Song Qiang, eds. 1999. *Quanqiuhua Yinyingxia de Zhongguo Zhilu* (China's Path under the Shadow of Globalization). Beijing: Shehui Kexue Chubanshe.

*Fazhi Ribao* (Legal Daily). 1999. "Minzhu bu neng chaoyue falu." January 19.

Fewsmith, Joseph. 2001a. *China Since Tiananmen*. Cambridge: Cambridge University Press.

———. 2001b. "Rethinking the role of the CCP: Explicating Jiang Zemin's Party anniversary speech." *China Leadership Monitor* 2 (December). www.chinaleadershipmonitor.org.

Foreign Languages Press. 1994. *Selected Works of Deng Xiaoping III (1982–1992)*. Beijing: Foreign Languages Press.

"Foreign Trade Law of the PRC." 1994. Adopted at the Seventh Session of the Standing Committee of the Eighth National People's Congress and promulgated on May 12, 1994, effective from July 1, 1994.

Foucault, Michel. 1983. "Governmentality." In *Michel Foucault: Beyond Structuralism and Hermeneutics* edited by Hubert L. Dreyfus and Paul Rabinow. Chicago: University of Chicago Press.

Fouchereau, Bruno. 2001. "Secular society at stake." *Le Monde Diplomatique* (June):10.

Fox Piven, Frances, and Richard Cloward. 1971. *Regulating the Poor: The Functions of Public Welfare*. New York: Vintage.

Fraser, Nancy. 1997. *Justice Interruptus: Critical Reflections on the 'Post-Socialist' Condition*. New York: Routledge.

Friedman, Milton, and Rose Friedman.1979. *Free to Choose: A Personal Statement*. New York: Harcourt Brace Jovanovich. Chinese translation version, *Ziyou Xianze*. Beijing Shangwu Press, 1998.

Friedman, Thomas L. 2000. *The Lexus and the Olive Tree*. New York: Anchor Books.

Gao Xinjun. 1998. "Woguo xian xiang liang ji zhengzhi tizhi gaige de shuguang—Henan sheng Xinmi shi cunji minzhu zhengzhi zhidu jianshe diaocha (Dawn of the reform of the political system at the two levels of county and township in our country—survey on the establishment of the democratic political system at the village level in Xinmi City, Henan Province)." *Jingji shehui tizhi bijiao* 6.

General Office of the CCP CC and General Office of the SC Issue Circular. 1999. *Journal of the Shenzhen Special Economic Zone*, trans. in *CLG*, 32, 5. August 24.

Ge Youli. 1999. "East meets West feminist translation group." Paper for Women Organizing in China workshop. Oxford, UK. July 12–16.

Gibney, Frank. 1993. "Breaking new ground in farm country." *Newsweek*. February 15.

Gold, T. 1990. "The resurgence of civil society in China." *Journal of Democracy*. Winter: 18–31.

Gu Xiuliang. 2000. "Strengthening organizational building of women's federation, push forward the new century women-work to higher level." Paper presented at the Workshop of Directors of Women's Federations at Provinces, Municipalities, ACWF. *Chinese Women's Movement* 8. Beijing: The All-China Women's Federation, 2001.

Habermas, Jürgen. 1998. "Gonggong lingyu (The public sphere)." *Wenhua yu Gongongxing* (Cultures and Publicity), Wanghui, Chen and Yan Gu, eds. Beijing: Sanlian Publishing House.

———. *The Structural Transformation of the Public Sphere*. Cambridge: Polity Press.

Harding, Harry. 1998. "Will China democratize? The road from socialism." *Journal of Democracy* 9, 1: 11–17.

He Baogang. 2003. "From village to township: Will China move elections one level up?" East Asian Institute, National University of Singapore, Background Brief 126. February 24. www.nus.edu.sg/NUSinfo/EAI/es126.

He Baogang and Lang Youxing. 2001. "China's first direct election of the township head: A case study of Buyun." *Japanese Journal of Political Science* 2, 1 (May): 1–22.

Heberer, Thomas. 2001. "Falungong—Religion, Sekte oder Kult? Eine Heilsgemeinschaft als Manifestation von Modernisierungsproblemen und sozialen Entfremdungsprozessen." *Duisburger Arbeitspapiere Ostasienwissenschaften* 36.

He Chong. 2001. "'Falun Gong' has degenerated into an anti-China tool for the West." *Zhongguo Tongxun She*. January 21.

He Min. 2001. Head of the Administration for China Offices of Foreign Law Firms under the Ministry of Justice. Quoted in *China Daily* on December 29.

Hershatter, Gail. 1986. *The Workers of Tianjin, 1900–1949*. Stanford: Stanford University Press.

Hewitt De Alcantara, Cynthia. 2001. "The development divide in a digital age: An issues paper." *Technology, Business and Society Programme* 4 (August). New York: United Nations Research Institute for Social Development.

He Xiaopei. 1999. "Chinese women tongzhi organising in the 1990s." Paper presented at the Women Organizing in China workshop, Oxford, UK. July 12–16.

Hindess, Barry. 2001. "The liberal government of unfreedom." Paper presented at the Forum on Governmentality. Griffith University, July 13.

Holbig, Heike. 2001. "The evolution of China's political system: New rules for CCP rule?" Presented at the Fourth ECAN Annual Conference China's WTO Accession: National and International Perspectives, Hamburg, Germany. February 1–2.

———. 2000. "Falungong. Genese und alternative Deutungen eines politischen Konflikts." *CHINA Aktuell* (February): 135–47.

Hom, Sharon K., and Xin Chunying.1995. *English-Chinese Lexicon of Women and Law*. Beijing: CTPC.

Hong Da Yong and Kang Xiaoguang. 2001. *NGO Fupin Xingwei Yanjiu* (Research on NGO Action in Poverty Alleviation). Beijing: China Economics Press.

Hong Yung Lee. 1991. *From Revolutionary Cadres to Party Technocrats in Socialist China*. Berkeley: University of California Press.

Honig, Emily. 1986. *Sisters and Strangers: Women in the Shanghai Cotton Mills, 1919–1949*. Stanford: Stanford University Press.

Howell, Jude. 2003. "Gender and civil society in China. Making a difference." *International Journal of Feminist Politics* 2.

———. 2000. "Organising around women and labour in China: Uneasy shadows, uncomfortable alliances." *Communist and Post-Communist Studies* 33: 355–77.

———. 1998a. "An unholy trinity? Civil society, economic liberalization and democratization in post-Mao China." *Government and Opposition* 33 1. Winter: 56–80.

———. 1998b. "Gender, civil society, and the state in China." *Gender, Politics, and the State*. V. Randall and G. Waylen, eds. London: Routledge.

———. 1997. "Post-Beijing reflections: Creating ripples, but not waves in China." *Women's Studies International Forum* 20, 2: 235–52.

———. 1996. "The struggle for survival: Prospects for the Women's Federation in post-Mao China." *World Development* 24, 1: 129–43.

Howell, Jude, and Diane Mulligan. 2003. "Gender and civil society. Editorial introduction." *International Journal of Feminist Politics* 2.

Howell, Jude, and Jenny Pearce. 2001. *Civil Society and Development: A Critical Exploration.* Boulder, Colo.: Lynne Rienner Publishers.

Hsiung, Ping-Chun, Maria Jaschok, and Cecilia Milwertz with Red Chan, eds. 2001. *Chinese Women Organizing: Cadres, Feminists, Muslims and Queers.* Oxford and New York: Berg.

Hu Angang. 2001. *Zhongguo: Tiaozhan Fubai* (China: Fighting against Corruption). Hangzhou: Zhejiang renmin chubanshe.

Huang Qizao. 2000. *Messages of Spring: Huang Qizao on Women and Children's Work.* Beijing: Chinese Women's Publishing House.

Huang, Philip C. C. 1993. "'Public sphere'/'civil society' in China? The third realm between state and society." *Modern China* 19, 2 (April): 216–40.

Huang, Weiping, ed. 2000. *Zhongguo jiceng minzhu fazhan de zuixin tupo.* Beijing: Shehui kexue wenxian chubanshe.

Hung-yee Chen, Albert. 1998. *An Introduction to the Legal System of the People's Republic of China,* 2nd ed. Singapore, Malaysia, and Hong Kong: Butterworths.

Hu Ningsheng. 1998. *Zhongguo Zhengfu Xingxiang Zhanlue* (Strategic Images of China's Government). Beijing: Zhonggong zhongyang dangxiao chubanshe.

Hurst, William, and Kevin J. O'Brien. 2002. "China's contentious pensioners." *China Quarterly* 170 (June): 345–60.

Hutzler, Charles. 2002. "Winding road to reform." *Far Eastern Economic Review.* September 5: 27–31.

*International Herald Tribune.* 1999. "Beijing's law and order problem." January 19.

Jakobson, Linda. 1999. *Blazing New Trails: Village Committees' Elections in the P.R. China.* UPI Working Papers 19/1999. Helsinki: Finnish Institute of International Affairs.

———. 1998. *A Million Truths. A Decade in China.* New York: M. Evans.

Jayasuriya, Kanishka. 1999. "A framework for the analysis of legal institutions in East Asia." *Law, Capitalism and Power in Asia.* Kanishka Jayasuriya, ed. London: Routledge.

Jiang, Wandi. 1996. "Grassroots democracy taking root." *Beijing Review.* March 11–17.

Jiang Yongping. 2001. "Review of the debate on 'phased employment' and the argument of 'women returning home': Crossing centuries." *Women's Studies* D423, 4. Beijing: China People's University Social Sciences Information Center.

Jiang Zemin. 2002. "Quanmian jianshe xiaokang shehui, kaichuang Zhongguo tese shehui zhuyi shiye xinjumian (Comprehensively build a comparatively well-off society, open up a new phase in socialism with Chinese characteristics)." news.xinhuanet.com/newscenter/2002–11/17/content.

———. 2000. "Hold high the great banner of Deng Xiaoping theory: Carrying the cause of building socialism with Chinese characteristics to the twenty-first century." *Xinhua.* September 21, 1997. In Thomas G. Moore. "China and Globalization." *Globalization and East Asia.* Samuel Kim, ed. Lanham, Md.: Rowman and Littlefield.

———. 1998a. "Welcome speech on the opening ceremony of the UN Fourth World Conference on women." 1995. In *Treatise of Top Leaders of the Party and the State on Works Concerning Women and Children.* National Working Commission on Women and Children, ed. Beijing.

———. 1998b. "The whole party and society should build up the perspective of Marxist women's liberation. A speech at the commemoration of the 80th anniversary of the Eighth March International Women's Day." 1990. In *Treatise of Top Leaders of the Party and the State on Works Concerning Women and Children*. National Working Commission on Women and Children, ed. Beijing.

———. 1997. Report at the 15th Party Congress of the Chinese Communist Party, delivered on September 12. www.chinadaily.net/cndy/history/15/fulltext.

———. 1992. "Accelerating reform and opening-up." *Beijing Review* 35, 43. October 26: 9–32.

———. 1991. "Zai qingzhu Zhonghua remin gongheguo chengli sishi zhounian dahui shangde jianghua (Talk at the meeting celebrating the fortieth anniversary of the establishment of the PRC)." In *Shisanda Yilai Zhongyao Wenxian Xuanbian* (Selected Important Documents Since the Thirteenth Party Congress) 2. Beijing: Renmin Chubanshe.

Jin Yihong. 2000. "The organization of the Women's Federation: Challenge and future." *Collection of Women's Studies* 2: 28–33.

Johnson, Ian. 2000. "Death trap: How one Chinese city (Weifang) resorted to atrocities to control Falun Dafa." *Wall Street Journal*. December 26.

Katznelson, Ira. 1981. *City Trenches*. New York: Pantheon.

Kaye, Lincoln. 1995. "Flourishing grassroots: Village-level democracy blooms." *Far East Economic Review*. January 19.

Keane, Michael. 2003. "Creativity and complexity in post-WTO China." *Continuum* 1, 3.

———. 2002. "Facing off on the final frontier: The WTO accession and the re-branding of China's national champions." *Media International Australia* 105 (November): 130–47.

———. 2001. "Cultural technology transfer: Redefining content in the Chinese television industry." *Emergences: Journal for the Study of Media and Composite Cultures* 11, 2, November 1: 223–36.

Kelliher, Daniel. 1997. "The Chinese debate over village self-government." *China Journal*, 37: 63–86.

Khan, Azizur Rahman, and Carl Riskin. 2001. *Inequality and Poverty in China in the Age of Globalization*. Oxford: Oxford University Press.

Kim, Samuel, ed. 2000. *Globalization and East Asia*. Lanham, Md.: Rowman and Littlefield.

Kipnis, Andrew B. 2001. "The flourishing of religion in post-Mao China and the anthropological category of religion." *Australian Journal of Anthropology* 12, 1 (April): 32–47.

Kolb, Eugene. 1978. *A Framework for Political Analysis*. Englewood Cliffs, N.J.: Prentice Hall.

Kunming Declaration. 2001. Passed at the First Chinese Lawyers' Forum. Kunming city, December 9–10.

Lam, T. C., and H. S. Chan. 1995. "The civil service system: Policy formulation and implementation." *China Review*. I. C. K. Lo, S. Pepper, and T. K. Yuen, eds. Hong Kong: Chinese University Press.

Lampton, David M. 1977. *The Politics of Medicine in China*. Boulder, CO: Westview Press.

Lawrence, Susan V. 2002a."A Chinese academic addresses the issue of Party leadership: Daring to raise a taboo topic." *Far Eastern Economic Review*. September 12: 37.

———. 2002b. "Corporate accountability: Gagged by big business." *Far Eastern Economic Review*. August 1: 24–27.

———. 1994. "Democracy, Chinese style." *Australian Journal of Chinese Affairs*, 32: 61–68.

Lee, Jin-Weo. 1987. "Religiüse Bewegurgen." In *Pipers Wörterbuch zur Polink, Bd. 6, Dritic Weit. Gesellsehaft, Kultur, Entwicklung*. Münehen, Zürich.

Leftwich, Adrian. 1993. "Governance, democracy and development in the Third World." *Third World Quarterly* 14, 3: 605–24.

Leung, Beatrice. 2001. "China and Falun Gong: Party and society relations in modern era." Mimeo, presented at conference organized by Berend ter Haar, June 7.

*Liaowang* (Outlook). 2001. FBIS-CHI-2001–0619. June 11 and 19.

———. 1998. FBIS-CHI-98–044. February 17.

———. 1997. FBIS-CHI-97–071. March 10.

———. 1993. FBIS-CHI 93–034. February 23.

Li Changhong. 2001. "Renmin shiping: Tan 'cungong jiti pizhi' (The people's comment: Discussion of 'joint resignation by village heads')." *Renminwang zhuangao* (special report of *People's Daily* Internet edition). http://peopledaily.com.cn.

Li Conghua. 1998. *China: The Consumer Revolution*. Singapore: John Wiley and Sons.

Lieberthal, Kenneth. *Governing China: From Revolution through Reform*. New York and London: W. W. Norton and Company, 1995.

Li Fan, Shou Huisheng, Peng Zongchao, and Xiao Lihui. 2000. *Chuangxin yu fazha—Xiangzhenchang xuanju zhidu gaige*. Beijing: Dongfang chubanshe.

Li Hongzhi. 2001a. *Essentials for Further Advancement. A Falun Gong Practitioners Guide*. Gloucester, Mass.: Fairwind Press.

———. 2001b. *Zhuan Falun: The Complete Teachings of Falun Gong*. Gloucester, Mass.: Fairwind Press.

———. 1998. *Zhuan Falun*. Bad Pyrmont.

Li Jialu. 2001. "Woguo yidong tongxin de fazhan (China's communications development trends)." *Xinhua News Agency*. August 15.

Li Lianjiang. 2002. "The politics of introducing direct township elections in China." *China Quarterly* 171 (September): 704–23.

———. 1999. "The two ballot system in Shanxi Province: Subjecting Party secretaries to a popular vote." *China Journal* 42: 103–18.

Li Lianjiang and Kevin J. O'Brien. 1999. "The struggle over village elections." *The Paradox of China's Post-Mao Reforms*. Merle Goldman and Roderick MacFarquhar, eds. Cambridge, Mass.: Harvard University Press.

Li Nian-ting. 2001. "By combining with and taking in capitalists, CPC is changing into a Social Democratic Party." *Hong Kong Sing Tao Jih Pao*. FBIS-CHI-2001–0703. July 3.

Li Peilin. 2002. "Jiaru WTO hou Zhongguo shehui keneng de bianhua (Possible changes in Chinese society after China joins the WTO)." *2002 nian: Zhongguo shehui xingshi fenxi yu yuce* (The Circumstances of Chinese Society: Analysis and Prediction, 2002). Ru Xin, Lu Xueyi, and Li Peilin, eds. Beijing hehuikexue wenxian chubanshe, 2002.

Lipset, S. M. 1959. "Some social requisites of democracy: Economic development and political legitimacy." *The American Political Science Review* 53, 1: 69–105.

Liquidation Committee. 1999. *Guangdong International Trust and Investment Corporation: Second Meeting of Creditors Liquidation Progress Report*. Hong Kong, mimeo. October 22.

Liu Bohong. 2001. "The development of Chinese women's non-governmental organizations." *The Non-Profit Sector and Development*. Zhao Liqing and Carolyn Lyoya Irving, eds. Hong Kong: Hang Kong Press for Social Sciences.

———. 1995. "Zhongguo funu yanjiu qushi (Trends in China's women's studies)." *Funu Yanjiu Luncong* 1: 9–11.

Li Xiao Jiang. 1993. "Xin shiqi funu yanjiu he funu yundong zhi wo jian (My views on women's studies and the women's movement in the new era)." *Zhongguo Funu Yu Fazhan. Diwei Jiankang, Jiuye* (Chinese Women and Development. Status, Health, and Employment). Tianjin: Henan's People's Publishing House.

Li Xiaoyun. 2000. "China rural women's issues in the globalization." *Chinese Women's Movement* 9. The All-China Women's Federation: 41.

Li Yangfen. 2000. "The development and problems of the work on organizational construction." *Chinese Women's Movement* 6. The All-China Women's Federation: 24–26.

Lubman, Stanley. 1999. *Bird in a Cage: Legal Reform in China after Mao*. Stanford: Stanford University Press.

Luo Bing. 1999. "The secret plot to suppress Falun Gong: The inside story." *Zheng Ming* (Hong Kong). August. Translated in *Chinese Law and Government* 32, 6: 91–98.

Lu Xueyi, ed. 2001. *Dangdai Zhongguo Shehui Jieceng Yanjiu Baogao* (Research Report on China's Social Strata). Beijing: Shehui kexue wenxian chubanshe.

MacFarquhar, Roderick, ed. 1997. *The Politics of China: The Eras of Mao and Deng*. Cambridge: Cambridge University Press.

Madsen, Richard. 1993. "The public sphere, civil society and moral community: A research agenda for contemporary China studies." *Modern China* 19, 2 (April): 183–98.

Manion, Melanie. 1993. *Retirement of Revolutionaries in China: Public Policies, Social Norms, Private Interests*. Princeton: Princeton University Press.

———. 1991. "Policy implementation in the People's Republic of China: Authoritative decisions versus individual interests." *The Journal of Asian Studies* 50, 2: 253–79.

Marshall, T. H. 1964. "Citizenship and social class." *Class, Citizenship and Social Development*. T. H. Marshall, ed. New York: Doubleday and Company. Chinese translation manuscript by Li Yongxin, 2001.

Ma Shu Yun. 1994. "The Chinese discourse on civil society." *China Quarterly* 137 (March): 180–93.

Medard, Jean-Francois. 1991. "The historical trajectories of the Ivorian and Kenyan states." *Rethinking Third World Politics*. James Manor, ed. London and New York: Longman.

*Ming Pao* (Hong Kong). 1998. FBIS-CHI-98–301. October 28.

Ministry of Civil Affairs. 2000. *China Civil Affairs' Statistical Yearbook*. Beijing: China Statistics Press.

———. 1990. *Peng Zhen tongzhi guanyu cunmin weiyuanhui jumin weiyuanhui de zhongyao jianghua* (Important Speeches by Comrade Peng Zhen on Villagers' Committees and Residents' Committees). Mimeograph compiled by Department of Basic-Level Governance. Beijing: Ministry of Civil Affairs.

Ministry of Information Industry. 2002. January 30. www.chinaonline.com/issues/internet_policy.

Ministry of Justice, Supreme People's Court. 2001. "The Supreme People's Procuracy and the implementing measure for the National Judicial Examination (trial provisions)." Issued jointly on October 31, 2001, and effective as of January 1, 2002.

———. 1998. Circular of the China Securities Regulatory Commission on the Strengthening of Lawyers Engaging in Securities Legal Business. Issued on July 3.

———. 1997. Measures on Punishment of Lawyers' Illegal Activities. Issued on January 31.

———. 1996a. The Measures on the Administration of State-funded Law Firms.

———. 1996b. The Measures on the Administration of Cooperative Law Firms.

———. 1996c. The Measures on the Administration of Partnership Law Firms.

———. 1996d. Lawyers Law of the PRC.

———. 1995a. Circular on Further Improvement of the System for the Punishment of Lawyers and Strengthening Work on the Punishment of Lawyers. Issued on May 20.

———. 1995b. Several Provisions Concerning Legal Profession Against Unfair Competition Activities. Issued on February 20.

———. 1994. "What attention should be paid in the process of deepening reforms on lawyers' work?" Issued on March 3.

———. 1993. Provisions Concerning Lawyers' Professional Ethics and Practising Disciplines. Issued on December 27.

———. 1992. Rules for the Punishment of Lawyers. Issued on October 22.

———. 1980. Provisional Regulations of the PRC on Lawyers.

Ministry of Labor and Personnel. 1984. "Guanyu jianli guojia xingzheng jiguan gongzuo renyuan gangwei zirenzhide tongzhi (Notice on establishing a responsibility system for state administrative personnel)." *Laoren* 162. *Renshi gongzuo wenjian xuanbian* (Selected personnel work documents) 5. Ministry of Labor and Personnel Policy and Research Office, ed. Beijing: Laodong renshi chubanshe.

Ministry of Personnel. 1999. "Renshibu banshi gongkai zanxing guiding (Temporary regulations on transparency in handling ministry of personnel matters)." *Renshi gongzuo wenjian xuanbian* (Selection of Personnel Work Documents) 21. Ministry of Personnel, ed. Beijing: Zhongguo renshi chubanshe.

———. 1993. Provisional Regulations on Civil Servants. Beijing: Ministry of Personnel.

———, ed. *Renshi gongzuo wenjian xuanbian (Selection of Personnel Work Documents)* (various volumes). Beijing: Renshi chubanshe, various years.

Ministry of Personnel and Ministry of Finance. 2001. "Guanyu diaozheng jiguan gongzuo renyuan gongzi biaojunde shishi fangan (Implementation plan for the adjustment of the wage standard for government employees)." September 7. In *Gazette of the Ministry of Personnel of the People's Republic of China* 11. Ministry of Personnel General Office, ed. Zhonghua renmin gongheguo renshibu gongbao. November 15.

Molyneux, M. 1998. "Analysing women's movements." *Feminist Vision of Development: Gender, Analysis and Polity*. R. Pearson and C. Jackson, eds. London and New York: Routledge.

Moore, Barrington. 1966. *Social Origins of Dictatorship and Democracy*. Boston: Beacon Press.

Moore, M. 1993. "Introduction." *IDS Bulletin* 24, 1: 39–50.

Moore, Thomas G. 2002. *China in the World Market: Chinese Industry and International Sources of Reform in the Post-Mao Era*. New York: Cambridge University Press.

———. 2000. "China and globalization." *Globalization and East Asia.* Samuel Kim, ed. Lanham, MD: Rowman and Littlefield.

Moser, C. 1993. *Gender Planning and Development: Theory, Practice and Training.* London and New York: Routledge.

Mufson, Steven. 1995. "China dabbles in democracy to run village, reform Party." *Washington Post.* January 26.

Mykkänen, Pekka. 2001. "Haaveet demokratiasta murentuneet Kiinan lukuisissa pikkukylissä (The dream of democracy shattered in scores of China's small villages)." *Helsingin Sanomat* (Finland's Largest Daily). July 9.

*Nanfang zhoumo (Southern Weekend).* 1999. "Falun Gong: A 'folk heresy' with cult characteristics." BBC SWB. April 27. March 13. www.arts.ubc.ca/polisci/chab/p321/private/flg

———. 1999. "Zhi xuan xiangzhang." January 15.

Narayan, Francis B., and Barry Reid. 2000. *Financial Management and Governance Issues in the People's Republic of China: Diagnostic Study of Accounting and Auditing.* Manila: Asian Development Bank.

Nolan, Peter. 2001. *China and the Global Economy.* Basingstoke: Palgrave.

O'Brien, Kevin J. 1996. "Rightful resistance." *World Politics* 49, 1: 31–55.

———. 1994. "Implementing political reform in China's villages." *Australian Journal of Chinese Affairs*: 33–59.

O'Brien, Kevin J., and Li Lianjiang. 2000. "Accommodating 'democracy' in a one-party state: Introducing village elections in China." *China Quarterly* 162: 465–89.

OECD. 2000a. *The Creative Society of the 21st Century.* OECD: Paris.

———. 2000b. *Towards the Creative Society of the 21st Century.* OECD: Paris.

———. 1998. Working Party on the Information Economy. "Content as a new growth industry." Directorate for Science, Technology and Industry; Committee for Information, Computer and Technology Policy. Paris: OECD.

Oksenberg, Michael. 2001. "China's political system: Challenges of the twenty-first century." *The China Journal* 45 (January): 21–36.

———. 1998. "Will China democratize? Confronting a classic dilemma." *Journal of Democracy* 9, 1: 27–34.

Ong, Aihwa. 1999. *Flexible Citizenship: The Cultural Logics of Transnationality.* Durham and London: Duke University Press.

O'Regan, Tom. 2001. "Cultural policy: rejuvenate or wither." Presented at the Australian Key Centre for Cultural Policy Professorial Lecture, Griffith University. July 26.

Organization Department (Zhonggong zhongyang zuzhibu), Ministry of Personnel. 1999. *Dangzheng lingdao ganbu tongji ziliao huibian 1954–1998* (Collection of statistical information on party and government leading cadres). Beijing: Dangjian duwu chubanshe.

———. 1998. "Guanyu zuohao xiangzhen jiguan shishi guojia gongwuyuan zhidu he canzhao guanli gongzuo de yijian (Opinion on doing well the implementation of the civil service system in towns and townships and related management work)." *Zutongzi*, 48. 1997. In *Renshi gongzuo wenjian xuanbian (Selection of Personnel Work Documents)* 20. Ministry of Personnel, ed. Beijing: Zhongguo renshi chubanshe.

Østergaard, Clemens Stubbe. 1989. "Citizens, groups and a nascent civil society in China: Towards an understanding of the 1989 student demonstrations." *China Information* 4, 2: 28–41.

Ownby, David. 2001. "China's war against itself." *New York Times*. February 15.

———. 2000. "Falungong as a cultural revitalization movement: An historian looks at contemporary China." Talk at Rice University. October 20, 2000. www.ruf.rice. edu/~tnchina/commentary/ownby1000.

Palmer, David. 2001. "The doctrine of Li Hongzhi. Falun Gong: Between sectarianism and universal salvation." *China Perspectives* 35. (2001): 14–23.

Pan, Philip P. 2002. "When workers organise, China's party-run unions resist." *Washington Post Foreign Service*. October 15.

Pei Minxin. 1998. "Chinese civic associations: An empirical analysis." *Modern China* 24, 3 (July): 285–318.

Peng Peiyun. 2001a. "Bringing women's organizations into full play in the new historical era." Speech at the Workshop of Directors of Women's Federations at Provinces, Municipalities, ACWF. 2000. In *Chinese Women's Movement* 8. The All-China Women's Federation, Beijing.

———. 2001b. "Promoting women to fully participate in the implementation of the national Fifth Ten Year Plan: Peng Peiyun made four proposals." *China Women's News*. March 14.

———. 2000. "Provide women's development supportive theories." *People's Daily*. February 15. *People's Daily*. 1999a. November 1.

———. 1999b. August 20.

———. 1999c. Overseas edition (Doc. 17 in *CLG*, 1999). July 23.

Perry, Elizabeth J. 2001. "Challenging the mandate of heaven: Popular protest in modern China." *Critical Asian Studies* 33, 2: 163–80.

———. 2000. "Reinventing the wheel? The campaign against Falun Gong." *Harvard China Review* 2, 2: 68–71.

———. 1999. "Crime, corruption and contention." *The Paradox of China's Post-Mao Reforms*. Merle Goldman and Roderick MacFarquhar, eds. Cambridge, MA: Harvard University Press.

———. 1994. "Shanghai's strike wave of 1957." *China Quarterly* 137 (March): 1–27.

———. 1993. *Shanghai on Strike: The Politics of Chinese Labor*. Stanford: Stanford University Press.

Perry, Elizabeth J., and Li Xun. 1997. *Proletarian Power: Shanghai in the Cultural Revolution*. Boulder, CO: Westview.

Pierre, Jon, and B. Guy Peters. 2000. *Governance, Politics and the State*. New York: St. Martin's Press.

Protocol on the Accession of the People's Republic of China: Schedule of Specific Commitments on Services. 2001. November 10.

Provisional Regulations on the Establishment of Representative Office in China by Foreign Law Firms. 1992. Passed in 2001.

Putnam, R.D. 1993. "The prosperous community: Social capital and public life." *American Prospect* 13: 35–42.

Pu Xingzu. 1999. *Zhonghua renmin gongheguo zhengzhi zhidu* (Political System of the People's Republic of China). Shanghai: Renmin chubanshe.

Qing Lianbin. 2003. "Zhongguo dangzheng lingdao ganbu dui 2002–2003 nian shehui xingshi de jiben kanfa (Opinions on social situation in 2002 by some officials)." *2003 nian: Zhongguo shehui xingshi fenxi yu yuce* (China's Social Situation: Analysis and Forecast, 2003). Ru Xin, Lu Xueyi and Li Peixin, eds. Beijing: Shehui kexue wenxian chubanshe.

Qingdao Women's Federation. 2000. "Investigation into women's participation in the sixth election in Qingdao." Selected Documents of Work on Women and Children. 1998–1999. ACWF, ed. Beijing: China Women's Press.

Quah, Danny. 1996. "Growth and dematerialisation: Why non-stick frying pans have lost the edge." CEP's CentrePiece 1, 3. (October): 20–25.

Raboy, Marc. 1999. "Communication policy and globalization as a social project." Communication, Citizenship and Social Policy: Rethinking the Limits of the Welfare State. Andrew Calabrese and Jean-Claude Burgelman, eds. Lanham, MD: Rowman and Littlefield.

Rankin, Mary Backus. 1993. "Some observations on a Chinese public sphere." Modern China 19, 2 (April): 158–82.

Rawls, John. 1999. "The public reason: Revisited." Law Review 62, 3. The University of Chicago. (Summer 1997): 765–807. Chinese translation version "GongGong Lixing." In Gonggong Lixing yu Xiandai Xueshu (Public Reason and Modern Academic Research). Harvard Yanching School and Beijing Sanlian Publishing House.

Report on China's Legal Profession. 2000. Submitted to the Chinese Lawyer Millennium Conference, held in Beijing on November 26.

Renmin Ribao (People's Daily). 2001. "Zhongguo quanmian tuijin nongcun jiceng minzhu." April 9. www.peopledaily.com.

——. 1999a. "On revealing Falungong multiple echelons." FBIS-CHI-1999–1101. November 1.

——. 1998. FBIS-CHI-98–097. March 9 and 24.

——. 1997a. "System of self-rule explained." FBIS-CHI-97–358. November 20.

——. 1997b. FBIS-CHI-96–034. January 17.

——. 1994. August 1.

Research Group on the System of Village Self-government in Rural China and the China Research Society of Basic-Level Governance. 1994. Study on the Election of Villagers' Committees in Rural China. Beijing: China Society Publishing House.

Riskin, Carl, Zhao Renwei, and Li Shi, eds. 2000. China's Retreat from Equality: Income Distribution and Economic Transition. Armonk, N. Y.: M. E. Sharpe.

Romzek, Barbara, and Melvin Dubnick. 1987. "Accountability in the public sector: Lessons from the Challenger tragedy." Public Administration Review 47. (May/June): 227–38.

Rong Jiben, et al. 1998. Cong yali xing tizhi xiang minzhu hezuo tizhi de zhuanbian (Transformation of the Pressurized System to the Democratic System of Cooperation). Beijing: Zhongyang Bianyi Chubanshe.

Rowe, William. 1993. "The problem of 'civil society' in late imperial China." Modern China 19, 2. (April): 139–57.

——. 1990. "The public sphere in modern China." Modern China 16, 3: 309–29.

Ru Xin, ed. 1998. "Xiao Zhengfu Da Shehui" de Lilun yu Shiqian (Theory and Practice of Small Government and Small Society). Beijing: Social Sciences Collections Publishing House.

Saich, Tony, ed. 2000. "Negotiating the state: The development of social organisations in China." The China Quarterly 161 (March): 124–41.

——. 1996. The Rise to Power of the Chinese Communist Party: Documents and Analysis. Armonk, N.Y.: M. E. Sharpe.

Saich, Tony, and Yang Xuedong. 2002. "Selecting within the rules: Institutional innovation in China's governance." Presented at conference on local government reform in China and India, Kennedy School of Government, Harvard University. March.

Scalapino, Robert. 1998. "Will China democratize? Current trends and future prospects." *Journal of Democracy* 9, 1: 35–40. Updated in 2000.

Schmitter, Philippe. 1974. "Still the century of corporatism?" *Review of Politics* 36, 1 (January): 85–131.

Schumpeter, Joseph A. 1934. *The Theory of Economic Development.* Cambridge: Harvard University Press.

Selya, Roger Mark. 1995. "Taiwan as a service economy." *Geoforum* 25, 3: 305–22.

Shambaugh, David, ed. 2000. *Is China Unstable?* Armonk, N.Y.: M. E. Sharpe.

Shanghai shi dangjian yanjiuhui ketizu. 2001. "Zhongshi jiaru WTO dui ganbu renshi gongzuo de tiaozhan (Pay attention to the challenge WTO poses to cadre and personnel work)." *Dangjian yanjiu neican* 11: 5–7.

Shao Ren. 1999. "Zhongguo: Ruguan buru tao (China: Joining the WTO without falling into the trap)." *Tianya* 3 (May): 5–15, 90.

*Sing Tao Daily (Sing Tao Jib Pao)*.1998. FBIS-CHI-98-133. May 13.

Shi Shuren. 2001. "Xiangzhen zhengfu wu quan chehuan 'cungong' (Township government has no right to dismiss 'village head')." *Beijing Qingnianbao*. March 30. www.peopledaily.com.cn/GB/shizheng

Shi Tianjian. 1999. "Village committee elections in China: Institutionalist tactics for democracy." *World Politics* 51, 3: 385–412.

Shi Wen. 2001. "Putian shi shixing 'santui liangkao yixuan' xuanba xiangzhen lingdaobanzi chengyuan (Putian municipality implemented on a trial basis the three recommendations, two examinations, and one selection system to select members of the leading group of administrative villages and townships)." *Dangjian yanjiu neican* (Studies on Party Building, Internal Reference) 11: 8–9.

Shou Beibei. 2001. "Cungong de dang jia quan. Shandong 57 ming 'cungong' jiti yaoqiu cizhi yinchu de huati (Acting village heads without power)." *Renmin ribao.* March 30. www.peopledaily.com.cn/GB/guandian/26/20010330/429329

Smith, Craig S. 2001a. "Sect clings to the web in the face of Beijing's ban." *New York Times.* July 5.

———. 2001b. "Falun Gong manages skimpy rally: Is sect fading?" *New York Times.* July 23.

Solinger, Dorothy. 2000. "Sudden sackings and the mirage of the market: Unemployment, reemployment, and survival in Wuhan, summer 1999." *Institute Reports, East Asian Institute.* New York: Columbia University.

———. 1999. *Contesting Citizenship in Urban China: Peasant Migrants, the State, and the Logic of the Market.* Berkeley: University of California Press.

Song Qiang, Zhang Zangzang, and Qiao Bian. 1996. *Zhongguo Keyi Shuobu* (China Can Say No). Beijing: Zhonghua Gongshan Lianhe Chubanshe.

*South China Morning Post* (Hong Kong). 2001. March 24, May 15 and 18, June 19 and 20, and September 7 and 9.

———. 1999a. "Historic township vote in Shenzhen." April 30.

———. 1999b. "Beijing indicates recognition of landmark election." March 1.

————. 1999c. "Media blackout ordered on poll." January 31.

Spaeth, Anthony. 1996. "Surprise: Democracy is taking root in China too." *Time.* April 1.

State Council. 2002. "The regulation on the administration of representative offices set up in China by foreign law firms." December 19, 2001. Came into effect on January 1.

————. 1994. "Law on the protection of state secrets of the People's Republic of China." 1988. *Renshi Dang'an* (China's Cadre Dossier System) in *Chinese Law and Government* 27, 2. J. P. Burns, ed: 79–83.

State Statistical Bureau. 1997. *China Statistical Yearbook 1997.* Beijing: Zongguo tonji chubanshe.

*Straits Times Interactive.* 2000. January 20.

Strand, David. 1990. "Protest in Beijing: Civil society and public sphere in China." *Problems of Communism* 39: 1–19.

Straubhaar, Joseph D. 2000. "Culture, language and social class in the globalization of television." *The New Communications Landscape: Demystifying Media Globalization.* Georgette Wang, Jan Servaes, and Anura Goonerasekera, eds. London: Routledge.

Sun Liping. 2002. "Women zai kaishi miandui yige duanlie de shehui? (Are we starting to face a fragmented society?)" *Strategy and Management* 2: 9–15.

Sun Yingbao. 1994. "Zhongguo shehui tuanti guanmin erchongxing wenti (The issue of the dualism of Chinese civic associations)." *Chinese Social Science Quarterly.* Hong Kong. (February): 17–23.

Sutton, Rebecca. 1999. "The Policy Process: An overview." *ODI.* August.

Tacchi, Jo. 2001. "Developing convergence: Spaces for innovation and enterprise." Presented to the second radiocracy conference Predicting Pathways and Pulling Together. Durban, South Africa. September 20–24.

Tang, Wenfang, and William Parish. 2000. *Chinese Urban Life under Reform.* Cambridge: Cambridge Univeristy Press.

Tang Dahuan. 2002. "Yijuezhi minzhu yu piaojuezhi minzhu (The resolution system democracy and the voting system democracy)." *Gaige Neican (Internal reference)* 10: 17–19.

Tanner, Murray Scot. 2001. "Cracks in the Wall: China's eroding coercive state." *Current History* 100, 647 (September): 243–249.

Tarrow, Sidney. 1998. *Power in Movement,* 2nd ed. Cambridge: Cambridge University Press.

*Time* magazine. 1999. Interview with Li Hongzhi, May 10, 1999. www.time.com/time/asia/magazine/1999/990510/inerview1.

Tipson, Frederick S. 1999. "China and the Information Revolution." *China Joins the World: Progress and Reports.* Michel Oksenberg, ed. New York: Council of Foreign Relations.

Transparency International Corruption Perception. 2001. September 7. www.transparency.org/documents/cpi2001.

Turner, Bryan S., ed. 1993. *Citizenship and Social Theory.* London: Sage Publications.

Turner, Mark, and David Hulme. 1997. *Governance, Administration and Development: Making the State Work.* Basingstoke: MacMillan Press.

UNDP. 2002. *Human Development Report 2002: Deepening Democracy in a Fragmented World.* New York and London: Oxford University Press.

————. 1998. *Governance in China: A Compendium of Donor Activities (1995–1997).* Beijing: UNDP (July).

————. 1997. *Reconceptualizing Governance Discussion Paper No. 2.* New York: UNDP.

———. 1995. *Public Sector Management, Governance, and Sustainable Human Development: A Discussion Paper.* New York: UNDP.

UNESCO. 1996. *Our Creative Diversity: Report of the World Commission on Culture and Development.* Paris: UNESCO Publications.

Unger, Jonathan, and Anita Chan. 1996. "Corporatism in China: A developmental state in an East Asian context." *China After Socialism: In the Footsteps of Eastern Europe or East Asia?* Barrett McCormick and Jonathan Unger, eds. Armonk, N.Y.: M. E. Sharpe.

———. 1995. "China, corporatism and the East Asian model." *The Australian Journal of Chinese Affairs* 33. (January): 29–53.

Ure, John, and Liang Xiong-Jian. 2000. "Convergence and China's national information infrastructure." *Electronic Communication Convergence: Policy Challenges in Asia.* Mark Hukill, Ryoto Ono, and C. Vallath, eds. New Delhi: Sage.

Vermander, Benoit. 2001. "Looking at China through the mirror of Falun Gong." *China Perspectives* 35: 4–13.

Von Hayek, Friedrich. 1978. "Liberalism." *New Study in Philosophy: Politics, Economics and the History of Ideas.* Chicago: The University of Chicago Press.

Wakeman, Frederic, Jr. 1993. "The civil society and public sphere debate: Western reflections on Chinese political culture." *Modern China* 19 (April): 108–38.

Wang, Xu. 1997. "Mutual empowerment of state and peasantry: Grassroots democracy in rural China." *World Development* 25, 9: 1431–42.

Wang Hui. 1998. "Dangdai Zhongguo de sixiang zhuangkuang yu xiandaixing wenti (The circumstances of contemporary Chinese thought and the problem of modernity)." *Wenyi zhengming* 6. (November): 7–26.

Wang Ying. 1994. "Zhongguo de shehui zhongjian ceng: shetuan fazhan yu zuzhi tixi chongguo (The intermediary level of society: The development of social organisations and the reconstruction of organisational systems)." *Chinese Social Science Quarterly.* Hong Kong. (February): 24–36.

Wang Ying, Zhe Xiaoye, and Sun Bing Yao. 1992. *Zhongguo shehui zhongjian ceng: gaige yu Zhongguo de shetuan zuzhi* (The Intermediary Level of Society: Reform and China's Social Organizations). Beijing: Zhongguo Fazhan Chubanshe.

Wang Zheng. 2000. "The application of the gender concept in China." *China Women's News.* May 2.

Wasserstrom, Jeffrey. 2000. "The year of living anxiously: China's 1999." *Dissent* 47, 1: 17–22.

Watts, Craig. 2000. "China's 'take' on business incubators." *Interfax Information Services.* May 17. Reprinted on China Online, January 30, 2002. www.chinaonline.com

Wei Luo. 2002. "Jiaru WTO dui dangde lingdao fangshi he huodong fangshi de yingxiang (The influence of joining the WTO on the leadership method and activity method of the CCP)." *Dangjian yanjiu neican* 3: 1–3.

Weldon, Jim.2001/2002. "New moves for pearly Delta migrants." *China Development Brief* IV, 3. (winter): 25–27.

Weller, Robert. 2001. *Time* magazine. July 1.

*Wenhui bao (Hong Kong).* 2001. July 2; September 15, 1997; and February 7, 1993.

White, Gordon. 1998. "Social security reforms in China: Towards an East Asian model?" *The East Asian Welfare Model: Welfare Orientalism and the State.* Roger Goodman, Gordon White, and Huck-ju Kwon, eds. London and New York: Routledge.

———. 1994. "Democratization and economic reform in China." *Australian Journal of Chinese Affairs* 31: 73–94.

White, Gordon, Jude Howell, and Shang Xiaoyuan. 1996. *In Search of Civil Society. Market Reform and Social Change in Contemporary China.* Oxford: Clarendon Press.

White, Tyrene. 1992. "Reforming the countryside." *Current History* 91, 566: 273–77.

Whyte, Martin K. 2000. "Chinese social trends: Stability or chaos?" *Is China Unstable? Assessing the Factors.* David Shambaugh, ed. Armonk, N.Y.: M. E. Sharpe.

The Women's Studies Institute of China (WSIC) and Department of Social, Science and Technology Statistics, State Statistics Bureau. 1998. *Gender Statistics in China (1990–1995).* Beijing: China Statistic Publishing House.

Wong, John, and William Liu. 1999. "The mystery of China's Falun Gong." Singapore University Press, East Asian Institute. *Contemporary China Series* 22. Singapore.

Woodman, Sophia. 1999. "Less dressed up as more? Promoting non-profit organisations by regulating away freedom of association." *China Perspectives* 222: 17–27.

World Bank. 1997. *China 2020: Disparities in China: Sharing Rising Incomes.* Washington, D.C.: World Bank.

———. 1994. *Governance: The World Bank's Experience.* Washington, D.C.: World Bank.

———. 1992. *Governance and Development.* Washington, D.C.: World Bank.

World Summit on the Information Society. 2003. (The convening organization is the Platform for Communication Rights.) www.itu.int/wsis/about/about_WhatIsWsis_Print.

World Trade Organization Council for Trade in Services. 1998. "Audiovisual services: Background notes by the secretariat." June 15.

Wright, Teresa. 2002. "The China democracy party and the politics of protest in the 1980s–1990s." *China Quarterly* 172 (December): 906–26.

Wu Mingde. 2000. Secretary-general of the All-China Lawyers Association, quoted in *China Daily* on November 27.

Xiao Yang. 2000. "Take basic construction of the people's courts to a new stage." Delivered at the National Judicial Basic Construction Work Conference. June 23, 2000. In *Zhonghua renmin gongheguo zuigao renmin fayuan gongbao* (Supreme People's Court Gazette). April.

Xie Chun Lei. 2002. "Wailai gong zizhi zuzhi chuxian Zhejiang Ruian (Outside workers self-organization first appears in Ruian, Zhejiang)." *Nanfang Zhoumo* (Southern Weekend). April 7.

*Xinhua.* 2001. Reports (Chinese and English) on the Beijing Lawyers Association. "Beijing lawyers' code of conduct for practice (trial)." First brought to light in February 2001 for public consultation and later implemented on a trial basis. July 4.

———. 2000a. "Ministry of Personnel issues notice stipulating that state functionaries may not practice Falun Dafa." Translated in *CLG* 32, 5. July 23: 26.

———. 2000b. FBIS-CHI-2001–0105. January 5, 2001. In FBIS-CHI-2000–0914, September 14, 2000; in FBIS-CHI-2000–0913, September 13, 2000; and in FBIS-CHI-2000 0717, July 17, 2000.

———. 1999a. "Police crack Falungong illicit publication cases." FBIS–CHI-1999–1021. October 21.

———. 1999b "Using Falun Gong."

———. 1998. FBIS-CHI-98–310. November 6, 1998 and October 29, 1998. In FBIS-CHI-98–217, July 31 and August 5, 1998.

*Xinhua* (New China News Agency). 2001a. FBIS-CHI-2001–0701. July 1, 2001. In FBIS-CHI-2001–0615, June 15, 2001 and in FBIS-CHI=2001–0308, March 8, 2001.

———. 2001b. "Expose the vicious political motives of Li Hongzhi and his 'Falun Gong.'" *Renmin Ribao Commentators*. FBIS-CHI-2001–0107. January 7.

———. 2001c. "One more ironclad evidence of trampling upon human rights: The facts of Li Hongzhi and his evil cult Falungong covering up crime of dumping corpse, destroying evidence." FBIS-CHI-2001–0719. July 19.

———. 2001d. "Xinhua interviews former Falun Gong member on Li Hongzhi's 'tricks.'" FBIS-CHI-2001–0726. July 26.

———. 2001e. "Embassy spokesman says fight against Falungong proceeding 'smoothly.'" FBIS-CHI-2001–0719. July 19.

———. 2001f. "China's fight against Falungong part of worldwide fight against cults." FBIS-CHI-2001–0212. February 12.

———. 2001g. "Coming out of a haze, remolding ones life: Analysis of typical cases of transformation of obsessed 'Falungong' adherents." FBIS-CHI-2001–0524. May 22.

*Xinhua Domestic Service*. 1997. "Decision on alleviating peasants' burdens." Foreign Broadcasting Information Service, FBIS-CHI-97–065. March 31.

Xu Dejin. 2001. "Falungong activities in Washington were to oppose China." *Beijing Zhongguo Xinwen She*. FBIS-CHI-2001–0723.

Xue Muqiao. 1998. "Establish and develop non-governmental self-management organisations in various trades." *Renmin Ribao* (People's Daily). October 10. Translated in FBIS, China Report, 88/201.

Xu Xin, ed. 2001. "Zhongguo Suehui Yingxi fengsi yu yuece (An analysis and forecast of China's society)." Beijing, 1999. Cited in Leung.

Yan Yuxiang. 2000. "The politics of consumerism in Chinese society." *China Briefing 2000: The Continuing Transformation*. Tyrenne White, ed. Armonk, N.Y.: M. E. Sharpe.

Yi Ying. 2000. "A preliminary study of women's studies organizations in contemporary China." *Collection of Women's Studies* 2. Beijing: Women's Studies Institute of China.

You Ji. 1999. *The China Challenge in the New Millenium*. Strategic Update '99. Canberra. idun.itsc.adfa.edu.au/ADSC/Strat99/paper_y_ji.

Yue, Yan, and Hai Zhen. 1997. "China: System of self-rule by village explained." *Renmin Ribao*. FBIS-CHI-97–358. November 20.

Yu Ning. 2000. "The development of China's legal profession." Paper presented by vice president of the All-China Lawyers' Association at China-UK Legal Development Seminar, London. April 3.

Zhang, Junzuo. 1994. "Development in a Chinese reality: Rural women's organisations in China." *Journal of Communist Studies* 10, 4: 71–92.

Zhang, Naihua. 1999. "NGO, national policy machinery, and the All-China Women's Federation: Renegotiating space and position in between women and the state in post-Mao China." Prepared for Women Organising in China workshop, Oxford.

Zhang Jing. 1996. "Zhidu Beijing xia de jiandu xioayong (Different effect for supervision at institutional background)." *Zhanlue yu Guanli* (Strategy and management) 6: 94–98.

Zhang Ping. 2001. "Rural interregional inequality and off-farm employment in China." *China's Retreat from Equality: Income Distribution and Economic Transition*. Carl Riskin, Zhao Renwei, and Li Shi, eds. Armonk, N.Y.: M.E. Sharpe.

Zhao Hongjun. 2001. "Quanguo gedi gongkai xuanba lingdao ganbu gongzuo qingkuang zongshu (A summary of the work of open selection of leading cadres in areas throughout the country)." *Dangjian yanjiu,* 1–2: 18–21.

Zhao Liqing. 2001. "The emergence of China's non-profit sector and governance." Presented at International Forum on Governance in China, Institute of Development Studies. September.

———. 1998. *NGOs. Feizhengfu Zuzhi yu Kechixu Fazhan* (NGOs and Sustainable Development). Beijing: China Economics Press.

Zhao Liqing and Carolyn Iyoya Irving, eds. 2001. *The Non-Profit Sector and Development.* Hong Kong: Hong Kong Press for Social Sciences Ltd.

Zhaoying Chen. 2000. "High-tech parks in China." World Bank, Washington, D.C.. Cited in *China and the Knowledge Economy: Seizing the 21st Century,* Carl J. Dahlman and Jean-Eric Aubert, eds. Washington, D.C.: WBI Development Studies. January 16, 2002: 108 www.worldbank.org/html/fpd/technet/dahlman_china.

Zhao Yuezhi. "Enter the world: Neo-liberal globalisation, the dream for a strong nation, and Chinese press discourses on the WTO." *Chinese Media, Global Contexts.* Chin-Chuan Lee, ed. London: Routledge, forthcoming.

Zhao Ziyang. 1987. "Advance along the Road of socialism with Chinese characteristics." *Beijing Review* 30, 45. November 9–15: i–xxvii.

Zheng Yongnian. 2001. "Ideological decline, the rise of an interest-based social order, and the demise of communism in China." *The Nanxun Legacy and China's Development in the Post-Deng Era.* John Wong and Zheng Yongnian, eds. Singapore: Singapore University Press and World Scientific Publishing.

Zhi Xuan Dang Daibias [Direct-Election of Party Delegates]. 2003: Zhong Guo Xinwen She, Xinwen Zhoukan [China News Agency, News Weekly]. 20 January.

Zhonggong Zhongyang Zuzhibu Ketizu, ed. 2001. *Zhongguo diaocha baogao (2000–2001)* (China Investigation Report, [2000–2001]). Beijing: Zhongyang Bianyiju.

Zhongguo dalu yanjiu jiaoxue tongxun. 1995. "Cunweihui yi xianshi chu qi shengmingli: cunweihui zuzhifa diaocha baogao zhi yi (Villagers have already demonstrated their vitality: Investigative report on the Organic Law of Villagers' Committees)." Beijing: Zhongguo dalu yanjiu jiaoxue tongxun.

*Zhongguo laodong tongji nianjan* (China's Labour Statistics Yearbook). Beijing: Zhongguo laodong chubanshe, various years.

*Zhongguo qingnian.* 1997. FBIS-CHI-97–046. January 1.

Zhongguo shehui chubanshe. 1994. "Zhongguo nongcun cunmin weiyuanhui huanjie zhidu (The system of change of office and elections in China's rural village committees)." Beijing: Zhongguo shehui chubanshe.

Zhongguo siying qiye fazhan baogao (Report on the Development of China's Privately-Managed Enterprises). 2000. Beijing: Shehui kexue wenxian chubanshe.

*Zhongguo tongji nianjian* (China Statistical Yearbook). 2001. Beijing: China Statistics Press.

———. 2000. Beijing: China Statistics Press.

———. 1997. Beijing, China Statistics Press.

———. 1995. Beijing, China Statistics Press.

———. 1992. Beijing: China Statistics Press.

Zhonghua renmin gongehuo xianfa (Constitution of the People's Republic of China). 1999. Beijing: Renmin chubanshe.

————. 1982. Beijing: Renmin chubanshe.

Zhongyang jiwei bangongting (General Office of the Central Discipline Inspection Commission), ed. 2001. *Zhengwu gongkai* (Openness in political affairs). Beijing: Zhongguo fangzheng chubanshe.

Zhu Qingfang, ed. 2000. *Guojia gongwuyuan luyong kaoshi baokao xunzhi* (State civil servant recruitment and examination: Information for applicants). Beijing: Zhongguo renshi chubanshe.

Ziteng and Asia Monitor Resource Center. 2000. Conference for Sex Workers in East and South East Asia, Hong Kong. January.

Zweig, David. 1997. "Rural people, the politicians, and power." *The China Journal* 38: 153–68.

Zweig, David, and Fing Chung Siu. 2002. "Strengthening democracy: Direct nominations and electoral legitimacy in rural China." Paper presented at conference on legal and political reform in the PRC, Lund University. June.

# Index

\

# About the Contributors

**Marc Blecher** is a professor of Politics and East Asian Studies at Oberlin College. He is the author of *China Against the Tides* (2003, second edition); *Tethered Deer: Government and Economy in a Chinese County* (1997); *China: Politics, Economics and Society* (1986); and with Gordon White *Micropolitics in Contemporary China* (1979), as well as numerous articles on Chinese politics, political economy, and political sociology. He is now at work on a book tentatively entitled *A World to Lose: Workers' Politics and the Chinese State*. He lives in Oberlin, Ohio, and in London.

**John P. Burns** is the chair professor of Politics and Public Administration at the University of Hong Kong, where he does research on civil service management, administrative reform, and Party-state relations in China, including Hong Kong. His most recent book is *Civil Service Systems in Asia* (coedited with B. Bowornwathana) (2001). He is completing a book on Hong Kong's civil service system, *Government Capacity and the Hong Kong Civil Service*.

**Du Jie** is a research fellow at the Women's Studies Institute of China, the All-China Women's Federation. She has an academic background in gender and development, comparative culture and philosophy, and Chinese philosophy. She has been working for many years in the areas of women and development in China, providing policy and regulatory advice and consultation on women's political participation and women's reproductive health. She is a member of the Gender Training Group based in Beijing and has facilitated numerous participatory gender training workshops in China. She is also the gender advisor for CIDA in China.

**Joseph Fewsmith** is a professor of International Relations and Political Science as well as the director of the East Asia Interdisciplinary Studies Program at Boston University. He is the author of four books: *China Since Tiananmen: The Politics of Transition* (2001); *Elite Politics in Contemporary China* (2001); *The Dilemmas of Reform in China: Political Conflict and Economic Debate* (1994); and *Party, State, and Local Elites in Republican China: Merchant Organizations and Politics in Shanghai, 1890–1930* (1985). His articles have appeared in such journals as *Asian Survey, Comparative Studies in Society and History, The China Journal, The China Quarterly, Current History, The Journal of Contemporary China*, and *Modern China*. He is also a research associate of the John King Fairbank Center for East Asian Studies at Harvard University.

**Jude Howell** is a professor and the director of the Centre for Civil Society in the Department of Social Policy, London School of Economics, and is a former fellow at the Institute of Development Studies, University of Sussex, UK. She is the author of three books: *China Opens Its Doors: The Politics of Transition* (1993); *In Search of Civil Society: Market Reform and Social Change in Contemporary China* (with Gordon White and Shang Xiaoyuan) (1996); and *Civil Society and Development: A Critical Exploration* (with Jenny Pearce) (2001). She has also written over 45 refereed articles and book chapters on civil society, development, gender, labor, and the state. Her current research interests are gender and political participation, new developments in civil society, and labor organization in China.

**Linda Jakobson** is a senior researcher at the Finnish Institute of International Affairs (FIIA) in Helsinki. She spent nearly a decade in the P.R. China (1987–1997) and is now based in Hong Kong. She is the author of several books on China and East Asia, among others, *A Million Truths: A Decade in China* (1998). The Finnish edition of the book won the National Publication Award in 1998. In 1990 Jakobson was a fellow at the Kennedy School at Harvard University, where she wrote a paper about the Chinese media's role and impact during the Beijing Spring of 1989. She started research on village elections in China in 1995.

**Michael Keane** is a post-doctoral research fellow at the Creative Industries Research and Application Centre (CIRAC) at the Queensland University of Technology, Australia. Current research interests include television format trade in Asia and creative industries internationalization in China and East Asia. He is the editor (with Stephanie H. Donald and Yin Hong) of *Media in China: Consumption, Content and Crisis* (2002) and (with Albert Moran) of *Television Across Asia: Formats, Television Industries and National Cultures* (2003).

**Clemens Stubbe Østergaard** is the head of the Department of International Politics and associate professor at the Institute of Political Science at the University of Aarhus in Denmark. In addition he is the longtime director of East Asian Area Studies at Aarhus University. He is also an external examiner for Danish departments of Science of Religion. His research interests are U.S.-China relations, Chinese political reform, and East Asian political economy and security. His publications cover Chinese foreign policy, Sino-U.S. relations, Chinese rural institutions, civil society, and political corruption. He is the coeditor of the journal *Politica*.

**Zhu Sanzhu** (BA, LLM, PhD) is a lecturer in Chinese Commercial Law, Department of Law, School of Oriental and Studies (SOAS), University of London. He is also the deputy chair of the Centre of East Asian Law, SOAS. He teaches and convenes various courses at both undergraduate and postgraduate levels on Chinese Commercial Law, Modern Chinese Law, Foreign Trade, and Investment Law of Asia. He is the author of *Securities Regulation in China* (2000.)

**Zhang Jing** is a professor in the Department of Sociology at Peking University. She is the author of *The Unit of Organized Interests: A Case Study of Workers' Congresses in the Factory* (2001); *Problems of Rural Level Governance in China* (2000); and *Corporatism* (1998). She is the editor of *The State and Society* (1998). Her research interests include political sociology, sociology of law, and transition in China.